RAFFAELLO PANTUCCI

'We Love Death as You Love Life'

Britain's Suburban Terrorists

HURST & COMPANY, LONDON

First published in the United Kingdom in 2015 by
C. Hurst & Co. (Publishers) Ltd.,
41 Great Russell Street, London, WC1B 3PL
© Raffaello Pantucci, 2015
All rights reserved.
Printed in England

The right of Raffaello Pantucci to be identified as the author
of this publication is asserted by him in accordance with the
Copyright, Designs and Patents Act, 1988.

A Cataloguing-in-Publication data record for this book
is available from the British Library.

ISBN: 9781849041652 *paperback*

This book is printed using paper from registered sustainable
and managed sources.

www.hurstpublishers.com

For Leslie, Gabriele, Niccolo and Sue Anne
Grazie per tutto

CONTENTS

PREFACE AND ACKNOWLEDGEMENTS

When this book was initiated, the Arab Spring had not taken place. As research and writing on the volume progressed, the flame of insurrection spread around the Arab world and finally caught light in Syria. And as the Syrian conflict expanded and metastasised, it became the brightest spot on the global jihadist map, drawing to it fighters from across the world, including some 700 or so (according to the latest official count) from the United Kingdom. In many ways the flow of fighters we see going to Syria and Iraq and the narratives they espouse are an extension of the history of Britain's jihad told in this book. Yet theirs is a distinct tale. Britain's Levantine jihad is still ongoing, and it will likely be scrutinised intensively and generate a new body of literature that is beyond the scope of this text.

'*We Love Death as you Love Life*' instead seeks to tell the background story of Britain's first domestic jihad and to explain how and why the July 7 2005 London bombings took place and the broader context in which they occurred. It is based on interviews, conversations, briefings, court documents, published sources and much more that were drawn together over years of research as I sought to understand what it was that had fostered a generation of extremists who sought to destroy the United Kingdom from within.

* * *

As with any book, I am indebted to innumerable people for their support in pulling it all together. First, my family have been a constant source of support and encouragement, and in particular my mother and agent Leslie Gardner. Sue Anne, Gabriele and Niccolo have all enquired politely over the years about how things were going and whether we were near-

PREFACE AND ACKNOWLEDGEMENTS

ing conclusion—gentle harassment that helped keep me moving forwards. To Michael Dwyer and Jon de Peyer of Hurst I owe a great debt of thanks for their patience and editorial support.

At a substantive level, I wish to thank Nigel Inkster, CMG and Professor Peter Neumann who helped me to develop my ideas and offered great support in my time at the International Institute for Strategic Studies (IISS) and the International Centre for the Study of Radicalisation and Political Violence (ICSR) respectively. Innes Bowen, Richard Lambert and James Brandon all read earlier drafts of the manuscript and helped me to fill in some of the gaps. Many others have helped me dig into the various plots and narratives captured in this study. To list them all would almost entail a book in itself, so I reserve the right here to thank you anonymously. You know who you are, and even if you do not, you have my gratitude and friendship unknowingly.

This is a work of contemporary history, and a history that is constantly evolving and about which more is being learned almost every day. As a result, some details and facts will later emerge which I was unfortunately unable to uncover in time. Similarly, I have more information about some plots and characters than I could cram in for fear of losing narrative coherence. Books consist of an author's choices, and while I have tried to weave everything in to capture the full tapestry of Britain's suburban mujahedeen, some parts were omitted. I hope that the interested reader will explore some of this writing, much of which is republished on my personal site www.raffaellopantucci.com , which contains more tales from Britain's jihad.

Finally, all mistakes and errata are my own.

Raffaello Pantucci   *London, January 2015*

INTRODUCTION

JIHAD UK

Before 7 July 2005 Mohammed Siddique Khan had a good reputation. Popular among local youth, he had helped to run a local Islamic bookshop, had a wife and young child, and was seen as a local community leader in Beeston West Yorkshire. But this public image concealed another side of his character, one that drove him to lead a group of friends who blew themselves up on London's public transport system, killing themselves and as many of their fellow citizens as they could. In the weeks and months that followed, as Britain tried to comprehend why these young men chose to carry out such an act, Mohammed and his co-conspirator Shehzad Tanweer spoke from beyond the grave. Through videos released by al-Qaeda's media wing, As Sahab, the two men told the world of why they had chosen this path. Speaking in a strong Yorkshire accent, Siddique Khan announced:

I and thousands like me are forsaking everything for what we believe.

Our driving motivation doesn't come from tangible commodities that this world has to offer.

Our religion is Islam: obedience to the one true God, Allah, and following the footsteps of the final prophet and messenger Muhammad… This is how our ethical stances are dictated.

Your democratically elected governments continuously perpetuate atrocities against my people all over the world.

And your support of them makes you directly responsible, just as I am directly responsible for protecting and avenging my Muslim brothers and sisters.

Until we feel security, you will be our targets. And until you stop the bombing, gassing, imprisonment and torture of my people we will not stop this fight.

1

We are at war and I am a soldier. Now you too will taste the reality of this situation.[1]

While Siddique Khan's rationale is specific to his narrative, the wider explanation of expressing anger against the British government's foreign policy is one that many Britons may be able to appreciate; the key difference being that they would choose political forms of expression, rejecting the extreme method of a self-immolating bomb. Some of the members of Siddique Khan's group did in fact participate in these protests: Germaine Lindsay had met his future wife at an October 2002 Stop the War rally, while Muktar Said Ibrahim and Yassin Omar, two of the key plotters behind the subsequent copycat 21 July 2005 attempt on London's public transport system, claimed to have decided to carry out their act after a demonstration in September 2004. They concluded that such protests were pointless as the politicians 'don't listen' and that instead they should 'do something that would stand out, carry out a demonstration that would make people think there was going to be some sort of explosion.'[2] His fellow al-Qaeda conspirator Abdulla Ahmed Ali would echo this explanation years later when on trial for his role in an alleged plot to bring down several transatlantic flights, claiming that their's was merely an attempt to make a controversial video highlighting the wars in Afghanistan and Iraq, given that their political activism was clearly not working. In both cases, the men were calling upon a defence that they thought would help them tap into the general sense of rage that existed in the United Kingdom against the government's foreign policy, but neither jury believed them and they are currently serving long prison sentences for terrorism and attempted murder.

The question that has since plagued Britain is what drove this group of young men to such extreme action. Given the volume of people in the country also angry at the government's foreign policy who chose other forms of protest to express themselves, anger at foreign policy alone is clearly not a sufficient explanation. Since July 2005 an increasing number of people have been arrested, and in November 2007 security services declared that they believed there were up to 4,000 individuals of concern and some thirty plots.[3] The sense of public alarm grew accordingly, producing a cyclical effect of anger and fear. The far right capitalised on this unease, and a new conversation began about Britishness, questioning whether a multicultural society could function faced with the threat of Islamist terrorism.

Most prominently, the public discourse on terrorism shifted: the British government stopped talking about counter-terrorism in terms of traditional policing or military operations as it had done during the conflict in Northern Ireland, referring instead to winning hearts and minds. The word 'radicalisation' entered the public vocabulary, acting as a shorthand explanation for the multifaceted reasons that drove young men to extreme acts of self-destruction in religio-political protest. The term 'home-grown' was adopted in the press and among academics and strategists to explain the phenomenon of these individuals coming from within a particular society and yet seeking to destroy it. A new strategy was designed by the British government to counter this blossoming phenomenon, using a four-pillar approach: 'Prevent, Pursue, Protect and Prepare.'[4] The aim was both to protect the British public from the menace of Islamist terrorists, but also to stop young Britons from being attracted to the extremists' narrative in the first place.

This book aims to understand the extremists' narrative and its history in the United Kingdom, and to peel away some of the complexity around the issue of 'radicalisation' by telling the story of Britain's suburban mujahedeen. In doing so, it analyses what drove Mohammed Siddique Khan and his friends to carry out their attack, and seeks to understand the roots of Britain's jihadist culture that emboldened them to pursue this path. Eschewing the polemical approach often favoured in discussions of terrorism, the book aims to shed light on what prompted Siddique Khan and his fellow conspirators to make their fateful choices. The manifestation of anger that occurred on 7 July 2005 was not merely a knee-jerk reaction to British foreign policy, but rather the product of a confluence of global and local events that in the minds of the perpetrators of the attacks were symmetrical. They concluded that God had made it their duty to assume responsibility for the global Muslim community, and moreover to express this by killing as many of their fellow Britons as they could.

The point here is not only to better explain Siddique Khan's actions, but also to highlight the many other individuals who participated in similar activity and thus to contextualise the wider story of Britain's jihad. The extent of the links between different sets of plots and groups is only clear to those within the security services or a few journalists and academics who focus intently on the subject. Furthermore, the degree to which al-Qaeda tapped into this interconnected community of radicalised British Muslims to recruit willing footsoldiers is something that has been underestimated by the public, given that the full stories of plots often only emerge piecemeal, many years after the individuals have been arrested and incarcerated.[5]

And the trends that are laid out here are ones that will ultimately prove incomplete in the final account of Britain's jihad. At the time of writing Syria was the biggest landmark on the jihadist map, drawing in hundreds of young Britons and threatening the possibility of prolonging a domestic problem that many analysts had felt was in decline. The Syrian civil war and and its repercussions are for another book that will be written only once some historical perspective and consideration can be included. Nevertheless, the trends playing out in Syria resonate with the many narratives and personal histories laid out in this volume.

It is also necessary to highlight from the outset that it was a tiny minority within a minority who chose the path of violence. The broader community of British Muslims—both those born as Muslims and those who converted to Islam—from which they emerged should not be tarred with the same brush. It may be a cliché, but it is undeniably true that the overwhelming majority of British Muslims are peace-loving and have nothing to do with terrorism. Nevertheless, it is also true that most of the most dangerous and ambitious recent terrorist acts and plots in the United Kingdom are perpetrated by people professing an Islamist outlook.[6]

* * *

The story starts in this introductory chapter with some explanation of how radicalisation works. Notions of a linear path to radicalisation have been belied by events: instead, the central thrust of this narrative is to show how a confluence of historical trends and local dynamics created a social movement that resulted in the terrorist networks that carried out the attacks of 7 July 2005. For the reader who has not spent many years immersed in the intricacies of academic debate on terrorism and radicalisation, this chapter offers a rapid primer to the major themes and ideas that have emerged over the past decade as causal explanations of why people become attracted to violent Islamism.

Most of Chapter 1 will be devoted to exploring the roots of Britain's Muslim population: where they came from, how they established themselves and how they spread around the country. It will also explore how, among and after the wave of economic migrants, there emerged a community of dissidents and activists fleeing persecution in their homelands, who benefited from the United Kingdom's long tradition as a home for foreign political activists. While most were secularists, Muslim fundamentalist ideas were among those also brought to Britain as part of this big burst of migration.

In Chapter 2 we will look in greater detail at the establishment and socialisation of Britain's Muslims: as the 'myth of return' faded, communities were established that retained strong links with their original homelands in Pakistan, India and elsewhere. Drawing on social reports, documents and interviews, the chapter paints a picture of the state of Muslim communities and the social tensions they confronted in the 1980s and 1990s. It also ties these wider social experiences into the broader radicalisation narrative. Whilst focusing in particular on a few communities, the lessons highlighted refer to a wider national trend.

Chapter 3 will explore the late 1980s and the 1990s, the years in which the strands of fundamentalism and social confusion first fused together with dramatic consequences. The Rushdie Affair provided the loudest expression of the discontent within Britain's Muslim communities, but also demonstrated the power of Muslim identity, bringing to the fore a growing number of Muslim revivalist groups who found a constituency among Britain's young. These groups were founded by Islamist dissidents, some of whom translated ideologies that focused on broader issues in the Muslim world to a domestic audience in Britain. The ideas they espoused were reinforced by the global wave of optimism that gripped the Islamic world as the overthrow of the Shah of Iran and defeat of the Soviet Union in Afghanistan were held to demonstrate the power of Allah and faith. The trickle of young British men who went to fight in Afghanistan was soon overtaken by the arrival of a 'holy war' in Bosnia, thus making jihad a mere bus ride away.

In Chapter 4 we see how the threat of Islamist terrorism was first manifested in the United Kingdom around the turn of century. A group of British plotters were tracked down in Yemen in 1999, and then a waiter in Birmingham was discovered building a large bomb. In the wake of 9/11, Richard Reid attempted to destroy a transatlantic flight using an explosive device he was most likely given in Afghanistan by senior members of al-Qaeda. The threat had come home, although most attention was paid to the North African network operating out of the jihadist safe haven that Abu Hamza created in Finsbury Park, North London.

In Chapter 5 we shall see how this threat evolved and expanded, driven into a renewed frenzy after the invasions of Afghanistan and Iraq, as a network of radicals previously established by Abu Hamza, Omar Bakri Mohammed and Abdullah el-Faisal (and other less high profile individuals). Young Britons continued to travel abroad to participate in combat as part of what they interpreted as the obligation of jihad, and eventually some found themselves being redirected back home: if they really wanted to help the cause, they started to be told by their al-Qaeda contacts, they should return home and do something in Britain. The result was the attacks of 7 July 2005 and a wave of prior and subsequent interlinked plots.

Just as these networks were penetrated by the police and security services, new plots continued to emerge, this time powered by the internet. Chapter 6 explores subsequent jihadist battlefields, especially online clerics like the late Anwar al-Awlaki, the phenomenon of 'lone wolves', the attempt to import Iraqi-style terror to London's streets and the growing importance of Somalia, Yemen and al-Qaeda affiliates to Islamist terrorists in Britain, rather than the core organisation based in Pakistan. Jihadist ideas have now taken firm hold and express themselves in an ever more complex and random fashion, unlike the relatively stable trajectories they followed in earlier years.

Chapter 7 will finally take stock of where things stand today and reflect on the new manifestations of the jihadist terrorist threat. As this book was being completed, the complicated threat from Syria was just starting to manifest itself back at home, with the first cases involving Syrian returnees allegedly plotting terrorism coming to court in the United Kingdom.

Radicalisation

There has been much discussion in the academic and policy world on how best to explain the radicalisation process, with debate focusing on the correct blend of grievance and ideology,[7] but also on the degree to which external links influence the process or whether individuals 'self-radicalise' and then seek out al-Qaeda.[8] Marc Sageman in particular has provided an intensively researched, data-based, understanding of how cells formed in the West.[9] Prominent experts have focused on the relative importance of economics in the radicalisation narrative,[10] while others have instead explored the salience of foreign policy as a driver.[11] Scholars of Islam like Olivier Roy have focused on the dislocation between young Western Muslims and their antecedent generations, offering a fissure in which extremist ideology can take root.[12] In a British context, Jonathan Githens-Mazer and Robert Lambert have highlighted how religious curiosity and piety may play a positive role in diverting people from a path of violence.[13] Others have instead fixed on research being conducted by demographers, sociologists or psychologists looking at how religious cults may offer options for countering radicalisation. While acknowledging and to various degrees incorporating such erudite research, the purpose of this book is not to stray too far into niche debates, but rather to offer a prism through which to understand radicalisation within a specifically British context, using a historical approach.

If one were to sum up in a sentence this book's key argument, it is that behind the terrorist threat lay various social, political and religious factors which were catalysed by the impact of an external ideology that created a new form of jihadist mini-movement in Britain. Quintan Wiktorowicz has provided the best informed and subtlest understanding of how extremist ideas can take hold in the West,[14] and in the United Kingdom in particular, while Peter Neumann has offered a comprehensive outline of what he contends are the three main drivers underlying radicalisation—ideology, grievance and mobilisation. This text draws heavily on both these models in order to narrate the history of how jihadist ideas were propagated in Britain, incubated here and later galvanised a social movement that culminated in a cult of death directed by al-Qaeda.

Understanding what drives individuals to carry out acts of terrorism is usually difficult to fathom in that motivating factors are often felt by many but violence as a mode of expression is deployed only by very few. Furthermore, the same apparent level of motivation can express itself very differently among those people who get involved. Some march or demonstrate, others set up websites to express their rage, while a hard core opts to fight overseas and an even smaller, self-appointed select core chooses to carry out acts of terrorism at home. It may also take wildly different lengths of time for people to radicalise to the point of violence: for some it takes decades, for others merely weeks. That there is no single terrorist biography has added to the confusion: bar very broad generalisations, it is impossible to make predictions based on the available data in any useful way. In a final distracting twist, some individuals may experience all the necessary elements yet choose to abjure the path to violence.

Three main drivers usually have to be in place before individuals become involved in terrorism: ideology, grievance and mobilisation. How they coalesce is dictated by random events and how individuals respond to a given situation, factors that are difficult to forecast, much as a fruit machine, with three wheels spinning in tandem and occasionally lining up, is hard to predict.[15] The process is one that is predicated upon a series of contributory factors, but there is no clear way accurately of measuring which one has a greater direct impact than the others. All three drivers need to be in place in order for some sort of connection, however tenuous, to prompt an individual to turn from a disenfranchised member of society into an adherent of a violent cause. By focusing on the history of jihadism in tandem with the biographies of those young men who opted for violence, this book aims to show how these drivers play out in order to illustrate the reality of Britain's jihad.

The radicalisation narrative presented in this book is by no means prescriptive (the specifics of how Mohammed Siddique Khan went from Beeston boy to international terrorist have gone with him to the grave, and undoubtedly differ from those of Nicky Reilly, the mentally disadvantaged young convert who tried and failed to detonate a bomb in an Exeter restaurant in May 2008), but is instead offered as the backdrop against which the author illustrates how Siddique Khan and other young British Muslims got involved in jihad abroad and at home. It is almost impossible to categorise all those individuals who became involved in this sort of terrorism in the United Kingdom into a single group, beyond the fact that they are Muslim and mostly male, neither of which is a particularly helpful category given the number of innocent individuals who comprise such a dataset nationally. This is a conclusion one could reach simply by reading publicly available information on terror plots in the United Kingdom, but it was most clearly expressed in a leaked MI5 report covered in the *Guardian*.[16] Some broad themes are identifiable among the stories of individuals who signed up to Britain's jihad, but before mapping this pattern in its local context, we should clarify what exactly is meant by ideology, grievance and mobilisation.

Ideology

Ideology is in many ways the most important of the three drivers, and within a British context can best be described as the external agent that brought al-Qaeda terrorism to Britain's shores. It can be understood as the philosophy that enables individuals to become involved in extremist

Islamist terrorism, a supremacist, *takfirist*[17] ideology that seeks to impose a global Caliphate and holds that its goals can be achieved by means of terrorism. Such ideas have fused with hatred towards specific governments: Osama bin Laden, the greatest advocate of this approach, was motivated by these ideas but also by his anger at the corruption of the Saudi government, while his deputy Ayman al-Zawahiri, leader of al-Qaeda at the time of writing, was inspired by the desire to overthrow the Mubarak regime in Egypt. The religious aspect of the ideology provides a way to channel this narrative and to broaden it out to draw in recruits. These particular religious ideas have evolved from ideologies born in the Middle East and South Asia, which provide key elements of the supporting literature and belief system, in the form of ideologues like Abu Ala Maududi, Muhammad ibn Abd al-Wahhab or Sayyid Qutb. These revivalist ideologues look back to Islam's roots as an answer to the modernity that they believe has weakened it, drawing on a literalist interpretation of Islam that rigidly follow the words of the Koran and the *hadith* (saying and deeds) of the Prophet, taking them as immutable truths. It also dismisses mysticism, the worship of saints or shrines, as *bidah* (innovation) and thus ungodly and *haram* (forbidden). This also leads to extreme views on the accoutrements of modern society: music and television are held by some extremists to be forbidden.

For an example of a society founded on these beliefs, in many ways one need only look to the Taliban's rule in Afghanistan prior to their ousting by American and allied forces in late 2001. As Ahmed Rashid wrote in his seminal book on the Taliban, 'the Taliban had closed down all girls' schools and women were rarely permitted to venture out of their houses, even for shopping. The Taliban had banned every conceivable kind of entertainment including music, TV, videos, cards, kite-flying and most sports and games.'[18] Life was instead ruled by a set of religious edicts drawing on a literal reading of the Koran and echoing the lives of the Prophet and his companions in pre-medieval times. Echoes of this joyless perspective are found in statements made by Omar Bakri Mohammed, the head of Al-Muhajiroun, who told an interviewer in the mid-1990s that British girl band Spice Girls would be 'arrested immediately' in an Islamic nation;[19] or a ruling issued by Al-Muhajiroun's descendent group in Britain, www.islam4uk.com, which in December 2008 outlawed clapping.[20]

While Omar Bakri Mohammed preached his exclusionary ideology from the comfort of the British welfare state (and then online from

Lebanon where he is believed to be at the time of writing),[21] men like ibn Wahhab, Maududi or Sayyid Qutb usually preached their purist and exclusionary ideology at times of conflict. Ibn Wahhab may not have drafted his ideas under fire, but, rather, later used them during the Nejdi warriors' conquest of what is now Saudi Arabia; Qutb was jailed for allegedly trying to overthrow the Egyptian government; while Maududi was embedded in the turmoil of the early years of Pakistan. A similar strain of anti-establishment Islam is already extant in the backdrop of many Britons of Pakistani descent who are Deobandis. Forged in resistance to British colonial rule in India, Deobandism is one of the foremost denominations of Islamic teaching in Britain. According to sources cited in *The Times* in 2007, of 1,350 mosques in Britain, 600 were run by followers of the Deobandi movement.[22] It is important also to mention two offshoots of the Deobandi movement within this context: Ahl-e-Hadith (people of the *hadith*, the statements or actions of the prophet Muhammad) and Tablighi Jamaat (the society for spreading faith), which both command many followers in the United Kingdom and offer purist interpretations of Islam based on active proselytisation. They will be covered in greater detail later.

Of course, not all individuals following these movements are terrorists or inclined to be terrorists (it is certainly not true that Deobandism equates to terrorism; and the same can be said for Salafism, a term used almost synonymously with the idea of a purist form of Islam, signifying the followers of the 'Salaf', the first followers of the Prophet).[23] However, the unavoidable conclusion is that adherence to more literal readings of Islam—writings and beliefs that can be construed as 'Salafi'—and adding further interpretations to them are what those involved in terrorism often see as the ideological cover for carrying out such activities. British individuals who get involved in Islamist terrorism are attracted to an ideology which places them within a global community of Muslims, while at the same time providing them with a religious worldview which is revivalist and purist, rejecting anything but selective and extreme readings of religious texts.

What distinguishes those who become involved in terrorism from those who merely follow these schools is their *takfirism*, legitimising the excommunication and even killing of others. *Takfiris* also believe that they can hide in plain sight, among those with whom they live, and justify suicide in the course of martyrdom attacks. Coupled with the purist beliefs outlined above, *takfirism* underpins a worldview that offers religious justification for slaughter on a large scale. Some individuals are drawn to this ideology, and the narrative plays out as one of the three drivers of radicalisation that warps their vision of Islam, gradually drawing or pushing them towards extremism.

There is a further non-religious element that needs to be borne in mind when considering ideology within the context that is explored in this book; what might be termed the jihadist 'cool factor'. Revisionist and obscurantist in their outlook, the ideas outlined above are drawn from texts in Arabic, a language unintelligible to most people in the United Kingdom. What else might explain why some young Britons are drawn to them? In some cases of course they may know Arabic and feel they can engage with *takfiri* ideas, but for most this seems not to be the case, mostly because they seem unable to really understand or engage with the ideas, and it is likely the appeal comes from other quarters. One factor may be that by subscribing to them, they see themselves as joining a global revolutionary movement, a vanguard that is leading the ideological fight and forging a new world as part of a secret community of believers. As well as this connection with ideas, there is the notion of becoming an international terrorist, a figure imbued with a sense of cool—an alternative James Bond—with concomitant visions of global travel, secret encounters overseas, participation in training camps with guns, all in aid of a world-changing ideology. Given the fusion of religious ideology with the insurgencies around the Muslim world often referred to by radical groups, transforming regional clashes into constituent parts of a global anti-establishmentarianism, it is easy to see why this ideology is one that might particularly appeal to a new generation of globalised youth: 'become a warrior fighting in God's name for a worthy cause in a foreign land'. These elements elevate the ancient religious ideas outlined above and place them in a modern context, making them more accessible to young men and women brought up in the West.

Access to such ideas is easier than ever, as they are always available and increasingly in English: thanks to 'Sheikh Google' all knowledge is merely a click away, and the radical preachers discussed herein have been the main transmitters of the ideas that feature in this book and continue to openly advertise themselves online. But while these ideas are crucial in forming a terrorist, they alone cannot push people into carrying out terrorist acts; this requires a complex set of features to be present as well in the individual's mind, leaving him receptive to such ideas.

Grievance

Grievance is often the most confusing driver, since it can encompass everything from the undeniable resentment of an individual finding he is unable to advance in society, to a perceived sense of grievance directed against the broader community he identifies with: for example, the narrative that the West is at war with Islam, and thus at war with Muslims as individuals. It is also the driver that is most broadly identifiable among communities more generally, as anyone may empathise with the problems that are articulated; Muslims in particular may feel the pain of the global Muslim community (or *ummah*[24]) to a higher degree. Disagreements with national policies may also contribute to grievances that are relevant to the radicalisation narrative, positions with which many British voters would largely agree. In other words: a not inconsiderable proportion of citizens, Muslim and non-Muslim, disagreed with Britain's decision to support the American invasion of Iraq and would thus appreciate, if not endorse, the rationale behind Mohammed Siddique Khan's anger at his impotence in trying to end the conflict.

For those who become involved with terrorism the motive grievance is a complex blend of all of these issues, best expressed by Mohammed Siddique Khan, who stated 'I am directly responsible for protecting and avenging my Muslim brothers and sisters', while damning the 'so-called knowledgeable people' who he claims were misled from the safety of their 'Toyotas and semi-detached houses'. Seeing himself as a 'true inheritor of the Prophet', Siddique Khan declares that he is 'at war' and that the time has come for the rest of us to 'taste the reality of this situation'.[25] That Siddique Khan links the globalised grievances associated with the alleged Western oppression of Islam with the failures of his local Muslim leadership highlights the capacity of radical ideology to provide him with an all-encompassing global outlook. He sees himself both as a warrior representative of the greater *ummah*, whilst also driven by a very local anger. Co-conspirator Shehzad Tanweer is blunter in his statement of where the grievances of the wider *ummah* lie, repeatedly invoking 'Falasteen' (Palestine), Afghanistan, Chechnya, Iraq and Kashmir. For him, the failures of his community are more manifest as they too see the problems but choose to ignore them. He chides the British public at large: 'day in and day out on your TV sets [you] hear about the oppression of the Muslims from the East and West. Yet you turn a blind eye, and carry on with your lives as though you never heard anything, or as if it does not concern you.'[26] Both men saw great injustice in the world around them, in particular against 'their people', but also in the fact that no one was doing anything about it; and both saw themselves as part of a select few who decided to act.

At no point in these videos is there a sense that the men's motivation stems from economic disenfranchisement. More broadly, care must be taken not to over-interpret grievance to suggest that social deprivation is necessarily at the root of terrorism. As Trotsky put it, 'the mere existence of privations is not enough to cause an insurrection: if it were, the masses would be always in revolt'.[27] Nevertheless, a sense of not being able effectively to participate in society may indeed play a role in some cases: according to conclusions reached by MI5, the loose term 'blocked mobility' apparently features as a running theme through the biographies of Britons who get involved in terrorist activity.[28] However, it would be erroneous to claim that all of those who become involved in terrorism had an economic impediment in their lives; as we shall see later, several individuals who absorbed jihadist ideas in Britain were from comfortable backgrounds. The narrative of grievance must be conceptualised as a driver that fosters the individual's sense that society is against them in some way.

Mobilisation

In many ways it is mobilisation—the most restricted of the three drivers—that enables this blend of ideology and grievance to mutate into action. While ideology and grievance can both be quite wide-ranging concepts, which have an impact on many individuals in society, the next step would then appear to be to take these two ingredients and move on to activity that might qualify as mobilisation. But this assumption overlooks the fact that individuals might involve themselves in activism before they have completely imbued the ideology, or that those who are active in mobilisation do not necessarily go on to become terrorists. According to his prison diaries, Omar Saeed Sheikh, the British-Pakistani who was convicted in Pakistan for the murder of *Wall Street Journal* reporter Daniel Pearl, says he was moved by the plight of Bosnians and threw himself into aid and support work on their behalf: an experience that exposed him to the suffering of the *ummah*, which later brought him into contact with extremists.[29] The grievance driver was already present in his desire to help the *ummah*, but it is unclear to what degree he had yet imbued the extreme ideology. Mobilisation afforded him activity to be involved in, which in turn led him further down the path he had taken.

Mobilisation brings the individual into contact with other like-minded individuals and groups, and the latter purposely target those for whom grievance is already an issue. In highlighting the importance of grievance as a tool for recruitment into his radical organisation, Al-Muhajiroun, Omar Bakri Mohammed said, 'people, when they suffer in the West, it makes them think. If there is no discrimination or racism, I think it would be very different for us.'[30] It is important to note that association with Al-Muhajiroun and related groups does not necessarily lead to radicalisation: some of those who joined the organisation abjure violence or have not been involved in any terrorist activity, suggesting that it is not membership of these groups *per se* which results in criminality.[31]

The internet as a new venue for mobilisation, one no longer requiring the tangible link or connection that previously appeared so essential, has been the subject of much discussion.[32] Given the almost limitless volume of extremist material, websites or forums that can be found online, it is easy to understand why this can appear to be the wave of the future. Any individual can almost self-mobilise through the active pursuit of and involvement in online extremist activism, for instance by getting involved in web forums, contributing to online publications and developing online friendships. The cases of the Moroccan diplomat's son Younis Tsouli, also known by his online handle 'Irhabi007' ('Terrorist007') and Bradford resident Aabid Khan offer some insights into the potential utility of the internet as a tool for mobilisation: the two men were part of a network of young Muslims online who plotted together and separately to carry out attacks and train abroad, using the internet as their principal method of interaction and exchange.[33] They had some offline interaction with radicals, but most of the offences for which they were convicted occurred online. Members of the online community around these two young men were involved in establishing websites, providing translation of Arabic material into English, collecting radical material, downloading information that might be useful for terrorism, committing acts of online fraud to support their activities and recruiting members to go to fight or train in Afghanistan or prepare terrorist acts at home. This list shows the sliding scale that can quickly be established online, from mobilisation or activism to active terrorism; indeed most of those imprisoned from among the fringes of the Khan–Tsouli network were convicted for real-world (rather than online) activity, though this was untrue of Tsouli and those directly convicted with him. However, while the group around Khan and Tsouli may have overstepped the mark, there is a substantial community of individuals who interact on these sites in very similar ways, and yet never cross the line into active terrorism.

Mobilisation is then not necessarily the spark driving individuals to terrorism, but it appears to be the most tangible external expression of the three drivers within an individual. Grievance and ideology can both be internalised to a high degree, and the fact that the wider public may often empathise with the grievance element means that it is difficult to distinguish a radicalised individual from the rest of society on that basis.

The usefulness of the fruit-machine analogy mentioned earlier is that while all three of these drivers may be present, they have to be aligned in order to drive an individual to terrorism. There is clearly a moment or an event that occurs in a person's mind to trigger the decision that terrorism is the path forward. This might take the form of a specific event in an individual's life, or an external one (a national foreign policy decision) which drives the individual, or 'bunch of guys', to quote Sageman,[34] to conclude that something must be done.

In some cases, it is hard to distinguish mobilisation from the spark caused by alignment: an individual (or group) might have other radicalising elements present, but it is actual contact with 'real' jihadis (those individuals who are connected to al-Qaeda or affiliated groups) that spurs the move from talk to action.

As we shall see through the story in later chapters, time and again, it is necessary for all three elements to be present to drive an individual to action. Without grievance, the individual lacks the empathy or the 'cognitive opening'[35] to be convinced by ideology. Similarly, without ideology or mobilisation, the individual will merely be a member of an angry crowd. What is important for the broader narrative of terrorism explored in this book is that a confluence of factors occurred in Britain which brought together several crucial strands at one time: a community of people encountered while young, impressionable and open to ideas, and an external ideology which drove them to movements that catalysed their involvement in terrorism, a convergence of circumstances that prompted Mohammed Siddique Khan's videotaped epitaph: 'our words are dead until we give them life with our blood'.

Confluence

Understanding what causes a confluence of the three drivers and leads to terrorism is the fundamental question at the heart of counter-radicalisation. What makes a man like Mohammed Siddique Khan turn from being 'content with Toyotas and semi-detached houses' to taking on the job for 'the real men, the true inheritors of the Prophet'[36] and leading a group to attack the London transport system? This book attempts to answer this question by looking not only at individual motivations, but also at the historical and social events and trends that coalesced in Britain through the 1990s and which were accelerated in the period following September 11. The central idea is that an environment evolved within Britain that was conducive for a radical ideology to take hold that persuaded a community of young people that they needed to take action through violence.

Given the opacity or confusion in most terrorists' biographies, and the internalisation of much of the radicalisation narrative—dead individuals can tell us no tales, and even those who agree to be interviewed find it hard to enunciate exactly what drove them to act—it is almost impossible to determine why some individuals take the fateful step while others do not. Yet if one surveys the various jihadist battlefields of the 1990s and 2000s, it is hard to find one that has not attracted to it a substantial body of British fighters. Yemen, the southern Arabian country long plagued by civil war, was an early draw for international British jihadists, and it continues to attract young men to train at madrassas and connect with al-Qaeda's local affiliates. Omar Sharif and Asif Hanif, who carried out a terrorist attack in Hamas' name in Tel Aviv in 2003, had previously been to Afghanistan and the Balkans, and were trying to join the caravan of individuals going to Iraq before they were redirected to Israel. Mohammed Siddique Khan and his team first tried Kashmir, then decided that Afghanistan post-September 11 was where they wanted to fight. Mohammed Bilal, Britain's first officially recorded suicide bomber, blew himself up in a car next to an Indian army checkpoint in Kashmir in December 2000.[37] Convert Andrew Rowe, who was jailed on terrorism charges in 2005, was drawn to both Bosnia and Chechnya. In March 2008 a video emerged from Somalia that included a young Ealing resident who used the *nom de guerre* Abdul Ayoub al-Muhajir and claimed responsibility for a suicide attack in Somalia in October 2007. In 2011, there were reports of young British Libyans returning home to fight against Colonel Gaddafi's forces, while a constant trickle has been reported in South Asia, Yemen and East Africa. More recently, all of these battlefields have been eclipsed by Syria where numbers at the time of writing were officially estimated at 500–1000 from the UK.

In part, the emergence of the United Kingdom as the heart of jihad in Europe was due to factors beyond Britain's control, like the 'Pakistanisation' of al-Qaeda following the invasion of Afghanistan and the shift of the group's bases into Pakistan's badlands. It was also fuelled by British foreign policy decisions such as involvement in the invasion of Iraq. Beyond this, it was due to a complex combination of social immobility and racism, a divide between the first and later generations of immigrant families, the influx of extremist ideologies and individuals, and a national policy of turning a blind eye to the active mobilisation of unknown numbers of British youths. These are the true causes of the British jihad, and the underlying drivers that culminated in the events of 7 July 2005. This is what led a young Beeston cricketer named Shehzad Tanweer to follow in bin Laden's footsteps and perpetrate a suicide attack in London, having already recorded a fateful epitaph echoing his Sheikh, Osama bin Laden: 'We love death as you love life.'

1

FROM ARABIA TO SOUTH ASIA

MIGRATION

'In Britain we have 56 nationalities of Muslims, who speak over 100 languages.'[1]

Unlike continental Europe, where roving bands of Moors seized control of large parts of what are now Spain and Italy, and in 732 reached as far as Poitiers in France, Muslim warriors never reached British shores.[2] Humayun Ansari's authoritative account identifies Muhammad al-Idrisi (1100–66), the fabled Moroccan cartographer, as one of the first Muslims recorded in Britain.[3] Before this, coins with Arabic inscriptions were found there as early as 796, while a cross bearing Arabic script was found in Ireland dating back to the ninth century.[4] It seems as though there is evidence of a variety of encounters between Islam and Britons from this point onwards.

The earliest Muslim arrivals who settled were mostly sailors and adventurers, who tended consequently to congregate near port cities like London, Liverpool, Cardiff and Glasgow. Among the first settled individuals identified was a freed slave called Ayuba Suleiman Diallo from what is now Gambia, who in 1731 wrote out the Koran from memory and travelled around the country regaling Britain's aristocracy with exotic tales. In 1777 a Bengali named Monshee Mahomet Saeed was apparently 'advertising for pupils'. One of the more notable Muslims was Sake Dean Mahomet from Patna, who landed in Ireland in 1784 with an officer from the East India Regiment, learned English and married a pretty Irish girl from a good family. He soon left Ireland and migrated to the mainland where he ran an 'Indian Vapour Bath and Shampooing Establishment', which went on to receive a royal endorsement and was appointed 'Shampooing Surgeon to His Majesty George IV', a title that continued under King William IV. He holds the distinction of opening Britain's first curry house, the Hindoostane Coffee House in Portman Square, London, and wrote the first book published in English by a Muslim in the United Kingdom, *The Travels of Dean Mahomet*.[5] These individuals aside, there are numerous accounts of small groups of Muslims showing up in Britain, mostly from imperial locations around the globe, with their arrivals echoing the expansion of Empire and British alliances.

It is not until the 1800s that the first substantial wave of Muslim immigration to the United Kingdom can be charted, though, as Ansari points out, 'the pattern of Muslim arrival in Britain did not follow a uniformly rising curve'.[6] These small pockets of communities, coupled with some early converts to the cause, including William H. Quilliam, a Liverpudlian who converted in Morocco in 1887 and upon his return to England established one of the first Muslim centres in the United Kingdom, cannot be said to have had a substantial impact on the country.[7] Quilliam was openly supported by foreign rulers (including the Ottomans who at the time were enemies of England) and backed his fellow Muslims resisting Britain's imperial forces in the Sudan.[8] Despite his activism, it is unclear how many people he attracted to the cause, and much of the support for his mosque ebbed with his passing.[9] The case is useful to highlight, as it shows both the importance of individual preachers in passing on religious ideas, but also that the ideas we see later finding a home among Britain's young Muslims are ones that have a historical resonance, which may in part be responsible for their continued appeal.

Quilliam's activities aside, the numbers of converts and born Muslims in Britain remained relatively small for quite some time; by the early 1920s it is estimated that there may have been some 10,000 born Muslims in the United Kingdom, with perhaps another 1,000 converts.[10] It was not until the end of the Second World War that substantial migrations started to occur, laying the foundations of communities that make up a large part of Britain's Muslim population today. During the war itself, many Muslim soldiers from South Asia volunteered to fight on the Allied side and served valiantly; many of their names are inscribed on war memorials in Britain and at battlefields in Europe. An unknown number of those who survived the war returned to settle in the United Kingdom.[11] Another significant factor driving immigration was the labour shortage that followed in the wake of the Second World War—the result not only of deaths during combat but of the massive reconstruction required in the post-war period.

Both the war and the links of colonialism played an important role in drawing people to the Britain. Germany, Italy, Spain and the Scandinavian countries, were obliged to actively recruit workers from the third world to replace the ranks of men who had been lost in combat. In the United Kingdom migration was also driven by unfavourable economic conditions in its former colonies (in particular Cyprus and the Indian subcontinent), and the free migration allowed under the Commonwealth encouraged many mobile Muslims to choose to move to Britain to seek a better life.[12] Many came to do menial labour, filling the ranks of waiters, street cleaners, porters and the like in London and other major cities, while others instead streamed up to the northern textile mills, where tight price margins meant that only immigrant labourers would take such low paid jobs.[13]

South Asian Migration

South Asians from Bangladesh, Pakistan and India accounted for the biggest influx of Muslims into Britain. According to Philip Lewis, the numbers of Pakistanis and Bangladeshis in the United Kingdom grew at the following rate (based on British Census figures and compared to estimates of the total Muslim population):

Year	Pakistani–Bangladeshi population[14]	Total Muslims[15]	Percentage of total[16]
1951	5,000	23,000	21.7%
1961	24,900 (1.2% British born)	82,000	30.4%
1971	170,000 (23.5% British born)	369,000	46.1%
1981	360,000 (37.5% British born)	690,000	52.2%
1991	640,000 (47% British born)	1,133,000	56.5%
2001	980,000	1,545,000	64.0%
2011	1,550,000 (55% British born)	2,660,000	58.3%

Until 1971 Bangladesh was part of Pakistan: the two were called East Pakistan and West Pakistan until the conflict of 1971 firmly cleaved politically the two already physically detached regions. Whether this had an impact on the number of migrants is unclear, as the rate of influx from 1961 to 1971 accelerated mostly in anticipation of legislation to close the door on the growing numbers of immigrants coming to the United Kingdom from former colonies. The split between Pakistan and Bangladesh, however, did have a depressing social impact upon the South Asian Muslim community in Britain, demonstrating the fracturing of the great experiment to create a Muslim homeland in the subcontinent.[17]

Nowadays families whose roots can be traced back to Bangladesh or Pakistan account for over half of Britain's Muslim communities. In fact another layer of specificity can be added to refine this quite general national definition. Roughly a quarter of Britain's Muslims trace their roots to the Kashmiri part of Pakistan, around Mirpur. Among British Bangladeshis there is a similar trend, with a majority of individuals tracing their roots to Sylhet. This by no means accounts for the totality of migrants coming from these two countries to the United Kingdom, but it does account for an overwhelming majority.

That so many migrants came from just two locations in South Asia was not of course part of some organised social experiment or government strategy; instead, as with many historical migrations, it was the product of a combination of 'pull' and 'push' factors. On the 'push' side, the biggest impact of the post Second World War period on South Asia was the partition of India and Pakistan following the British imperial decision to step back from its dominions in South Asia and to create a separate nation for the region's Muslim populations. Sir Cyril Redcliffe's most controversial border decision took place in Kashmir, where, like Solomon, he overnight cleaved historically disputed areas of land in two. When in 1947 the official declaration of Partition was announced, floods of migrants moved each way seeking to establish themselves in their new respective nations. Countless people were killed in the orgy of internecine violence that followed. Some estimates have placed the casualties at around one million, though accurate figures are impossible to calculate.

Aside from laying the foundations for tensions between India and Pakistan that persist to this day,[18] this massive human dislocation also made many re-evaluate their opportunities. As Humayun Ansari describes it, 'many of those who had to move from Indian Punjab—Julludhar,

Ludhiana and Hoshiapur—to Pakistan [felt] that migrating to Britain was probably one of the more desirable ways of recouping their losses. Similarly Bengali Muslim peasants, who had moved from Sylhet to Assam [in Bangladesh] to take advantage of the more favourable land-tenure system introduced in the British period, returned to their home districts as refugees without land once Assam became a province of the new India at Partition.'[19] For many of these individuals, migration to the United Kingdom would have seemed as attractive a prospect as any other; especially when one considers that they were likely to have heard positive stories from ancestors who had travelled there previously, either as what were called 'lascars'[20] on British merchant ships or as soldiers who had fought for Britain in either of the World Wars and then decided to try their luck there.[21]

But while there are undoubtedly roots to the Pakistani population among these pioneer soldiers and post-Partition migrants,[22] one of the biggest links between Britain and its Pakistani population comes from the decision in 1961 to build the Mangala Dam in Mirpur, a construction which led to the destruction of hundreds of villages. Feeling some obligation to its former imperial subjects, and in the belief that few would want to settle on a permanent basis, the United Kingdom agreed to accept a substantial volume of the displaced, a gesture that the Pakistani government encouraged by issuing some 5,000 passports to individuals from the region.[23] While this number does not account for the entire increase, it probably contributes strongly to the first huge surge in figures indicated previously. A more recent report by the Department of Communities and Local Government (DCLG) in the United Kingdom concludes that the 'majority' of the 100,000 displaced by the construction of the dam chose to come to Britain.[24]

For the Bangladeshi community, the link to Sylhet results from the fact that when the British navy was recruiting there, it drew from the communities that were close to local rivers. This created a pioneer group who de-mobilised once in England and settled in East London, thus providing an initial community for others to follow. Eade and Garbin cite local caste traditions that would have enabled specific communities to generate enough income to pay for a first young man to track a path that others would then follow.[25] The natural preference for this community was to go where they knew people, leading to the concentration of Britain's Bangladeshi population. According to Peach, the majority of the Bangladeshi community came roughly ten years later than the Pakistanis, peaking in the 1980s.[26]

Drawn to where the work was, these men for the most part went to the industrial centres, and in particular areas where pioneer individuals (earlier migrants) had already trodden a path. So, many Pakistanis went to the northern industrial communities where former fellow villagers were finding prosperity as labourers.[27] The later arrival of Bangladeshis in London's East End might also explain why many went to work in the restaurant industry rather than taking up the factory jobs that were one of the major sources of employment in the 1970s, and the tendency for 'curry houses' in Britain to be Bangladeshi-owned. Arriving after the factory jobs had run out, they would have found employment in the restaurant industry, and eventually carried on the trade they already knew, often moving around the country to where there was less competition.

A further dimension to this picture can be added by looking at the economy of post-war Britain, where extra job opportunities emerged as labour shortages became more acute, but were matched by a general surfeit in production capacity as a result of the wartime ramping up of production. Factories globally had increased their outputs during the World War to help feed a demand that largely shrank again in the post-war period. Moreover the war had created new industrial centres, but when hostilities ceased those industries were obliged to economise and find ways of staying competitive in what was now a globalised marketplace. This naturally led to a push towards longer working hours and lower wages, neither of which particularly appealed to British workers who felt a greater sense of entitlement having survived the rigours of a world war. For migrant workers from the Indian subcontinent, the depressed wages still presented a substantial opportunity and improvement in lifestyle compared with what they had earned in Pakistan. For example, while in Birmingham the average Pakistani weekly wage was a meagre £13, this was still considerably more than the £0.37 that was the average weekly wage in Mirpur.[28] As an anonymous Bengali shopkeeper put it in 1979: 'Many illegal immigrants think they're coming to the Promised Land. But the reality is much different. Even so, for many of these people it's better working 18 hours a day washing dishes in London or Birmingham for a few pounds than doing the same thing in Karachi or Dacca.'[29]

A further 'push' factor was provided in 1972, when Idi Amin's 'Africanisation' policy in Uganda led to the expulsion of the predominantly Indian Gujarati trading class from that country. This mirrored earlier expulsions in Kenya and Tanzania, where the South Asian communities (who had for the most part migrated to these parts of the Empire under British rule to carry out white-collar jobs) had been harried out as Africa de-colonised. The numbers who chose to come to the United Kingdom were so high that in 1968, under pressure from right-wing politicians, the British government passed the Commonwealth Immigration Act that tightened up the previous Commonwealth immigration controls to allow entry only for those who had a grandparent or parent with British citizenship.[30] This legislation led to a great rush from around the Commonwealth, which explains in part the earlier surge in numbers. Public opinion regarding migration was highly unfavourable, with one newspaper in Leicester (where many of the African South Asian families had settled) taking out advertisements in the Ugandan press telling people 'not to come to Leicester'.[31] While the overwhelming majority of Indian migrants coming from Africa were Hindu, it has been estimated that some 20,000 were Muslim.[32] This group joined an extant Indian Muslim (predominantly Gujarati) population, who had migrated in much the same way as their Bangladeshi and Pakistani brethren.

Chain Migration

Among this influx of South Asian men in 1958 was a twenty-one-year-old from Pakistan called Anwar Pervez. Tracking his journey is instructive in showing the processes of chain migration that for the most part dictated how South Asians tended to come to Britain. Joining cousins from his *biradari* (clan) in Bradford, who gave him food and lodging in a terraced house that a group of them rented, he found a job at the local woollen mill so that he could quickly repay their generosity. However, demonstrating early an entrepreneurial flair which served him well later, he was eager to do more than simply cover his own expenses, and soon found a better job as a bus conductor. This eventually generated enough income to permit him to move further up the employment ladder and buy a corner shop. As he improved his prospects, he continually invested some portion of his income so that gradually he could bring over others from his clan or village. As he put it to the BBC years later:

I felt my first job was to bring the people here. First I brought my brother-in-law. Then another brother-in-law. Then my own brothers and my uncles...Then slowly and steadily I started calling friends as well. So first I looked after my immediate family, then very close friends….then I began to look further afield… [within my area]. So whenever I called anyone we became two, then two became four [and so on]…[33]

Anwar Pervez's small shop proved a success and he went on to establish a company called Bestway that supplied other corner shops, turning himself into the 'cash and carry king' of Britain. The firm has now diversified into a property business, as well as moving further up the food production ladder with rice mills in Britain. But Pervez has maintained the spirit of investing back home, with assets in Pakistani banking and cement production. In addition to helping 'my whole area come here', Sir Anwar (he was knighted in 1999) has helped run twenty-six schools in Pakistan and, according to figures published in 2005, was giving 2.5 per cent of Bestway's global profits to charity.[34] More recently, the company established a scholarship fund to help children from the war-torn Swat province of Pakistan.[35]

This may be an exceptional story, but it highlights quite effectively the process and importance to the community of chain migration, which is essential in understanding the British Pakistani and Bangladeshi experience as well as explaining how intimate connections remain to this day. In the process of chain migration, a first wave of pioneers arrives, predominantly men,[36] who discover that there are good opportunities in the chosen territory; then they call their communities back home, telling them about the bountiful prosperity that can be found in the new land. In some cases, families actively invest in young individuals in a community to send them abroad, cognisant of the opportunities that can be found.[37] These first individuals act as 'bridgeheads for chain migration flows', encouraging others through their success and gradually starting to attract families and dependants to join them.[38] This also helps explain why so many British South Asian Muslims can trace their roots to quite specific parts of South Asia (this is not something that is exclusive to these communities or to Muslims; Ansari highlights the case of an Italian community of 8,000 brick-makers in Bedfordshire, half of whom come from a series of adjacent villages in southern Italy).[39] The result of chain migration is that communities are rapidly established which have deep connections to quite specific parts of their home countries, and in many ways are in fact merely extensions of the home countries. This trend among Britain's Pakistani Muslims is charted in detail in Muhammad Anwar,[40]

Philip Lewis,[41] and Danièle Joly's research,[42] with each exploring the specific links to Rochdale, Bradford and Birmingham, respectively.

Another aspect of the *biradari* links in the Pakistani community is that not only are dependents and other relations brought over, but those who are born in the United Kingdom often marry family members back home.[43] Philip Lewis has argued that this practice is still very much the norm, with roughly 50 per cent of the now third or fourth generations being paired up with relations back in Pakistan.[44] All of this strengthens the community's connections in the sending country, but has the unfortunate impact of making communities living in the United Kingdom seem increasingly insular from the outside, hampering the natural integration that would happen through mixed marriages. In some cases, this practice can give the young a specific reason to rebel against his or her family. While undoubtedly not the only reason for his subsequent decisions, Mohammed Siddique Khan's initial break with his family stemmed in part from a refusal to submit to an arranged marriage.[45]

Arab Migration

While far fewer in number than South Asian migrants to the United Kingdom, a substantial number of Muslim Arabs or North African migrants came to Britain in the post-Second World War period. It is useful to look at this community in some detail, since it included a number of people who would turn out to be important radical figures, including senior dissidents who served as key conduits for radical ideas to the United Kingdom. As with the South Asian community, large numbers of young Arabs and North Africans came seeking jobs and livelihoods, later bringing over their families, relations or other fellow co-nationals through processes of chain migration. Reflecting the South Asian lascar experience, a number of Yemeni communities established themselves near ports, including one in Cardiff that also claims to have built the first mosque in the United Kingdom. However, the number of Yemenis in Britain has historically remained small; Fred Halliday estimates that the total number never exceeded 15,000.[46] The absolute size of other Arab communities is hard to define, with 2001 census figures drawing primarily on the respondents' nation of birth (meaning those born in the United Kingdom would necessarily classify themselves as Arabs), with other identities of individuals who identify themselves as Muslims being subsumed into the 'Arab', 'Black' or 'White' categories (for obvious reasons people tend to have different perceptions of what category they would fit into). Official figures in the 1991 census claimed that there were 22,582 Egyptians living in the United Kingdom, but this figure was roundly rebuffed, with actual figures in 1997 estimated as being possibly as high as 500,000 (though this is a figure provided in an interview without any statistical basis), while other estimates vary between 50,000 and 200,000 (including an official guess by an individual at the Egyptian Embassy in London of 100,000).[47]

Whatever the actual number, compared to the earlier South Asian figures, the volumes are smaller and the timing of the arrivals considerably later. Until the 1960s, many of the migratory patterns were similar to those of South Asians in that they tended to follow the pattern of pioneers establishing 'bridgeheads' that would then lead to a condensed migration from their home community. Ansari cites the case of the Moroccan community, who were initially brought over to work in Arab-owned casinos, which led to them filling a variety of 'low-paid unskilled jobs in the hotel and catering trade and to a minor extent in the National Health Service as ancillary workers'. By the early 1990s this had grown into a community of up to 10,000 individuals, most of them tracing their roots to the city of Larache and its surrounding villages.[48] The lower number of Arab migrants reflects the fact that even those parts of the Arab world once under British rule were not part of the Commonwealth, and so its members were not entitled to the same freedom of movement to the United Kingdom that South Asians enjoyed.[49]

But not everyone fled to seek better economic conditions; some came as students who ended up staying. Mostafa Kamel Mostafa, who would later grow up to become the infamous hook-handed cleric Abu Hamza al-Masri, arrived in the late 1970s as a student having abandoned his studies at Alexandria University or fleeing military service. While he arrived in the United Kingdom as a student, he quickly morphed into one of the working class, doing odd jobs to make ends meet in London while hanging about with the other young Arabs. It would thus be hard to distinguish him demographically from other young Egyptian and Arab men who had arrived with no student qualifications.

At the other end of the scale, in the wake of the 1973–4 oil crisis, a number of Arabs from the Gulf chose to invest their new found wealth in London property and other assets. One specialist at the time estimated that Middle Eastern investment had injected roughly £500 million into the London property market during the boom between 1975 and 1978.[50] This episode was followed in 1975 by a wave of wealthy Lebanese businessmen and traders, fleeing the upheaval caused by the outbreak of civil war in their country. The displacement from Beirut affected not only the Lebanese, but also the community of wealthy Arabs who used the city as a holiday resort. For them, this displacement was merely temporary, with London replacing Lebanon as a holiday destination. One report from 1976 in *The Economist* spoke in breathless terms of a 'bonanza of big spenders' descending on London, spending '£156m (nearly half as much again as last year) during their average stay of 20 days'.[51] But while many came through only to enjoy the shopping and high life that London had to offer, some chose to stay, drawn by the fact that many of them already spoke English (a legacy in some cases of a British education) while the time difference with the Arab world is such that staying in contact (both electronically and physically) was manageable. Finally, the Western lifestyles they enjoyed in London stood in contrast to the 'increasingly narrow Islamic fundamentalism back home'.[52]

The late Mai Ghoussoub, a Lebanese bookshop owner, typifies this group: migrating to Paris in 1976 as a result of the troubles in Beirut, she found herself frequently travelling back and forth to visit friends in London. Eventually those friends suggested they set up a bookshop in London together, and, drawn by 'the Anglo-Saxon respect for individuality', she moved over in 1979. As she put it in an interview with the *Guardian* years later, in 1994, 'In Lebanon you live between conformity and a crazy kind of freedom. In France, even among intellectuals, the way you dress, what you read, how you think, has to fit. But here you don't have to follow a group.'[53] This spirit of openness and permissiveness was highly attractive to numerous Arab migrants at the time, whose homelands were affected by civil wars and repressive or dictatorial governments. Ansari writes that:

By the 1970s Arabs coming to Britain not only increased substantially, but also seemed to come from more diverse national and class backgrounds. Writers, poets and journalists, living in exile after having escaped the censorship in much of the Arab world and challenging it from a safe haven such as London, proceeded to form an important part of a culturally variegated and intellectually polymorphic community.[54]

Unlike the economic migrants who had followed large chain migration patterns to come to Britain to take on menial jobs, many Arab migrants from this period were educated and often more affluent, enabling them to pursue careers higher up the economic ladder. While some economic considerations no doubt played a role in their decisions to emigrate, most of them also saw in Britain an opportunity both to enjoy some freedom and to advance their prospects. Migrating from war-torn Beirut in 1975 after his family's earlier eviction from Haifa, Palestinian writer and academic Abbas Shiblak declared, 'London gives all groups a chance to broaden their scope.' Shiblak later incurred some infamy when he was interned during the first Gulf War because of his role as the public representative for the Arab League in London. In an interesting twist on the issue of alienation that will be looked at in greater detail in a later chapter, he was astounded by the outpouring of public support for his case: 'English neighbours here in Queen's Park and friends all over the place began protesting, plus people we didn't know.'[55]

Another prominent Egyptian to land in London around this time was Dr Zaki Badawi, who in 1976 returned permanently to London after a lifetime as an itinerant religious man of letters. After graduating in 1947 from Islam's cradle of education at Al Azhar University in Cairo, Badawi taught at the venerable institution, before coming to Britain for the first time in 1951 as a student of psychology at London University. Having completed his course, he took off around the world with a British wife in tow, teaching Islamic studies in Malaysia, Singapore and finally Nigeria for twelve years. Returning to London in 1976, he was appointed as the first chief imam at London's new Regent's Park Mosque in 1978, saying that he had been drawn to making London his home thanks to its religious tolerance and 'tremendous self-assurance' he found when dealing with the British.[56]

Dr Badawi was to assume a major role in the evolution of British Islam and acted as the standard-bearer for moderate Islam for many years. He epitomised the high end of the 'intellectually polymorphic' community to which Ansari refers. But it is also clear that this influx of educated Arabs who were fleeing persecution and rising Islamist fundamentalism also prepared the ground for what later emerged, and would be perjoratively termed, 'Londonistan'. These early migrants were attracted to the freedom that London afforded them intellectually and turned the capital into an outpost of Arab thought. In much the same way that the moneyed Arab classes shifted their itineraries to go through London as Beirut descended into chaos, the journalistic class who had enjoyed Beirut's relative freedom shifted their bases to London. This led to the flourishing of Arab media and publishing in London, turning the city into a base from which many of the pan-Arabic newspapers that flourished in the 1980s and 1990s were first established. In 1977 alone, three major newspapers were launched in London that remain in existence and are still influential to some degree today: *Asharq al-Awsat* (the Middle East), *Al-Zaman* (the Times), and *Al-Arab* (the Arab). Just over a decade later, they were joined by *Al-Hayat* (the Life) in 1988 and *Al Quds al-Arabi* (Arab Jerusalem) in 1989. This Arab media centre was emulated by the jihadist community, with radicals like Abu Musab al-Suri and Abu Qatada running magazines supporting jihad in Algeria and elsewhere from bases in London. Osama bin Laden further capitalised on this by inviting members of the media community to publish his press releases, to visit him in Afghanistan or, using local representatives, to propagate his agenda.

London provided a hub of intellectual thought, free speech and refuge within easy reach of the Middle East and North America. As well as being a diplomatic and business centre, it was also home to a growing and diverse community of Arabs who used positions in London to spread ideas back home and raise money for causes. But while the freedom that London afforded meant that it flourished as a centre for Arab media, this fact also attracted the wrath of the Arab governments, who regarded London as a home for radical publications and a haven for dissidents who continued to instigate trouble at home. This in turn attracted the interest of intelligence and security agencies across the Arab world, turning the city into a battlefield in which Arab dissidents were gunned down and blew each other up with frightening regularity.

Arab terrorism comes to Britain

The 1970s were marked by a wave of international terrorist incidents as left-wing groups across Europe took up arms and Middle Eastern terrorism began, fuelled by Palestinian anger. Both developments were set against the backdrop of the ideological struggle between Communist and Western agencies. At the heart of this international intrigue was London, with warring factions shooting at each other, hurling bombs, and even resorting to poisoned umbrella tips. While Britain was largely spared the problems seen in continental Europe from left-wing groups like the Brigate Rosse in Italy, Action Directe in France and the Rote Armee Fraktion (RAF) in Germany, London became a battleground for Middle Eastern score-settling and assassination. Naturally this was all eclipsed by problems associated with the Irish Troubles, but the regularity of Middle Eastern terrorism and killings on London's streets was a cause for concern. One report from 1980 highlighted that: 'Since 1977, former premiers of North Yemen and Iraq have been killed here [in London]; so has the London representative of the Palestine Liberation Organization. This spring saw the takeover of the Iranian Embassy, the killing of two Libyan exiles, and several bombings of Arab targets. Iraqi intelligence and Libyan hit-squads are said to be particularly active here, and one longtime observer speaks of "bitter factions" among the "underground organizations" in the Arab community.'[57]

The attacks were often audacious and involved public shootings or car bombs with little regard for what was going on around them. In a particularly brazen attack on 10 July 1978, a hit-man hiding behind a potted plant outside the Intercontinental Hotel in Mayfair leapt out and shot former Iraqi Prime Minister Colonel Abdul-Razak al-Naif in the back of the head with a 0.38 caliber revolver. A doorman at the hotel and a couple of other passersby gave chase and apprehended the assassin, who proved to be an agent of Saddam Hussein's Ba'ath party. This was not the first time that there had been an attempt on Colonel Naif's life: in 1972 Arab gunmen had sprayed his London apartment with gunfire, injuring his wife.

Other assassinations, however, did not appear to have the same sort of state sanction behind them, and instead heralded a development that would become more common in later years. In his definitive history of the Baader-Meinhof gang, Stefan Aust recounts the story of Zohair Youssif Akache, a young Palestinian who in 1973 enrolled as a student at the Chelsea College of Aeronautical Engineering. A known supporter of the Popular Front for the Liberation of Palestine (PFLP), he was a regular agitator at Palestinian rallies in London during his student days and was twice arrested: the second time serving a sentence that only ended in 1975 when he went on hunger strike and was finally ejected from the country. In early 1977, however, he sneaked back in and took lodgings in a flat opposite the Royal Lancaster Hotel in Hyde Park, to plot his next action. Aust's account tells how: 'On 10 April, the ex-prime minister [of North Yemen, Kadhi Abdullah al-Hajri], with his wife and a member of the staff of the Yemeni embassy, got into a Mercedes outside the hotel. Akache had been in wait behind the car. He walked around the vehicle, opened the right-hand front door, and fired a pistol fitted with a silencer at the three occupants. They died instantly. Akache managed to fly out of London the same day.'[58]

While the motives behind the assassination were never completely established, in October of the same year Akache resurfaced as the leader of a PFLP commando unit that hijacked Lufthansa flight 181 en route from Palma de Mallorca to Frankfurt. The group demanded the release of imprisoned RAF leaders, a couple of Palestinian colleagues in Turkish custody, and $15 million. Whether what Akache learned at the Chelsea College of Aeronautical Engineering was of use to him during the 122-hour hijack 'action' is unknown, but he was undeniably one of the first globe-trotting ideological terrorists at the heart of the nexus between Palestinian subversive organisations and European far-left networks for whom London was an occasional base. In many ways this fusion of global ideologies (Western left-wingers and Palestinian anger), the internationalisation of terrorism, and the benefits of the British education system that we see on display in Akache's experience are all markers that find parallels in the later profile of British terrorists in the early 2000s. Among the community of British jihadis, there is evidence of a fusion of Middle Eastern ideologies and Western anger, terrorist plots and networks stretching across Europe and the United States with connections across the Muslim world, and finally the relatively high instance of highly educated British graduates becoming involved in terrorism. To highlight just one example, Umar Farouk Abdulmutallab, the Nigerian 'underwear bomber' attempted on Christmas Day 2009 to detonate an explosive device that was sewn into his clothes. He had served as president of the Islamic Society at University College London, which he attended as an undergraduate student of engineering with business finance from 2005 to 2008, and appears to have been driven by a combination of international ideologies and schooled into action by the Yemeni al-Qaeda in the Arabian Peninsula (AQAP).

South Asian Politics and Islam come to Britain

Given their proportionately large size and relatively homogeneous ethnicity, it is not surprising that the first intimations of Muslim identity politics emerged from among Britain's South Asian communities. Those from the Pakistani community of Kashmir were among the earliest arrivals, and so it follows that the first expressions of ethnicity-based politics emerged among them, often linked to political issues back home in South Asia. Political parties in the subcontinent recognised the value and importance of Kashmiri diaspora communities in the United Kingdom, and as early as 1966 the All Jammu and Kashmir Muslim Conference (UK) opened its offices in Bradford.[59] Both Birmingham and Bradford, major conurbations with substantial Pakistani populations, became pit stops for parties like the Bhutto family's Pakistan People's Party (PPP), the Pakistan Muslim League (PML) and the Jamaat Islami (JI, Party of Islam).[60] Undoubtedly, these parties had seen the substantial remittances that were by now flowing back to Pakistan from Britain and were eager to tap directly into this funding source. But this relationship was an odd two-way street at times, with the strength of support that they found locally sometimes causing some parties to overreach themselves. In 1970 a PPP candidate chose to stand in local ward elections in Manningham, Bradford (the later site of the 2001 riots), though it was unclear what exactly they would be able to represent citizens living in Britain.[61]

The arrival of Pakistani domestic party politics into the United Kingdom was by no means a phenomenon that was unique to Britain's South Asians—or indeed to any large diaspora community. What distinguished this community's politicians was that they were not only traditional politicians seeking votes, but also that they came hand in hand with politico-religious groups whose work was to save souls as well as to win votes. These secular political parties were merely following in the footsteps of their religious predecessors, who had arrived much earlier and already put down deep roots among their fellow believers. Most prominent among these was the Jamaat Islami, a politico-religious party established in 1941 by Abdul Ala Maududi in Lahore (then still in India) to 'instil in them [the Muslim community] the fact that Islam has a code of life of its own, its own culture, its own political and economic systems and a philosophy and an educational system which are all superior to anything that Western civilization had to offer'.[62] Disenchanted by the fossilised Muslim intelligentsia and leadership, as well as the gradual leaking of Western ideologies into the Muslim world, Maududi instead saw Islam as a defining creed that offered a complete perspective and approach to life. In many ways similar to the Egyptian Muslim

Brotherhood (established by Hassan al-Banna in 1928), JI saw a need to return to a purer form of Islam that would help solve many of the problems that beset the global *umma*.[63] But unlike fundamentalist religious groups who sought to use the purifying force of violence to achieve this goal, groups like the Muslim Brotherhood or Jamaat Islami instead aimed to infiltrate political institutions slowly through more traditional political routes.[64]

JI first officially established itself in the United Kingdom in 1962, when a small group of middle-class South Asians led by a student taking the bar, Korban Ali, established the UK Islamic Mission (UKIM) out of a study circle that they used to hold in East London.[65] While initially something of a home-grown British movement, by 1964 it was holding its first major conference with a keynote speaker invited from South Asia. A prominent Indian JI scholar, Abul Hasan Nadvi, spoke to the group about the importance of *dawah* (call to Islam).[66] The group also elected Mohammed Khan Kayani president.[67] Philip Lewis recounts how this emphasis on call to prayer became a major feature of the UKIM's work, reporting a brochure that opened with the words: 'The UK Islamic Mission is an ideological movement. It stands for the establishment of the will of Allah in the life of the individual as well as society. Islam is a faith and a way of life, a world view and a socio-political order. ... a complete and all embracing order of life based on the unity of God.'[68]

JI enjoyed a certain prominence among the white-collar classes in Britain's growing South Asian Muslim community, but for the vast majority it was a cerebral organisation driven to persuading them that the Maududist approach to Islam was the correct one, with little connection to day-to-day problems.[69] Over time UKIM would assume a prominent role in British Islam, with the Islamic Foundation in Leicester, the Federation of Student Islamic Societies (FOSIS) and the Muslim Council of Britain (MCB) springing for the most part from the work of UKIM individuals in Britain. And as we shall see later, groups affiliated to UKIM played an important role in funnelling Saudi influence to the United Kingdom, particularly during the Rushdie Affair.

For most South Asian British Muslims, their religious choices were ones that were defined by their places of provenance, as a result of the same strong *biradari* connection that had initially provided them with bed and board upon their arrival in the United Kingdom. In much the same way as they brought over their family members and extended relations from the subcontinent, they soon decided to bring over religious leaders from their home provinces too. As what Anwar has called the 'myth of return'[70] started to fade and the communities became increasingly established, they realised that some provision would need to be made for the growing communities in Britain. This meant pooling funds to pay for a common location in which the community could gather and pray together, and second to bring over an imam (prayer leader) or *alim* (scholar) well-versed in their particular branch of Islam to ensure the proper religious education of the young.

Given that most of the South Asian community at this time traced their roots to Sylhet and Mirpur, they followed the same religious identities that defined Islam back home: the Barelwi and Deobandi traditions, and a few followers of the Ahl-e-Hadith (literally, people of the sayings of the Prophet; *hadith* refers to the sayings of the Prophet which have survived and can serve as commentaries on the Koran) and Tablighi Jamaat (society for spreading faith) schools. As each community established itself, for the most part along the aforementioned homogeneous lines as defined by their shared *biradari*, it invariably sought also to replicate those same religious practices that they were accustomed to back home. Ansari quotes Sher Azam, the prominent Bradford leader who took leadership of the Council of Mosques and later played a major role in the Rushdie Affair: 'whoever established [these organisations] was going to do it his own way, in his own tradition'.[71]

A substantial number of South Asian Muslims tend to be of the Barelwi tradition—an Islamic sect originating in the village of Bareilly, Uttar Pradesh, birthplace of founder Ahmad Raza Khan, which fuses mystical Sufi beliefs with veneration of Muslim saints, shrines, and both living and dead *pirs* (guides)—which as a result rapidly became one of the major religious orders among Britain's Muslims.[72] In his seminal book on Bradford's South Asian Muslim community, Philip Lewis provides a brief biography of Pir Maroof Hussain Shar, a Mirpuri-born Barelwi leader whose story gives a snapshot of Barelwi influence in the United Kingdom. Born in Mirpur in 1936 to a family with deep Islamic roots, he came to Britain in 1961 through *biradari* links to work in Bradford's textile mills. After taking a couple of years to establish himself, he set up the Jamiat-i Tabligh al-Islam (Association for Preaching Islam) in Southfield Square, which rapidly became one of the most influential Barelwi mosques in the city (by 1989, eight mosques and six schools out of eleven mosques and seven schools in Bradford had followed him). In 1974, he ambitiously established a missionary college in Pakistan, which he hoped would help cement his followers' importance and continue the growth of the sect. He also invested further in establishing schools and mosques back in Mirpur, Pakistan, to ensure that his following contin- ued there and also to provide his followers in Europe (beyond Britain, his congregation was scattered through Belgium, France, Germany and Holland) with appropriate leadership. Proof of his large following was provided when in 1987 and 1988 he organised large celebrations in hon- our of the Prophet's birthday in Hyde Park, London, which drew crowds of 25,000. The 1988 gathering was given front-page coverage by the *Daily Jang*, the main Urdu language newspaper.

That Pir Maroof was able to draw such a crowd in the United Kingdom is again a reflection of the intense homogeneity of Britain's South Asian community. His ability to build such a large congregation so quickly most likely occurred because when he arrived he found himself living among a community of individuals who were familiar with his deep religious roots and knowledge. While he later went on to publish a magazine which included some articles in English, initially no doubt he was communi- cating solely in Punjabi to his flock, something reinforced by a later prob- lem he encountered when trying to recruit teachers to educate his con- gregation's young people. Although it was mostly a Punjabi-speaking community, he was forced to rely on eight teachers (out of a total of four- teen) who were originally of Gujarati extraction, and thus spoke Gujarati as their first language.[73]

This experience of intense localisation in the United Kingdom, reflect- ing an equally intense geographical particularity from their point of ori- gin, was repeated across the community, with similar stories emerging from the Deobandi and Ahl-e-Hadith groups. Depending on the major- ity sect in any given area, this would be the one that the local mosque adhered to, with further fracturing of the community as different sects in the same city established competing mosques with imams and teachers brought over to run them, each eager to maintain the purity of their given belief structure. While on the one hand this facilitated cohesion within the limited group, provided for the community's spiritual nourishment and ensured the proper education of the young, on the other it failed to provide a convenient tool for integration with the wider British commu- nity. Instead it had the effect of creating quite distinct communities that tended towards self-segregation with little interaction with the wider public except through the mosque, which became the most visible symbol of the community. For politicians looking to secure election, the mosque was often the first port of call where local leaders could be identified who could then be relied upon to deliver the local vote. Such 'clientelism' is an approach to politics that is typical of the subcontinent, where family dynasties tend to rule political parties and people faithfully vote for their local leader with little attention to the policies being offered.[74]

While the Deobandi and Ahl-e-Hadith traditions offer different interpretations of Islam, their interaction with the local community and the community structures they established were very similar. In order to understand their significance, however, some historical background is called for. Deoband is a village in India that in 1867 became the founding place of the deeply anti-Western sect that rejected all worship of shrines and *pirs* as a form of heretical polytheism. Aware of Islam's decline in the world, the group that emanated from there sought to preserve and promote Islam through a more unifying form of Islam that would bring the *ummah* of believers closer together.[75] Ahl-e-Hadith are even more doctrinaire in their outlook and take a deeply literalist approach to the Koran, believing in living in a manner similar to that of the Prophet in his time and basing their lifestyle around his exact words. An interesting element to add about the Ahl-e-Hadith movement is its apparent interconnectedness in Pakistan with the terrorist group Lashkar-e-Taiba (LeT). In his authoritative account of LeT, Stephen Tankel describes the groups' ideological proximity and use of the Ahl-e-Hadith school in their training for both jihad and *dawah* (propagation).[76] This linkage is particularly interesting within a British context as one of the first clerics to be pursued on charges of terrorism in Britain was an Ahl-e-Hadith preacher who was allegedly running a fundraising and recruitment network for Lashkar-e-Taiba until the Security Services uncovered him and attempted to have him deported in 1998.

A third group within this context is Tablighi Jamaat, an evangelical movement which seeks to persuade Muslims to live their lives in total accordance with God's wishes. As Yoginder Sikand has described them, 'Tablighi Jamaat is a world-wide Islamic movement that seeks to revive Islam by encouraging Muslims to lead their lives in accordance with the injunctions of Islamic law.'[77] Avowedly apolitical in their outlook, they are an offshoot of the Deoband School, though Tablighi's main thrust is to bring people back to God and to spread the good word. Described by one Muslim academic in conversation as 'hippies' who go on forty day 'wanders' preaching, they are uninterested in worldly pleasures and are instead focused on life in the hereafter.[78] Their Deobandi roots mean that the group is largely concentrated among the South Asian community in the United Kingdom, with their main headquarters in Dewsbury, but large mosques are found on the fringes of London as well.

Tablighi Jamaat is particularly important within the context of the broader narrative of the emergence of extremist Islamist terrorism within the United Kingdom, as several individuals who became involved in terrorism or extremist activity appear to have had some connection to the organisation. Both radical preachers Abu Qatada and Abdullah el-Faisal were apparently involved in Tablighi work, while Mohammed Siddique Khan was a congregant at a Tablighi mosque in Dewsbury.[79] The group featured repeatedly in the backdrop of a major plot to bring down a series of airlines on transatlantic routes that was disrupted in August 2006. An allegedly key plotter in East London was an active Tablighi member who was seen performing *dawah* with one of the convicted plotters on television, while a number of the others were regulars at a Tablighi mosque in Walthamstow. A man who was quizzed about the plot but was cleared of involvement in it told the police he entered Britain in order to pursue Tablighi missionary work and had previously been involved in the group at university.[80] Even further back, on-the-ground cell leader Ahmed Ali Khan told a court in 2008 that he had initially been drawn to the Tablighis as a teenager when exploring his Muslim identity.[81]

Nevertheless, it is unclear how much Tablighi can be held responsible for any of these plots. Given the group's avowedly apolitical nature, it would seem surprising that members would become involved in something as real-world as terrorism. As Ziauddin Sardar put it, 'most young Muslims in Britain have spent some time "going out on a Tabligh"', and while there is some danger that the 'unquestioning mind' the group produces 'can easily be redirected towards nefarious ends', it is unlikely that the group *per se* will actively promote terrorism.[82] Rather, the stimulation to purist Islamist activism might be a reflection of individual's curiosity that might later be exploited in other directions. A possible explanation for their repeated presence in the background of plots is provided by Omar Nasiri, who says that the guides to al-Qaeda training camps in Afghanistan recommend first connecting with a Tablighi group, as they would not turn away fellow Muslims while their proselytism offered plausible cover for travelling jihadis.[83] The fact that the group has no rigid membership, and members will always stand behind fellow Muslims, makes it very hard for an outsider to determine an individual's involvement or not in the movement.

A final important detail to note in regard to all these movements is their state of inherent propagation. These are all religious movements that espouse active propagation (*dawah*) as a key facet of religious observance, something that is in contrast to the Barelwi movement, which instead has a greater personal and traditionally more spiritual focus. Many of the earliest mosques or centres of religious learning in the United Kingdom were affiliated with one of these movements, mostly because they were the schools of Islam followed by British South Asian communities. As pioneer settlers realised that their new lives in Britain needed religious leadership, they would naturally bring over their own denominations of Islam.

Infused by, or at least adjacent to, these religious movements is the Kashmiri struggle. As mentioned above, the Ahl-e-Hadith school has considerable influence over Lashkar-e-Taiba, which began as a group that focused on jihad in Indian Kashmir,[84] and for the Deobandi movement, whose origins lay in the anti-British struggle, means it is a relatively easy transference ideologically to move to support their Muslim brothers in Kashmir against Hindu India. More recently, the Deobandi movement (and the Jamaat Islami) were seen as major supporters in Pakistan of the jihad in Kashmir; and some of their cadres participated in the post-2001 conflict in Afghanistan.[85]

Kashmir

'Kashmiri is not recognized in this country [the United Kingdom] as an ethnicity, but *it is* for a lot of people.'[86]

On 3 February 1984, Ravindra Mhatre was returning to his home in Bartley Green, Birmingham with a birthday cake for his daughter. A diplomat serving in the Indian consulate in the city, Mhatre had just stepped off the number 12 bus when he was bundled into the back of a car by gunmen and taken to a location in Alum Rock, a predominantly Muslim South Asian part of the city. There he was tied up and beaten, while his kidnappers made contact with the Reuters Press Agency in London.

Calling themselves the Kashmir Liberation Army, they stated that they would shoot an Indian diplomat they had seized unless the Indian authorities released specified Kashmiri prisoners and paid a £1 million cash ransom. A day after the snatch, the kidnappers contacted their appointed mediators, the Jammu Kashmir Liberation Front (JKLF, then also known as the Kashmir Liberation Front, a Kashmiri independence group that had been established in 1977 in Birmingham), and demanded to know what had been achieved. When asked for an extension, they granted a further three hours and hung up. This was the last that was heard from the group. The next evening, the kidnappers drove Mr Mhatre to a dairy farm in rural Leicestershire, marched him from the car before gunning him down and abandoning the body, which was discovered by a farmer and his wife when they returned at 10pm that evening.[87]

The Indian response to the assassination was rapid and decisive, with Prime Minister Indira Gandhi calling an emergency meeting of the cabinet and denouncing the murder as a 'cowardly and brutal outrage'.[88] They also expedited the much delayed execution of Kashmiri leader Maqbool Butt, who had been held in Indian custody for around eight years awaiting execution for the murder of a bank manager during a 1976 robbery. Butt, a founder of the Jammu Kashmir Plebiscite Front (JKPF), a precursor to the JKLF, was top of a list of Kashmiri separatists that the Birmingham kidnappers had demanded be released, and his rapid execution (after a long-standing delay on the grounds of a 'mercy petition' and a review of India's death penalty legislation) was widely seen as a reaction to Mhatre's murder; it marked a further ratcheting of tensions between India and Pakistan.[89] On his way to Moscow at the time, Pakistani President General Muhammad Zia-ul-Haq expressed his solidarity with his Muslim Kashmiri brethren, describing Butt's death as 'depriving the Kashmiri people of a freedom-loving person'.[90]

As shocking as this event was, it had little impact on the broader perception of British Muslims at the time, resulting for the most part in local crackdowns on Kashmiri populations. The men held as responsible for the murder, Mohammed Bhatti, Mussarat Iqbal, Aslam Mirza, Abdul Quayyum Raja and Mohammed Riaz, were all Pakistani-born and the reason they gave for committing their crime was a foreign political dispute. Some had been involved in previous protests at the Indian High Commission in London and were well-connected among Birmingham's politically active Kashmiri community. None of this would have particularly resonated among the wider British community at the time, and while people were surprised by the brutality of the act, few locals found the murder or those accused of it particularly remarkable. However as news emerged of Butt's impending execution the local Kashmiri population became enraged.[91]

In many ways this early murder in Birmingham was the most significant of the many Muslim-on-Muslim murders and assassinations that took place in Britain during the 1970s and 1980s. Unlike the Palestinian-inspired assassinations or the intra-ethnic Middle Eastern killings, where the murder was most likely directed from outside and the impact mostly felt abroad, this was a conflict that had a substantial resonance among a large constituency within Britain and the action was seemingly carried out independently by a group in the United Kingdom. Anger among the Kashmiri community was palpable. By this point there was a community of just under 400,000 South Asians in the United Kingdom, accounting for more than 50 per cent of Britain's Muslims, with the overwhelming majority tracing their roots to Azad Kashmir. In addition, Britain had absorbed a substantial Indian population, who were likely to be shocked that the sectarianism they thought they had left behind in the subcontinent was apparently following them to Britain. An earlier display of political passion was manifested when riots broke out after Friday prayers in April 1979 after news emerged that Pakistan's newly installed military dictator Zia-ul-Haq had hanged his deposed predecessor Zulfikar Ali Bhutto.

The legacy of the Mhatre murder was seen again decades later, when a political party emerged to challenge the ruling Labour party in its heartland Birmingham constituencies. Initially named the Free (Mohammed) Riaz and Quayyam (Raja) (FRAQ) campaign, after two of the imprisoned men, it eventually evolved into a political party which in 1998 changed its name once again to Justice for the Kashmiri Community (JFKC) and later contested elections in a number of inner-city wards, winning several council seats. Their interests were twofold: that the British government was not doing enough to persuade India to address the Kashmir issue; and that the Labour party had abandoned the inner-city Birmingham wards where many British-Kashmiris lived. By April 2000 *The Economist* was describing it as the 'most successful ethnically-based party, outside Northern Ireland', and it had accumulated enough support and credibility to re-launch itself once again under the less exclusionary name of People's Justice Party (PJP).[92] Local MPs from the larger parties are well aware of the importance of Mirpuri Kashmiri identity politics: as Oldham Labour MP and then-minister of state for local government and community cohesion put it, 'I have situations in my constituency whereby family disputes in Mirpur come up at my advice surgeries.'[93]

Against this backdrop it is therefore unsurprising that from within Britain's Kashmiri community there should also be some level of active support for Kashmiri separatist groups like Harakat ul-Mujahedeen, Jaish-e-Mohammed (Army of Mohammed) or Lashkar-e-Taiba (Army of God). In later chapters we shall look in greater detail at the individuals who went to fight under the banner of these groups, but at this point it is more important to note the existence of a strong connection between the two communities, and in particular the deep-rooted tradition of support for Kashmiri causes and the strong Kashmiri identity that there has been in the United Kingdom. This comes in a variety of forms, not only political but also violent.

At the softer end of the scale there has been a long-standing tradition of sending money home to relations who stay behind in Pakistan. Such remittances are a key source of income for families back home and account for a substantial portion of the GDP of provinces where these connections exist. We saw earlier the specific case of Anwar Pervez, and his is but one of many instances, many of which are at the smaller end of the scale. One former British diplomat reported visiting parts of Mirpur with many historical family connections and seeing large, prosperous houses which had clearly been built thanks to remittances.[94] Furthermore, in times of need, there are large outpourings of support: unknown millions are said to have flowed back to Pakistan in the wake of the 2005 Kashmir earthquake.

But these funding flows sometimes seem to have darker connotations too: an Oldham imam was stopped as he was coming back from Pakistan in 1998 and interrogated by security officers who asked him to be an informant for them. According to court documents, the home secretary and MI5 believed that the imam 'has been involved in the recruitment of British Muslims to undergo military training and in fund-raising for LeT' but he was ultimately cleared of any involvement and remains in the United Kingdom.[95] The Indian government has long complained of the funding flow between Britain's Kashmiri community and their brethren in Pakistan; in 2006, after the series of bombings in Mumbai that killed 182 people, the government accused British Kashmiri charities and businessmen of funnelling some £8 million a year to militants.[96] Similarly, prior to the death in 2005 of Dr Ayub Thakur, the Indian government would regularly demand that Britain hand him over; Dr Thakur was a Pakistani nuclear scientist of Kashmiri descent living in London who helped run a charity organisation called Mercy Universal, which the Indian government believed was a front for terrorist funding. Dr Thakur was a long-term vocal supporter of the Kashmiri cause: he had been an activist when a student at the University of Kashmir and continued his activity in the United Kingdom, lobbying the government and parliament to help bring about a political solution for the troubled province.[97]

That such Indian claims are real is hard to verify independently, but certainly they do not seem surprising given the high level of scepticism and antagonism towards India that can be found among Britain's Pakistani community. In one instance, a young British Kashmiri reported to the author that his father was convinced that Indian forces were behind the 2008 attack on Mumbai that had been credited to Lashkar-e-Taiba.[98] Former government officials have stated to the author that concerns about the repercussions of events in South Asia among Britain's Pakistani and Indian communities were often high on their minds.[99] According to demographer Ceri Peach, drawing on figures from the 2001 census, there are just over 1,000,000 Indians and 747,000 Pakistanis in the United Kingdom (it is not clear whether the East African Gujaratis are included in the Indian figure).[100]

In much the same way that Pakistani politicians would come to seek backing from among Britain's community, extremist group leaders would equally come looking for funding and support. Their already strong Kashmiri identity would have been called upon periodically to provide tangible evidence of their support for the cause back home. Specific instances are hard to verify, though it is known that at some point during the early 1990s Maulana Masood Azhar came to the United Kingdom and visited the West Midlands. At the time a relatively junior member of Harakat ul-Mujahedeen (HuM), he was later captured by Indian forces only to be released alongside British HuM member Omar Saeed Sheikh as part of an exchange for a hijacked Indian Airlines craft. It has been reported that another later prominent British radical named Rashid Rauf came in contact with Azhar during this trip.[101] It also seems likely that it was during this trip that he helped establish the connections that later turned into a veritable conveyor-belt of Britons joining the group he founded—Jaish-e-Mohammed—in its war against India in Kashmir.[102] A passionate speaker and ideologue, one local journalist reported talking to people who saw him speak in Birmingham who told him that women at the event were so moved by his fiery rhetoric that they took off jewellery they were wearing to hand it over for the cause.[103] Another prominent leader who visited in 1995 was founder of Lashkar-e-Taiba Hafiz Saeed who delivered speeches entitled 'Kashmir: a disputed issue' and 'Violations of United Nations Resolutions' at Islamic centers in Birmingham, London and Rochdale.[104]

More recent than this is the case of the thirty-one-year-old taxi driver Mohammed Ajmal Khan who exemplifies the mechanics of the latter-day link between Britain's Kashmiri community and the struggle back home. Khan was born in Coventry, but spent much of his childhood in Pakistan. Having completed a three-month training course at a Lashkar-e-Taiba training camp, he returned to the West as a fundraiser and recruiter for the group. Described by prosecutors in the United Kingdom as a LeT 'quartermaster', he coordinated the purchase of equipment including wireless cameras, Kevlar and paintballs to be sent back to Pakistan.[105] Khan pleaded guilty to being a director of a terrorist organisation, being a member of LeT and conspiring to provide funds for the group. He was convicted in March 2006 and jailed for nine years. With a complex network of individuals in both the United Kingdom (though Khan was the only one actually convicted, he elected to stay silent on the stand rather than incriminate his alleged co-conspirators) and the United States, the investigation into his activities showed the complexity of the LeT's fundraising and recruiting networks among the diaspora in the West. According to one account, Khan's case is a prime example of how LeT manipulates members of the Kashmiri diaspora: it provides individuals with some training to raise their familiarity of the group and experience, and then sends them back home to raise money and awareness among the community.[106]

Jihad comes to London

It was, of course, not only Kashmiri extremists and fighters who were coming through the United Kingdom. The 1970s and 1980s were a period of great empowerment and success for global Islamist movements; the Iranian revolution and the anti-Soviet war in Afghanistan showed what could happen when holy warriors took up arms against oppressive secular governments. Both events had a direct impact, in a number of different ways, on the United Kingdom. As we shall see in a later chapter, the Iranian revolution helped foster the creation and growth of the Muslim Parliament and stoked trouble during the Rushdie Affair, while the war in Afghanistan helped bring together the individuals who would later establish al-Qaeda and provided a place where young Britons could get a taste of jihad, connect with radical groups and join the global struggle.

During the Soviet-Afghan conflict, mujahedeen leaders, then friendly to the West, would regularly come through London for political meetings and for fundraising junkets. Often during these trips they would proselytise at local community centres. Syed Ayad Ghylani is one such example, a mujahedeen leader of the Afghan Islamic National Front who in July 1980 came through London seeking government support and funding, and was welcomed both in official settings and among migrant communities in London.[107] Similarly, the British government tolerated a constant flow of Saudi emissaries coming to Britain to preach jihad, recruit young Britons and raise funds to support the Afghan mujahedeen and refugees.[108] CIA officials reported instances of British Special Forces training mujahedeen warriors in the Scottish Highlands.[109] In some extreme cases, British converts to Islam travelled to fight alongside the mujahedeen: the case of James McLintock, also known as the 'Tartan Taliban', a man who helped found a radical bookshop in Beeston that Mohammed Siddique Khan used to frequent, was an early example. He claims that he was not recruited to fight, but rather decided to join the anti-Soviet jihad after meeting a group of Saudis on a flight to Pakistan in the late 1980s.[110]

The importance of this connection would only become apparent later, when it was revealed that a path had been established by which extremists recruited in London, and in some cases established themselves among the community of Arab and Muslim dissidents in London.[111] The net result was that, as the war in Afghanistan wound down, or at least the initial glorious jihad against the Soviets concluded and the nation descended into a grim factional civil war, many of those who had been to London before, or knew others who had, returned once again, this time seeking refuge. For most Islamist warriors, the trip to London was not a direct one. Initially many sought to return home, but they found a hostile reception from their secular governments who had no desire to allow trained Islamist warriors back into the country. This pushed them towards Europe and in many cases to London. Many members of the leadership committees of the Libyan Islamic Fighting Group (LIFG) and the Front Islamique du Salut (FIS) arrived in Britain, and they were joined by dissidents linked to Osama bin Laden like Khaled al-Fawwaz, a man who seemed to act as his representative and point of contact and support in London.[112] These individuals and groups were, like the earlier groups of dissidents and journalists, attracted to London because of its welcoming environment for Arab dissenters. But unlike their more secular counterparts, many of these men were coming to the United Kingdom to use it as a base to espouse the violent overthrow of governments that would have probably tried to execute them had they returned. And unlike the secularists who had come before, seeking in some cases to escape the rise of Islamism in their home countries, these were fundamentalists bent on imposing religious extremism back home. Crucially, for most of these activists the priority was to instigate action in the Muslim world.

In the end not all of those who arrived maintained this division, and many simply saw London as a staging point for activity elsewhere; but over time a number decided that Britain was equally a target. When one considers the global nature of the message that they espoused this is not entirely surprising, but it is important to recall that at the time knowledge about radical Islamist groups was very sparse. The world's experience of them thus far had been as the fanatically brave mujahedeen in Afghanistan, who had used mules and rocket-propelled grenades to tame the Soviet empire. Later in the narrative we shall encounter individuals like Abu Qatada and Omar Bakri Mohammed who arrived during this period, but at this point it is most useful to note the names of Dr Mohammed al-Massari and his colleagues Dr Sa'ad al-Faqih and Yasser al-Sirri. All three men were linked into the network of Islamists around Osama bin Laden, but unlike those who arrived to establish themselves in the United Kingdom solely to instigate activity elsewhere, their actions eventually effected their new home.

Al-Faqih and al-Massari established in London a base from which to rail against the Saudi regime under the auspices of the Committee for the Defense of Legitimate Rights (CDLR); while al-Sirri was the media representative for Egyptian Islamic Jihad (EIJ). All of them spoke reasonable English and became active in the evolution of Islamism in the United Kingdom. Dr al-Massari was a close friend of Omar Bakri Mohammed (as well as being a former Hizb ut-Tahrir member, it is likely that Bakri was the reason al-Massari came to London[113]), who later became a co-sponsor of the Global Jihad Fund that claimed to be sending money and warriors to fight abroad. Al-Massari also played a key role in helping nurture the early days of the Islamic Gateway community of websites, a key online resource that served as a home for the online web presence of many of Britain's homegrown extremist groups that we shall encounter later.[114] He was also at the centre of a clash between the British and Saudi governments when the Saudis became angered by his campaign against the al-Saud family and threatened to cut off links with the United Kingdom. However, the government was unable to deport him, and al-Massari continues to live in the United Kingdom rallying against the ruling regime in Saudi Arabia. Yasser al-Sirri was charged, but ultimately cleared, of involvement in the sending of a team to kill Northern Alliance leader Ahmed Shah Masood on the eve of the September 11 attacks, though he appears to have remained engaged with Britain's radical scene. He appeared leading a crowd of Al-Muhajiroun protesters outside the Danish Embassy after the infamous cartoons scandal of 2006, and then again on the telephone next to Abu Qatada when Qatada was caught on camera by a tabloid newspaper while living under a restrictive control order.[115]

The point here is that there is something of a continuous flow from the initial communities that arrived in the United Kingdom, to the 1970s, when London became a haven for dissidents from the Arab world, to the shift in the 1980s and 1990s as the city became a refuge for extremists who were attracted for the same reasons that the more secular-minded dissidents had been before them. In some cases, the government appeared happy to allow such extremists to flourish. Commentators like Melanie Phillips now take great pride in hammering home the shortsightedness of this approach,[116] but at the time some perceived that it might actually be a way of encouraging some movement towards democracy in states where there was none. This at least appears to be part of the rationale behind allowing Dr al-Massari to stay in the face of furious rage from Saudi Arabia.[117] This also helps explain somewhat why later activity around the radical preachers who were far more actively proselytising and recruiting in Britain was initially allowed to pass by unnoticed; the assumption was that their focus was overseas and that these individuals would at worst be leaving the country and therefore be of no concern domestically.[118] This, unfortunately, was a misreading both of these groups' rhetoric but also of the relatively easy transference whereby an individual who had persuaded himself that killing innocent people abroad is acceptable could later decide (or be persuaded) that killing them at home is equally *halal* (permissible).

2

ALIENATION AND THE
SUBURBAN MUJAHEDEEN

'I were born here but I don't belong. I don't feel like I belong like some people feel they belong.'[1]

In order for a person to be persuaded that he ought to attack the society in which he lives, he must convincingly believe that the latter is already against him. This chapter explores the issues that led to the radicalisation of individuals in the United Kingdom by looking in some depth at the social environment that evolved from the migrations described in the last chapter. Far from being solely a political or ideological tale, the radical story in the United Kingdom is one that has also reflected social tensions. This can be seen in the official government response that has sometimes treated social cohesion and counter-terrorism almost interchangeably.

For many of Britain's self-appointed Muslim warriors, one of the roots of the anger they feel is the backdrop of real or perceived racism emanating from the country in which many of them were raised. Former Hizb ut-Tahrir leader Maajid Nawaz, who ended up in prison in Egypt as a result of his activism there on behalf of the group, has repeatedly highlighted the impact of racist attacks upon him as a child as one of the reasons that he became involved in the group as a young man.[2] Similarly, a Birmingham gang of British Muslims that produced one person who was later convicted of terrorism in Yemen and another who was detained in Guantanamo was in part the legacy of a common experience of racism.[3] Perhaps less reliably, a former cellmate of Omar Saeed Sheikh reported that 'Omar spoke of his childhood and of racism in the playground, of being rejected by his peer group, who used to call him a "Paki bastard"'.[4] But it is equally clear that this cannot be the sole cause; quite aside from the involvement of white converts, it is also possible to find anecdotal evidence of individuals who do not appear to have faced a constant onslaught of racism in their upbringing. The Beeston in which Mohammed Siddique Khan was brought up was periodically stricken by riots pitting local white and South Asian communities against each other, probably spilling into his daily life in small ways. School friends recall Siddique Khan staying away from trouble,[5] and he was described as a well-integrated young man who found it easy to mix with white school friends.[6] In contrast, his co-conspirator Shehzad Tanweer was more actively involved in the local clashes that Siddique Khan seemed to avoid.

A stronger underlying reason why it is hard to identify racism as the only or main driver of radicalisation among Britain's young Muslims is simply that it is a problem experienced by any number of individuals who never become even vaguely involved in extremist or terrorist activity. Racism is regrettably common to the Muslim experience in the United Kingdom. In 1968, at a Conservative Association meeting in Birmingham, Enoch Powell made his famous 'Rivers of Blood' speech in which he stoked public fears with inflammatory rhetoric about how 'in fifteen or twenty years' time the black man will have the whip hand over the white man'.[7] Yasmin Alibhai-Brown, a journalist who arrived as a young woman in the United Kingdom as part of the wave of East Africans from Uganda at around this time, recalled how she 'would never forget the raw, crude racism we were all subjected to.'[8] What is not clear is that the hatred she felt was directed at her religion, rather than her skin tone. Racism projected towards Muslims at the time was mostly a product of the fact that they were from foreign countries and had dark skin, making it easy for white supremacists to brand them as part of Britain's non-white communities and thus a target for racism. While these issues had improved somewhat once the first generation of children were born in Britain, as evidenced by Mohammed Siddique Khan's apparently relatively well-integrated experience and reflected anecdotally in conversations with other young Muslims from the same area,[9] there were still underlying issues and tensions. As we shall see later in this chapter, the 1984

Honeyford Affair in Bradford, when a teacher complained about the authorities turning a blind eye to South Asian families' tendency to pull their children out of school for long periods of time, rapidly spilled over into a bitter and acrimonious racial debate. But this environment alone did not cause the emergence of a wave of Bradford-based terrorists.

Nevertheless, racism, or the perception of exclusion that it implies, can be a radicalising factor, even if it is perceived in a less overt way and has faded from the fever pitch that Enoch Powell espoused. Anjem Choudary, a leader of Al-Muhajiroun in the United Kingdom, has pointed out that while the overt racism of the earlier generations might have died down: 'despite the fact that you have just as many qualifications as the next man and [have] gone to the same universities, there is still a feeling that you are disadvantaged or people are still discriminating against you.'[10]

Radical leaders like Choudary preyed on this sense, employing it as the opening they can fill with dangerous ideas. A leader at the East London Mosque closely links Al-Muhajiroun's local success in later years with the rise of groups such as the English Defence League (EDL) and other right-leaning organisations.[11] There was a sense of struggle between the races that made dark-skinned young South Asians (or other Muslims) feel that society was against them. As Choudary's leader, Omar Bakri Mohammed, has put it: 'People are looking for an Islamic identity. You find someone called Muhammad, who grew up in Western society, he changes his name to Mike, he has a girlfriend, he drinks alcohol, he dances, he has sex, raves, rock and roll, then they say, "You are a Paki." After everything he gave up to be accepted, they tell him he is a bloody Arab, or a Paki.'[12]

The opening on which Omar Bakri sees himself focusing is in part also born of the sense of missing a Muslim, as well as a racial, identity. For young, second-generation British Muslims, there is the confusion of having their religious and racial identities fused together in hostility. But there is a generational gap between the parents who arrived from the Muslim world where religious notions were embedded in everyday life and their children who find themselves living in a very different world. The home and mosque may still be imbued with the ethos of the Muslim world from which they emigrated, but the school these children attend, the television they watch and the games they play are most likely not. And besides, they have a skin colour that separates them from the world around them.

This is a complex breach to understand, as it not only appears to have acted as an opening into which radical ideas could flow, but also as a key driver of community cohesion problems that have plagued parts of the United Kingdom since the 1980s. But it is clearly not a complete explanation for the inculcation of jihadism, since not all of those who have been affected by it end up taking a path that leads to terrorist activity. Instead, it must be understood as a part of the context in which the radical ideas that have led to terrorism have taken root. That is to say, it has provided a catalyst for ideas to develop and grow to a point where they become a movement and develop a momentum beyond this community. This helps explain why it is that individuals who become involved in terrorist activity are drawn from a pool far wider than just the community this chapter deals with.

To better understand this context, this chapter will look in particular at the case of Bradford, the northern British city a twenty minute drive away from Beeston and Huddersfield from which the 7 July 2005 group emerged, which has been at the heart of British concerns about community cohesion and British Muslim identity. As prominent British Muslim writer Hanif Kureishi has put it, the Bradford experience is a 'microcosm of a larger British society that [is] struggling to find a sense of itself, even as it [is] undergoing radical change'.[13]

Bradford

The Bradford riots of 7 July 2001 were the culmination of a long history of trouble and social conflict in the northern British city. While the rage that erupted onto the streets was surprising in its violence—it is considered the most violent rioting to have struck the British Isles for over twenty years—its occurrence was not. Tensions in the city had long been creeping towards some sort of boiling point, and the parallel civil disturbances in nearby Burnley and Oldham at the instigation of local far-right groups merely provided the spark to the kindling. In total some 400 people were arrested across the three cities,[14] and in Bradford in particular 90 per cent of the rioters were of Pakistani ethnicity.[15] Bradford was not unfamiliar with such clashes: in April 1976, twenty-four Asian youths were arrested after clashes with far-right National Front groups; in 1982, another twelve were arrested (and later cleared) after they were caught making petrol bombs, which they had planned to use against far-right groups; and then in June 1995 intense rioting in the Manningham part of the city presaged the 2001 troubles.

Significant about the riots and their aftermath in the context of this narrative is that many of the social drivers are similar to those that underlie the alienation we see in evidence on those who are drawn to terrorist activity. This is not to say that public affray and rioting are equal to self-immolating mass murder, but there are parallels in the motivations. The anger and disaffection evident among a community with high unemployment and riven with social tensions comes from the same pool as the social grievances that motivate some individuals to become involved in terrorism. And many of the issues that were crystallised in the riots in Bradford are to be found as issues throughout the broader Muslim community.

It is also worth noting that radicalisation, while an issue nationally, appears to have had particular resonance in this part of the country: the 7 July 2005 group came from Beeston and Huddersfield, towns close to Bradford, and other groups of young men who became involved in terrorism emerged from nearby Dewsbury and Tipton. In the late 1990s intelligence agencies were focusing on an imam at Ahl-e-Hadith mosque in Oldham, which they believed was involved in a network sending funding and recruits to Lashkar-e-Taiba in Kashmir. And as we shall see in greater detail in later chapters, there were numerous young men from this part of the country who were drawn to the narrative espoused by radical preachers and other extremists living in Britain.

Even more relevant for the narrative at hand, the riots were part of a continuum of events that include the Rushdie affair (which in part emerged from the city and will be dealt with in greater detail later) and the later 7 July 2005 bombings. Elements of both events passed through the area around the city, highlighting Hanif Kureishi's earlier point about the city as a 'microcosm' of broader trends. As Bradford resident and long-time observer Philip Lewis has put it, implicitly at the heart of all of these public conversations are questions about 'the loyalty of British Muslims'.[16] Bradford has a long history at the heart of conversations about Britain's Muslim communities, in large part because it is the city with the second largest Muslim community in the United Kingdom (if London is counted by separate local authorities). According to the 2001 and 2011 census:

Local authority	Muslim population/ total population		% of population
	2001	2011	
Birmingham	140,000	234,000	14/22
Bradford	75,000	129,000	16/25
Tower Hamlets (London)	71,000	88,000	36/35
Newham	59,000	98,000	24/32
Kirklees	39,000	61,000	10/15
Waltham Forest	33,000	57,000	15/22
Brent	32,000	58,000	12/19
Leicester	31,000	61,000	11/19
Redbridge	29,000	65,000	12/23
Hackney	28,000	35,000	14/14
Blackburn	27,000	40,000	19/27
Luton	27,000	50,000	15/25
Haringey	24,000	36,000	11/14
Camden	23,000	27,000	12/12
Westminster	21,000	40,000	12/18
Slough	16,000	33,000	13/23
Pendle	12,000	16,000	13/17

It is also important to note that the overwhelming majority of the Muslim community in Bradford is from Pakistan, or more specifically Azad (Free) Kashmir. According to figures provided by the Bradford local authorities, updating the 2001 census figures, 73,900 of South Asians in Bradford were from Pakistani Kashmir.[17] Given that Bradford's Muslim community was made up primarily of families whose roots were in the same part of Pakistan, and who had mostly come over through a process of chain migration which over time turned into bringing over families and relations, the result has been to produce a Muslim community that was highly concentrated, resulting in a 'clustering' that meant that 'the inner city appears to visitors as mainly Asian'.[18]

This has not resulted from any sort of local government social engineering, but is rather a community-led choice that evolved over time alongside the chain migration patterns. As an interview subject explains in M. Y. Alam's fascinating book of a series of research interviews he conducted in Bradford in 2004–5 as part of a project exploring young Muslim men in the city after the riots:

If she [a white older woman still living in the area] did want to move, she wouldn't even need to put a "For Sale" sign on, her house would sell no messing around. We like the area and because we have families and need more space, we end up buying the houses. We're the only ones who are left ... If I had to, I really had to, I could move, but why should I? It's a good area if you know it.[19]

As was shown in Chapter 1, this clustering is enhanced by the emphasis on *biradari* (clan) links back home. In the first instance, this means a very closely related set of men moving over together to earn a living: according to the 1961 census there were 81 women among the 3,376 Pakistanis in Bradford.[20] But as this community became more established, its members started to bring over relations, wives, children and extended families; by the 1971 census, of 12,250 Pakistanis in Bradford, 3,160 were women. This influx of females meant that children invariably followed, and from being a community of men eking out a living to send home, whole families started to be established. Increasingly, some provision needed to be made for life-cycle events, religious observance and the education of the young, meaning that religious leaders came to Britain too. Whereas the first mosques 'had no obvious affiliation to any particular school of Islamic thought', as the communities became more substantial a specialisation started to occur.[21] Given the tight clan links already extant among the communities, it makes equal sense that religious leadership would be sought to cater specifically to individual groups' beliefs. All of which would lead to the creation of a very close-knit and seemingly self-segregated community that would interact with the world around it in only the most limited fashion. None of this, it should be noted, is particularly specific to either Muslims in general or those in Bradford in particular; such ethnic clustering is quite common among any immigrant communities living abroad.

But distinct frictions were generated between the Bradford Pakistanis and their surroundings, in part as a result of this close connection with home in South Asia and the tendency for high levels of mobility back and forth among family members. In 1984 Ray Honeyford, a headteacher in Bradford, wrote an article that caused great controversy and stirred up a fearsome debate about race issues. Among other complaints, he mentioned specifically the fact that parents from the Indian subcontinent tended to withdraw their children from schools for long periods in the middle of term-time to send them back home to South Asia. When an attempt was made to confront the parents about this in a public event, the event degenerated into a shouting match to which most parents were unable to contribute since they could not speak English, even 'though there have been freely available English classes in the area for at least a decade'.[22] While Honeyford's observations were troublingly interspersed with statements meandering close to racism, his observations about parents' inability to communicate with the local authorities are supported by other researchers.[23] And his overall point about children being withdrawn home for extended periods, or even for marriages to occur at a relatively young age, are negative practices that have also been observed by others.[24] Many from the community across England report sending troubled children back to Pakistan to try to instill some old fashioned 'family values' and in some cases to wean them off drugs.[25] Others see marriage as something determined by older generations, in line with tradition, when parents alight upon a suitable match and moment. The parents' intentions may be admirable, but they are nonetheless not conducive to supporting deeper integration of their children into British society.

The Honeyford affair marked an early turning-point in the debate on integration and multiculturalism in Britain, raising questions which in time came to be seen as ever more salient. When they emerged, however, little actually happened and Honeyford was obliged to resign his post, drummed out in a heated debate that focused mostly around questions of race. Twenty years later, an article published in *The Daily Telegraph* pointed out that many of the issues Honeyford had raised in the early 1980s remained concerns in the mid-2000s, and the new headteacher at the school, herself the daughter of immigrants, spoke to the paper about problems not dissimilar from those her predecessor had raised two decades before. The problems had not gone away, as school absence is still not permitted, but now there was a capacity to discuss the issues in a less shrill manner, as parties could now converse in a shared language.[26]

Economic conditions

These were not the only issues which led to clashes and rioting in the city. Bradford's South Asian community (and in fact the north of England more generally) was faced soon after its arrival with a dramatic economic crisis as globalisation all but destroyed the local textile industry, which shed 61,000 jobs between 1961 and 1991 (about 80 per cent of the total number formerly employed).[27] 'One of the wealthier parts of the country when the textile industry was at its peak, Bradford had become by

[2008] among the most deprived. ... More than 80 per cent of Pakistanis lived in areas defined as affected by multiple deprivation.'[28] This was clearly a problem for the older generations, who found their new home no longer as bountiful as before; but it was even worse for the younger generations that were to follow. This was a community founded on hard labour and on the backs of a generation of young Kashmiri men who had left their homelands to work in local industries where they could make a much better living than they could back home. Once money had been raised, families and friends and others were also brought over, all demonstrating the success of the individual. So pride in work was a key element of society. As another of M. Y. Alam's subjects put it: 'My dad got off the plane, got a bus here to Bradford and on the same day he got a job: believe that, if you can. In them days you could walk into a mill and they'd set you on. Even if you couldn't speak English, they'd give you a job; that's how plentiful work was.'[29]

But for the younger generation things were not that easy, and instead they found themselves living in communities where jobs were few and far between, and they felt under the shadow of parents. The region generally fell slowly into decay, sapping employment possibilities and growth, something quite visible elsewhere if one makes the journey from slightly run-down Beeston to Leeds. These trends drew already isolated communities further into themselves, with tight *biradari* structures dominating the social matrix of the community.[30]

What initially was prompted by necessity, to provide a welcoming environment for the non-English-speaking young men who came over by themselves, slowly developed into a parallel social structure as families became more established. Over time this was transformed from boon into burden as the children of these tight-knit communities found themselves to be both a product of their parents, but naturally also highly influenced by the society in which they were growing up. Speaking with strong local accents these youngsters cannot be mistaken for anything but natives, but at the same time their skin tone and occasional use of Urdu or Punjabi phrases mark them as outsiders. Similarly, in Pakistan their Westernised manners and fluent English mean that they are not entirely accepted there either, leaving them in a comparative void in between:

I don't know what I am. I'm just lost, that's what I am. I haven't got a recognized identity. I don't associate with what's been set. I don't associate with totally British: I'm not *gora* [a South Asian term for pale-skinned person] and yet if someone says I'm Pakistani, I'm not. British Asian, but I don't think that term justifies it. It doesn't mean much, man. People can't understand that because for me going back there ... was a shocker—the people and everything.[31]

Mohammed Siddique Khan's brother recognised this particular problem when his brother tried to find a mosque to connect with: 'Siddique had found that the traditional, community-run mosque of Hardy Street had nothing to offer him; it was run by Kashmiri Muslims, who had no idea how to connect with the second generation. They spoke and wrote in Urdu, and the only time they interacted with the younger Muslims was when they taught them to recite the Koran by rote—in Arabic.'[32]

Siddique Khan later recounted to a fellow British-Pakistani extremist in Waziristan how he had clashed with his parents about the *pir* they would follow. As the other extremist recounted it: 'he [Siddique Khan] had travelled around Pakistan with his *pir* and often used to tell me of the ridiculousness of the sayings of his *pir*. After he left his *pir*, Siddique's family were furious with him and threw him out of the family home. They were always waiting for Siddique to be destroyed and covered with misery because of his rebellion towards the *pir*.'[33] Of course, this is a biased telling of events, but it demonstrates the pressures that affected these young Muslims. Additionally, the *biradari* strictures mean that second generation British-born Muslims frequently come under great pressure from their parents from a young age to enter into arranged marriages with cousins.[34] This locks the generation born in the United Kingdom with one still adapted to customs in agrarian Pakistan, deepening the confusion among the generation marrying, and also continuing this into the next generation. The older generations look upon the children as recipients of the generous advantage of being born (or brought up) in modern Britain, as opposed to the rural backwaters from which they came. Parents recall the struggle of moving to a new country on the other side of the world where they lived in communal spaces and did manual labour, sending money back home to bring over relations, friends and fellow villagers, and in some cases leaving behind a life that was now completely destroyed. (For those who migrated in the wake of the Mangla Dam displacement, they had literally nothing to go back to with everything now submerged under water.) All of which means they place a great sense of responsibility and debt upon the next generation.

The entire older generation's experience, however, is one that is completely alien to youngsters brought up in a cold and damp northern British city, educated in English and surrounded by un-Islamic vice and temptation. This results in a very different set of core concerns for both generations. As a pair of anthropological researchers exploring the Bradford situation describe:

> The younger generation born here were seen by themselves and felt by their parents to be *British citizens* with the same 'rights' as any other British citizen. The older generation express what we would term 'denizen identities': they feel that their presence in Britain is not one of a citizenship 'right', and consequently the younger generation see them, and the first-generation migrants feel themselves, as not having a legitimate voice. They feel that they lack the 'full citizenship' of their sons and daughters and the political rights associated with it. They fear deportation, and this expresses the core of being a denizen. Language is central to these differences.[35]

Identity

It is easy to understand how a deep generational divide can be engendered, and it is also easy to imagine how this is exacerbated by the lack of opportunity that is offered to the youngsters who grow up in this confused environment. Within the context of the riots specifically, one set of researchers analysed this generational gap as expressing itself in a particularly striking way: for the older generation the sense is that the youth are being impetuous and misguided; while among the younger generation, the driving motivation appears to be that they are attempting to protect their community. In this reading, the young disagree with the parents' attitude of simply trying to get by in British society while overlooking racism; they feel instead an ownership and identity that they want to fight for. Yet at the same time, the younger generation remain heavily influenced by their elders, which explains the post-riot phenomenon of horrified parents who had seen pictures of their children on 'Wanted' posters marching them down to the police station.[36] The high level of confessions and of individuals turning themselves in highlighted not only the parents' faith in the system but also the strong family links still extant among the community in Bradford.

For researchers Bagguley and Hussain, the reality is that these young men were expressing a new identity for themselves, forged from both their birthright from South Asia and experiences in the United Kingdom. An example of how this identity is formed is given in a reported conversation between a group of British Kashmiri fourteen-year-olds in Rotherham: 'Do you like being called British Asian?' Shakeel asks a group of friends. 'I like Paki better. I'm a Paki. What do you think?' Kiran replies: 'I think of myself as a British Asian Muslim.' Samina says: 'I'm a Muslim, I believe in Islam.' And Shazad: 'I don't think of myself as a Muslim and I don't think of myself as a Pakistani... I may be a Muslim, but I don't think of myself as Muslim. I think of myself as a British Asian, that is what I think of myself.'[37]

Clearly displaying the bravado of youth, this group demonstrates confidence in blending all of their identities together. As a result of their assuredness about their place in the United Kingdom they are eager to stand up and be counted, rather than simply lie down and meekly take the racist abuse that earlier generations might have suffered. To return to Bradford, the notion of fighting for empowerment has precedence in the Asian Youth Movement (AYM) that was born in 1978 out of early racist clashes: it attempted to unite all minority communities, not simply Pakistanis. It was, however, a short-lived experience. Different community interests tore it in different directions. In other words, Afro-Caribbean, Hindu and Pakistani community interests diverged, causing a fracturing of the pan-minority identity that the AYM sought to protect.[38]

Instead the identity forged by the generation involved in the riots focused upon their Pakistani (Kashmiri) identity and, to some degree, their religion. In Lewis' authoritative account of the Bradford Pakistani experience, he highlights how a part of this identity is gained from their inherited religion, Islam. Yet strangely it is bereft of any liturgical manifestations. Using the example of strong popular support for Muslim Iraq among young Muslims at schools in Bradford during the 'Gulf crisis', Lewis points out that only 'two or three' also took advantage of prayer space that had been put aside for them.[39] So while they enjoy citing their religious identity, there is little evidence that it is seen within a Muslim-specific context, but rather is perceived as an ethnic identity-marker. This in many ways reflects the reported conversation from Rotherham, where religion is treated as merely another badge of identity. However, this becomes important when we consider that the narrative espoused by extremists is one that calls repeatedly upon a globalised Muslim identity as the rationale for action. This identity, which connects the individual to the global, stands in contrast to the ritualised versions their parents may have brought over, instead appealing to the young by offering empowerment in a package related to their multi-faceted identity. While the parents focus on Barelwi *pirs* and the restricted view of religion with which they were brought up, the globalised identity offered by extremists immediately brings the individual into contact with a world well beyond his or her periphery. As Omar Bakri's quotes earlier in the chapter show, the appeal is to a complex individual identity formed in response to the environment in which they live.

Religion

Ultimately, this is as close as religion gets to being an integral cause of the Bradford riots. But there are broader issues behind the fact that this identity is formed to contrast with the religious identity of their parents' generation, for whom religion was seen in a clear-cut fashion, in the spirit of an inherited tradition that was a cornerstone of their national identity. Still imbued with Islam as taught in the subcontinent, the older generations would not have been confused by the other identity questions mentioned earlier, and would in fact want to continue bringing up the next generations with a clear religious identity. At the other end of the scale, as we shall see in later chapters, it would seem as though parental extremist leanings would be reflected in later generations. But this was not the norm.

For Muslims in Bradford, as in much of the rest of Britain, religious leadership was (and for the most part still is) founded very much on the sects and schools that the older generations adhered to in their home countries. Thus a number of schools of Islam that prevail in Britain also dominated the Indian subcontinent; and these function here in many ways as a by-product of the *biradari* structures.[40] As these communities of Muslims became more established and the reality that they were staying in Britain set in, religious ministers needed to be brought over to provide guidance. Families in the same area would pool their resources to buy a property to be used as a mosque and then find funds to bring over a trained individual to lead the prayers. Unsurprisingly, the communities tended to bring over individuals reflecting their personal beliefs, often from rural parts of Pakistan, with only the rote training typical of madrassas in the countryside and little experience of the world beyond their immediate vicinity. Upon arrival in the United Kingdom they found themselves essentially in the bondage of the community that had brought them over (their salary came from community leaders), and in an alien environment. A dissident Iranian journalist living in London put it rather cruelly: 'Even in their own countries, these Bengalis and Pakistanis are regarded as hillbillies. They are not even from the capitals, but from the backward countryside, they come without a word of English and the British allow them to bring their own Mullahs who are extremely hostile to the spirit of enlightenment.'[41]

Whether they know they are 'hostile to the spirit of enlightenment' is unclear. But there is nevertheless a kernel of truth in this description, particularly the lack of English, and the lack of familiarity on the part of imams with the environment to which they are moving.[42] This all has implications for the role of a religious minister, who is expected not only to ensure the good observance of rites and the religious education of the young (who will be quite unlike the children he may have taught back home), but also to offer pastoral guidance for his congregation. As we saw earlier, Mohammed Siddique Khan in particular had been noticeably frustrated by his experiences and similar complaints can be found elsewhere among Britain's Muslim communities.[43]

For youth looking for answers to the vicissitudes of daily life, such an individual will have little advice to offer and may not even be able to communicate properly with them. And where communication is possible, a rigid approach emanating from a school of education that favours mindless repetition, will reject and stifle the spirit of inquisitiveness that is fostered in the British education system. Dilwar Hussain, a second-generation Bangladeshi now head of the Policy Research Centre at the Islamic Foundation, reported that 'asking questions in the mosque… seemed only to inflame the tempers of the impatient, doctrinally rigid imams'.[44] Naturally this state of affairs is not universal, and there are doubtlessly some imams who play a vital role in their communities; but this is not necessarily the priority demand when the community is identifying a candidate. For the community of local leaders who have brought him over, the imam's role is to educate the young in rote learning of the Koran and to preserve that specific mosque and community's school of Islam.[45] Unlike the vicar who in a Christian parish has a clear pastoral role in the community, this is something that only coincidentally falls on the imam's shoulders.

It is also important to understand the role of the imam within Islam. Unlike Christianity, where the religious leader has a specific role in a defined hierarchy, in Islam the imam's role is largely that of a caretaker. The individual is essentially expected to lead the correct observation of the relevant rites, ensure the transmission of this doctrine to the next generation and to tend the property of the mosque. The real power in the mosque lies more with the trustees, who will actually guide the decisions that define what social activities are undertaken under its aegis. And the individuals who take a trusteeship role tend to be self-appointed local leaders or simply representatives from the most important families or *biradaris* within the catchment area of a specific mosque. As described in an academic study of Bradford, the leadership of a specific mosque on York Road can be taken as standard in this situation:

> York Road's mosque committee is not elected on a democratic basis. Rather, it is made up of representatives of the two main *biradaris* represented at the mosque—the Choudhurys and the Rajas. Men like Shabbir, who actually lead mosques like York Road in Britain, therefore tend to combine good family connections with respect as a strong character, and some general education including competence in English. However, even for the most enlightened of mosque leaders like Shabbir, there is a general difficulty in responding creatively to the pressing social needs of the community, most especially in terms of provision for the youth. Even if they have the cultural capital themselves, their main constituency still tends to be the first generation of migrants—the *babas* (old men)—whose primary orientation is still very much towards the Indian subcontinent.[46]

Another angle on the generational religious dislocation is offered by Lewis, who (citing a anthropologist writing about Keighley, a town adjacent to Bradford) contends that the missing grandparent generation among these communities is at the root of the problem. Traditionally, 'in Pakistan and Bangladesh, many facets of religious nurture are in the hands of grandparents who see the children daily'. Since the parents in Britain know less, or feel less confident, about teaching their religion than their elders did, they suggest the establishment of a religious school (madrassa) which then leads to the decision to bring over a religious teacher from home.[47] This explanation reinforces the proposition that the older generation understands the importance of a religious identity and outlook, but feels unprepared to provide direction, preferring instead to sub-contract this role to a third party. This leads to the formation of a religious leadership in the United Kingdom that is imported and which has no direct sense of connection or understanding of the environment in which it operates.

This absence of religious leadership within the family is of course not entirely universal. In several cases among the roster of Britain's suburban mujahedeen, individuals from quite religious families ended up embracing the path of jihad. There is the case of Hammad Munshi, the boy from Dewsbury with the distinction of being the youngest person in Britain to be convicted on terrorism charges, and who came from a family with very strong religious credentials in the community. Similarly, Usama Hasan, now a religious leader in London, was brought up in a religious family with a strict Muslim father, but chose to fight in Afghanistan alongside the mujahedeen during his university holidays, something he calls his own spiritual voyage.[48] And then there are instances like that of Abu Hamza al-Masri, the hook-handed cleric who, while clearly radical in his views, has at least one son who has grown up to become a religious figure in London.

But in most cases there is a lack of such structured religious leadership that in turn feeds into the previously identified issues of restless youth with a confused cthno-religious identity. They live in a city with few prospects and with an older generation that has its roots still firmly back in the home country, and have little effective religious pastoral care. Poor economic prospects have an impact beyond the Muslim community, which helps make host-regions an attractive target for far-right groups seeking political support and willing to deploy the old mantra of 'blame the foreigners'. This exacerbates the prevailing social problems, not only sparking off rioting, but also creating the sort of opening into which extremist groups can flow, be they far-right or extreme Islamist. For example, Tahir Abbas highlighted that the 2001 riots 'open[ed] the door' for the British National Party and Hizb ut-Tahrir, both of which flowed into Bradford 'intent on capitalizing on a widespread feeling of malaise'.[49]

Beyond Bradford

A similar picture can be found in many of Britain's other northern communities with substantial South Asian Muslim populations. Burnley and Oldham have both faced economic problems almost identical to Bradford's, while Birmingham's predominantly Pakistani Sparkbrook area experienced unemployment in 2003 of 21% overall (26% for men and 12% for women), compared to 7.8% for the city as a whole (and 3% for the region, the West Midlands).[50] Similarly, in East London boroughs or satellite cities like Luton where large concentrations of South Asian communities live, we can see replicating patterns of low employment or poor economic prospects and concentrated communities living closed-off lives. Those Muslim communities tend to be tight-knit and with equally strong links back to their home communities, facts that far-right groups attempt to capitalise upon to suggest that they are the root of local problems. In a way, far-right rhetoric is a reaction among the white community to many of the same problems faced within the Muslim community. Additionally, these white communities often feel their sense of identity is challenged by this influx of foreigners and a sense of the land being theirs and not something to be ceded to others. This is what informed the activities of the National Front (NF), which sparked the 2001 riots (as well as earlier clashes in Bradford and other cities), and more recently the inroads that the British National Party (BNP) has made into many of these troubled areas. Their ability to capitalise on such discontent and focus it in the form of anger against Islam is as much a product of their xenophobia as it is a failure of government to address these local problems.

The point here is not to identify economic misery and deprivation as a direct cause of extremism; as was highlighted before, this proposition certainly does not fit a world where economic disenfranchisement is high but violent radicalisation is relatively low. It is important to bear in mind the earlier reaction that was seen among the young rioters in Bradford, the products of their local environment, who felt that their actions were steps taken to protect their community. This is directly comparable to what we hear of the Muslim-majority gangs that emerged in the 1990s, established by young men who were confronting local racist groups. One particular example is the Lynx gang in Birmingham that, according to member Moazzam Begg, was made up mostly of young men from Pakistani Kashmir (he himself is from an Indian Muslim family).[51] It was established by, among others, Begg and Shahid Butt, a tall and imposing British-Pakistani who went on to be Abu Hamza's bodyguard and eventually served time in a Yemeni jail as part of a group accused of plotting a series of attacks in that country.[52] The gang provided the diminutive but charismatic figure of Begg with the safety of being part of a larger group, but also fostered a sense of protecting local South Asians from outside racists. This role was apparently recognised by the community, who in later years, as reported by other figures, still held Begg in high esteem thanks to his long history as a champion of local interests, his later life experiences and ongoing community work thereafter.[53]

At the time, according to Begg, his father's response to him getting into trouble with the gang was to recount his own experiences in India during Partition, highlighting to young Moazzam 'just how good [he] had it' now. This narrative exemplifies the generational gap mentioned above: undoubtedly the young man's experiences dealing with racism in Britain were nothing compared to the bloody massacres attending the Partition of India and Pakistan; but at the same time this comparison meant little to the youngsters who had not witnessed this appalling history at first hand. For the younger generation, brought up in Britain and facing racist assaults, the gang provided a means by which they can both take on their aggressors and protect their family and friends.

A different sort of empowering gang, the Mullah Boys, was allegedly formed to help address the rampant drugs problem that plagued Beeston's Asian community. While it is unclear the degree to which Mohammed Siddique Khan and Shehzad Tanweer were involved, both apparently played a role at one point or another.[54] The group was a grass-roots effort to address a local drug problem, and, apparently with parental consent, they seized young drug addicts and forced them to endure 'cold turkey' in a flat above a laundrette.[55] Run by young men who went on to become youth workers, it took a proactive role in improving the community, thus illustrating the point that the response to local conditions is not necessarily simply to fall into the predefined path of misery that seems to be mapped out.

While this may not be a causal link, such rationalisation is similar to that espoused by extremists who involve themselves in terrorism, claiming that their actions are an attempt to protect the global *ummah* of believers. They do not see themselves as nihilists, but instead as taking on the role of protectors. In court young Waheed Ali, a Bangladeshi-Briton who went to a training camp in Afghanistan with one of the 7 July bombers and was convicted of plotting to go to another, was unrepentant in his desire to fight against British soldiers in Afghanistan in order to protect his fellow Muslims.[56] On the witness stand he highlighted the popularity of such views among the community: 'a lot of brothers used to go to Kashmir training camps. It's just the whole romantic idea of going there, training, helping your brothers, because we all used to just come back.'[57] Mohammed Siddique Khan and Waheed Ali were both drawn in by this narrative and opted in 2001 for a camp run by Harakat ul Mujahedeen (HuM), a Kashmiri-oriented terrorist group. In his subsequent martyrdom video, Siddique Khan described himself as assuming a responsibility that others were failing to take, and his group as 'the real men, the true inheritors of the prophet'. Later in this narrative we shall see how a desire to help beleaguered Bosnian Muslims, whom many British Muslims saw as brothers, inspired a number of convoys of aid and fighters to set out from the United Kingdom. And this is a narrative justification that lies at the heart of almost every individual story of why they become attracted to extremist activity—or at least how they appear to justify their actions to themselves. For them, the words of Abdullah Azzam resonated clearly: 'It is the few that carry the burden of carrying Islam to mankind, then a few from among them offer their wealth and their lives in the path of Allah, and it is a few from among a few from among a few who sacrifice their lives for Islam.'[58]

Azzam was the key ideologue of the Afghan mujahedeen, a mentor of Osama bin Laden and a perennial jihadist icon. His popularity among the English-speaking world and particularly the United Kingdom was made apparent when, in the 1990s, a website was established in Britain that provided a portal for the dissemination of English-language extremist material and information using the URL www.azzam.com.

Building their own structures

Aside from joining gangs and standing up for their own communities, the younger generation's desire to redefine their environment expresses itself in other ways too. One interesting reaction can be seen in the attempt to create a new religious architecture which is their own and thus more accessible than that which their parents built. Unknowingly, they were emulating their parent's generation in doing this—Khurshid Ahmed and other founder members of the Islamic Foundation in Leicester initially established the institution to provide the growing Muslim community with 'a fresh set of thinking about how Muslims should live in the west.'[59] Within the context of the 7 July group, they were all involved quite intimately in the establishment of the Iqra bookshop in their local area, which they would use as a place of congregation and radicalisation. According to declarations filed with the charity commission in 2002, Mohammed Siddique Khan, Khalid Khaliq, Waheed Ali and Sadeer Saleem were all listed as trustees: Siddique Khan went on to lead the 7 July group; Khaliq pleaded guilty to possessing an al-Qaeda manual; Ali was incarcerated for plotting to go to a training camp in Pakistan, and in court revealed he had been there previously with Siddique Khan; and Saleem admitted to attending a training camp in Pakistan with Ali, though was cleared of having any involvement in terrorist activity.[60] Shehzad Tanweer was another name later added to the list of trustees at the bookshop, while Hasib Hussain (one of the 7 July bombers) and Mohammed Shakil, who was also convicted of plotting to attend a training camp in Pakistan and admitted to having been there before, were apparently regular visitors.[61]

This bookshop was a focus for local youths, in particular a group associated with the local Mullah Boys gang. Within its walls, young Muslims would follow their own religion, marrying people of their own choice rather than submitting to arranged marriages to cousins, as well as bringing in their own preachers and speakers who were not of their parents' schools of belief.[62] Shehzad Tanweer reported to his uncle that they were teaching young children at the Iqra bookshop.[63] During the Coroner's Inquest into the July 7 bombings, it was revealed that Khan had tried to convert an eleven-year-old boy he had brought under his wing. He would bring the young man with him to the local bookstores and at one point after 9/11 told him that 'they' would 'pay' for what they were doing to Pakistan.[64] The institution had an open-door policy: anyone could use the computers in the back room if they needed to.[65] Established by a group of local radicals, the bookshop was one of several Muslim community organisations that James McClintock, a Dundee-born convert who spent time in Afghanistan alongside the mujahedeen and later went to Bosnia, and who was also known as the 'Tartan Taliban,' and fellow convert Martin 'Abdullah' McDaid, had set up in the community and through which they appear to have influenced to some degree its impressionable young men.[66]

The bookshop was a centre for spreading radical ideas and tales of jihad, with the local community rife with rumours of what was going on inside.[67] One local IT expert helped them set up their computer systems and reproduce some CDs, before becoming disgusted at some of the extremist videos he saw them disseminating. Most telling, however, is the experience that Waheed Ali reported when he was on trial for being part of a support cell of the 7 July group. As a teenager, at the time known as Shippon Ullah, he was drawn to the community at the bookshop after being approached by Sadeer Saleem at a bus stop. Saleem apparently knew him from the local community and could see that the young man was having difficulty finding his way in life and invited him to the bookshop. Ali reported hearing about Bosnia and the plight of Chechen Muslims, watching videos about them, and within a week 'had taken down his posters of hip hop stars and footballers and replaced them with pictures of Kalashnikov rifles'. As he put it in court, 'my life rapidly changed. I started praying three to four times a day. I saw my goal in life as helping my Muslim brothers.'[68] Hearing stories of jihad first-hand from people like occasional preacher James McClintock, the young man was rapidly drawn into the romantic world of jihad.[69] Eventually, for Mohammed Siddique Khan, the bookshop was not hardline enough, and when they started stocking videos and cassettes by a preacher who condemned suicide bombing in 2003, he fell out with the owners and apparently started to appear there less often.[70]

A few years prior to the setting up of the Iqra bookshop in Beeston, former Bosnian aid worker, Moazzam Begg, and his friend Shakeel established a similar endeavour in Birmingham. Founded in 1997 or 1998, the Maktabah al-Ansar (Library of the Faithful) bookshop was an attempt to create a space in which discussions could be held about religious and political issues that were frowned upon in the mosque.[71] As Begg put it in a later interview, the bookshop 'attracted people, bringing people to the forefront, discussing issues there that we wanted to talk about, many of which were political, and I don't shy away from that'.[72] As well as offering a forum in which politics could be discussed and empowering individuals to learn more about their religion in their own terms, the bookshop also provided translations of important works by authors such as Abdullah Azzam, whose *Defence of the Muslim Lands* was apparently the bookshop's best-seller.[73] In 1999 they published a book by a Hindu convert named Dhiren Barot entitled *The Army of Madinah in Kashmir*, under his pseudonym Esa al-Hindi, which detailed his exploits fighting alongside the Kashmiri liberation group Lashkar-e-Taiba.

Such books naturally attracted the attention of the security services, and the bookshop has been repeatedly raided over the years. It also proved a draw for local youths seeking to learn more about jihad: Ruhal Ahmed, a young local Bangladeshi, told his captors in Guantanamo Bay that he found books, videos and cassettes on Afghanistan, the Taliban, and jihad in Chechnya at the bookshop in 2000.[74] Now primarily an online forum, the bookshop remains at the forefront of republishing literature by the likes of Abdullah Azzam and other ideologues. In 2007 and then again in 2010 the chief operator at the bookshop, Ahmed Faraz, a local Birmingham Pakistani who used the name Abu Bakr was arrested: the first time in connection with a plot to behead a soldier (of which he was cleared), and the second on charges of disseminating terrorist publications and owning material of use to terrorists. He was convicted in December 2011 on charges of disseminating terrorist material and was sentenced to three years incarceration, though part of this conviction was later quashed. A long time elapsed between his arrest and trial, because, according to investigators, the volume of radical material collected during police raids was so large (during raids in 2007 and 2010, police seized some nineteen computers, twenty-five hard drives, 15,000 books, and over 9,000 DVDs and videos). In press coverage of the trial it was highlighted that copies of books produced by the shop had been found in the possession of the 7 July bombers and their wider network. These books were also quoted in the martyrdom video made by one of the men who allegedly participated in the August 2006 plot to bring down an unspecified number of aeroplanes on transatlantic flights with liquid bombs.[75] During the trial the judge recognised Faraz's contributions to society in Sparkhill as a mentor and anti-drug worker—a similar narrative to those we have seen before. This mitigated somewhat the judge's severe statements that 'it is grossly irresponsible to publish these books in the way that you have published them,' pointing out how clearly inflammatory the texts were even though there were no specific links to any terrorist plots on display during the case.[76] In late 2012 an appeals court quashed part of Faraz's conviction, highlighting the difficulty in proving the specific texts he had been convicted of had driven others to terrorism. His conviction relating to possession of material useful to someone preparing a terrorist attack still stood.

In Begg's telling, the bookstore gave him a first-hand insight into what he saw as a religious revival going on around him: 'I found too there were many people that were struggling to fill the spiritual vacuum that existed, and yet shunned what they knew of organised religion. Despite that rejection, Islam was attracting thousands of indigenous Britons, some of whom converted right in front of me in the bookshop.'[77]

This detail is significant for several reasons. First it captures the sense of collective religious revival that existed in the late 1990s, but it also highlights the role of these bookshops as centres of religious revivalism.

Young men who have recently discovered (or rediscovered) their religion will naturally want to spread the good word further. Fighting a jihad is only one way of proving your faith to God. Bringing others to the cause is also a key part: *dawah,* or propagation, is a key tenet of Islamists' work. And a religious bookstore offers an excellent location to propagate these ideas further: not only is it a place of contemplation and erudition, but all of the relevant literature is available to be passed on to the prospective follower.

In Chatsworth Road, London a similar organisation was established near a charity store run by a former mujahedeen fighter who would regale the young men who visited his shop with tales of jihadi derring-do and organise aid missions to Afghanistan, which the security services believed were a cover for trips to training camps. Nearby, and drawing in the same community, was the Al Koran bookshop, established by Mohammed Hamid, an older man from West Yorkshire but born in Tanzania. It was established after he rediscovered his religious roots in his thirties. Within the bookshop Hamid created an environment in which all aspects of religion could be discussed free from the strictures of traditional religious spaces, and this became a congregation point in East London for radicals from up and down the country—at least one of his assistants in the shop ended up blowing himself up in a failed bomb making experiment alongside al-Qaeda trainers in Pakistan.

In an evolution of this model, in November 2009, police in Manchester arrested a group of men who were all connected to a series of *dawah* stalls in Manchester and Longsight. The leader of the group, Munir Farooqi, was an ex-Taliban fighter who had returned to Afghanistan after 9/11 to fight alongside the group. Captured by Uzbek General Rashid Dostum's forces, he was held until his wife came over from England with a ransom fee to have him freed. Once back in Britain he seems to have continued to actively support the fighters in Afghanistan, raising money for them as well as travelling back and forth more than once. At the same time, he established a home-based recording and duplication system in order to produce DVDs and CDs of extremist material that he would then sell at his stalls. Using these as his first point of contact, he would draw in seemingly susceptible young men (for example, individuals with criminal records and converts) with his first-hand tales of jihad and gradually brought them into his circle, continually talking about the 'sweetness' of jihad. As he put it to an undercover officer, 'you know when you've tasted the honey...then you only want more...until Allah takes you from this earth.'[78] Farooqi had created a locus like a bookshop (when he was arrested he had some 5,000 DVDs and 50,000 books and pamphlets), to use as a way to draw new Muslims to his cause.

Unlike a mosque, a bookshop does not require a religiously trained leader to be there permanently; instead a religious leadership can be invited in as and when required and the rest of the time ideas and ideology are simply shared among those who frequent the place. The problem is that the self-selecting and concentrated nature of such environments means they can act as echo chambers for ideas introduced there, the participants blindly accepting and repeating those ideas in a similar manner to the rote-learning madrassas they thought they were leaving behind. The Iqra bookshop appears to have been home to numerous study circles led by former Bosnia veterans such as James McClintock, and travelling preachers like Abu Hamza or Abdullah el-Faisal would have been in touch with the shops when they visited Beeston, if they were not specifically invited by the groups there.

For bored young men living in the quiet British heartland, facing the array of local tensions and pressures listed above, the temptation of a created persona which they can immediately identify with and which at the same time offers a much more exciting version of reality than what they had found before, is highly appealing.

Orphans of Islam[79]

The young people drawn in by these structures and personalities have been called the 'orphans of Islam'. No longer anchored to a traditional religious outlook, they are drawn by others to more extreme versions. In some cases, individuals are attracted or shepherded towards a radical view from a young age, making the 'orphans' description seem inaccurate, but nor are they being directed towards mainstream Islam, and more often than not end up drifting away from that to which they had been sent.[80] In other cases, they are brought up in a religious environment, find it lacking or missing some element and instead seek out newer ideas, different from those passed on to them by their parents or elder generations.

This leads us to the piece that is still missing from this picture: the element that makes the dislocated generation choose to look deeper into their religion as the answer. In the first instance it might be understandable that, when they are seeking to redefine themselves, they will pursue a facet of their identity that they may have previously buried: in other words, they rediscover their religious identity as a part of their ethnic identity. But to go from this stage to ideas of seeking jihad is a leap that requires greater motivation than simply reading about it. While in later chapters we shall see how the internet has in some cases come to replace this element, earlier on (and most likely today in many cases) an external connection is necessary. This could come in the form of a contact with the community of radical preachers, ideologues and former fighters who streamed into the United Kingdom during the 1980s and 1990s. The specific phenomenon of how the ideologies transferred to Britain will be addressed in greater detail later, but the aim of this chapter is more to lay out the backdrop which provides the opening into which the radical ideas can flow, and also to show how some of the misguided activism that expresses itself in terrorism has also taken form in other ways.

But there is a deeper question which also needs to be addressed, and this is the reality that not all individuals who become involved in terrorist activity in the United Kingdom are drawn from the sort of ethnic or religious backdrop that we see laid out in this chapter. In fact, while Bradford has been used as a kind of generality, a report published in 2010 that provided a comprehensive overview of convicted British jihadists from 1999 to 2009 showed that only two individuals out of 124 convicted were from Bradford.[81] The overwhelming majority were from London and the surrounding areas, though Birmingham and the cities around Bradford made up most of the remaining community profiled.[82] The correlation between the size of the communities and where convicted terrorists come from is close, with the complication that in some locations where radical activity has been noted it may not have crossed the threshold of criminal activity, and would not necessarily have been registered. The focus on Bradford is symptomatic of the fact that the city's experience is one that has parallels in Muslim communities elsewhere in Britain. Luton has undergone a series of spats as a result of racial tension that led to clashes between local communities and created a space for both extremists descending from Al-Muhajiroun, and also for the enduring presence of hardcore elements supposedly linked to jihadi networks in Pakistan. Similar stories can be written about parts of London and Birmingham, creating a narrative that would not be dissimilar from that seen in Bradford.

Converts who become involved in extremist activity in Britain is another noteworthy issue. Witness the specific cases of Terence Kelly and Trevor Brooks, who as Khalid Kelly and Abu Izzadeen were leaders of Al-Muhajiroun in Ireland and England respectively: at one point Kelly was interviewed by the *The Sunday Times*, announcing he was in the mountains of Waziristan trying to find a British soldier to kill, while Brooks was incarcerated for raising money for terrorism and for inciting terrorism abroad; he claims to have previously trained in Pakistan. Brooks was born to a Jamaican family in East London and was training as an electrician when, just before his eighteenth birthday, he found Islam. Kelly's story is more circuitous: he was born Catholic and was a male nurse in Saudi Arabia running a small bootlegging operation on the side when he was caught by Saudi authorities. Imprisoned for the offence, he was introduced to Islam through an English translation of the Koran and fellow inmates. In 2002 he was released and deported back to the United Kingdom, where he continued pursuing his new faith. Both of these men encountered Omar Bakri Mohammed and his Al-Muhajiroun group at an early stage in their Islamic lives, Brooks when Omar Bakri was still in charge of Hizb ut-Tahrir. He also features prominently in the 1997 documentary about Omar Bakri called 'Tottenham Ayatollah', while Kelly seems to have come across him upon his return to Britain in 2002.[83]

Such cases appear to disrupt the flow of this chapter: nothing in either man's history (bar the likelihood that Brooks, a black convert, encountered racism) particularly compares to the narrative that is laid out hitherto. But the reality is that radicalisation and the spread of jihadist ideas occurs in many different ways. There is no single path to radicalisation, and nor is there a single narrative story for those who become involved in terrorism. While many have a history which fits into the overall pattern of generational dislocation, alienation and youthful confusion which was discussed above, many individuals do not, or instead have followed a trajectory which has few if any commonalities with those we have examined. These individuals are instead more traditional religious seekers, who encounter a radical ideology at a particular moment of disorientation. In some cases, like Khalid Kelly or Richard Reid (the infamous shoe bomber), this occurs in the wake of a brush with the law;[84] while for others, like Dhiren Barot (the Hindu convert whom we encountered before as the author Esa al-Hindi) or Trevor Brooks, it occurs as young men who are trying to define their identity. Both Barot and Brooks appear to have found religion while living humdrum lives: Brooks was training to be an electrician, while Barot was working at a travel agency. The key difference between this community of converts and traditional religious seekers in the wider world is that most of those who become involved in violent Islamist extremism are in fact religiously illiterate. Very few appear to be either genuine religious scholars or attuned to the finer debates of Islamic jurisprudence, except at a superficial level.

There are further divergences, with some extremists having abandoned relatively comfortable lives for a far more questionable lifestyle. The case of Omar Saeed Sheikh is instructive in this regard: educated at a public school, a student at the London School of Economics (LSE), he is now in a Pakistani jail charged with some role in the murder of *Wall Street Journal* reporter Daniel Pearl. Omar came from a comfortable middle-class family in East London, was bright enough to secure a scholarship to his fee-paying school, and spent some time at the Pakistani version of Eton, Aitchison College, in Lahore.[85] His brother went to Cambridge while his sister went to Oxford, and beyond some statements to a fellow prison inmate while he was serving time in India for the kidnap of a group of tourists in New Delhi, it is hard to find much evidence of either deprivation or racism in his past.[86] He may well have encountered negative racial messages at some point, but it is hard to imagine that they would necessarily have been a defining feature of his life. Instead, we see in Omar evidence of an early seeker who was on a path that would have taken him down a traditional middle-class route, before he rebelled as a young man and instead sought to take an active role in fighting for Islam.

And yet, enough of those who become involved in terrorism have a life story that does bear some connection to the narrative of grievance outlined in this chapter, and the larger point is that this narrative has helped radical ideas take root and multiply. And this common Muslim disenfranchisement has further effects on the broader community, whether or not they have a sense of deprivation, making them feel part of a collective that is perceived to be downtrodden. But what binds the 'orphans of Islam', the 'reverts' (converts in Islam are considered reverts, on the grounds that we are all originally Muslims) and 'seekers' like Omar are the individuals who furnish the radical ideas and ideology that offer the answers or solutions they are seeking. The role of the ideologue in transmitting such ideas is essential, but as we shall see in later chapters, it is not always clear that the ideologue inspires them to move from radical activism to active terrorism. Marc Sageman has defined such individuals as 'Fabulists', or forty-year-old men who fill the younger generation's heads with romantic stories of jihad and fighting in foreign lands.[87] Though some may be fantasists, some are the real thing, actual former fighters or individuals who had genuine jihadist connections.

As we saw in the opening chapter, from the 1970s onwards Britain became a safe haven for individuals who espoused anti-establishment ideologies, religious or otherwise. This happened first as secular Arab dissidents made Britain their home after Beirut's descent into chaos, but over time, extremist and fundamentalist individuals followed them, bringing violent ideologies and a propensity for propagation. From early nationalists like those involved in the Kashmiri struggle, to post-Afghan jihad fighters who were no longer welcome in their own nations, and finally to individuals linked into terrorist networks who saw Britain as a base from which to launch operations elsewhere—the United Kingdom over time became a hub of extreme ideas from the Muslim world. And while these individuals' primary preoccupation was originally jihad abroad, over time their ideas filtered into the community around them, attracting recruits, but ultimately also threatening the United Kingdom. The leap from being willing to kill abroad in the name of your religion to being convinced that your act will have more meaning if you conduct it in Britain is probably less substantial than one might think.

3

EARLY EXPRESSIONS

FROM THE RUSHDIE AFFAIR TO JIHAD IN BOSNIA

'Death perhaps is a bit too easy for him; his mind must be tormented for the rest of his life unless he asks for forgiveness to Almighty Allah.'[1]

Salman Rushdie and Kalim Siddiqui were both Muslims born in India but it was the cultural clash of which they were at the heart in 1989 that highlighted the very different faces of British Islam that they represented. On one side stood Salman Rushdie with his novel *The Satanic Verses,* written after the critical success of *Midnight's Children.* On the other stood Kalim Siddiqui, one of the first prominent British Muslim activists, who was at the forefront of the campaign against the book and may even have helped inspire the *fatwa* (legal opinion or ruling), which amounted to a death sentence, passed by Ayatollah Khomeini against Rushdie. The cultural clash of which they stood on either side is widely credited as one of the harbingers of what later culminated in the events of 11 September 2001 and 7 July 2005.

The 'Rushdie Affair', as it has become known, is one of the most written about moments in recent British history.[2] Events since seem only to have magnified its importance, with the Queen's award of a knighthood to Rushdie in 2007 leading to a replay of the anger seen in 1989 upon the book's publication, with protests around the world and a pledge by al-Qaeda's number two, Dr Ayman al-Zawahiri, to carry out a 'very

79

precise response' to the decision 'because he [Rushdie] insulted the Prophet'.[3] While no such 'precise response' took place, the threat echoed the importance of the first set of protests against the book and their particular impact on British Muslim identity. For one young Birmingham-born Muslim whom we have briefly encountered before, Shahid Butt, the protests against Rushdie's book in 1989 marked the first step on a path which led to a Yemeni jail cell as part of a group of British plotters linked to Abu Hamza al-Masri. As Butt put it in an interview twenty years after the Rushdie Affair, 'In 1989 I was twenty-three years old. I knew I was a Muslim, but I think I would have been considered what people would say a Muslim by name, not by actions or deeds.' Hearing about the protests in London, Butt went along and found himself targeted by a police snatch team who treated him roughly, mocking him as a 'part-time Muslim' and threatened to force him to eat a 'pork sandwich' and drink a 'pint'.[4] According to Butt's account, the end result of this abuse was for him to revisit his Muslim roots and eventually join the ranks of supporters around Abu Hamza al-Masri. Having already helped establish the anti-racist Lynx gang mentioned earlier, he then went to Bosnia and ultimately emerged, as we shall see later, as one of seven Britons arrested in Yemen as part of an alleged plot to carry out a bombing campaign—the first such plot known to have emerged from networks in the United Kingdom.

The Rushdie Affair

Doubtless Shahid Butt's tale is not unique, and it is perfectly possible that others who later opted for violence were among the 20,000-odd Muslims who protested in London on 27 May 1989. Others opted for mainstream political activity, like Asghar Bukhari, who went on to found the Muslim Public Affairs Committee UK (MPACUK). He recalls that during the Rushdie protest he 'bought some spray cans of paint and then we sprayed the local library because they had a copy of Salman Rushdie's book in it'.[5] But many of those among the protestors were not from these younger generations, but rather were the older generation, who were deeply offended by the harm they thought that Rushdie had done to their religion. Very few of them had actually read *The Satanic Verses*: instead articles about it were circulated widely. As one of the leaders of the protests against the book in India put it, 'I have not read it, nor do I intend to. I do not have to wade through a filthy drain to know what filth is.'[6] The writer Malise Ruthven described the protesters as strangers in a strange land: 'They wore white hats and long baggy trousers with flapping shirt tails. Most of them were bearded; the older men looked wild and craggy with curly grey-flecked beards—they were mountain men from the Punjab, farmers from the Ganges delta, peasants from the hills of Mirpur and Campbellpur.'[7]

This evocative description captures well one of the roots of the Rushdie protests, where much of the most fervent anger was first stirred up in the north of the country. According to Kenan Malik's authoritative account of events, the first major protest in Britain took place in Bolton on 2 December 1988, when 7,000 Muslims marched across the city and burned the book in a Deobandi-led protest.[8] Likely to have been inspired by messages received from South Asia, the intention was, according to Bolton Action Committee 'supporter' Ismael Lorgat, to burn the book 'to try and attract public attention'.[9] This had little impact, and it was not until the scene shifted to Bradford that the protests gained wide attention.

On a cold January morning in 1989 a small gathering of mostly male Bradford natives got together in the town square to stage a protest. Their hope in taking this step in such a public place was to highlight that as a community of faith they mattered, and they owned a part of the 'police station, town hall, Magistrate's court' that surround the square. Rushdie's book provided them with a vector and reason to stage this protest that was about more than just the book, but also their sense of identity in modern England. But the book was difficult to burn.

As Ishtiaq Ahmed, a Pakistani-born leader at the Bradford Council of Mosques, recalls, 'it was a very thick book, particularly the hardcopies, and it was very difficult to actually set fire to it. So we had to find a can of petrol to pour on the book.'[10] While for Ahmed and his fellow book burners this was a dramatic moment, the press were less interested in it and while the protest garnered far more attention than its Bolton predecessor it was not until the fatwa was issued by the Ayatollah Khomeini in Iran that the Rushdie affair took on the proportions that are now retrospectively ascribed to it.

The point of the demonstration in Bradford, according to Ishtiaq Ahmed, was to make a statement to Britain at large that 'we matter, we exist, we are here, our presence matters'.[11] While undoubtedly some religious sensibilities were key to the decision to burn the book, the groups involved were not extremists; as Philip Lewis puts it, 'perplexingly...it was a moderate community who burned the book'.[12] For them the protests were as much a social statement as an expression of religious anger. Sher Azam, the chairman of the Bradford Council of Mosques, described it at the time in an interview in the weeks before the *fatwa* had been issued: 'Salman Rushdie has been good for us Muslims...we used to have questions about who we are and where we were going. Now we know. We've found ourselves as Muslims. There are action committees in every city up and down the country. It's bringing us together. Muslims are becoming much more united.' Even more positive was the impact that it was having upon Muslim youth: 'for a long time we thought we had lost our children, they were growing up hating our culture. They were angry, withdrawn, we could not reach them. Now they're coming back to us.'[13] For these Bradford elders, the cathartic effect of the Rushdie book burning was to bind together a community that they had helped found in the United Kingdom and that they could see was starting to fragment.

On Valentine's Day 1989, events were wrenched from their hands by the Ayatollah's declaration: 'I inform all zealous Muslims of the world that the author of the book entitled *The Satanic Verses*—which has been compiled, printed and published in opposition to Islam, the Prophet and the Qur'an—and all those involved in its publication who were aware of its contents are sentenced to death.'[14]

The issuing of the *fatwa* (a legal ruling) sentencing Rushdie to death changed the dynamic of the debate around the book. Rushdie went into hiding, embassies withdrew their ambassadors, and an issue that had been quietly simmering in the background since the book was published in late 1988 was transformed into a global event.

For Muslims in Britain, the issuing of the *fatwa* was an empowering moment. As Inayat Bunglawala put it to *The Guardian*: 'when the Iranian Islamic leader, Imam Khomeini, delivered his *fatwa* calling for Salman Rushdie's death, I was truly elated. It was a very welcome reminder that British Muslims did not have to regard themselves just as a small, vulnerable minority; they were part of a truly global and powerful movement. If we were not treated with respect, then we were capable of forcing others to respect us.'[15]

Yet while Mr Bunglawala and others may have felt that the Ayatollah's *fatwa* brought British Muslims back into the fold, the truth was that for the Iranian regime the intention was simply to manipulate a situation to their benefit. Still consolidating power after the 1979 toppling of the Shah, the regime in Tehran was keen to deflect attention from problems at home and ensure that their revolution continued. As Fred Halliday has argued, the *fatwa* 'was a means of meeting his [the Ayatollah's] two main policy goals—mobilization at home, confrontation internationally'. Reporters at the time highlighted that 'Khomeini's revolution is in trouble, with the war against Iraq ended but not won, and a bitter struggle underway in Tehran between the "pragmatists" and the "radicals"…a crusade—or perhaps jihad is a better word—against blasphemy is a good way to unite the Islamic world.'[16]

None of this analysis points to the importance of the role of British Islam within the Ayatollah's thinking; instead, the Iranian regime was taking advantage of the opportunity to get involved and usurp the role of protector of Islam from the Kingdom of Saudi Arabia. For the underdog Shiite regime in Iran, the opportunity to receive global validation and support from the fervour being whipped up around *The Satanic Verses* was too good an opportunity to miss. Up to this point, the Saudi Arabian government had been taking the lead in protests through its support of a network of Jamaat Islami (JI) groups in Britain. One of the first to publicly take up the cause of banning the book in the United Kingdom was the Islamic Foundation in Leicester, an early cradle of Islamic learning in Europe which was first established in 1973 as a way of trying to provide the increasingly permanent British Muslim community with an academic institution to 'think at a more holistic Muslim community level as to what the challenges, what the issues, what the debates would be for Muslim minorities living here [in the United Kingdom]'.[17] The Islamic Foundation was one of the first major Muslim institutions established in the United Kingdom aimed specifically at British (and European) Islam.

Seeing itself primarily as an academic institution of letters, the Foundation was aware of the book, and was made further aware of its scandalous content though contacts with JI groups in South Asia that had been at the forefront of the protests there. With funding and ideological support from the Saudi Arabian government, the Islamic Foundation, the UK Islamic Mission, the Saudi Islamic Cultural Centre and a whole host of other Saudi-funded Muslim organisations in Britain banded together to establish the United Kingdom Action Committee on Islamic Affairs (UKACIA). They put Iqbal Sacranie, a Malawi-born Gujarati who had migrated with his family as part of the East African

Asian contingent that came in the 1960s and 1970s, in charge alongside a Saudi diplomat, Mughram al-Ghamdi. Supported by Saudi funding and driven by individuals of Jamaat Islami or Muslim Brotherhood training, this group wrote angry letters to all mosques telling them to reach out to their communities and lobby politicians to get the book banned. None of this had the desired effect, with little attention being paid by the press or British society more generally, who were appalled at the notion of banning a book. Instead, in an apparent slap in the face to Muslims, *The Satanic Verses* was awarded the 1988 Whitbread Novel Award and was shortlisted for that year's Booker Prize (though it did not win).

It was not until the 'Iranians rolled a grenade under the door'[18] in the form of the *fatwa* that the protests around the book moved into a higher gear. Using their own proxy organisations in the United Kingdom, primarily Kalim Siddiqui's Muslim Institute in Bloomsbury, the Iranian government quickly took control of the ideological battlefield and seized the agenda. Prior to the *fatwa*, Siddiqui's interest in the Rushdie Affair had been minimal, but as he wrote, 'the Imam's intervention on February 14th will go down in history as one of the greatest acts of leadership of the umma by any political or religious leader in the history of Islam'.[19] Siddiqui was originally a Jamaat Islami affiliated individual who established the Muslim Institute in 1972 with mostly Saudi money, but over time he grew tired of such groups' political approaches, and when in 1979 the Iranian revolution shook the Muslim world, he was an early convert to their cause. As one of Kalim Siddiqui's fellow founders of the Institute pointed out, they were 'the first Sunni organization to support the revolution' a fact that gave them 'privileged access to the revolutionaries'.[20] In fact, according to Siddiqui's own account, he may have been in part responsible for the issuing of the *fatwa*, as on 13 February he was in the lounge at Tehran Airport when an Iranian minister approached him and asked about the book. He told the minister what he 'knew of the book and the man' and told his interviewer years later that he 'was absolutely' proud of the possible role he may have played in the *fatwa*'s drafting.[21] Whether the *fatwa* was inspired by Siddiqui's comments, images of a violent protest in Islamabad outside the US consulate, or readings from the book delivered by a group of scholars from Qom to the Ayatollah 'designed to send the old boy incandescent,'[22] by the next morning, the world had heard the ruling.

Amidst the furore that came in its wake, the fundamental message of anger from Bradford Muslims at their lack of a public voice was largely ignored; the entire exchange took on the aspect of an international incident focused on the religious clash of civilisations. But for many British Muslims in the wake of the Rushdie Affair, a renewed sense of activism was awakened. As one Muslim academic put it years later, at the time he was a teenager and for him 'the Rushdie Affair was almost like the arrival of Islam'. Born into a largely non-practising Muslim household, the book came along during his religious awakening, throwing up a series of questions in his mind: 'Why is this guy [Rushdie] saying such offensive and ridiculous things about Islam? And why is the rest of society defending that and promoting it and refusing to take seriously the sentiments and the hurt that Muslims feel?'[23]

The Muslim Parliament

Within the United Kingdom, the competing poles of Iranian- or Saudi-backed organisations used the event to burnish their credentials as the true representatives of British Islam. For the Saudi government, its multiplicity of Muslim Brotherhood or Jamaat Islami organisations continued to advance their cause, but it was the Iranian-supported Muslim Institute that ended up taking most of the limelight. In particular, the head of the Muslim Institute, Kalim Siddiqui, was elevated from an aspirational former *Guardian* journalist to being the leading voice of Islam in Britain—although it is unclear how many people he actually spoke for. As another of his former Muslim Institute co-founders, Ziauddin Sardar, sarcastically pointed out, Siddiqui 'could not believe his luck: he was handed a conflict on a platter…He took over the Muslim leadership—not a difficult task since most Muslims are inarticulate and terrified of the media—and projected himself as *the* Muslim leader ("I have been advising the Muslim community…" is his favourite opening line).'[24] Nevertheless, Siddiqui was vocal, well-funded and media-friendly, meaning he was accepted as a Muslim spokesman by the press. He realised that in order to profit properly from this explosion of interest, he would have to capitalise on it rapidly. He did this through the establishment in 1992 of the Muslim Parliament, an organisation preceded by the grandly titled 'The Muslim Manifesto—A Strategy for Survival'. In this thirty-two-page manifesto, Siddiqui laid out a plan to enable Muslims in Britain to 'develop their own identity and culture within Britain and as part of the global Muslim community'. With swipes at other 'cosmetic and hypocritical creation[s] of the Saudi regime', and couched in exclusionary terms, he declared that action must be taken to prevent a 'surrender to the demands of rampant immoral secularism'.[25]

Much of the manifesto was dedicated to expressing anger at the fact that the Muslim community's view was so roundly disregarded during the Rushdie crisis—a defining moment in Siddiqui's mind—from which he hoped that an array of Muslim institutions would blossom to foster and protect a British Muslim identity: from a 'Muslim Education Commission, the Muslim Law Commission, a Loan Fund for Students in Higher Education, Muslim Weekend Colleges' to finally an International Islamic University out of the 'intellectual foundations' laid by the Muslim Institute. First among these was the creation of the Muslim Parliament, which was founded in 1992 and held its first meeting to controversy in Kensington Town Hall.[26] In his first speech to the assembled 155 Muslim Members of Parliament, Siddiqui declared 'let us make it quite clear that Muslims will oppose, and if necessary defy, any public policy or legislation that we regard as inimical to our interests', and that this new body would take 'up the role and duty of leadership, organisation and discipline within the Muslim community in Britain'.

More salient for the narrative at hand is a passage buried in the Muslim Manifesto about 'jihad': *Jihad* is a basic requirement of Islam and living in Britain or having British nationality by birth or naturalisation does not absolve the Muslim from his or her duty to participate in *jihad*: this participation can be active service in armed struggle abroad and/or the provision of material and moral support to those engaged in such struggle anywhere in the world.'[27]

This document cannot be described as a jihadist screed in the same way one refers to the writings of Sayid Qutb or other jihadi theologians, but the casual way in which it affirms the duty of Muslims to armed jihad struggle is significant. While not wanting to exaggerate the importance of a document that was not widely disseminated among British Muslims, its inclusion of the duty of jihad in such terms is highly significant. At the time, people claiming to be part of Britain's Muslim community would declare to the press that any of them would proudly follow the Ayatollah's commandments to kill Rushdie—a sentiment most infamously reflected in Iqbal Sacranie's comment that 'death, perhaps, is a bit too easy for him;

his mind must be tormented for the rest of his life unless he asks forgiveness to Almighty Allah.'[28] Cognisant of the power of the anger he was stirring up, Kalim Siddiqi asked audiences whether they agreed that Rushdie should be killed and would be met with a sea of raised hands. All of which would set a violent tone around the Rushdie controversy, blending vindictive and violent imagery with Islam. Ultimately, no British assassins appear to have tried their luck against Rushdie, but this very public fusion fostered an image in the common imagination.[29]

As the Rushdie Affair gradually faded into the backround, a new sort of Muslim activism started to take hold. Kenan Malik rightly observed that among the young anti-Rushdie demonstrators, 'Many were not that religious, only a handful could recite the Koran, and most flouted traditional Muslim taboos on sex and drink. They felt resentful about the treatment of Muslims, disenchanted by left-wing politics and were looking for new ways of expressing their disaffection.' But the response they heard from their older generations was tinged with fiery zealous rhetoric, and in the wake of the events new religious groups started to find their feet and draw an audience.

It is a combination of religious naïveté and disaffection that groups on the radical fringe thrive upon and, as we saw in Chapter 2 and in the backdrop of the Rushdie protests, both were in abundant supply. As Shahid put it, the protests in London were for him the first step on a path that ended in a Yemeni jail. However, in between a variety of groups like Jam'iat Ihyaa Minhaaj Al-Sunnah (JIMAS) or Hizb ut-Tahrir (HuT) started to come into their own, espousing rhetoric aimed at a younger generation that offered them individual empowerment packaged with an overarching global solution to the world's problems. Speaking directly to youngsters in a language that they could understand, and exuding an aura of religious knowledge that they claimed came directly from the words of the Prophet, these groups found a fertile ground among the growing generation of young Muslims. In his memoir from the period, Ed Husain, a second-generation Bangladeshi who in the early 1990s was an organising force for a local Jamaat Islami group in East London, recalls that the speakers from JIMAS 'were mostly dynamic speakers, able to stir a crowd and plant genuine interest in Islam'. This was in contrast to the 'absence of strong intellectual leadership skills'[30] in the group he was working with, and completely different from the Islam he experienced when he went to the mosque with his father, where the adults literally spoke over his head. As Ehsan Masood, a journalist for *Q-News* (the first independently funded Muslim publication in the United Kingdom) put it, Hizb ut-Tahrir 'is very attractive to young people, this pre-packaged Islam, particularly for those young Muslims who want to break out of the *biradari* (clan) politics which dominate the society of their parents'.[31] Naturally, this analysis was completely rejected by the young men or women drawn to the radical message, who in a cultish manner would say, 'it is not a question of attraction...we come because we realize it's a reality; there is no God but Allah, and Mohammed is his messenger'.[32]

Hizb ut-Tahrir and Omar Bakri Mohammed

The timeline of Hizb ut-Tahrir's arrival in the United Kingdom is a little vague,[33] but its emergence into the public eye definitely seems to be linked to the arrival in Britain of Omar Bakri Mohammed Fostok, a Syrian refugee who was fleeing persecution in the Arab world and who ultimately played an important role in this narrative. Born in Aleppo in 1958, 'he came from a wealthy family of twenty-eight brothers and sisters. His father had made a fortune selling sheep and pigs and cows. They had chauffeurs and servants and palaces in Syria, Turkey and Beirut.'[34] Young Omar was sent to the Al-Kutaab Islamic Boarding School at the age of five, where he became a Hafiz al Koran (one who memorises the Koran), a feat he allegedly completed by the age of twelve.[35] An activist from early on, something maybe reflected in his ability later to attract and organise youngsters to the cause, he joined the Muslim Brotherhood at fifteen, fleeing (or being expelled by) Syrian authorities at nineteen (in 1977, exactly when the Assad regime was cracking down on dissidents) to go to Beirut where he first joined Hizb ut-Tahrir.[36] After some time in Cairo, briefly at Al-Azhar University (a fact which has been disputed by some of his opponents),[37] he moved to Mecca where he studied at the Islamic School of Saltiyah and started actively working towards advancing HuT.

Omar Bakri claimed to have been under the wing of contacts of the royal family in Saudi Arabia, who would protect him as he countered their official line on such groups, his proselytisation in the kingdom was not popular among the HuT leadership, who were eager not to incur the wrath of the Saudi monarch. Nevertheless, Omar Bakri claims that he managed to recruit some thirty-eight members by 1983, though 'most of

the members were foreign students studying at different Islamic universities, including a number of activists formerly affiliated with Juhaiman
al-Utaiba'.[38] But when he wrote to request some leaflets from the regional
Kuwait branch of HuT, the request was denied and he was commanded
to desist from promoting HuT in the country.[39]

This announcement from his HuT masters came as 'a huge shock' to
Omar Bakri, and as a result caused a 'serious dispute [to break] out
between me and HT organizers in Kuwait who subsequently suspended
my membership of the party'.[40] At this point, he claims to have established Al-Muhajiroun for the first time—choosing the significant date
of 3rd March 1983 (the fifty-ninth anniversary of the abolition of the
Ottoman Caliphate)—along with his thirty-eight 'brothers' to continue
the work he had been doing under HuT. As he was no longer a member
of HuT, Omar Bakri now felt freer to operate in an open fashion, and by
his own account his activities became much bolder:

We started a stickers and leaflet campaign in the major cities, attacking all Kufr
systems [i.e. man-made regimes], including the al-Saud Regime…we pasted and
distributed stickers and leaflets in an underground manner. The regime was not
able to trace the massive sticker campaign to Al-Muhajiroun as we worked fur-
tively and were skilled in these activities. We built up dedicated cells. Our people studied Islam during the day and engaged in distributions and other activities during the night.[41]

Such activity was not appreciated by the Saudi monarchy, and led to
confrontations with the regime. Wiktorowicz's account, based on interviews with Omar Bakri, picks up the narrative:

The movement grew to seventy members and issued a total of sixty-one leaflets
before going undergoing a series of arrests in 1984. Omar used his position at a
Saudi business to get himself and thirteen others released, but two members
were remanded after they physically attacked their interrogators. Membership
dropped to forty-four. In December 1985, the regime launched a second series
of arrests after movement activists were seen distributing leaflets at a local market in Jeddah. During a raid, Omar was caught teaching from a book written by
Abdul Qadeem Zalloom, one of the early leaders of HT, and the regime concluded that there was a connection. After a week of rough interrogation at the
al-Malaz detention center, seven activists, including Omar, were deported.[42]

It is unclear where the other six were sent to, but for Omar Bakri
Mohammed this marked the beginning of his time in the United
Kingdom. Having briefly been there in 1984 on business, his passport

still had an open entry visa that he used to flee Saudi Arabia, though he claims his final destination was intended to be Pakistan or Malaysia.[43] It is worth highlighting that during this time, in which he was allegedly working under his new aegis of al-Muhajiroun, Omar Bakri claims to have told his followers that 'his use of the al-Muhajiroun banner was purely an administrative issue and that they were still acting on behalf of the movement [HuT]'.[44] When they were arrested, Omar Bakri said 'we simply presented ourselves as Muhajiroun (emigrants) who had left their countries in the hope of security sanctuary in Saudi Arabia'; however, when caught with the Zalloom book, their alibi was destroyed.[45]

This is a significant detail, as when in 1996 Omar Bakri Mohammed's disputes with the HuT central leadership led him to separate from the group once again, he apparently started to tell this tale, one that had not been heard before by many HuT activists. As one active HuT member in the 1990s put it:

In 1996 they [HuT central leadership] kicked him out the group. Then he [Omar Bakri] started saying that he'd established a group in Saudi Arabia in 1983 called Al-Muhajiroun, but a lot of members doubted this, they said he made it up, because to become a member of Hizb ut-Tahrir you cannot be a member of any other organisation. So they said if he had already set up a group, why didn't he declare it? When he became a member, how come nobody knew about it? That means he's either lying, or he's being deceitful...I think that Al-Muhajiroun was created in Tottenham in 1996. Personally, I think that. He [Omar Bakri] claims that it was set up in 1983 in Saudi Arabia, but no-one else can verify this prior to 1996, apart from him.[46]

This questionable timing is commonplace in the recounting of events by Omar Bakri Mohammed. What is clear however is that on 14 January 1986 he landed in Britain. A little time later he was approached by the Amir of HuT in Germany who expressed his regrets that he had previously broken from the group and asked him to 'operate as a "member" of Hizb ut-Tahrir' alongside the other 'two brothers' who were already in the United Kingdom. In Omar Bakri's telling, he never actually broke from the group in the first place, so this was not so much a re-instatement into the organisation, but rather a re-activating; and he claims to have told the remaining Saudi members of Al-Muhajiroun to re-start their operations now as HuT members, while he took on the role of establishing operations in the United Kingdom.[47] While it has been repeatedly suggested that Hizb ut-Tahrir in Britain was established by

Omar Bakri Mohammed, it does not seem as though this was actually the case. In an angry press release of 9 August 2005, issued in response to noxious press coverage after the London bombings in which Omar Bakri was frequently referred to as a British member, Hizb ut-Tahrir Britain claimed: 'Omar Bakri Mohammed was not the founder of Hizb ut-Tahrir in Britain.'[48] According to scholar Suha Taji-Farouki's account of HuT's establishment in the United Kingdom (an account based on reporting from within the group), 'the movement established a presence in Britain during the early 1980s when a handful of experienced activists came to live and work in the country', though she does not go into any greater detail.[49]

Whatever the case, by the late 1980s and early 1990s Hizb ut-Tahrir was a growing force in the United Kingdom with Omar Bakri proudly taking credit for much of its success. He later commented, 'my activities in the UK (from 1987 to 1996) awakened all the sleeping cells of HT around the world'.[50] Boastful claims aside, it was not until 1989–90 that notice started to be paid to the group in any sort of serious way. An early story in the *Guardian* from 1989 describes a HuT meeting in East London in quite positive terms, describing the 'serious young men' sitting around discussing what a 'halalicised' financial system would look like, being addressed by one of HuT's key leaders at the time: Jamal Hardwood, a Canadian convert. For this 'earnest' group, 'the sights and sounds of a Friday-night disco are never a temptation. To them the message of Islam has far more attraction.' Unburdened by its later infamy, the article focuses precisely on questions of HuT's appeal, offering this by way of insight: 'while older generations of Muslims have been, and continue to be, mainly concerned with worship, the young have become more interested in Islam as an ideology and a way of life'. The journalist Sean O'Neill, who went on to document Abu Hamza's activity at the Finsbury Park Mosque, places HuT within the context of being part of a 'boom period' in 'youthful fundamentalism' that had been taking place in Britain 'since the late 1970s'. For the youngsters attracted to HuT, 'Islam isn't a religion where you can only adopt a part of it and just talk about that. You have to adopt the whole Islamic viewpoint on society. There can be no compromise with the divine system which has been revealed to us.'[51] The sense of HuT offering a political vision that was absent at the time is something that members of the group have mentioned. Its former leader Maajid Nawaz has spoken of how, had it been a couple of decades earlier, he would have 'become a Marxist,' but the absence of any other voices led him to find HuT.[52] Another former member told the author that in the early 1990s he found that very few other voices were addressing political issues in a way that was appealing. As he put it, 'there were no other useful political movements at the time.'[53] An aspiring young drama student, he found himself reading both Bertold Brecht and HuT materials and was drawn to the latter's narrative because of the political debate that they were bringing into the public narrative.

The political message that they were referring to was first laid out by Mohammed Taqiuddin al-Nabhani, a Palestinian dissident and scholar who studied at Al Azhar in Cairo and established Hizb ut-Tahrir in 1953 in Jerusalem. Dr Suha Taji Farouki, an academic who has produced the official history of HuT (official in that she had the group's sanction and access to internal documents and discussions), offers this description of the group: it 'was conceived as a modern political party having Islam as ideology and the resumption of an Islamic way of life as its goal'.[54] According to Hizb ut-Tahrir Britain's own literature: 'Exclusive to the Muslim world, our political aim is the re-establishment of the Islamic Caliphate as an independent state—having an elected and accountable ruler, an independent judiciary, political parties, the rule of law and equal rights for minority groups. Citizens of the Caliphate have every right to be involved in politics and accounting the ruler—as the role of the ruler (*Khilafah*) is that of a servant to the masses, governing them with justice.'[55]

In its earlier days, the group was more radical in its approach, offering a far more confrontational approach to establishing the Caliphate, harking back to its zenith under the Ottoman Empire. While the rhetoric may have changed over the years, the fundamental objective is to gain control of a Muslim majority country by infiltration of its government and then slowly take over the world from there. According to many researchers and former members, one specific aim is to infiltrate the military (Pakistan is often considered to be the group's main target, given its nuclear capability) and then from there facilitate a complete takeover that is the beginning of the return of the globe to Allah. Previous attempts against governments in Jordan and Egypt have been linked to HuT members, though recently the group has gone to great lengths to distance itself from its violent past. With a centralised ruling body in the Arab world, which dispenses wisdom and guidance to its regional parties and to which individual members may write and receive replies, the group provides its members with a vision of the world and offers them an opportunity to play a role in its creation. According to one twenty-four-year-old female convert in London, who joined HuT almost immediately after converting, put it: 'Hizb ut-Tahrir, the fundamentalist Party of Liberation, looks at every known political and economic system, capitalism, socialism, communism and Islam. It questions how they work and analyses them Islamically, using the evidence of the Koran. It's very rational.'[56]

Married to a Libyan man, she seems happy adopting the strictures of life mandated by a fundamentalist interpretation of Islam, unconcerned by the fact that she can no longer eat with male friends in a private place. The package offered by HuT and Islam appealed to her after she became 'disillusioned with the NHS, where money matters more than people', finding the order now imposed upon her life as more spiritually fulfilling. This sort of account is commonplace among converts in groups like HuT,[57] but it is also part of the appeal among born Muslims. Ed Husain recalls an early encounter with a HuT activist in East London called David, a convert research student described as being 'a tall, thin man with glasses' who 'cared little for social graces', whose 'brimming confidence and radical vision for a future world order' were highly attractive to 'a disillusioned teenage Islamist' like Husain.[58] Offering a vision for a world order rather than simply a more puritanical religious life, HuT's rhetoric found fertile ground among Britain's young men and women. As another activist from East London at the time put it, HuT had a 'wow factor' that made them very successful.[59]

Key to HuT's success was the driving force of Omar Bakri Mohammed, who recognised that there were many potential recruits among young British Muslims. With a natural magnetism and humour that drew people in, he impressed his young acolytes with his knowledge, fiery speeches and willingness to engage with them in personal debates.[60] Having established himself in 1987, he and Farid Qassim, an Iraqi who was then a town planner in London, quickly expanded the organisation, establishing cells up and down the country in universities among communities of 'orphans of Islam'. These young men and women had been brought up, as Shahid Butt put it at the beginning of this chapter, 'Muslim by name,' but were not practising. Instead, as was seen in the last chapter, they confronted social immobility and a generation gap and found themselves lost in between, an opening that Hizb ut-Tahrir thrived on in the early 1990s.

They were not the only group around. As was mentioned earlier, JIMAS (Jam'iat Ihyaa Minhaaj Al-Sunnah, or the Association to Revive the Way of the Messenger, a name which reflects their Salafi roots) was also very active. Established at the University of Kingston in Surrey in 1984 'by four brothers', the group was one of the first major Salafi organisations in the United Kingdom and its head, Abu Muntasir, was 'the father fig-ure of UK Salafism'.[61] Earlier Salafi graduates had joined up with Ahl-e-Hadith groups in the Midlands—the groups' outlooks are very simi-lar—but Abu Muntasir and his group became 'impatient with what they saw as a lack of dynamism and relevance, and an unwillingness to prefer English over Urdu' so they instead formed JIMAS.[62] Encountering them as a young Islamist working with the Jamaat Islami groups in East London, Ed Husain was initially impressed by the group, describing them as sending 'black, white, and Asian converts who had studied Islam in Saudi Arabia to live and preach in the UK. They spoke passionately about the idea of one God, *tawheed* [oneness of God] in Arabic, and ceaselessly warned against *shirk* [worship of false gods].' Dressed in attire more suited to the Saudi desert, 'they had huge, bushy beards and their trousers were very short, just below their knees. They looked like people from another era, austere in their ways, harsh in their conduct, and constantly repri-manding us for our own.'[63]

In much the same way as Hizb ut-Tahrir appealed to the confused identity that lay within Britain's Muslim youth, JIMAS would tell its fol-lowers 'you don't feel at home in Britain, but you can't go "home" to a country you have never visited. So we have a third identity for you—a pan national Islamism that knows no boundaries and can envelop you entirely.'[64] This provided the youngsters with meaning and internal bond-ing to the group, as former member Usama Hasan put it: 'we had a strong sense of being under siege. It was all a conspiracy against Islam, and we were the guardians of Islam.' Coming from a religious family that had moved to Pakistan during Partition, his father was a Pakistani cleric who was later sent to the United Kingdom by the Saudi Ministry of Religious Affairs. Hasan arrived in Britain when he was four years old and by age eleven he had memorised the Koran. Brought up in North London he encountered racism on the streets, and the camaraderie of numbers offered by JIMAS offered a practical shield against this. A bright student, he managed to obtain a scholarship to the private City of London School and a place to study physics at Cambridge University. Unlike his

Cambridge peers, however, Usama chose to spend his 1990 holidays at an Arab-run training camp in eastern Afghanistan. Alongside two of his JIMAS brothers, they 'learned how to use guns', got to fire AK-47s and were brought to frontline positions where the mujahedeen were fighting the last hold-out communist groups.[65]

JIMAS's decision to go to Afghanistan in late 1990 was precipitated by the growing number of inquiries they were getting from British Muslims about whether it was permissible to join the jihad in Afghanistan. The London-based JIMAS members had been hearing mixed reports about what was going on in Afghanistan and thought it best to investigate for themselves. This would not be the first trip for Abu Muntasir, who had initially made contact with Afghan fighters through contacts in Holland in 1988–89, subsequently travelling to fight in Kunar in 1989.[66] Armed with a point of contact in Islamabad, the group headed off, only to be re-directed by an Egyptian they met in Peshawar, from where they took a bus through Bajaur to Kunar province in Afghanistan; Bajaur, Kunar and neighbouring Nuristan were all areas heavily influenced by Ahl-e-Hadith Salafism. Here they were warmly welcomed by the Palestinian head of the group they connected with, who was exited to find such bearded and faithful Muslims from the United Kingdom. As the most proficient Arabic speaker among the group, Hasan acted as translator for much of the trip, helping conduct an interview with the camp leader to understand better what was taking place in Afghanistan. At the camp they found a mix of Saudis, Kuwaitis and Algerians, with a group of Malaysians and Filipinos who were unable to communicate with anyone else and were thus left to themselves. Although the usual requirement was for a three to six month training period before they were allowed to go to the front, a special dispensation was given to the British group after a week's training. Having seen the front and spoken to the camp leader, the trio returned home, where they subsequently provide peopled who asked with an accurate assessment of the situation in Afghanistan. By Hasan and Abu Muntasir's count, from 1989 onwards, JIMAS sent some 50–100 fighters to the battlefields of Afghanistan, Kashmir, Bosnia, Burma and the Philippines.[67]

While Usama Hasan's is a first-hand account of leaving the comforts of England for a foreign battlefield, among many individuals involved in extremist groups or indeed among the wider Muslim community there were many rumours of similar stories. Largely unverifiable, they merely served to strengthen the mystique of armed jihad. Husain recalls 'one student who left for what was increasingly being called "jihad" never returned to Britain. He was considered a martyr. Increasingly there were reports of individual Muslims from different cities going to join the jihad.'[68] The family of Hasib Hussain, one of the 7 July bombers, reported that they had heard rumours that Shehzad Tanweer had apparently been involved in the fighting in Afghanistan.[69] Defending his actions on the witness stand, Waheed Ali, another member of the community in Beeston told of how 'a lot of brothers used to go to Kashmir training camps. ... out of a hundred brothers, ninety-five would come back and do their normal day-to-day job, or they go back again, and five or six brothers would fight.'[70] Thus while many might go over to Kashmir or Afghanistan, it was a smaller number who would become combatants.

There were also important doctrinal differences between Hizb ut-Tahrir's approach to armed jihad and JIMAS's. While the former would refuse to condemn jihad or armed activity by Muslims—during repeated interviews in the 1990s Farid Qassim abjured from criticising terrorist actions abroad, and was quoted as saying 'there are 123 verses in the Koran about fighting and killing. Ours is not a passive religion'[71]—it did not mobilise its members to participate either. JIMAS, on the other hand, appears to have taken a far more active role in getting people to fight. Usama Hasan recalls returning from Afghanistan and spending his time recruiting Muslim students to Wahhabism and trying 'to persuade people to go to fight in Afghanistan and later Bosnia, since the Afghan jihad was ending.' By Hasan's count some two dozen or more members of the group were believed to have gone to Afghanistan.[72] Underlying all of this was a message similar to Hizb ut-Tahrir's, offering the mirage of the Caliphate as the final objective and 'easy answers' to the complex identity questions felt by young British Muslims: 'go back to the original sources, and [follow them] literally'.[73]

Since these early days, both Hizb ut-Tahrir and JIMAS have changed: JIMAS in particular has rejected many of its former postures and support for armed jihad, while HuT has gone to great lengths to reform its image in the United Kingdom. Three of the individuals cited, Ed Husain, Usama Hasan and Maajid Nawaz, have now switched sides and condemn the extremism they formerly espoused. Yet, it seems hard not to conclude that during the early 1990s both groups to some degree played an important role in the radicalisation of British Muslim youth. In JIMAS's particular case, Usama Hasan points to a young man he met at a JIMAS-influenced LSE Islamic Society study circle: Omar Saeed Sheikh, the young Pakistani Briton who became one of Britain's first terrorist exports, first as a fighter with a Kashmiri group, Harakat ul-Mujahedeen, and later as the man convicted for the kidnapping of *Wall Street Journal* reporter Daniel Pearl. Hasan's enduring memory of Sheikh is 'that he was a clean-shaven, well-educated public schoolboy'.[74] The two young men, both Pakistani-Britons, privately educated and students at two of the nation's most prestigious universities rejected the path of their peers and instead pursued a life of religious struggle. Hasan believes that he may have been the one to first turn Sheikh onto the violent radical life: when he met him at a JIMAS study circle at LSE, Sheikh asked about Bosnia and was surprised to hear from Hasan that one could go to fight there. It was years before Hasan saw Sheikh again. Encountering him at an event at Imperial College, Hasan was struck to find the young man now had a long beard, wore a Pakistani-style shalwar kameez and claimed to have fought alongside Harakat ul-Mujahedeen.[75]

Hizb ut-Tahrir's alleged role in nurturing terrorists is a more complex tale, with anecdotes pointing to individuals who passed through the group and then on to terrorism—with it remaining unclear whether HuT had any involvement in these individuals' decisions. As a former HuT member put it, 'HT's paradigms justify jihadist activity…as soon as you start declaring the world *dar al harb* (land of war) and *dar al kufr* (land of non-Muslim), and you starting using this language…then it justifies a militant approach.'[76] A review of press coverage at the time points to a high instance of anti-Semitic and anti-Israeli statements on HuT's part, and in public statements both Farid Qassim and Omar Bakri expressed strong opinions. In February 1991, at a London anti-war protest, speakers stirred the crowd with the apocalyptic pronouncement, 'We will never rest until the forces of the allies are destroyed … until the desert sands are wet with their blood.'[77] Calling itself the International Islamic Front, and led by 'Omar Mohammed', the group was at the forefront of a number of protests that year, and appears to have been one of several extremist organisations drawing some, albeit limited, support from Britain's domestic Muslim population.[78] In one instance during a Hizb ut-Tahrir rally at the time, members were reported to have called for 'holy war' alongside Saddam Hussein.[79] But it is not clear how much this ideology was infused in the group's ideology, or something driven by its leaders. Moazzam

Begg ascribed the group's radicalism to Omar Bakri, 'to be fair to Hizb ut-Tahrir, at the time when Omar Bakri was their leader, then, yes, they were a bit of a crackpot lunatic-type organisation'.[80] Certainly, without Omar Bakri at the helm, it became a different entity.

In the early 1990s, both JIMAS and HuT capitalised upon the revival of interest in Islam that occurred after the Rushdie Affair erupted and later dominated the Islamic scene in Britain. While it was the Muslim Parliament that was the most visible Islamic organisation that emerged in the wake of the Rushdie Affair (not forgetting the UK Action Committee on Islamic Affairs, which went on to become the Muslim Council of Britain many years later), it was groups like Hizb ut-Tahrir that found a constituency among some young British Muslims. Dr Zaki Badawi, an Egyptian Muslim immigrant encountered earlier, and usually referred to at the time as one of the most senior 'moderate' Muslim voices in the United Kingdom, observed in 1993 that 'Hizb ut-Tahrir is not that significant a force. But, interestingly, it's getting a stronger following than the Muslim Parliament…it's talking quite a lot especially to young people, and is becoming quite active in the mosques around London.'[81] This account is supported by the testimony of one young Muslim student. In 1990, he attended King's College London, choosing this university as it was going to take him to the capital, the cradle of Islamic activism at the time. Once he got to campus, however, he found:

The next three years were a nightmare, you kept banging your head against these sorts of organisations … we were stuck between four forces on campus … Hizb ut-Tahrir, which was gaining ground about 1990; Salafis, who had a sustained and significant presence and were still quite hardline, people like JIMAS; organisations like the Young Muslims, broadly inspired from the revivalist Islamist message; and finally, those who didn't want to have anything to do with these groups.

He chose the moderate line espoused by the Young Muslims, which led him to a lifetime as an academic in Muslim affairs, but he could see that the main forces on campus were clearly the radical fringe 'political activists' (Hizb ut-Tahrir) or the 'theologically conservative' (JIMAS).[82]

Bosnia

Events in the former Yugoslavia reached a tipping-point in 1991 when Croatia and Slovenia broke away from the Serbian-dominated Yugoslav federation. After a series of bloody clashes, a semblance of peace was finally imposed in January 1992. It was only a temporary respite, and the stirring separatism in Bosnia-Herzogovina finally spilled over into open conflict when in April 1992 Bosnia declared independence from Serbia. Ethnic Serbs left in Bosnia were unhappy with this state of affairs, as were their brethren on the other side of the new border in Serbia, and fighting soon broke out. As stories emerged of Serbian forces easily overrunning their under-gunned Bosnian enemies, the West looked away, refusing to move on the arms blockade imposed in 1991. US Secretary of State James Baker famously declared, 'We don't have a dog in the fight.'[83]

In the Muslim world, the conflict was seen in a completely different light. As Zaki Badawi put it, 'Bosnia has shaken public opinion throughout the Muslim world more deeply than anything since the creation of Israel in 1948.'[84] Soon enough, men from across the Muslim world were arriving in Bosnia to cast their lot with their brothers in a defensive jihad. As analyst Evan Kohlmann put it in his book analysing the phenomenon of foreign fighters who arrived there from around the world, 'thousands of young men driven by a warped sense of religious chivalry travelled to Bosnia ostensibly in the hope of defending the ancient and threatened Muslim community in the Balkans'.[85] Muslim governments also saw this as a propitious opportunity to demonstrate once again that they were the defenders of the faithful: King Fahd of Saudi Arabia reportedly donated $8 million of his personal fortune to the Bosnians, while Sheikh Jaber Ahmed al-Sabah, the Emir of Kuwait, gave $3 million. By 1993, one report stated that Saudi Arabia had given a total of $65 million, the United Arab Emirates $5 million, while Pakistan had pledged $30 million. Iran rapidly followed suit, setting up an Embassy in 1994 and openly flouting the arms embargo.[86]

In June 1993, during the seventh session of the Muslim Parliament, a proposal was tabled to raise money for fellow Muslims suffering in Bosnia. However, one group went a step further, and sought to link this to a proposal to establish 'a body of Muslim fighters' that would be trained and 'ready to defend Muslims in Bosnia or anywhere else in the world'.[87] Under the supervision of Parliament spokesman Massoud Shadjareh, a former campus radical in the United States of Iranian descent who moved to Britain in 1971 and is now head of the Islamic Human Rights Commission (IHRC), the Human Rights Committee (HRC) of the Parliament took the lead in activities with regard to Bosnia. According to Iqbal Siddiqui, Kalim Siddiqui's son, writing in a magazine he edited, *Crescent International*: '[Great] importance was given to the Human Rights Committee (HRC) in the early years of the Parliament. It was this committee which was largely responsible for the Parliament's work on Bosnia, which was arguably the most important and successful work the Parliament ever undertook. The HRC's "Arms for Bosnia" fund was later up-graded to a "Jihad Fund" which collected for the mujahideen working in Algeria, Kashmir and other parts of the world.'[88]

Events to raise money for the fund took place around the country. In one instance in the small town of Chesham, in southern England, the County Council were obliged to close a fete that was openly raising money for the 'Arms for Bosnia' appeal.[89] Years later, in 1999, this 'Global Jihad Fund' (GJF) achieved some notoriety when it was revealed that the webmaster Mohammed Sohail, a second-generation Pakistani, was rallying for global jihad and Osama bin Laden through the GJF, using his work email account at Railtrack. In an interview when he was exposed in 1999, Mr Sohail baldly admitted: 'I work for two people really, Mr Massari and Osama bin Laden.'[90] The Mr Massari he referred to was Mohammed al-Massari, the Saudi dissident and leader of the Committee for the Defence of Legitimate Rights (CDLR), whom we encountered towards the end of Chapter 1. Sohail was further linked to the Muslim Parliament through the website he helped establish, the Islamic Gateway, which he claimed was 'sponsored by both Kalim Siddiqui and Mohammed al-Massari'.[91] The two are natural allies: an anti-Saudi dissident and a deeply pro-Iranian (and thus anti-Saudi) organisation. That the Muslim Parliament was pro-Iranian and later anti-Saudi cannot be doubted: aside from Kalim Siddiqui's known passion for the revolution in Iran, one Muslim recalled attending an event in the 1990s where the audience were encouraged to participate in anti-Saudi chanting.[92]

To return to the Balkans, however, the British Muslim community (as well as the community at large) joined the many other Muslim communities across the globe raising money and sending relief supplies through to the beleaguered Bosnian Muslims. Much of this was undoubtedly innocuous charity fundraising and relief, but Ed Husain recalls being involved in meetings at London universities where funds were raised and individuals sent to join the mujahedeen in Bosnia. One video that he and some friends obtained entitled 'The Killing Fields of Bosnia' portrayed atrocities like 'the serving of men's testicles on trays, Serbs slaughtering pregnant Muslim women'.[93] Most distressing of all was that it was taking place 'less than two hours from Heathrow' while their government did nothing about it.[94] The dilemma for many British Muslims was a deep one:

The Bosnian issue had a profound impact on the psyche of British Muslims. In positive ways, but largely negative ways unfortunately—in the radicalisation process. ... Bosnia came in as part of that broader negative narrative that because you're Muslims you'll never really be accepted in Europe, and here is an example of people who have been in Europe for centuries, who are white, who have ... gone beyond integration into assimilation. Who are not religious, necessarily, but just because they are Muslims, they are being picked on and slaughtered and raped and expelled from their communities and brutally murdered. This fed into the narrative that Europe has a deep problem with Islam, and it's a Christian problem partly, but it is also a cultural European problem. And this was a sort of argument that was being put forward by people. Not just extremist groups, this was a mainstream narrative in the Muslim community.[95]

After the bruising Rushdie Affair and the religious revivalism that came in its wake, here once again was evidence that the fears of persecution that plagued Britain's Muslims were in fact real. Muslims, and society as a whole, watched as massacres and sectarian fighting not seen since the Second World War once again occurred in Europe; and all the while Western governments stood by and did nothing. Highlighting that this was taking place at around the same point that he started to re-engage with his religious identity, Mohammed Shakil, a Beeston native who went to a training camp alongside Mohammed Siddique Khan and was later convicted on terrorism charges, reported:

Back when I started practising is when I first saw actual footage of what had happened in Bosnia and places like Kosovo and Albania and these sorts of countries, I mean these are sorts of things I had never been exposed to before and when I see this videos, especially the Bosnia video which is nearby here, I think that really had an effect on me and when I seen the massacre and the mass killing I mean I could not believe that one human being could do this to another—do you understand?—and it was like happening everywhere in Bosnia, Kosovo.[96]

One young Pakistani-Briton growing up in Sheffield as a teenager at the time recalls going to ask his father about the situation in Bosnia and being told that there was nothing that could be done, that 'political situations will get better by themselves'. While the issue was a topical one at the mosque, a similar line would be repeated there, with invocations that 'we need to pray for these people and send them clothes'. But this was not enough for a young man: 'when you're that age you're a teenager and you're a bit more rebellious and you want to do more than just pray and send clothes'.[97] Hizb ut-Tahrir clearly saw an opening here that they could profit from. One former member told of how 'Bosnia tipped [the group] over into political radicalisation.' In one instance, he recalled listening to Omar Bakri Mohammed's *khutbah* (sermon) at a mosque in Turnpike Lane and a weeping Bangladeshi present in the audience drawing everyone's attention to a group of Bosnian refugees in the back of the room. Omar Bakri used this opportunity to hammer home his message: 'The Muslim ummah is like a body, if you hit it in the arm then the body will hurt over.'[98] The willingness of Hizb ut-Tahrir to engage with these ideas and talk openly about what the meaning of Bosnia helped them grow:

HT organised a talk in the mosque about Bosnia, specifically about this issue, so I went down to that. What was interesting to me about that talk was, you know for the very first time someone had explained in detail where is Bosnia, what's the history of the place, what's the geography of the place, what kind of people live there, no-one had really explained this to me before. And also, their narrative into why this conflict was happening and not just this conflict, but why all these type of conflicts like Iraq, Kashmir, and wherever else. And their narrative was, that the West, America and Britain, didn't really like Muslims, and they were orchestrating these kinds of wars. ... In the absence of any other explanation, I started getting more interested in this group.[99]

For this young man, confronting the identity crisis experienced by most teenagers, but exacerbated by the fact that he found he felt at home neither in the United Kingdom nor among his relations in Pakistan, Bosnia appears to have played the crucial catalytic role in getting him involved in Hizb ut-Tahrir. Slightly older youths, however, felt that, rather than simply sending clothing, they could be involved in the supply convoys and play a more proactive role in helping their Muslim brothers and sisters. Omar Saeed Sheikh, the eager young Muslim whom Usama Hasan had met at a JIMAS study circle, chose to join one of these convoys. By Hasan's account, 'Sheikh was furious about the massacres of Muslims in Bosnia, and demanded the study group lay down their Koranic debates and act.'[100] As mentioned above, he found the young man surprised to learn that one could join the fighting in Bosnia. A senior member of the Muslim Parliament at the time recalls having to dissuade young Omar from seeking to connect to jihadist groups in Bosnia through trips they were organising.[101] Finally Omar got his wish to go through Asad Khan, one of the coordinators of 'Convoy of Mercy', which was running regular missions into the war-torn country.[102] Sheikh approached him after a speech he had given in 1993 saying he was interested in going along to help. He was never to reach Bosnia, however, and by Croatia was apparently 'sick as a puppy'.[103]

According to Sheikh's diary from the period, it was at this point that he made a crucial connection: unable to go on, 'due to indisposition and fatigue', Sheikh stayed in Split, Croatia, where he met Abdur Rauf, a Pakistani member of Harakat ul-Mujahedeen (HuM). Rauf saw a potential recruit in young Sheikh, and told him not to waste his time with aid convoys to Bosnia, but instead to pursue armed jihad in Pakistan. A fellow Pakistani, Rauf realised the importance of family ties to the young Briton, and suggested he went to the Clifton Mosque in North London where he could contact a preacher who would help persuade his father to allow him to join the jihadi warriors.[104] Soon after his return from Bosnia, Omar did just as he was instructed. This is unlikely to have been a unique instance: the presence of British Muslims and parallel activities of South Asian militants like HuM or Lashkar-e-Taiba (LeT) fighting in Bosnia means that it is likely other, similar, connections were made.

Convoys and fundraising efforts took place around the country.[105] Moazzam Begg first encountered Bosnian Muslim refugees at the Birmingham Central Mosque, at this point fired up by earlier experiences in Afghanistan where he had travelled to find out more about jihad. He later recalled that the Bosnians 'fascinated me because they were these blonde-haired, blue-eyed Caucasians who I had never heard of. I felt a great affinity towards them.'[106] This led to a series of trips to Bosnia, by Begg's count between six and eight, during which time he both engaged with 'development projects and delivering aid and food', but also giving financial donations which went to the Bosnian Army. By his own account, he did not, however, take up arms himself; as he put it, 'I wasn't ready to die.'[107] In his autobiography Begg recounts visiting training camps in Zenica along with two other British participants in the 'Convoy of Mercy' aid effort. He does not mention participating in fighting.[108]

Others were less bound by such restraints and, drawn by the mystique of jihad and driven by youthful exuberance, opted to fight alongside the Bosnian forces and the growing international brigade.[109] While the actual numbers involved are hard to determine, cassettes released by Azzam

Publications at the time highlight the cases of at least three Britons who allegedly fell on the battlefields of Bosnia. The tapes, amateurish recordings with an electronic-sounding voice reading a text interspersed with sounds from the battlefield and *nasheeds* (religious songs) in Arabic, tell the tales of individual Bosnian mujahedeen operations and detail the biographies of those men who died. The voice-over is provided by an unidentified, but clearly British, individual who intones, 'Azzam recordings in London UK presents to you the first cassette in a series of cassettes on real life experiences in Jihad.' Entitled 'In the Hearts of Green Birds', the tapes detail one British casualty: David Sinclair, a twenty-nine-year-old IT worker who converted to Islam, changed his name to Dawood al-Brittani, and encountered trouble at work in his new Muslim attire. After quitting his job he went to Bosnia, apparently giving away two passports to other non-British fighters who were seeking some respite from the conflict. Then, sometime in the summer of 1993, he experienced an odd dream in which he apparently saw the house of another fallen mujahid, 'Abu Ibrahim, the Turkish brother from Britain who was killed by the French United Nations in Sarajevo Airport'. The following morning Sinclair was killed during an operation against Croat forces.[110]

Two further British mujahedeen martyrs are detailed in the sequel cassette, 'Under the Shade of Swords': Abu Mujahid and Sayyad al-Falastini (doubtless not their real names, though al-Falastini denotes he is of Palestinian extraction). Both fell at about the same time: Abu Mujahid on the battlefield, but Sayyad al-Falastini in an accident at base-camp. A twenty-five-year-old engineering graduate from London University, Abu Mujahid postponed getting a job to get involved in aid work for Bosnia instead:

The war in Bosnia was into its second year and there was much shouting and screaming still going on in the Muslim community in Britain. Abu Mujahid, however, was one who firmly believed that actions speak louder than words; he made his first journey to Bosnia in 1993 in an aid convoy carrying supplies, food and medicine. Over the next two years, Abu Mujahid hurried back and forth between Bosnia and Britain carrying valuable supplies to the brothers who are there. Between trips, he travelled the length of Britain reaching its smallest parts in his efforts to raise money for the cause and increase awareness among Muslims there. In the summer of 1995, he postponed his marriage arrangements to go and fight in Bosnia. For the last two years he had been helping with aid work and now he realized that aid work without fighting was a lost cause. He arrived in August 1995 and joined the training camp of the mujahedeen soon after that.[111]

At the camp he proved an adept warrior and impressed the others with his zeal, declaring that he would 'stay until we get victory or I get martyred'. Eventually, on 10 September 1995, he got his wish when he was killed during 'Badar', a major operation named for a famous clash as told in the Koran, in which the prophet Mohammed led a smaller army of the faithful to victory against the Meccans. Told in romantic and mythological language reminiscent of biblical tales or saints' biographies, Abu Mujahid apparently appeared to a fellow comrade in a dream soon after his death. Back in London in the meantime, his sister reported having a dream six days before his body was found in which she saw him 'lying down with a white sheet covering him'. Similar hagiographical language is deployed in the case of Sayyad al-Falastini 'from South London':

Born in Britain he migrated at an early age with his family to Saudi Arabia; after spending most of his youth there he returned to Britain when he was twelve. A very intelligent and physically fit young boy, Sayyad enjoyed making his friends laugh and playing practical jokes on them. He was of Palestinian origin so there was a background of realising the importance of jihad in his family. Sayyad's first desire in going to Bosnia for jihad was when he was only sixteen, after hearing an inspiring Friday sermon by a young brother who had fought there. Unfortunately, this did not bear any fruit. After being selected as the leader of the Islamic society at his college and becoming a fully practising Muslim, Sayyad again became interested in partaking in jihad somewhere around the world. He set about saving up his money from his part-time job, from which he would give some of his earnings to his family, and the rest he would save for jihad. He refused to take even a penny from donated funds, insisting that it all came from his own pocket. In the summer of 1995, after months of patience and preparation and the full support of his mother, Sayyad finally left England and travelled to Bosnia. The two brothers who took him to the coach station in London noticed an unusually sad expression on Sayyad's otherwise smiling face. Upon being pressed why he was sad, he mentioned his sorrow at leaving his mother. It seemed that he knew he was not going to see her again in this life.[112]

According to the recording, Sayyad was the fifth British mujahedeen to be martyred, killed when a truck blew up next to him on 12 December 1995, two days short of his nineteenth birthday. In the days before he died his mother reported dreaming of an empty house, and after he was killed she reported that a green bird with camouflaged wings apparently kissed her on the cheek in a dream; according to a *hadith* (saying) of the prophet, martyrs 'souls are inside green birds', and Sayyad was apparently wearing his trademark camouflage trousers when he met his death.

Recorded for recruiting purposes, and still venerated on extremist web-sites years later, these hagiographies have clearly been composed with another purpose in mind, and the details are difficult to confirm inde-pendently. The man accused of being Azzam.com's webmaster, Babar Ahmad, admitted years later in court that he had fought in Bosnia a number of times in the 1992–1995 war.[113] Officially reported deaths of British citizens in Bosnia lacked this mythology and occurred in far murk-ier circumstances: in one case Serb shelling of a supposed aid convoy resulted in the death of a Briton, Gulam (or Ghulam) Jilani Soobiah, aged forty-four, from Leicester. A sympathetic obituary in the *Guardian* newspaper described Mr Soobiah as 'a hippie turned Muslim activist' who had trekked around the Muslim world as well as working for a time in Saudi Arabia as a director in a plastics company and establishing a newspaper in Mauritius called *La Renaissance Islamique*. A King's College graduate in engineering, he had established 'Helping Hands', the Peterborough-based charitable organisation whose convoy he was with when he was killed, as well as earlier founding another organisation involved in promoting exchanges between children in Britain and Yugoslavia.[114] However, in a report in the *Daily Mail* that was later dis-missed by the charity, another individual who survived the attack on the convoy, a Turkish Kurd named Hakan Uzun, claimed that 'they were in a convoy of 12 mujahedeen…and that they were carrying rifles and gre-nades'. Whichever the case, this example nonetheless highlights the inter-est among the British Muslim community in helping out their brethren in Bosnia.[115]

Other instances of foreign British fighters appear more clear-cut. In one report, a British army unit outside Guca Gora came across a fear-some band of armed men wearing 'Afghan turbans and green headbands with Islamic script'. The two sides prepared for a stand-off until one of the men, 'whose face was largely covered by a blue bandana', stood for-ward and told the British peacekeepers 'in a strong Yorkshire accent' to 'be cool, these people won't fire until I give them the order'.[116] Maybe less conclusive, but demonstrating nevertheless the sort of light in which some young British Muslims viewed Bosnia and the recruitment efforts underway in the United Kingdom, researcher Evan Kohlmann reported in 2002 coming across a video at the notorious Finsbury Park Mosque which featured a masked man identifying himself as 'Abu Ibrahim'. Undated, the video shows the twenty-one-year-old third-year medical student at Birmingham University living in Golders Green, North London, condemning his fellow Muslims who fail to take up arms, while extolling the virtues of his own participation: 'I watch the TV and tears roll down my face when I see the Muslims in Bosnia, Muslims in Palestine, Muslims in Kashmir. And then I come [to Bosnia] and you feel a sense of satisfaction. You feel that you are fulfilling your duty. You feel that you are doing what the Prophet and his companions done [sic] 1400 years ago.'[117]

This is the sort of emotion that Ed Husain was seeking to mobilise when he showed videos from Bosnia at his school in East London, and was an early influence on young Abdulla Ahmed Ali, who was growing up at the time in nearby Waltham Forest, East London. Later convicted as a key plotter in the August 2006 plot to blow up an unspecified number of planes on transatlantic routes, he recalled in court that 'when I was about fifteen or sixteen I remember the Bosnian war going on and I remember images of concentration camps, of people looking like skeletons and things like that. I was aware they were Muslims.'[118] This testimony echoes the earlier statements by Mohammed Shakil in Beeston who found Bosnia brought it all home for him: 'it was so close that it made me feel that it's Muslims that are getting slaughtered by disbelievers in them countries.'[119]

With leaders like Kalim Siddiqui openly calling for individuals to fight and support their Muslim brothers in Bosnia, while television was filled with daily images of death and misery, it is hardly surprising that some young men answered the call. As the case of Sayyad al-Falastini showed, 'for the price of a coach ticket, young British Muslims were able to travel to the Balkans to fight alongside these Arab volunteers'[120] and do their bit to support the cause. Exact figures are not known, but estimates suggest that a few hundred may have gone over to fight. And while some fell in battle, and some decided the experience had been enough, others returned home having tasted jihad determined to pursue it further.

The impact of Bosnia

Bosnia's impact on Britain's Muslim community should be understood on two levels: ideological and practical. As we saw before, the persecution of Muslims in Bosnia and the absence of a rapid Western response were seen by many British Muslims as evidence that there was no role for them in Europe, indeed that Europeans did not care about Muslims, and were content to let them be slaughtered. In fact, for many it seemed as though the Western arms embargo suggested support for the massacres. For the generation of Muslims growing up in the post-Rushdie Affair world and rediscovering their roots, this further confirmed their sense of alienation.

For some of those who were blooded in the Bosnian conflict, it was the beginning of a path that led to terrorism convictions in Britain. Prominent among former British Bosnian jihadists is Andrew Rowe, who was picked up in 2003 on the French side of the Channel Tunnel having apparently met with another Muslim convert and former Bosnia fighter, Lionel Dumont, in Frankfurt.[121] An aimless young Londoner living a life of drugs and partying, Rowe converted to Islam in 1990 and in 1995 offered himself as a driver to aid convoys to Bosnia. He flew into Croatia, at which point he says he changed his mind and decided to become a fighter.

Rowe: I wanted to participate and help people defend themselves against an aggressive force.

Prosecution: Were you prepared to fight?

Rowe: Yes. The situation in Bosnia required more than aid, it needed able-bodied people to help defend the Bosnians. It was accepted that I was there to help these people defend themselves and their lands.[122]

Once in Bosnia he connected with local fighters and was taken to an armoury where he got a sense of the thrill that in part appears to have driven him. 'I thought, "I've arrived now." That was the first time I'd seen rifles.' Having undergone some training, Rowe appears to have thrown himself into the conflict and fought alongside Bosnian forces. His efforts were to be short-lived, as he was soon caught in a Serb rocket attack, ended up in a field hospital and eventually returned to Britain in July 1995, proudly brandishing his wounds and *nom de guerre*, 'Yussuf Abdullah the Jamaican'.[123] Somewhere along the way he met Lionel Dumont, a French convert who served in Bosnia and later tried to set up a terror cell in Japan. This attempt by Dumont failed, and he instead became involved with a gang of former Bosnian fighters connected to Algerian jihadists who carried out a series of armed robberies in France in 1996. Rowe's involvement in these activities is unknown, but by the early 2000s police across Europe suspected him of involvement in a terror network and placed him under surveillance. Admittedly while under Guantanamo Bay interrogators claimed that Binyam Mohamn Ethiopian with British residency who was captured in Pakistan in April 2002, reported how in London he had watched radical videos with Rowe, identifying him by his adopted battlefield name, or *kunya*, 'Yusuf al-Jamaiki'.[124] In later correspondence with his lawyer, Clive Stafford Smith, Mohammed made it clear he did not know Yusuf.[125] The British government later awarded Mohammed £1 million compensation in a 2011 legal settlement on account of the torture to which he had been subjected.

Subsequent to Rowe's arrest and conviction, it was discovered that he had used four passports in eight years, some of which were found to have had pages and visas ripped from them. This was a crude method by which he attempted to mask his globetrotting travel, encompassing Thailand, Slovenia, Pakistan and Afghanistan. In 2000 he was turned away from Gatwick Airport as a suspected drug dealer with $12,000 in cash (a surprising amount given that he was living on benefits at the time) and a large collection of batteries. He later admitted that he was attempting to enter Chechnya via Georgia and that the money and batteries were intended for Islamic fighters in the breakaway Russian province. In another scrape with the law, he was briefly detained at Dover after travelling through the Channel Tunnel on a coach when a bag near him was found to contain a gun and two hand grenades—though no fingerprints or other forensic evidence linked him to it.[126]

Police were never able to pinpoint exactly what Rowe was up to in terms of plotting, but it seems clear that his activities in the wake of his experience in Bosnia were geared towards the goal of global jihad. A senior police officer from the time described him as a 'nasty piece of work' who was up to 'some serious stuff,' and was a 'very, very dangerous individual'.[127] While he spent a considerable amount of time travelling, possibly as a courier between al-Qaeda cells across Europe, he probably also played something of a role as a local radicaliser in Britain.[128]

A hint of how Rowe might have acted as a radicaliser is offered in the case of an individual named Michael Jean-Pierre, of allegedly North African origin, who in 1999 moved onto a housing estate in Lisson Green or Grove, North London, after a spell in prison. A former Bosnian veteran with injuries to show for his experience, it was suspected that Jean-Pierre was behind a spate of conversions to radical Islam on the Lisson Green estate in 1999. The families of the local youngsters involved initially welcomed this newfound faith, preferring that these young men were turning to Islam rather than drugs; but inevitably tensions started to develop as the youngsters were persuaded to travel abroad to learn more about their faith. A number ended up in Yemen at training camps which doubled as religious schools, and eventually tragedy struck when one young man was killed in an accident involving a gun.[129] There is a final twist to this tale: subsequent to Andrew Rowe's imprisonment, the Metropolitan Police released information that the possessions found in his flat were a number of *curricula vitae* in the name Michael Jean-Pierre—'a name Rowe had used in 2000 securing work as a security officer at the London Business School in Regent's Park'.[130]

Whatever the specifics of this connection, for Andrew Rowe Bosnia was a key catalyst in eventual graduation into international terrorist networks. The war provided him with tangible proof of the West's lack of concern for Muslims, and a battlefield on which he was able to vent his anger. It gave him access to a network of individuals with whom he was able to plot for unclear purposes, and back in the United Kingdom it provided him with a meaningful past to replace his previous existence as a drug dealer. With his war stories and wounds to back them up, a past that they could empathise with, it is easy to imagine how bored youngsters on a North London housing estate would have been impressed by him.

Abu Hamza al-Masri and Supporters of Shariah

Another important figure whose prominence was accounted for in part by his actions in Bosnia was Abu Hamza al-Masri, the infamous Egyptian preacher whose fearsome aspect and reign at the Finsbury Park Mosque dominated headlines in the late 1990s and early 2000s. He has already appeared in our narrative as a younger man arriving in London, having fled Egypt in the late 1970s, but at that point he was, by his own account, a very 'undisciplined Muslim' unable to resist the pleasures of the flesh. As he put it, 'the more you give your body, the more your body asks for'.[131] Born in Alexandria in 1958, he was from an average middle-class family with a father who was a navy officer and a mother who was a teacher. He was halfway through his engineering course at Alexandria University when he decided in 1979 to leave Egypt for Britain. This was very much the fashion among young Egyptian men at the time: as was explained in Chapter 1, unlike the migrations from South Asia, many of those who came to the United Kingdom from Arab or Gulf nations were from middle-class backgrounds. Another reason that has been suggested for his arrival is that Abu Hamza, then still Mostafa Kemal Mostafa, would have been a young man of military age in a nation where conscription was still the norm—as is supported by a later application in 1982 to the Home Office, in which he declared that he could not regularise his Egyptian papers (which had by then expired) as the Egyptian government would have summoned him home to do his military service.[132]

Once in London, he quickly fell into the life of a young man in a new land, hanging out with other Egyptians and taking on odd jobs to support himself. One of Abu Hamza's Egyptian acquaintances from the time, Zak Hassan, described their lives:

we used to hang around in coffee shops in Queensway to talk and chat and eat. Everyone wore jeans, no one had a beard and nobody talked politics or religion, it wasn't an issue any of us was interested in. Abu Hamza sat in the corner and joined in with everybody else … we were just ordinary young men looking for work. At night a lot of us went to pubs, not to drink but to chat up girls.[133]

From his job as a porter in a London hotel he managed to meet Valerie Traveso, a British–Spanish woman working as a receptionist who was attracted to the big Egyptian with an infectious smile.

The two married soon afterwards, in 1980, and the relationship was cemented a year later in October 1981 when she gave birth to his son, Mohammed. Domestic life was not, however, of great interest to the young Egyptian, who worked part-time as a bouncer in a Soho nightclub (where in December 1980 he was picked up during a police raid on unlicensed premises). Surrounded by temptation, he succumbed at least once to an affair with someone he had met through the club. In the ensuing row that followed, Abu Hamza promised Valerie that he would improve his life, and it is at this point that he started to rediscover his Muslim roots. The two of them started to study the Koran together, and Valerie began to adopt some Muslim traditions. This was not enough for the marriage to survive, and in June 1984 Abu Hamza petitioned for a divorce: the break-up appears to have been amicable enough, with Valerie agreeing to allow him to take their son Mohammed with him. She was not to see him again until December 1999, when he was revealed as being one of the infamous Yemen Seven who were accused of being behind a bombing campaign in Sana'a. When the two finally met up afterwards, the long-lost son revealed that his father had told him that she was dead.

Back in 1984, however, it did not take Abu Hamza long to find a new wife, marrying Nagat Chaffe two months later, a Moroccan divorcee with a child. They have remained together ever since, and have had six further children (four boys and two girls). Marital bliss was followed by further good fortune with the Home Office, who first allowed him indefinite leave and then later granted his application for citizenship in the spring of 1986. Settled into this new life, Hamza decided to return to his studies, applying to read civil engineering at Brighton Polytechnic, to which he would commute from his growing family in London. It is here that he first started to find the ideas that would become the foundation of his future infamy, among the other Muslim students in similar situations at the time who shared accommodation and food at the Dyke Road Mosque.[134] It was not until 1987, when he decided to go on Hajj to Mecca, that he found out properly about jihad, learning about it at the feet of the fabled mujahedeen leader and ideologue, Abdullah Azzam. The two allegedly bonded, with Azzam recognising the young Egyptian's potential and charisma: something that gave Abu Hamza the ability years later to fill his sermons with the impressive boast, 'I sat with Sheikh Abdullah Azzam.'[135]

He did not, however, choose to go to fight, deciding instead to return to Britain where he propagated his newfound ideologies to the Muslims he encountered in Brighton and London. Having imbibed jihad at the feet of the great Abdullah Azzam, his religious quest now moved in a new direction, and he contacted Sheikh Omar Abdel Rahman, the 'Blind Sheikh' who was travelling around the world espousing jihad, and who was later imprisoned for his part in instigating the first terrorist attack on the World Trade Center in New York in 1993. He also took on a role as translator for the numerous warriors from the Afghan front who were being treated in private Harley Street hospitals, paid for by wealthy Gulf Arabs eager to do their part for the Afghan mujahedeen. This contact inspired young Abu Hamza further, and he started to preach to small circles at the Regent's Park Mosque in London, calling for jihad in Afghanistan. Finally, in 1991, he left his job and moved to Afghanistan.

While his time there is not well accounted for, in early August 1993 he was involved in an accident which would result in the hideous scarring that marked him from then on. The actual accounts of how this happened vary, with Sean O'Neill and Daniel McGrory's account offering two possible versions from several sources: Hamza himself claimed to the *Daily Mail* that it was a result of clearing minefields in Afghanistan; while one of his acolytes claimed it was the product of an accident while mixing explosives at the Darunta training camp. Providing a particularly vivid mythological description, the student reported that 'there was no screaming and crying from him, not a whimper. He just looked down at his arms, totally calm, and said: "I did a lot of bad with these hands and Allah has taken them away."'[136] This second account in which Abu Hamza is reported as having suffered an accident while handling explosives is confirmed by an FBI agent's account of debriefing another Algerian al-Qaeda operator from the camp, and also by Omar Nasiri's account of his experiences at the training camps where he met others who told him of someone who had lost his hands and his sight in Darunta and was now a preacher in London. Nasiri claims that Hamza specifically asked him to keep this story to himself.[137] His prosthetic hook hand, while possibly imposed in the short-term by the relatively rudimentary conditions in which he would have been first hospitalised in Pakistan, could surely have been replaced with more suitable aids relatively quickly. That he chose to retain it years afterwards is likely to be a demonstration of the *grand guignol* character he appears to have enjoyed playing.

Advised by doctors in Pakistan to return for treatment in Britain, he arrived back just when the final wave of former Afghan–Arab fighters were descending on Britain (and elsewhere in Europe), having been summarily ejected by the Pakistanis and finding no warm welcome in their home nations. Among these men was Abu Qatada, a Jordanian (he was born in Bethlehem when it was still part of that nation), under whom the young Egyptian studied and helped to run the *al-Ansar* newsletter. By 1997 Abu Hamza had become the official spokesman for the newsletter, announcing that in the wake of a Groupe islamique armé (GIA) communique that 'denounced the Algerian people as unfaithful for not backing the GIA', the newsletter 'will only contain general information on how to pursue (the holy war) and will not have any news from within Algeria'.[138]

Back in 1994, however, Abu Hamza decided that if he was going to be a serious leader he would need an organisation behind him, and so in 1994 he set up the Supporters of Shariah (SoS). By his own description,

Supporters of Shariah (SoS) was formed in 1994, following a *mashura* (constitution) between some brothers, who have been involved in jihad in Bosnia, Afghanistan and to give the message to the average Muslims ... we are established to defend the Shari'ah, the Islamic law, and also to defend the people who are defending Islamic law...we also give people advice to go for training to help fellow Muslims, and not to be deceived by the Western European society.[139]

The support of an organisation gave him the beginnings of some credibility towards his later claims of being a Sheikh. More impressive than the organisation, however, was Abu Hamza's decision in 1995 to leave London again and, despite his substantial disabilities, seek jihad once more on the battlefields of Bosnia. Suspecting his movements were likely to be watched or curtailed, he chose to make the journey under an adopted British name, Adam Ramsey Eaman, going first as a part of an aid convoy, before separating himself near the frontline to seek out the jihadis. Given his support of the Algerian cause back home, it made sense for him to gravitate towards the Algerian camps in Bosnia, and he quickly threw himself into the ideological fray. In later years Abu Hamza would openly admit his role in supporting the mujahedeen in Bosnia, saying he helped 'rebuild the [mujahedeen] battalion' through, among other things, collecting donations, ideological support and 'this and that'.[140]

It is not entirely clear how many journeys he may have made to Bosnia, though it would appear that he left the nation under a shadow. Having arrived in Bosnia as the fighting was beginning to wind down with the Dayton Accords being drafted in the US, he positioned himself firmly within the camp of fighters who believed that the conflict should not end and that Allah's warriors should head for the hills and continue to fight. This was not well received by some of the others in the jihadi camps, who did not appreciate the loud Egyptian's sudden arrival and claimed that he was trying to set up a group within a group—a claim that Abu Hamza later vehemently denied.[141] A competing perspective is offered in an account from French court documents linked to an investigation of a group of former Bosnian fighters who returned to cause havoc in France. According to those documents, a rival leader in the Bosnian mujahedeen had grown envious of Abu Hamza's popularity and saw him as a competitor 'to the point of inviting him to leave the 'Moujahiddin Battalion'.[142]

Whichever was the case, by late 1995 he had returned to the United Kingdom, where his celebrity among the growing extremist community was high. Alongside the fact that he was a veteran of two jihadi conflicts and with injuries to show for it, Hamza was now increasingly finding his voice as an extremist preacher and was able to quote the Koran in its proper language. This biography would have made him a particularly attractive catch, and it is thus unsurprising that a group from Luton asked him to lead prayers in their congregation sometime in 1996. Who specifically these individuals were is unclear,[143] but the city has a history of strong Muslim sentiment and in the early 1990s trouble between rival factions over who controlled the new central mosque spilled over into street fights. Imam Qazi Abdul Aziz, a local leader who espoused fierce anti-Rushdie and pro-Saddam Hussein rhetoric, had claimed the mosque as his domain after it was completed, which others disagreed with; the case ended up being taken to the High Court, while local police were obliged to come and patrol the area around the mosque.[144] Whether linked to Hamza or not, in September 1996 posters and stickers started appearing all over Luton, some advertising the 'Rally for Revival' that Al-Muhajiroun was organising in central London, and others talking about 'jihad'.[145]

This seemed quite an appropriate perch for Hamza and, using this base just outside London as a springboard, he established himself as one of the leading lights of extremism in Britain, with his Supporters of Shariah (SoS) group rallying for jihadi causes around the world. As they put it on their website years later, SoS 'have been supporting the Mujahideen, as well as refugees, in Afghanistan, Bosnia, Kashmir, Palestine, Algeria, etc. Projects have included supporting the Front line soldiers, Islamic Education, Reconstruction, countering Anti-Islamic propaganda, as well as holding studies to learn from past mistakes.'[146]

For younger British Muslims who found their own preachers to be from another generation and often simply incomprehensible, such an individual would have seemed hugely appealing and accessible.[147] Here was a preacher who spoke to them in their own language (while not his first language, Hamza's English was fluent and accessible), could recite the Koran in good Arabic and was a veteran of two conflicts. In addition to all this, his appearance and fiery rhetoric were unlike anything they might have encountered at the mosque: a mountain of a man with an extraordinary appearance, screaming about jihad and telling war stories about Abdullah Azzam as he jabbed his fearsome hooks around. For young men and women caught up in the identity crisis mapped out in the last chapter, the rebellious fundamentalism he was declaiming would have been a hugely appealing message, as we shall see in greater detail in the next chapter.

Fin de siècle

1996–7 was a turning-point for both Omar Bakri Mohammed and Abu Hamza al-Masri. By now both men had been in the United Kingdom for over a decade and had been active in extremist circles for a long while. Abu Hamza had been first a follower, but was becoming increasingly a leader, as he turned his biography, affable manner and fiery speeches into a position of influence among the community of British believers. Omar Bakri, on the other hand, could lay claim to being one of the key men to establish Hizb ut-Tahrir in the United Kingdom, a fact he was not bashful about. When asked the question in 2005, 'why is it that HT has such a strong presence here in the UK?' he answered, smiling, 'because I set it up'.[148] From its humble beginnings, it had become the most talked about Islamist group in the United Kingdom. Thriving in the midst of such confrontation, Omar Bakri had increasingly raised the stakes, hosting dramatic conferences and making ever louder proclamations, including declaring as early as 1991 in the run-up to the first Gulf War: '[John] Major [then prime minister] is a legitimate target. If anyone gets the opportunity to assassinate him, I don't think they should save it. It is our Islamic duty and we will celebrate his death.'[149] He travelled up and down Britain debating at university unions and in any public forum where he could proselytise further, loudly bringing his message of confrontation and the Caliphate to all who would listen.

When he finally split from Hizb ut-Tahrir it was under awkward ideological circumstances. As one HuT member at the time described it, he began saying that the group should start trying to convert the United Kingdom to Islam, rather than simply focusing on recruiting people to support HuT efforts to take over Muslim majority nations. By Omar Bakri's logic, 'if the whole world is a *dar ul harb* (land of war), then why does it matter where we start', an approach that clashed fundamentally with the HuT leadership, who firmly told him that Britain was not the priority. The leadership gave Omar Bakri an ultimatum, which he responded to by re-establishing Al-Muhajiroun with two key individuals and roughly a tenth of the HuT membership at the time.[150] Unfettered by Hizb ut-Tahrir's politically prudent leadership, Omar Bakri moved swiftly to take Al-Muhajiroun to the extreme fringe of Islamist politics in Britain, including increasingly bizarre announcements, such as sending faxes to Welsh newspapers stating that the solution to the Royal

Family's image problems was to convert to Islam.[151] It was also around this time that Jon Ronson started filming Omar Bakri's activities, resulting in the documentary that endowed him with the sobriquet 'The Tottenham Ayatollah', and painting Omar Bakri in a comical light, or, as Omar Bakri put it, showing the world that 'I am delightful'.[152]

During the filming of the documentary about him Omar Bakri was organising the 'Rally for Revival' conference at the London Arena, to which he claimed to have invited a host of extremist leaders, from Osama bin Laden to Omar Abdel Rahman.[153] The event generated global notoriety, and many governments were appalled that the United Kingdom was willing to give a platform to the extremists that Omar Bakri had invited to vent their views. Ultimately the event was cancelled, though it marked the 'shock tactic' approach to self-promotion that has characterised Al-Muhajiroun's activities ever since. The film also showcased as younger men two individuals who would later play important roles in Al-Muhajiroun's evolution: Anjem Choudary, a young lawyer who assumed the mantle of leadership after Omar Bakri was evicted from the country, and Trevor Brooks, a convert we encountered earlier who adopted the name Abu Izzadeen and was later imprisoned on charges of funding terrorism and soliciting murder abroad. Hamza, while as visible as Omar Bakri, took a less confrontational approach. Invited to provide a presentation at Imperial College's Islamic Society (ISOC), Hamza reportedly told the Salafi head of the ISOC who disapproved of his rhetoric that while he may not agree with them, he would at least not publicly attack them.[154]

But in 1997 the radical clerics were in the ascendant: Omar Bakri rapidly transformed himself into a rallying-point for extremists, while Abu Hamza consolidated his position by persuading the trustees of the Finsbury Park Mosque to let him take it over. He then lent space to his friend Omar Bakri to use as a base for Al-Muhajiroun, though the two often also found themselves at loggerheads. More importantly, as we will see below, Abu Hamza transformed the mosque into one of the major stops on the European jihadist trail. It was to serve as a base from which to export one of the UK's first international terrorist cells to Yemen, in 1998; but at this stage there was little understanding of the threat that was being incubated. In Omar Bakri's account, relations between them and the British government remained good, disrupted finally by the arrest of Middle Eastern extremists in London in the wake of the US Embassy bombings in Africa in 1998.[155] In his later trial in the United States, Abu Hamza echoed this claim of contact, stating that as early as 1997 the British intelligence services had been in touch with him.[156]

Molten Lava

There were, however, indicators of problems on the horizon. On 3 February 1995, following lengthy surveillance, police arrested three students of South Asian descent in Manchester. At one of the houses they raided were found 'a large quantity of parts of firearms and air weapons, bullets, shotgun cartridges, bullet heads, rifle primers, timers, explosives of various sorts [and] a Sauer self-loading 0.23 pistol and ammunition'.[157] Two were cleared on trial, while the third, Faisal Mostafa, a Bangladeshi–British PhD student at UMIST, was convicted on charges of possessing the Sauer. While it was never clearly established what exactly the men were plotting to do with their arsenal they also had Hizb ut-Tahrir literature in their possession and had organised meetings for the group in Manchester.[158]

The most interesting link to emerge from this plot, however, is that of Dr Faisal Mostafa, who some five years later made another appearance in court as the alleged co-conspirator to Moinul Abedin. Code-named Operation Large, the investigation into the pair's activities was overseen by MI5's then-expert on al-Qaeda, (and former director general), Jonathan Evans. Initiated for reasons unknown in July 2000, the investigation into the pair's activities concluded that Abedin, a Bangladeshi-born but British-raised unemployed waiter in Birmingham, was assembling a series of explosive devices while trying to obtain other weaponry. His computer was found to contain both radical materials as well as plans for making improvised explosive devices. A note was further found in his handwriting (something he first admitted and then denied) that stated 'If I become a martyr, you should marry a "MOZAHID" God Willing.' Other documentation, seemingly in Abedin's handwriting was found, that was identified as having been written from a cave in Afghanistan in 1996, and appeared to be exercises in learning Arabic.[159] In the end Mostafa was cleared, while Abedin was found guilty and sentenced to twenty years in prison. It was not until 2002, however, that the potential importance of the case emerged publicly when during the investigation of David Courtailler, a French convert who was very active in Abu Hamza's circles at the Finsbury Park Mosque, it was discovered that an ID in his name was among Abedin's possessions. The link led to speculation that this was the first al-Qaeda plot in the United Kingdom, though the Security Service tempered this line in time, saying that it was an operation that was 'inspired' by al-Qaeda, but not 'tasked or directed'.[160] In 2010, former MI5 head Dame Eliza Manningham-Buller appeared to highlight the distinction in testimony before the Chilcot Inquiry into the Iraq War, pointing out that while at the time the perception was that Abedin may have been linked to al-Qaeda, the current assessment was that he was not.[161] Code-named Molten Lava by MI5, Abedin's accomplice Faisal Mostafa continued to be a fixture on Security Service radars, showing up in July 2008 trying to board an aeroplane to Bangladesh with a gas-fired pistol in his bag; finally in March 2009 he was arrested by Bangladeshi police during an investigation into a madrassa established by a charity he runs.[162]

But this was over a decade later. Throughout the 1990s, Al-Muhajiroun protested and agitated against events in Iraq, leading to some of the first expressions of violence from individuals associated with the group. On 17 December 1998, a young British-born Muslim called Amer Mirza threw a petrol bomb at a British Territorial Army base in West London. While the bomb did very little damage, Mirza rapidly admitted his guilt but refused to name those who had helped him get to his target. His stated reason was rage at the recent resumption of bombing in Iraq, something that the presiding judge took into account as a mitigating cause to give him a shortened six-month sentence. Mirza was allegedly a leader in the group, though details have been hard to verify.[163] Shortly before this, another prominent individual involved in the group, who was later imprisoned on terrorism charges, named Simon 'Suleyman' Keeler, was arrested for attacking a police officer at another Al-Muhajiroun rally. In 1997 both men were involved in a protest after Ealing Council banned an Al-Muhajiroun 'Rally Against Israel' meeting, promoted under the guise of the Society of Converts to Islam, from being held at the Southall Community Centre; Mirza was arrested during the protest for inciting racial hatred, while Keeler was quoted in the press afterwards as stating that 'this campaign refers strictly to Israeli Jews supporting the state of Israel'. Banners displayed by the group included slogans saying 'the hour will never come until the Muslims fight the Jews and kill them' and 'what holocaust?'.[164] But these were limited cases and largely regarded as noisy groups of protesters common to a democratic society. That Mirza was involved in an attempted firebombing at a barracks can now be seen as something of a forewarning,[165] but nevertheless at the time the appetite still did not really exist for large-scale violence in the United Kingdom. In the next chapters, however, we shall see how the radical preachers shaped and sharpened this anger, as global events gradually began to fit the 'clash of civilisations' narrative that they were espousing. In time, this would turn into a movement of young Britons who would not only be willing to fight abroad, as we have seen, but also would eventually be persuaded that Britain was an equally valid target.

4

9/11 AND THE LONDONISTAN LINKS

'That flag will be brought down on the day of judgment.'[1]

It was in the months before Christmas 1998 that a group of men from Finsbury Park Mosque set out for Yemen from London. In a possible preview of what was to come, the *Al Jihad* newsletter published by Abu Hamza's organisation, the Supporters of Shariah (SoS), ran a story in its October 1998 edition under the now-ominous title 'Supporters of Shariah after American marines', and then discussed the arrival in the country of a detachment of US marines on a 'specific secret operation to target "Muslim fundamentalists" in the region'.[2] The group of young men had strong direct connections to Abu Hamza: seventeen-year-old Mohammed Kamel Mostafa was his son; Mohsin Ghalain was his step-son; while big bruiser Shahid Butt (whom we have encountered in previous chapters) was a regular feature at Abu Hamza's side in the mosque. Finally, Sarmad Ahmed's phone number appeared as a point of contact on the SoS website.

Hamza's fixation with Yemen as the cradle of the global jihad was something that the security services had been alerted to by one of their agents. According to Omar Nasiri, a British–French agent who in the mid to late 1990s penetrated Abu Hamza's inner circle in Finsbury Park, 'Abu Hamza was obsessed with Yemen. He believed that the global Islamic revolution would begin there. "It will come out of Aden", he

121

always said. If sharia was established in Yemen, other secular regimes would fall like dominoes.'[3] An article published in the October 1998 *Al Jihad* reflected this belief; in response to the news that US marines had arrived in Yemen, the editor comments, 'we see this as a powerful detonator for Muslims to explode in the faces of the Snakes of America. This will hopefully trigger a domino effect in the Peninsula.'[4]

Having arrived in Yemen, the men contacted local jihadist leader Abu al-Hassan, whom Abu Hamza knew from his days in Afghanistan and for whose group, the Islamic Army of Aden-Abyan (IAAA), Abu Hamza operated as press secretary. It is likely that they spent some time training at camps run by Abu al-Hassan, before they headed to Aden to put their plan into action. While he already had a hotel room to stay in, Ghalain put down a £1,250 deposit to secure a house in Aden from which it was claimed they were planning to launch their unspecified attacks. They then started ferrying weapons and bomb-making equipment around the city. At this point events become murky, with most accounts suggesting that a group of the men crashed their Daewoo van laden with weaponry after trying to run a police checkpoint, while Yemeni versions at the time suggested they had been tipped off about a carload of explosives coming into the city from Abu al-Hassan's lair in the mountains. Whichever the case, the men crashed the car and ran into the night, sparking a manhunt for a group of 'dark-skinned Britons'.[5]

The men were unable to evade the Yemeni authorities for very long, and on Christmas Eve 1998 Yemeni police arrested six Britons and charged them with conspiring to carry out terrorist attacks. At this point, no doubt infuriated that they had got themselves caught, Abu al-Hassan decided to launch a counter-operation to try to secure their release, and ordered the kidnap of a random group of Western tourists. Using a satellite phone that had allegedly been given to him months earlier by Abu Hamza, Abu al-Hassan then called London to inform him that they had 'sixteen cartons marked Britain or America' and started the negotiation plan for the group of hostages to be exchanged for the group being held in custody. Yemeni authorities at this point informed their British counterparts of the fact that a group of nationals had been kidnapped, but they failed to mention the group of British nationals already in detention. Then, having ascertained where Abu al-Hassan and his group were hiding, the Yemeni government decided to act, moving in on the camp in a bloody firefight that cost the lives of four of the hostages.

Over the next few weeks further arrests were made, including that of Abu Hamza's son Mohammed Kamel Mostafa, who had fled into the mountains in the wake of the first batch of arrests. In one of the many interviews conducted at the time, Abu Hamza expressed joy upon hearing that the boy was safe, but remained adamant that the men were innocent. The event brought Hamza much press attention, something he would court, making brash pronouncements in SoS's name that 'demand[ed] all Muslim groups to rise and join bands to free the Yemeni people from oppression', and surprising British viewers with the image of a fearsome-looking cleric talking about holy war. Early online adventurers would have found a website for SoS with images of grenades, Osama bin Laden, and proclamations about 'shariah' and 'kafirs'. Unlike nowadays, when such terminology has become commonplace in public discourse, at the time this would have been a shocking and relatively incomprehensible incident, with most dismissing Hamza as an attention-seeker. For intelligence operatives who had been listening to Hamza and Hassan communicating regularly via satellite telephone, the connection between the mosque and the Yemen plotters must have seemed quite strong, though at the time sufficient legislation was not in place to pursue a conviction based on this link; it is likely also that Abu Hamza was feeding information to the Security Service, dampening their view of him as a threat. Furthermore, after initial approaches by British consular officials in Yemen to the imprisoned men had been met with violent opprobrium about 'kafirs' working for a 'kafir' government, they rapidly concluded there was little that could be done about the group, who appeared to have been caught red-handed. What public support did exist for them largely evaporated after footage was released of some of them playing with weapons at a training camp in Albania, somewhat contradicting their cover story of being ordinary tourists.[6]

What the coverage missed, however, was the importance of the group as a marker of what was to come much later. Here was a group of young British men who had all chosen to go to a distant country in order to carry out acts of terrorism, or at least training, in furtherance of the abstract goal of global jihad. Little in the biographies of the eight Britons distinguished them from the many other Muslims living in the United Kingdom. Six were born in Britain (of Pakistani or North African heritage), while the remaining two, Shahid Butt and Malik Nasser, were respectively born in Pakistan and Yemen and had moved to the United

Kingdom when they were very young. They were students, recent grad-uates or holders of low-end jobs (bus drivers, security guards, etc.) which reflected their relatively young ages and low levels of education: Hamza's children were the youngest at seventeen and eighteen, while Shahid Butt appears to have been the eldest at thirty-three.

The connection between them and the jihadists living in the moun-tains outside Aden was seemingly provided by Abu Hamza, the Finsbury Park Mosque and the Supporters of Shariah organisation. At the time few questions were asked about how these young men had been per-suaded to leave the comfort of England for an adventure in a lawless and far-off land, but with the benefit of hindsight and insights provided by those who were at the Finsbury Park mosque at the time, we are now better informed about the Egyptian cleric's charisma and presence. Offering understanding, assistance and shelter to all those who arrived, Hamza turned the mosque into a known place of sanctuary. For those who had nowhere to stay he could provide shelter and a bed; for those unable to speak any English, he could arrange translators or assistance; and for those lost and seeking direction, he offered a friendly ear.[7] Richard Reid was apparently attracted to the cleric by his willingness to talk directly with him, as well as by helping the rudderless young convert by standing down his tormentors at the mosque.[8] Stories of this warm wel-come had travelled far: 'for many North Africans arriving from or via France Abu Hamza had already become a folk hero'.[9] One young Algerian who trod this path was Nabil Hadjarab, who arrived in London from Paris in late 2000 and was picked up by American forces in Afghanistan a year later. Through a translator at his Combatant Status Tribunal in Guantanamo Bay, he reported that 'he went to London to work and was told that this [the Finsbury Park] mosque would help him get situated. Any Muslim could and would go there.'[10]

With the Yemen group, however, a plot appeared to have been directed by the radical preacher—so much so that US prosecutors made this one of the key charges in their request for Abu Hamza's extradition. According to the American documents, Abu Hamza received three phone calls at home from the kidnappers before they had carried out their action, and a further one soon after the action had been launched. The next day, 29 December, he purchased a further £500 worth of airtime for Abu al-Hassan's satellite phone while announcing to the world that he was to help negotiate the release of the hostages.[11] In May 2014, a jury in New

York found the preacher guilty of charges of involvement in the kidnapping operation as well as trying to establish a training camp in Bly, Oregon.[12] The Yemeni prosecutor leading the government's case against the men in January 1999 put it succinctly when he said, 'this offense started in London in the offices of SoS which is owned by Abu Hamza and who exports terrorism to other countries'.[13]

Training

The key question that has never been answered about the incident in Yemen in 1998 is what exactly the group was hoping to achieve there. As has been suggested in Omar Nasiri's point about the importance of Yemen to Abu Hamza, there is the possibility that this was his attempt to light the fires that would speed the return of the Mahdi, the Muslim messiah figure whose arrival will signal 'the end of days'. But at the same time, this does not appear to have been an end goal he pursued with any great determination. While a number of his followers were later linked to numerous terror plots, it is unclear how many of them were directed into action by Abu Hamza himself, rather than under the inspiration or direction of others who would seek recruits on the fringes of communities around Abu Hamza. There is the possibility that, in fact, the aim was not for the cell of young British Muslims to perpetrate terrorism, but instead to train with Abu al-Hassan's group, merely turning Yemen into the latest of many jihadi training fields.

This explanation certainly fits with Hamza's activity in Finsbury Park at the time, and the rhetoric he was espousing in which he endlessly exhorted his followers to train and prepare. From when he took over the mosque in March 1997, winning the position by undercutting his former teacher Abu Qatada, who had demanded a 50 per cent cut of all mosque collections for taking the role, Abu Hamza had rapidly turned it into a training ground and general flop-house for young Muslims from around the world and a staging point for warriors on the global jihad.[14] O'Neill and McGrory describe jihadists using the mosque as a 'secure retreat for rest and recreation after a tour of duty in the holy war.'[15] Within the mosque, videos and newsletters could be purchased, read or watched which provided grim updates from jihadist battlefields around the world. Returning warriors would regale newer recruits with tales of adventure and experiences fighting or training on the frontline, while posters would offer sign-up sheets for those who were eager to go abroad.

According to an MI5 agent who spoke to the press in early 2002, some parts of the mosque were turned into an open training school for fighters, with decommissioned AK-47s being used, while others openly discussed training and shared tactical information.[16] But most of the training took place beyond the mosque's four walls, with Abu Hamza regularly organising camping and adventure trips for his young warriors in the Brecon Beacons in Wales. In one instance, a group that included some of the men who would later be arrested in Yemen was stopped by police who were clearly watching out for them and searched their vehicle in a manner suggesting that they expected to find weapons.[17] But for the most part, these trips were essentially outward-bound training experiences, with men running around fields brandishing wooden weapons or going on paintballing missions. Similar events were being held up and down the country throughout the late 1990s and early 2000s; Mohammed Siddique Khan first appeared on police radars in October 2001 when he was spotted at a similar camp at Dalehead in the Lake District. According to police documents released during the 7 July coroner's inquest, this group was apparently run by Martin 'Abdullah' McDaid, a former soldier who had converted to Islam and ran, alongside a couple of radical friends, similar training camps in the British countryside.[18] Siddique Khan and his team that carried out their deadly strike on 7 July 2005 were so enamoured of the bodybuilding and training that by June 2005 Shehzad Tanweer was almost unrecognisable to friends, who noted that he had grown considerably more muscular.[19] Mohammed Siddique Khan's neighbour noted that he spent a lot of time going to the gym rather than with his wife.[20] It may even have been that the men participated in training with Abu Hamza's groups when they stayed at the mosque in 2002.

When police finally raided the Finsbury Park Mosque in 2003, all manner of camping and training equipment was found in the building and Abu Hamza and his acolytes were evicted. But this and the subsequent arrest of Abu Hamza did not in fact prevent the community based at the mosque from carrying out similar training. In February 2008 Atilla Ahmet, Hamza's former right-hand man who featured prominently at Hamza's side in the early 2000s, and Mohammed Hamid, who used the nickname Osama bin London, were convicted of running training camps in the Lake District and New Forest.[21] Following Hamza's conviction they had taken over running the mosque, and during the trial footage was played of the men supposedly training in the countryside in military manoeuvres, using branches as simulated weapons. While some rub-bished the supposed training that was going on, which was shown in the form of telephone video footage of men running around a forest, photo-graphic evidence showed that individuals involved in the 21 July 2005 copycat failed bomb attack on London's transport system and others who had fought in Afghanistan and Somalia had attended similar camps run by Hamid.

But Hamza's ambitions to run training camps went beyond organis-ing camping in the Lake District. Recognising that in the US people could more freely train with firearms, in October 1999 Hamza discussed with trusted American aide Earnest James Ujaama the possibility of establishing a jihad training camp in Bly, Oregon, to which he would subsequently dispatch followers to train prior to their eventual deploy-ment in Afghanistan. Impressed by Ujaama's accounts that the location looked 'just like Afghanistan', he sent out Oussama Kassir, an older Lebanese–Swedish national who had fought against the Israelis during the 1982 invasion of Lebanon and then later sought asylum in Sweden. Probably attracted by the stories that were spreading among the global Islamist community of Abu Hamza's safe haven in London, Kassir stayed at the Finsbury Park Mosque in the late 1990s and the two were caught talking together on camera in early 1999 during media coverage of the disastrous Yemen operation. In an unguarded media interview in September 2002, after the American charges were brought against him for helping establish the camp in Oregon, Kassir declared 'I love al-Qaida. I love Osama bin Laden' and that he would kill President Bush 'if I can'.[22] At Kassir's side when he went to Oregon was Haroon Rashid Aswat, a second-generation Gujarati Muslim who was often seen at Hamza's right-hand side and who was probably being groomed for a position of some importance within the transnational organisation that Abu Hamza was building.

Unfortunately for them, the entire experience was a disaster. Court documents report how, upon arrival, Kassir 'flew into a rage' when, instead of being met by an army of eager young warriors, he found an abandoned farm with a trailer, an 'Islamic leader from Seattle, a mentally impaired eighteen-year-old and two women more interested in canning jars than jihad'. He and Aswat made do with what they found, but within a few weeks abandoned the endeavour and returned to the comforts of urban Seattle. There they continued to try to train and recruit people at a local mosque, but found this equally fruitless and eventually gave up and returned to England.[23]

According to a report from within the mosque, the purpose of these 'outdoor training sessions [was] to separate young men with real potential to endure hardships from those who were intimately attached to their home comforts'.[24] For those who proved hardy enough to face these challenges, the next step was Afghanistan. They received funds and a ticket and were sent on their way to meet with individuals in Pakistan who would then help shepherd them across the border to the Afghan training camps. O'Neill and McGrory's account of Hamza's 'suicide factory' is replete with such tales, but the one that stands out is that of Feroz Abbasi, a young immigrant of mixed Pakistani–Ugandan heritage who had taken to travelling around Europe in an attempt to find some meaning in his life. After being mugged in Switzerland, he came across a Kashmiri man who provided him with all the answers he needed, which then set him off back to London in pursuit of Islam. Finding Hamza, Abbasi was almost immediately a fan, seeing in the cleric a replacement for the father figure who had left him as a child. After eagerly calling Abu Hamza and asking, 'I would like to know how I can go to jihad, please', he set off down a path which concluded with his capture by the Northern Alliance, while gripping a grenade in his underwear as he debated becoming a suicide bomber.[25]

The most interesting thing about Abbasi's account is the very practical role that Hamza appears to have played in it, at one point even providing Abbasi with an introduction to a senior individual in Afghanistan. According to US court documents, Hamza instructed Ujaama to take Feroz Abbasi to Pakistan and help introduce him to a contact there who would help facilitate both of their trips across the border into Afghanistan. Ujaama, who claimed to have previously made a trip to the camps in Afghanistan using a letter of introduction from Abu Hamza, was also given a compact disc containing messages that Abu Hamza wished to relay to senior individuals in Afghanistan.[26] This account is strengthened by the interviews given to the FBI by Ahmed Ressam, an Algerian terrorist who was intercepted crossing the border from Canada into America ahead of the millennium on his way allegedly to carry out an attack on Los Angeles International Airport; he claimed to have heard about Abu Hamza at the Afghan training camps, and Hamza had provided one of his cell with an introduction to the camp. All of which suggests that Abu

Hamza did have some weight and ability to provide access to the camps in Afghanistan.[27]

Some security analysts dispute that Abu Hamza had any ability to provide connections to the camps in Afghanistan. Many in the Arabic-speaking world simply dismissed him as a loudmouth and a clown, an attitude supported by his earlier disastrous foray into Bosnia and his relatively weak standing as a scholar. As Dr Muhammad al-Massari put it:

Abu Hamza started his scholarly development quite late in age and started [pause], he will not be happy with the way I say this, but on the wrong foot, started by studying, non-critically, classical *fiqh* books…Abu Hamza cannot overcome. He gets stuck in the scholarly opinions of the past and you have for a certain issue four or five points of view…it does not mean he cannot balance them and find the one that is more convincing on various grounds, but it is still not the critical approach in which you fully digest, assimilate and produce something new.[28]

Some pause must be taken to note that Dr al-Massari was a closer friend of Omar Bakri than of Abu Hamza (and as was highlighted earlier, the two preachers at various points competed for audiences), but his description of the relative vacuity of Hamza's preaching is also reflected in Omar Nasiri's account of hearing him speak. Furthermore, it is hard to find evidence of Abu Hamza's writings or *fatwas* having much impact beyond the English-speaking world. Wiktorowicz's account based on interviews with young radicals in London describes how Omar Bakri's followers tended to enjoy going to Hamza's speeches because they were inspirational and 'hot', but they preferred Omar Bakri's more erudite teaching for learning more about their religion.[29]

Whatever the specifics of Abu Hamza's ability to provide access to the camps and his stature within the international jihadist community, what is clear is that by the turn of the century he had established in London a jihadist base-camp on firm footings. It provided a haven for the global community of extremists, in particular offering shelter to the Algerians displaced by civil war in their own country. It became known throughout Europe and the US as a place where one could find contacts to get to jihadist training camps in Afghanistan. One report from a former official cites a group of Swedish converts who arrived hearing that they would be able to secure fake documentation and contacts at the mosque.[30] In his initial confession, 'Al Jaza'iri', who later claimed his name was Abd al-Rahman Said 'Amr, a member of the group who had gone to Yemen, claimed that he had arrived in London from Algeria in 1997 and had given up his passport. Having decided to go to Yemen, he obtained a French passport from a Tunisian associate of Hamza's at the mosque.[31] For the growing number of young British men drawn to Hamza, the mosque was where they could find understanding and shelter from trouble in their lives, and encounter a global movement of holy warriors. They could train, establish contacts, and in the first instance play a very active role in Supporters of Shariah, before being despatched to play a bigger role in the global struggle. Feroz Abbasi reports being appointed the head of SoS's 'Croydon Branch' (of which he was the sole member) during his first meeting with Hamza.

Hamza's gift appears to have been an ability to reach out to troubled young men of any background, to provide them with leadership and guidance supplemented with real-world support in the form of a roof over their heads and a role to play in his part of the global struggle to establish a Caliphate. It should be stressed that not all of his acolytes were hapless drifters like Richard Reid; he was also able to attract individuals like Saajid Badat, and his fellow second-generation Gujarati Muslim, Haroon Rashid Aswat. Currently in prison awaiting possible deportation to America,[32] Aswat was an important fixture at Abu Hamza's mosque. A native of Dewsbury, Aswat's name was apparently on a letter of introduction that 7 July leader Mohammed Siddique Khan had when he came to Finsbury Park in late 2002.[33] Aswat is regularly found at Hamza's side in images to have emerged from the mosque, and accompanied the cleric to court when he was first facing charges. Both Badat and Aswat are described as bookish and scholarly: Aswat was training to be an Islamic scholar before he came to Hamza, while Badat—who we will cover in more detail later—went down this path after he abandoned his terror plot. Both were drawn to Hamza's clear devotion to his task and the fact that he was actually doing something for Islam's advancement, rather than simply talking about it, which distinguished him from Omar Bakri Mohammed in the minds of aspirant young jihadis. In later trials it was made abundantly clear that a number of the young men who had passed through Al-Muhajiroun's ranks and then onto extremism found the group a source of ridicule, calling it all talk and no action.[34] The presence at the mosque of men like Aswat and Badat shows the important role that Abu Hamza played in bringing together the distinct worlds of global jihadist ideology and young British Muslims seeking something greater from their lives.

Abu Qatada

Abu Hamza was not, however, the only one who was helping foster extremist ideas from his position on the Londonistan map. Far more impressive, and important, according to undercover agent Omar Nasiri and others, was Abu Qatada, a Palestinian cleric who arrived in the United Kingdom on a forged passport from the United Arab Emirates on 16 September 1993.[35] Born in 1960 he moved to Peshawar in Pakistan in 1990 to be 'professor of Sharia sciences', before going to Afghanistan 'to visit some scholars after the fighting had ended'.[36] Once in London he rapidly established himself as a leader among the community of itinerant foreign extremists who were congregating there at the time. The Syrian Abu Musab al-Suri, another of the extremists drawn to London at the time, described Qatada's prayer hall as 'a place where bulletins were distributed, donations were collected, and a place where jihadis and zealots gathered'.[37] Others who attended his workshops found that the hall was filled with burly-looking men with visible battle injuries,[38] while Nasiri recounts hearing the same sort of language being spoken by Abu Qatada and his followers as he had heard being used at the camps in Afghanistan.

His prayer rooms were found at a youth club called the Four Feathers in Baker Street, in central London, which rapidly became known as one of the key meeting places of the global jihadi community. Later described by Spanish prosecuting judge Balthasar Garzon as 'al-Qaeda's Ambassador in Europe',[39] at this time most of Abu Qatada's efforts were focused on supporting jihad in Algeria. Alongside his student Abu Hamza and his fellow jihadi ideologue Abu Musab al-Suri (and a constellation of other Algerian and Arab extremists), Abu Qatada helped provide support for the jihadists in Algeria, running the *al-Ansar* newsletter and helping raise money among Muslims in London. As a scholar and religious leader, he was also able to provide ideological cover to the Algerian jihad, translating his experience in Afghanistan into credibility in jihadist circles, even though, as both Nasiri and al-Suri suggest, he had not actually seen any action there. This inexperience may have been at the root of some of his later problems, including *fatwas* he issued which later landed him in trouble. In particular one *fatwa*, in March 1995, which condoned the killing of the wives and children of 'apostates' in Algeria, was seen as giving the Groupe Islamique Armée (GIA) carte blanche to carry out horrendous massacres in Algeria.[40] While he later distanced himself from the more gruesome acts of the GIA, this act merely drove some of his congregants into Abu Hamza's arms, who cynically exploited this breach to embrace some of his former teacher's followers.

Unlike Abu Hamza, Omar Bakri and Abdullah el-Faisal, Qatada's command of English was relatively weak, and consequently his ability to reach out to British youth, who were for the most part unable to speak Arabic, was limited.[41] Richard Belmar, a tall St Lucian–British convert who was captured in Pakistan in February 2002, having trained the year before at the al-Farouk training camp in Afghanistan, admitted attending several of Abu Qatada's talks at the Four Feathers, though knowing no Arabic he found them hard to follow.[42] Abu Hamza provides an anecdote summarising the problem that Qatada would have faced when he recounts an event that Faisal and Qatada held together, in which Qatada admonished his former student for an excessive zeal in the invocation of *takfir*. Having little English, Qatada was reliant upon Faisal to act as his translator for the crowd. During the course of the presentation, by Abu Hamza's account, Faisal was somewhat selective in his translations of Qatada's words, meaning that while for the Arabic speakers in the room 'the end of the debate left brother Faisal a broken man', 'those that did not understand the Arabic (Faisal's students) went away feeling the same about Faisal'.[43]

Qatada's inability to communicate effectively in English did not detract from his role as a rallying-point for an itinerant body of post-Afghanistan jihadis who gravitated towards London. Djamel Beghal was a typical case: a handsome and charismatic Algerian–Frenchman who migrated to Britain in October 1997, bringing his wife and two children after Paris had become a hostile environment for extremists.[44] According to Nasiri, Beghal was attracted to London because of the presence of his idol Abu Qatada,[45] though once there Beghal quickly became a regular feature at the Finsbury Park mosque, where he talent-spotted for al-Qaeda. Providing late night lectures to the eager young men gathered in the mosque, Beghal would regale them with tales of jihad while emphasising the importance of martyrdom and 'that there was no higher duty than to offer themselves for suicide missions'.[46] Furthermore, his contacts with the core of al-Qaeda and its camps meant that he was also able to offer these excitable young men the means to ensure their secure passage to Afghanistan.

Beghal was only one of a number who were initially attracted to the city thanks to Qatada's presence, including, according to intelligence agencies, two other Algerians later picked up after fighting in Afghanistan, Nabil Hadjarab and Sufyian Barhoumi, both of whom were in Qatada's circle in London.[47] Neither denied knowing Qatada, and it would be surprising if the men did not in fact know the cleric given his prominent role as editor of the *al-Ansar* newsletter.[48]

Not a bashful man, Qatada boasted about his influence over the Algerian community in the United Kingdom as the basis for his claim to be able to 'protect' Britain, claiming in an interview with the Security Services in June 1996 that he 'wielded powerful, spiritual influence over the Algerian community in London'.[49] What is less clear is how much influence he wielded over the young British men who signed up for jihad and terrorism during the 1990s and 2000s, for whom leaders like Abu Hamza and Omar Bakri Mohammed were in fact more accessible. In this way, Abu Qatada is most likely seen in a similar light to Abu Baseer al-Tartousi, the influential Syrian jihadist ideologue about whom little is known, but who is believed to have arrived in the United Kingdom in the 1980s, probably attracted to the freedom that he saw other Arab dissidents enjoying in London at the time. His high profile among the extremist community meant that Abu Baseer was (and remains, particularly in light of the conflict in Syria—his homeland—to which he has returned to help the rebellion) an important and venerated figure; but, like Abu Qatada, his inability to speak English meant that he had less of an impact upon British Muslims (as opposed to foreigners drawn to Londonistan).[50]

For men like this, London was simply a backdrop against which they would carry out their activities overseas. Their targets and interests remained abroad, and their *fatwas* and commandments mostly concerned activities that occurred beyond Britain's borders. The receptive environment for jihadist ideologues drew another Syrian, Abu Musab al-Suri, an ideologue and thinker who came to the United Kingdom in 1994 with his Spanish wife, stating 'Among the Islamists, you will find everyone from Shaykh Muhammad Surur [a leading Syrian cleric who disagreed with using violence to create an Islamic state] to the jihadis, and lately it has become a refuge for everyone….I found that being in London during that period would place you at the centre of events'.[51] Working alongside Abu Qatada on the *al-Ansar* newsletter in support of the Algerian jihad, al-Suri was also a contributor to the Libyan Islamic Fighting Groups (LIFG) publication *Majallat al-Fajr* and the Egyptian Islamic Jihad (EIJ) publication *al-Mujahidun*. He also offered himself as a point of contact for Osama bin Laden, bringing journalists to Afghanistan as well as providing interviews on the activities of Islamist warriors around the world. Typical of the displaced foreign ideologues and warriors from this period, al-Suri does not appear to have had much contact or direct impact on the community of young British Muslims drawn by the radical preachers.[52]

Qatada played an equally active role in the jihadist scene: when he was arrested in February 2001 by counter-terrorism police, he was found to have in his possession 'UK and foreign currency to a value in excess of £170,000'—an impressive amount for a man living on welfare—and there was £805 in an envelope which recorded that it was 'for the mujahidin in Chechnya'.[53] He also appears to have acted as a contact point for al-Qaeda linked extremists in London; Nasiri recounts passing messages from Abu Zubaydah, the key contact in Pakistan for fighters seeking access to jihad in Afghanistan.[54] Reda Hassaine, another intelligence agent who penetrated the circles around Qatada, reported that the preacher held a prayer meeting in honour of Abu Walid, a Palestinian extremist who was apparently on his way from London to meet with Osama bin Laden.[55] He also provided *fatwas* in support of bin Laden,[56] and ideological support for both the Al Tawhid organisation in Germany and Ansar al-Islam, a Kurdish al-Qaeda affiliate.[57] His greatest contribution to jihad in the United Kingdom appears to have been the fact that he mentored two of the preachers mentioned above, Abu Hamza and Abdullah el-Faisal. He was particularly proud of his work with the former, to whom he would refer as 'the best student he ever had', boasting about how 'quickly Abu Hamza had memorised the Koran and the hadith' and that Hamza 'was a keen and quick learner and had an exploratory mind'.[58] Less is known about his work with Abdullah el-Faisal, though we learn from Abu Hamza's account that Faisal and Qatada went about London together debating 'the Salafis of Brixton', whom Qatada is forced to side with when Faisal over-zealously declares to the crowd 'you are Jews!', a comment that leads Qatada and the others in the room to believe he has accused them all of being apostates—a step too far even for jihadist ideologue Abu Qatada.[59]

Abdullah el-Faisal

A figure who is often viewed as marginal in the British Islamist scene, due to the fact that he did not manage to muster a mosque or organisation as did Omar Bakri Mohammed or Abu Hamza, Abdullah el-Faisal was nonetheless an important player, given that he was connected to the growing community community of West Indian converts and African Muslims in the United Kingdom as well as offering a fiery rhetorical style that was attractive to young men like Mohammed Siddique Khan. His tapes and recordings are consistently found among the possessions of individuals convicted of terrorism offences throughout the English-speaking world and he continues to produce a regular digest of material on the internet. Born William Trevor Forest in 1963 to an evangelical Christian family in Jamaica, he first discovered Islam when he met Saudi missionaries in his mid-teens (in one interview he mentions a specific teacher at school).[60] Leaving the Caribbean years later, he first went to Guyana, where he learned Arabic, before going to Saudi Arabia on a scholarship as part of a government programme to spread Islam. Having completed his studies in 1992, he was instructed by his teacher Sheikh Rajhi to move to Britain and spread the word there among the growing community of believers. He quickly found a berth as an imam at the Salafi Brixton Mosque, where he led Arabic and religious instruction and converted individuals from the local community to Islam.[61] It is also possible that he was sent specifically to the mosque as part of a Saudi programme to despatch missionaries worldwide; his training in the Saudi Kingdom and the fact that he went to a predominantly convert Salafi mosque in the heart of London's African community all point to a deliberate confluence. Usama Hasan recalls encountering the preacher at around this time and finding him particularly cocky and eager to flaunt his knowledge of Islam.[62]

Faisal was arriving to settle[63] in the West as the trend of conversion to Islam, and in particular conversion among individuals of West Indian descent, was becoming something of a fad among young men in the United Kingdom. The year 1993 saw the release of Spike Lee's film *Malcolm X*, a film which lionised the slain American Muslim leader, and also sparked off a greater level of interest in Islam among Africans in the West seeking a new identity. For many this identity was found through the vehicle of Islam, and specifically the group that Malcolm X used to speak for, the Nation of Islam; it was also paralleled in popular culture by the rap group Public Enemy, whose aggressive lyrics made reference to Islam. Capturing this zeitgeist, one *Sunday Times* reporter ventured to the Brixton Mosque in South London, where interviews with Abdul

Haqq Baker and Abdullah el-Faisal both featured prominently. During the piece, Faisal claimed that the congregation at the mosque had grown from 60 in 1987 to around 4,000 in 1993, while he personally claimed to have 'received three converts a day for the past six years'.[64] These figures are hard to substantiate, but it is undeniable that the charismatic prayer leader was able to draw people to his chosen religion.

When this interview took place in 1993, he still appeared to be in the mosque committee's good books. According to others at the mosque, there was a generally positive attitude towards Faisal among the community, who respected 'his willingness to challenge authority and stand up for black youths against the police', behaviour which 'appeared wholly consistent with the Malcolm X style of approach they admired so much'.[65] He was apparently particularly effective in turning young men away from dissolute lives dedicated to alcohol and drug abuse, a skill which led one South London Muslim leader to continue to doubt his guilt even after his trial and conviction in 2003, which exposed his violent views to the world.[66]

By 1994, however, he had moved on following a series of disagreements with the mosque committee. According to Abu Hamza, part of this falling out stemmed from the fact that he was apparently playing tapes of Hamza preaching in the mosque, which incensed the members of the community who disapproved of Hamza's jihadist rhetoric.[67] This led to a scuffle in which Faisal's nose was broken, an incident which Hamza cites as the root of a reference that appears a number of times in Faisal's lectures.[68] Abdul Haqq Baker, who recalls a stand-off with Faisal and his supporters in the Brixton mosque in November 1993, presents an alternative version of events. By now the mosque leaders had agreed to exclude Faisal, having determined that his *takfiri* views were not a positive contribution to the life of the mosque. Faisal then established a series of small study circles in Tower Hamlets, in the East End of London. In November 1993 he tried to make a forceful return to the Brixton mosque, entering the prayer area with about forty followers in an apparent attempt to 'take over'. Abdul Haqq Baker rallied a team of supporters 'who had a tough reputation' and confronted Faisal, leaving 'him and his team in no doubt they had entered without authority and in contravention of the ban'.[69] According to Baker's account, Faisal's group stood down, and the resulting victory by the Brixton Salafis strengthened their reputation in London.

This expulsion did not intimidate Faisal, and he moved on to leading prayer groups and giving presentations at university campuses. Unlike his fellow radical preachers Abu Hamza, Omar Bakri or Abu Qatada, Faisal did not have a permanent berth from which he would operate. Instead he became an itinerant preacher, moving about Britain preaching to crowds wherever he could find them. In many ways this reflected his training as a Tablighi Jamaat member, though he appears to have quickly moved on from the apolitical stance that Tablighis preach to a more confrontational posture that brought him into conflict even with his teacher Abu Qatada, for whom he had also acted as an interpreter.[70]

In his 'Be Aware of Takfir!' manuscript, Abu Hamza goes into some detail about the alleged clashes between Abu Qatada and Faisal, claiming that the teacher became astonished at some of his student's statements, to the point that he upbraided him for branding his audience 'Jews'.[71] There is some evidence of this clash still available in the public domain in the YouTube video of a debate between Faisal and Qatada in which Qatada appears to dominate his student with his superior Arabic and learning.[72] Whilst this debate between the two men remains relatively calm, later confrontations degenerated into violence. After 9/11, the two men held another conference, in Toynbee Hall in London, that attracted a broad cross-section of local Muslims, from supporters of the two clerics to members of Al-Muhajiroun, Hizb ut-Tahrir, and other more moderate groups. The discussion became heated and groups of supporters clashed outside afterwards, leading to the police being called.[73]

The wit and wisdom of Abdullah el-Faisal

In many ways, it is quite easy to understand why Abdullah el-Faisal would have been held in high regard among the African Muslim community (and is likely still to be so; Umar Farouk Abdulmutallab, the 2009 Christmas 'underwear bomber', was a follower of Faisal's speeches[74] and it was suspected that groups operating in Somalia in 2012 had been influenced by the preacher who continues, at the time of going to press, broadcasting speeches online and publishing his thoughts on various sites using the handle authentic tauheed).[75] While for those who spoke Arabic his diction might have been less persuasive, for those who did not he was an impressive linguist with religious bona fides thanks to his extensive training in Saudi Arabia; he also spoke a slang-laden 'street' English (he used to refer to his ideological opponents as 'dodgy sheikhs'). One East London Muslim recalled being impressed by a speech given by Faisal in Brixton in the mid-1990s, where he spoke of human rights and other 'moderate' themes: so much so that he helped organise an invitation for Faisal to speak at the prestigious East London mosque. At the time, American scholars and preachers were all the rage, and Faisal, his Jamaican roots notwithstanding, was similarly well-regarded. However, once in the mosque, Faisal 'revealed his true colours', launching into an intolerant and aggressive presentation. Fortunately, some more intellectual 'brothers' were also present at the session and were able to argue with Faisal and thus help blunt the impact of his words.[76]

However, most of those who came to his sessions and went on to become followers were far less sophisticated. While probably not as intellectually challenged as was painted in the press, Richard Reid did not shine academically. In fact, he is likely to be typical of the troubled former drug addicts and criminals to whom Faisal appears to have been able to reach out. Another such case is Richard Chinyoka, a Zimbabwean wanted for multiple rapes, who was found to have a series of recordings by Faisal in his car when police stopped him on 14 December 2001. Shocked by the contents of the tapes, police initiated an investigation that led to an undercover officer purchasing a number of similar recordings by Faisal openly on sale at an Islamic bookshop in Brick Lane, East London in February 2002. This ultimately led to Faisal's imprisonment and expulsion from Britain under the Offenses Against the Person Act of 1861; Chinyoka, on the other hand, was found guilty of raping and torturing teenage girls and given a twelve-year sentence in July 2003.[77]

Germaine Lindsay, who was born in Jamaica on 25 September 1985 and grew up in Yorkshire, was the non-Beestonite and non-British Pakistani among the 7 July bombers. He also became a troubled young man. It is unclear in what ways he had broken the law by the time he encountered the preacher, and was more likely to have been drawn by the two men's shared roots and by his mother's approval of Faisal. His mother recalled taking young Germaine to a speech by the preacher a few weeks after the two of them converted, though it was probably more than just this single contact that would have drawn the two men together. In an interview in South Africa many years after the attack, Faisal admitted teaching the young man and speaking to him (prior to his imprisonment) about Lindsay going 'to Saudi Arabia to become a sheikh'. When pushed about what he thought of Lindsay's action, Faisal refused to condemn it completely, instead declaring that 'I was hurt to see him on the news as one of the bombers, but I wasn't shocked as nothing shocks me any more'. Then, reprising a line he would often take with the men drawn to him, he said, 'The foreign policy of the unbelievers is so harsh, this racist, right-wing foreign policy. So when we have young angry Muslims who take matters into their own hands, it doesn't shock me any more.'[78]

Later on in his Londonistan career, Faisal became the object of ridicule even from within the extremist community. Quite aside from his increasingly vindictive and angry statements about 'Saudi Salafis' and those associated with the Brixton Mosque, his tendency to cast *takfir* (declaring people unbelievers) with impressive abandon led him to clash rhetorically with almost every other prominent extremist preacher. Beyond the aforementioned run-in with Abu Qatada, Faisal also criticised the 'Tooting and Finsbury Park' Muslims whom he dismissed as 'fake jihadis' who were 'using the word jihad for fame and fortune and to line their pockets'.[79] It was this tape that probably spurred Abu Hamza's response in the form of his manuscript 'Be Aware of Takfir!' In another tape, 'CIA Islam', Faisal launches a scathing attack on fellow extremist preacher Anwar al-Awlaki, whom he brands as a *kafir* (non-believer) for being too restrictive in his declarations of *takfir*. In fact, the rationale behind the title of the tape is that al-Awlaki's declarations offer a more restrictive view of the use of violence, and are thus a form of the 'acceptable' extremism that the CIA would push. It was later claimed by Faisal's followers online that the preacher had recanted this particular tape and made amends with al-Awlaki, but its existence demonstrates Faisal's somewhat erratic manner.

His fiery rhetoric may have stirred up followers like Germaine Lindsay, Zacarias Moussaoui (a French-Moroccan whom we shall hear more about later, and who was sent to America to participate in the 9/11 attacks), Richard Reid and Mohammed Siddique Khan, who told a jihadist contact in Pakistan that Faisal was one of his favourite preachers and who owned many of Faisal's tapes. However it is highly unlikely that Abdullah el-Faisal would have offered much practical help in putting them in touch with Osama bin Laden or al-Qaeda (whose 'every word is like [a] gem', as el-Faisal put it)[80] or indeed with the Taliban. His skill in radicalising young men and women, providing them with a sense of empowerment and connections around the United Kingdom, however, meant that he was nurturing the broader community of British Muslim radicals, from among whom were recruited several individuals who later became terrorists. Faisal's role appears to have been as a radicaliser, filling the men's minds with dreams of jihad which others then capitalised upon to turn them into warriors serving Osama bin Laden. Faisal was able to provide zealots like Moussaoui, Reid and Germaine Lindsay with a package of Islamist ideas that were easily accessible, playing a vital role in steering several young Britons (and others through his cassettes and recordings) further along the path of extremism.

Shoe bombers

Tensions remained high among passengers waiting for American Airlines flight 63 to Miami in the Paris terminal. Only a few weeks had passed since September 11 and security had been ratcheted up as people started slowly to adapt to the realities of the global terrorism that had abruptly become a major feature of their lives. Conscious of this new reality, some of them looked with some scepticism at the tall, unkempt individual who was waiting with them to board while muttering to himself. None of them would have known that just a day earlier he had attempted to board the same flight and had been turned away, his unkempt appearance and attempt to purchase a one-way ticket in cash arousing suspicions. He had been questioned for long enough to miss his flight, but no reason was found to detain him further. A day later and the workforce in Paris had been less suspicious, allowing Richard Reid past security with no check-in luggage; in fact all he had with him was a knapsack with a Walkman, cassettes, magazines and a Koran inside. His shoes, however, contained a deadly cargo in the form of a moulded piece of explosive that he planned to detonate mid-flight, bringing the aeroplane down somewhere over the Atlantic Ocean.

Richard Reid was unsuccessful in his attempt. A stewardess was alerted to his strange behaviour when she noticed a burning smell in the cabin and went to investigate. Seeing that Reid was lighting something in his shoe, she attempted to stop him while calling for help. Another steward ran forward and started throwing drinks in Reid's face while trying to douse the flame. By this time others in the cabin had been alerted to what was going on, and passengers leapt up to help pin him down. Tying Reid into his seat using spare seatbelts and other improvised restraints, they were finally able to subdue him when a doctor on board gave him a sedative injection. Aware of the danger, the pilot quickly redirected the flight to Boston airport where police and federal agents were there to meet the latest evolution of the terrorist threat.

Just over a year and a half later, in a Boston courtroom, Reid offered no apologies but rather a rambling justification of his actions:

I further admit my allegiance to Osama bin Laden, to Islam, and to the religion of Allah. Okay? With regards to what you said about killing innocent people, I will say one thing. Your government has killed 2 million children in Iraq. Okay? If you want to think about something, 20 against 2 million, I don't see no comparison. Okay? Your government has sponsored the rape and torture of Muslims in the prisons of Egypt and Turkey and Syria and Jordan with their money and with their weapons. Okay? I don't know, see, what I done as being equal to rape and to torture, or to the deaths of the 2 million children in Iraq. Okay? Thirdly. So, for this reason, I think I ought not to apologize for my actions. I am at war with your country. I'm at war with them not for personal reasons but because they have murdered more than so many children and they have oppressed my religion and they have oppressed people for no reason except that they say we believe in Allah. This is the only reason that America sponsors Egypt. It's the only reason they sponsor Turkey. It's the only reason they back Israel. Okay? As far as the sentence is concerned, it's in your hand. Only really it is not even in your hand. It's in Allah's hand. I put my trust in Allah totally and I know that he will give victory to his religion. And he will give victory to those who believe and he will destroy those who wish to oppress the people because they believe in Allah. So you can judge and I leave you to judge. And I don't mind. This is all I have to say. And I bear witness to Muhammad this is Allah's message.[81]

This uncompromising message appeared to be the ranting and raving of a lunatic, an interpretation supported by the generalised biographies of Reid that were being put out by the press at the time, but the truth appears to have been far more complex. Some digging into Reid's past uncovered that he had travelled widely around the world prior to the attack, in a series of movements that appeared to indicate reconnaissance planning. Reports written by Reid detailing his travels were found on a computer linked to al-Qaeda's number two Ayman al-Zawahiri after the fall of the Taliban in 2001.[82] Reid maintained his cover story throughout his trial, claiming that he had purchased the shoes and explosives in Amsterdam, rather than admitting that they had been given to him in an Afghan training camp.[83]

As he was dragged from the courtroom, he shouted 'that flag will be brought down on the day of judgment and you will see in front of your Lord and my Lord and then we will know'. Until this day comes, however, he will have to wait in ADX Florence, the maximum security prison in Colorado where America houses its worst offenders, including 1993 World Trade Center bomber Ramzi Yousef, the 'Blind Sheikh' Omar Abdel Rahman, notorious organised crime leaders of all stripes and 'Unabomber' Ted Kaczynski. Aside from his religious zeal, as he was being sent to prison Reid might have drawn some comfort from the fact that there was at least one prisoner there whom he would know, Zacarias Moussaoui, a French–Moroccan whom he had met earlier in London. Tried and convicted for involvement in the 11 September 2001 conspiracy, Moussaoui announced during his trial that 'I am al-Qaeda' and claimed that he and Reid were meant to make up a sixth hijacking team on that fateful day.

FBI investigators and 9/11 mastermind Khalid Sheikh Mohammed dismissed this far-fetched plot, without disputing the close connection between Moussaoui and Reid. In an undated letter that appeared to be a final will and testament found at the Tarnak Farms al-Qaeda training camp in Afghanistan, Richard Reid instructed his mother to pass on all his earthly belongings to Abu Khalid Sawahiri, an alias used by Moussaoui.[84] Both men have also been identified as regulars first at the Brixton Mosque[85] and then later at Finsbury Park.[86] In fact, their shared experiences in London are a textbook case of the influence that the radical preachers Abdullah el-Faisal and Abu Hamza had upon their followers and the threat from Londonistan that emerged in the post-9/11 world.

Born in 1973, Richard Reid got off to a difficult start in life.[87] His parents officially separated when he was just four and divorced six years later, leaving the boy fatherless while attending Thomas Tallis Secondary School in South London. Young Richard was spotted as a relatively accomplished artist, although his talent had little time to shine before he dabbled in petty crime, earning him several stretches in Feltham Young Offenders' Institution. Reid was never a leader among his peers and, like his father before him, was drawn to Islam during one of his stints in prison, where he adopted the name Abdul Rahim. On release from jail in 1996 he attended the Brixton Mosque, which at the time undertook support work for young released offenders.[88] According to people who knew Reid there, he was a happy congregant who sought to learn Arabic and immerse himself in his new faith, helping out at the mosque where he could. A fellow convert recalled: 'He loved Islam, he wanted to know everything about it. He was open and friendly. He didn't wear a *shalwar kameez* and didn't grow a beard; mostly he was just dressed in t-shirt and jeans, but he embraced the Koran. He told me he thought Islam was a religion of love and discipline.' It was clear to this friend, however, that Reid had only partially absorbed many of the messages he was repeating: 'he was par-roting others…he had not really understood what he read'.[89] So when Reid met and was impressed by a more forceful personality like Zacarias Moussaoui, who by this point had drifted towards a more extreme ver-sion of Islam, Reid was quickly drawn towards it himself.

Moussaoui was a French–Moroccan who had left Paris in the late 1980s, drawn to London to study business at South Bank University. It took Moussaoui almost seven years to complete his degree and it seems as though he was more intrigued by the Muslim life he found in London than pursuing his education. While he initially found a home for him-self at the Brixton Mosque, he was enticed away when he discovered the radical words of preachers like Abdullah el-Faisal or Abu Hamza. One preacher who was in contact with Moussaoui told a colleague that he received an email from Moussaoui in the late 1990s telling him what a great time he was having while on jihad in Chechnya.[90] Abdul Haqq Baker, a leader at the Brixton Mosque, identified both Moussaoui and Reid as individuals who used to attend the mosque before their extreme views and expressions of them meant they were asked to stop coming. By this time both men had apparently attended meetings hosted by Abdullah el-Faisal and had been drawn into the community that Abu Hamza had created at Finsbury Park.

By Reid's own account, he had already found jihadism before he came to the radical preachers Abdullah el-Faisal and Abu Hamza, 'through his own reading, experience and thinking about the world around him. But the sermons of Hamza and others gave him a greater understand-ing of how to interpret his faith in a way that supported the use of vio-lence.'[91] What is undeniable about both Moussaoui and Reid's paths to radicalisation is that both passed through the halls of Abu Hamza's Finsbury Park Mosque. As we saw above, by 1997 Abu Hamza had secured his position by force of personality, by his willingness to under-cut his former teacher, and later, thanks to his 'enforcers' who ensured that trustees and other concerned congregants were unable to wrest con-trol of the mosque away from him. In a candid recording that was later uncovered, Abu Hamza proudly boasted using his hard men to force his way into mosques:

Get some brothers, you don't need to be a majority, you need to be firm. ... I used to go to Regent's Park mosque. Three thousand people pray in Regent's Park mosque. And only ten people holy, ten people, and [the mosque authorities, elders tell us] we'll [Abu Hamza's men] never stand up and deliver the Khutbah. ... But if the people know you are firm, they will back down. They all back down. All what you need is somebody who's making himself [indecipherable] you give him a couple of slaps. You give him a flat tire outside, then the police take you and make you, give you a record. You go outside, somebody else the next day, finish, finish. They will all surrender: give me the keys for the mosque.[92]

As we saw earlier, his takeover of Finsbury Park Mosque was far less aggressive and mostly involved charming the trustees and offering himself as a cheaper option to Abu Qatada. Aside from making it the new headquarters for SoS, it also became an international hub for extremists. Radicalisers and recruiters operated side by side, drawing on the community of lost wanderers for recruits to direct towards camps in Afghanistan.

Both Moussaoui and Reid travelled along this path, where they were joined by Nizar Trabelsi, a tall Tunisian. Having blown a football career on women and the high life, he drifted into petty crime and drugs, before he found Islam and ultimately gravitated towards the Finsbury Park Mosque. By his own account it was after watching a video depicting the suffering of a Palestinian girl that he grew to hate the United States.[93] After allegedly meeting Osama bin Laden in Afghanistan, he was earmarked to be an al-Qaeda suicide bomber in Europe.[94] Trabelsi also seems to have played a role in Richard Reid's plot, with a phone-card that connected to both Reid and his accomplice Saajid Badat (who ultimately backed out of his part in the plot). According to Badat, in early September 2001 he had been directed by senior al-Qaeda men Abu Hafs al-Masri (Mohammed Atef), the then al-Qaeda number three, and Saif al Adl to meet with Nizar Trabelsi in Belgium. The latter had apparently been planning a 'terrorist operation'.[95] Both Reid and Badat at different times used the British Embassy in Brussels to obtain new passports, and it seems likely that they stayed with Trabelsi, or at least had contact with him, while they were doing so. Badat and Reid also shared email accounts that Badat had created, probably in order to help coordinate their action.[96] While one may generalise about Moussaoui, Reid and Trabelsi as troubled men who had encountered obstacles in life that left them susceptible to the path of extremism, this hardly applies to Saajid Badat.

Badat was a second-generation Gujarati Muslim, born in Gloucester after his family fled to the United Kingdom from Malawi, and bright enough to have memorised the Koran by the age of twelve.[97] He went on to get ten GCSEs and four A-levels, before moving to London in about 1997 when he was eighteen after he disagreed with his father's desire to send him to a madrassa immediately after he had finished his secondary education, in order to train to be an imam.[98] Drawn initially to a mosque in Tooting frequented by a number of radicals, he eventually became involved in the community around the Finsbury Park Mosque, where he was impressed by Abu Hamza's fiery rhetoric and the scars that were evidence of his personal commitment to jihad. While in Gloucester, Badat reported having first come across the Azzam.com tapes 'In the Hearts of Green Birds', about Bosnia, and when in London sought out those behind them. This led him to Tooting, and to Babar Ahmad, the alleged webmaster of Azzam.com.[99]

In 1998 Badat signed up for a trip to Sarajevo, and in early 1999 he travelled to the camps in Afghanistan along the same route taken by Richard Reid.[100] According to Badat, his intention was to go to 'Afghanistan in order to acquire military training for jihad, for violent jihad' though he was not intending to connect with al-Qaeda.[101] His first stop was a camp outside Kabul affiliated with 'Turkestanis'—Chinese Muslims— where he knew the camp trainer and trained for about four to six weeks. Rather than simply theory, the camp threw its recruits immediately into a tough regimen of physical activity.[102] It is surprising that he was able to survive this rigorous test, though the group seems to have seen his bookishness as an advantage, recruiting him to help with the production of magazines and translation of videos. According to Badat, from the beginning of 2000 he was receiving 1,000 Pakistani rupees a month from al-Qaeda to support his work with the group, and by the summer he was receiving a further 1,000 a month to help produce a magazine for the Taliban.[103] By the spring of 2001 he was well integrated into al-Qaeda and, returning from a period of recuperation in Karachi, was told by his minders Abu Hafs al-Masri and Saif al-Adl that they needed him to perform surveillance missions on potential Jewish targets in South Africa. The now well-trained young warrior took further courses of instruction, this time to teach him 'how to present ourselves, how to form our appearance, how to collect information on places, how to film places and even make reports on our findings.'[104]

It is not clear that Badat ever made the trip to South Africa (though he says he did some preliminary online research), and he went instead a few months later to Europe to meet Nizar Trablesi, as instructed by the same al-Qaeda leaders. Richard Reid on the other hand does seem to have made reconnaissance missions to the Netherlands, Israel, Egypt, Turkey and Pakistan in July 2001 for the group. A report found on a computer hard drive obtained by the *Wall Street Journal* in late 2001 identifies an individual called 'Abu Ra'uff' who travelled to these countries in the same order, and describes obtaining a new passport before flying to Israel by putting his old one through a washing machine and reporting to a British Consulate in Amsterdam to obtain a replacement. All this activity matches Reid's movements.[105] The report was filed in August 2001, meaning Reid must have returned to Afghanistan or Pakistan by then, but he came back to Europe soon after, where he connected with Trabelsi. It seems likely that Reid and Badat would have encountered one another at this point (if not beforehand). Both were in Europe at the time of the attacks and their immediate reaction seems to have been to head back to Afghanistan. On the day of the September 11 attacks, Badat's response was to visit the British Consulate in Brussels to obtain a new passport, and then on 20 September he flew to Pakistan and crossed the border into Afghanistan, heading for Kandahar.[106]

In the wake of 11 September 2001, al-Qaeda's leadership identified him and Richard Reid as individuals who were to take part in a second wave of terror attacks, in which terrorists with Western passports would strike a second blow to the West. The two men travelled through Amsterdam in September, before making their way to Pakistan and crossing the border into Afghanistan some time in November 2001.[107] According to Badat's account, having returned to Afghanistan Abu Hafs asked him whether he would take 'an explosive device onboard an airplane.'[108] He was then instructed by Saif al-Adl as to where to obtain the device in Kandahar, and was brought before Osama bin Laden who told him the justification for the attack and embraced the young man. As Badat later told an American courtroom:

He said that if you had—if you had a ton of weight on one side of the scale and a ton of weight on the other side of the scale, if you place one kilo on one side it would weigh everything down. So he said that the American economy is like a chain. If you break one—one link of the chain, the whole economy will be brought down. So after the 11 September attacks, this operation will ruin the aviation industry and in turn the whole economy will come down.[109]

At Abu Hafs' direction, Badat and Reid had a final meeting before leaving Afghanistan with Khalid Sheikh Mohammed who briefed them on how to handle themselves, communicate and to contact his nephew in Karachi who would act as their point of contact.[110] According to Khalid Sheikh Mohammed's statements to the FBI, Reid was an unkempt and shambolic individual who 'looked like trouble' and apparently declared to Mohammed that he had been a drug dealer.[111] Nevertheless, the two warriors were now armed and ready, and they set off back across the border to Karachi, with a group of 'families vacating Afghanistan' and a group of Malaysians who had apparently been tasked 'to perform a similar hijacking to 9/11.'[112] As Badat overheard Reid and the leader of the Malaysian cell talking about how the Malay group was simply going to hijack the plane, he decided to give them one of his shoes since this would ensure they had a way of getting into the cockpit in case it was locked. Linked to Southeast Asian al-Qaeda affiliate Jemaah Islamiyah, the Malaysian group was detected and arrested by the Malaysian authorities.[113] Confirmation of Reid and Badat's bombs being linked was provided by the fact that both devices used a piece from the same batch of detonator cord.[114]

Back in Europe, something in Badat changed. He developed a 'reluctance to perform the mission' due to 'fear of performing the mission and also the fear of the implication for [his] family.'[115] While he did not attempt to dissuade Reid from his mission, he wrote an email to his handler in Pakistan, Khalid Sheikh Mohammed's nephew, saying, 'You will have to tell Van Damme that he could be on his own.'[116] He then put his explosive device into a shoebox and placed it under his bed, signing up instead at the Blackburn Islamic College and re-starting the path on which he had initially set off, to become a religious teacher. This façade was maintained until in November 2003 anti-terrorism police came crashing through the door of his family home in Gloucester. He quickly admitted his guilt, directing police to the explosives, and was ultimately sentenced to thirteen years. While the judge accepted Badat's guilty plea and apparently 'genuine change of heart', Badat had not come forward after the failure of Reid's own attack or warned anyone of what he was about to do.[117] In explaining why he had not simply thrown away the explosives in his possession, Badat declared: 'whilst I had not undertaken the mission, the actual ideology, the al-Qaeda ideology or jihadist ideology I had not abandoned, so that principle of remaining armed stayed with me.' He had held onto the weapon in case he might use it again in the future 'in furtherance of jihad.'[118] Seemingly unshakeable in his view, he later relented, first pleading guilty to the charges against him, then agreeing to testify and help authorities in other cases. His about-face provided prosecutors in the United States with a very useful witness in a number of trials, as well as providing British investigators with a wealth of information and detail about jihadist structures in the United Kingdom.

The cast of characters involved in the shoe bomb plot reveals the extraordinary diversity of individuals drawn to the Finsbury Park mosque from around the world, including some British Muslims, all of whom were attracted by the safe haven that Abu Hamza had created. It further highlights the deep connections between this community and al-Qaeda in Afghanistan who found these young Westerners to be perfect as spies to reconnoitre potential targets, while also recognising their potential in supporting the group's media outreach. In Badat's testimony, he speaks at length of meeting others whom he believes are Americans at the camps, suggesting that the two Britons and the Belgian Trabelsi were not the only Westerners making the connections.[119] One prominent individual to feature repeatedly in Badat's account is Adnan Shukrijumah, an American jihadist who he knew as Jafar al-Tayyar and with whom he worked to translate extremist material into English.[120] At time of writing Shukrijumah remained at large. While the events of 11 September 2001 and the Shoe Bomber's attempt a couple of months later shone a bright light on the Finsbury Park Mosque, it was the North African community at the mosque that aroused the concern of the security services. Missing the importance of Reid and the others, British intelligence focused on the apparent danger that was emerging from the mosque and its community of North African radicals.

The Algerian Connection

French security services had long been worrying about Algerian terrorist networks and the fact that since the early 1990s, connections had been showing up in Algerian-linked terror plots in France that led back to Britain. In 1995 an Algerian extremist named Rashid Ramda had been linked to a series of bombings on the Paris metro system and was found to be living in London. Then in 1999 the arrest of Ahmed Ressam as he was trying to enter the United States from Canada, revealed the apparent importance of a figure living in London known as Abu Doha, whose real name is believed to be Amar Makhlulif, as a possible coordinator for the cell around Ressam. In time, it would be uncovered that Abu Doha was likely the head of a network of Algerian jihadists scattered across Europe and North America, who had trained at camps in Afghanistan and were linked directly to Osama bin Laden.[121]

The threat from terrorist activity in the United Kingdom drew directly through Finsbury Park and a former congregant called Djamel Beghal, arrested in July 2001 while in transit through Dubai. Beghal quickly opened up under questioning, and a series of arrests and investigations were instigated across Europe. In the wake of September 11, news of Beghal's arrest leaked to the media, and his roommate Kamel Daoudi panicked and fled across the Channel to England, heading to Leicester, where he contacted Baghdad Meziane and Brahim Benmerzouga. Meziane was an old friend of Beghal's from the late 1990s, both men having gravitated to Britain in order to be near their spiritual leader, Abu Qatada. Daoudi's arrival alerted security services to the cell in Leicester, and an operation codenamed Springbourne was launched to establish what they were up to. Police were particularly struck by the fact that the two men were involved in credit card fraud on a substantial scale, and yet were clearly not enjoying a commensurately lavish lifestyle. Instead, the proceeds of their credit cards scam were funding streams for European terrorist cells.[122]

The men were later found to be in possession of videos, training manuals and books about bin Laden (it should be remembered these arrests took place only two weeks after 9/11, before which such material was harder to obtain, highlighting the men's deepened involvement with the ideology. Subsequent to 9/11 such material was easily accessible on the internet, while beforehand it likely required contacts and knowledge), while Meziane was at the centre of a passport forging network. These links all coalesced in the Courtailler brothers, two French converts who were associated with the Finsbury Park mosque. David Courtailler admitted to French investigators that he had received fake documents, money and access to Afghan camps via the North London mosque, while his brother Jerome (another regular at Finsbury Park) stayed with Meziane in Leicester.[123] Earlier (in Chapter 3) we saw how David Courtailler was connected to Moinul Abedin, the Birmingham plotter from 2000. Courtailler had converted to Islam in Brighton in 1997 while living with a community of mainly Libyan extremists led by Abu Qatada, including at least one individual who ended up in Guantanamo Bay and others who were connected to the Libyan Islamic Fighting Group (LIFG).

The police and security service investigation into the network around Benmerzouga and Meziane opened up several lines of inquiry, including one that led to a farm in Thetford, Norfolk. When police raided the property, among the items they found were detailed recipes on how to make poisons including ricin and nicotine poison, all using items that would be easily available on most high streets. This discovery alarmed the authorities, as it revealed that the network being investigated was no longer simply fundraising for international terrorism targeted abroad, but plotting attacks within Britain. The next breakthrough in the case came after police received an intelligence briefing from the Algerian agencies who had intercepted a wanted terrorist named Mohammed Meguerba, trying to enter their country from Morocco. Meguerba's appearance in Algeria was no doubt something of a surprise to British services: they had picked him up and released him at an earlier stage in their investigation into the Algerian funding network. The initial information was received on 31 December 2002 and included the alarming message: 'The group of Algerian terrorists in London have a quantity of fatal poison (of the family of toxic products which act through the skin) which they intend to use in the next few days.'[124]

The briefing also provided non-existent addresses and phone numbers that left British security officials both alarmed and confused. Two days later new information arrived, this time leading police to an address in Wood Green, North London. While it seems highly likely that this intelligence was obtained under duress (Meguerba's family and other detainees report seeing him in an uncomfortable state while in Algerian custody),[125] police found '£4,000 in cash, copies of the poison recipes, various chemicals, latex gloves, thermometers, and electronic scales for measuring small weights'.[126] The owner of these materials, Kamel Bourgass, identified by Meguerba as 'Nadir', was not at home, having fled to Manchester after seeing numerous acquaintances in the Algerian community being picked up by the British police. Unfortunately for him he had mistakenly chosen to seek refuge with a friend who was also under scrutiny.

When police raided the Crumpsall Lane address in Manchester in the early hours of 14 January 2003, they were not expecting to find Bourgass there and initially he was simply held aside as a bystander to a separate investigation. As time went on, one of the officers thought they recognised the man from photographs that had been found with the poison recipes and the atmosphere became noticeably tense as he went to check in with his superiors. At this point Bourgass attempted to escape, grabbing a knife with which he lashed out, killing Detective Constable Steven Oake and causing serious injury to three other officers. Bourgass was convicted for the murder of DC Oake and, much to the dismay of police, was the only individual to be convicted in association with what became known as the 'Ricin plot'. Investigation into Bourgass' past turned up the revelation that he had initially used the name Nadir Habra (the name by which Meguarba knew him), an asylum-seeker who had dropped off the radar after he had failed to show up for a hearing in November 2001.[127] The address that Habra had used in his failed asylum claim was that of the Finsbury Park Mosque on Thomas Road in North London, also home of the photocopying machine that the plotters had used when they made copies of the poison recipes that Bourgass had written out. This provided police with a direct link between a terrorist plot in the United Kingdom and Hamza's hideout, and led less than a week later to the raid that evicted Abu Hamza from the premises.

The raid on the mosque uncovered a haul of evidence, including fake passports, identity cards, fraudulent credit cards, a stun gun, imitation weapons, a CS gas canister, as well as chemical and biological protective suits. Seven men were detained: six of Algerian extraction and a seventh from Eastern Europe, ranging in ages from twenty-three to forty-eight.[128] Nevertheless, all the leads from the case suggested that the foiled network was primarily of Algerian descent (up to that point, the overwhelming proportion of Islamist counter-terror arrests had been of Algerians). This missed a very crucial element in the story of Islamist radicalisation in Britain, happening both within the mosque but more prominently in cities just outside London, and among Britain's Muslim South Asian community.

Post 9/11 Afghanistan

America and Britain at an official and public level were largely as one in the wake of the September 11 attacks. So when the government supported the American decision to attack Afghanistan and unseat the Taliban and al-Qaeda, there was a general consensus that this was the right thing to do. All of which meant that there was some shock when it was discovered in late October 2001 that a group of Britons had been killed in Afghanistan, apparently fighting for the Taliban. The group, Aftab Manzoor, Afzal Munir and Yasir Khan, were all of Pakistani descent and from Luton and Crawley, towns just outside London with sizeable Kashmiri Pakistani populations. While for the families the news of their deaths was a tragedy, for Omar Bakri Mohammed's Al-Muhajiroun organisation they were celebrated as joyous events. The group lapped up the publicity as news spread of the three men's deaths, with one member, Qassim aged twenty-six, interviewed at an event featuring Omar Bakri at the Finsbury Park Mosque, ominously telling a reporter, 'I'd never have previously considered going off to fight. But this is serious. Very serious. And something has to be done.' His friend, Salim aged twenty-two, added, 'I think we should both go and fight. It's our duty to do it.'[129] Such statements were likely shows of bravado for the press, but the context of the interviews suggested that Qassim and Salim's hints were not that far-fetched.

The three dead men were all in their mid twenties, with decent education, holding down modest jobs as drivers or seeking employment as computer engineers (Afzal Munir was a recent graduate in computer sciences from Luton University). Two were married (one with his wife in Pakistan), and all three still lived with their families amid a bland suburban landscape. All three were fixtures at their local mosques and had been spotted regularly at Al-Muhajiroun meetings—which had gleefully claimed them as their own after their deaths. But in interviews subsequent to their deaths, there did not appear to be a great deal of surprise among the local community. In part this may have been because they already knew the men were fighting alongside the Taliban: Aftab's father, for instance, reported that he had spoken to his son in mid-October and that he had announced then that he was planning to go and join the fighting.[130]

In part it may also be a reflection of the fact that there was little novelty in young British Pakistanis going to fight or train in Kashmir, as we saw in Chapter 3. A year prior to the incident, in 2000, another Crawley boy, Omar Khyam, had run off to the mountains of Kashmir to join the holy warriors. Later imprisoned as the ringleader of a plot to detonate a massive fertiliser bomb in the United Kingdom, known by its police code name of Operation Crevice, Khyam came from a family with a strong military tradition in Pakistan and returned to Britain after his relations went to the camps in Pakistan to persuade the teenager to come home. He was met with a hero's welcome, which no doubt made him feel justified in his actions.[131]

The Al-Muhajiroun connection was not particularly new either. Khyam had signed up to the group in his teens, and while it was unclear whether it facilitated his travel to Pakistan, close relations blamed Omar Bakri for putting ideas in his head. The local leader of Al-Muhajiroun, Saleem Sultan, clarified at the time that 'we don't actually send people away to fight but we do encourage them to go if they want'.[132] Omar Bakri's name surfaced again in mid 2000 when an anonymous twenty-five-year-old calling himself Abu Yahya was interviewed by the BBC in which he claimed that he had spent four months in a training camp in Kashmir, 'in all kinds of warfare...I learned everything with respect to fighting: making bombs, using artillery, using a Kalashnikov, how to ambush.'[133] The training was called 'Ultimate Jihad Challenge' and the coordinating organisation 'Sakina Security Services' (sakina translates as 'peace' or 'tranquility'), though the owner denied all knowledge of events in Kashmir when confronted. He did, however, admit to being involved in the training of some of the individuals who ended up part of the fateful group that Abu Hamza sent to Yemen.[134] Omar Bakri Mohammed claimed to know Sakina well, 'as head of Al-Muhajiroun— meaning the eyes, the ears—I have overall responsibility for a number of organisations fighting for the Islamic cause. Sakina is one of those.'[135] Later that year, Omar Bakri claimed that he had been responsible for the recruitment of Mohammed Bilal,[136] a twenty-four-year old Birmingham-born man who had left the United Kingdom six years earlier to join Harakat ul-Mujahedeen, and who blew himself up in a suicide attack claimed by Kashmiri terrorist group Jaish-e-Mohammed (JeM) on Christmas Day 2000.[137] Established by Maulana Masood Azhar, whom we encountered earlier giving fiery speeches in Birmingham in advance of jihad, JeM became one of the focal step-off points for a number of British radicals with a network that Azhar likely was able to establish as a result of his trips to the United Kingdom.

For Omar Bakri, the experience of fighting abroad in Kashmir, Chechnya or Afghanistan was a 'obligation' for young Muslims that he compared to 'national service'.[138] A year earlier, he made similar pronouncements in response to an investigation by the *Sunday Telegraph* in relation to training people to join Osama bin Laden and to fight in Chechnya:

The military wing of the IIF [International Islamic Front] is run by Osama bin Laden. Volunteers from Britain are travelling abroad to join camps run by the IIF and other organisations. Once they are there they receive military training or take part in Jihad. Last week we sent thirty-eight people to Chechnya. Our volunteers are not terrorists. They are not targeting civilians and they do not target people in Britain.[139]

Other individuals in the article claimed that they had first been trained 'at the [Finsbury Park] mosque', while Abdul Wahid Majid claimed to have been on ten 'special training courses' in Britain before spending two months in the 'Pakistani hills'. As he put it: 'After my basic training with swords and sticks at the mosque, I then went on a number of courses where I was taught how to use real firearms and live ammunition. It is unlimited, the amount of things you can learn. Once in Pakistan I was introduced to a greater range of military hardware including guns like Kalashnikovs and M16s.'[140] Abdul Wahid Majid went on to be part of the wider community around the Crawley-based cell involved in plotting to detonate a large bomb outside the Bluewater shopping centre, including spending some time with the group in Pakistan in 2002. He gained greater notoriety when in February 2014 he became Britain's first known suicide bomber in Syria, blowing himself up in a truck full of explosives outside Aleppo prison. Initially drawn to Syria as part of an aid convoy, he decided to play a more kinetic role in the conflict. Talking to the press subsequently about Abdul Wahid, his friend Raheed Mahmood (whose brother was jailed during the fertilizer plot and with whom Abdul Wahid had travelled on the aid convoy to Syria) reported that the two of them had dabbled in Al-Muhajiroun as young men, but 'we disagreed with Al-Muhajiroun—the message, the styles and the means of how they put that out. So, just respectfully, as we did with many other movements, we moved on.'[141] But this was almost two decades later, and in the late 1990s, Abdul Majid's story was one that was typical of the community of individuals who were drawn to the training camps being run by the radical preachers as a way of engendering a sense of community among their acolytes.

In all of this it is unclear exactly where the defining line between Omar Bakri and Abu Hamza lies. Given that the organisational structures offered by Finsbury Park Mosque were not officially disrupted until 2003, it is hardly surprising that they were operational in late 2001. One report suggested the possibility that the three Al-Muhajiroun men who died in Afghanistan had been part of a unit that had been 'diverted from the guerrilla war in Kashmir', offering the possibility that they had started fighting there, but been left following the events of September 11.[142] This may have almost been the fate of Mohammed Siddique Khan and Waheed Ali, both of whom trained at a Harakat ul-Mujahedeen camp in June 2001 at the direction of an uncle of Siddique Khan's. At the camp, however, they had met a pair of Arabs who had redirected them towards Afghanistan, where what was perceived as a more genuine jihad was taking place. Both men fell sick, and while Siddique Khan recovered sufficiently to make it into Afghanistan, Ali waited at a base camp. The two men left Pakistan on 5 September 2011, and might have ended up alongside the Al-Muhajiroun men had they stayed a week longer.[143]

For those who had been listening to radical preachers like Abu Hamza, Abu Qatada, Omar Bakri or Abdullah el-Faisal, the events of 9/11 were a much needed 'punch in the nose' to the imperialist invaders in America, as Abu Hamza's Cypriot bodyguard put it years later to CNN.[144] Years of running camps, training, recruiting, fundraising and organising appeared suddenly to come to a climax, as the events of September 11 explosively catapulted the cause that they had been promoting into the public eye. Omar Bakri was quick to capitalise upon this and hosted a meeting at which the 'Magnificent 19' (a reference to the nineteen men who had taken part in the suicide attack on 11 September) were venerated. For young men like Aftab Manzoor, Afzal Munir and Yasir Khan, the cause they had long been supporting had suddenly and quite violently come to life, and they felt the need to take matters further. It was not only young men who were drawn back, and in October 2001, forty-odd-year-old Munir Farooqi of Manchester left his family to go and support the Taliban. Captured in Mazar-e-Sharif, he was freed only after his wife came over to buy his way out of detention in May 2002. He kept his passion for the cause and established, as was briefly mentioned in Chapter 2, a pipeline in Manchester sending young men whom he helped radicalise to fight alongside the Taliban.

The key question on many minds outside the radical community at this time was what exactly drove these men to make such decisions, in particular as individuals like Hassan Butt, the spokesman for Al-Muhajiroun, were boasting to the press of having facilitated 'hundreds' of British Muslims to cross the border from Pakistan into Afghanistan. In one high profile interview he claimed that:

News that the first Britons have been lost in the cause will not deter those who will follow. It will encourage many more. Those back home will see a chance for martyrdom—the greatest achievement possible in the Muslim faith. I have spoken to the families of the British men already martyred and they were happy for them. They were proud ... I've been in touch with a thousand British Muslims who are going to the Holy War. Hundreds have passed through here on their way.[145]

Later denounced as a fantasist after he told a prominent reporter that he made up considerable portions of a story, Butt nevertheless appears to be the archetypal young second-generation Pakistani who was attracted to Al-Muhajiroun. He helped establish the organisation at Wolverhampton University alongside his brother in the late 1990s, and quickly became one of its most prominent spokespeople in the wake of 9/11, claiming to be running a safe house for Al-Muhajiroun supporters in Pakistan. The public would have been all the more shocked to hear these pronouncements about the conflict in Afghanistan and Butt's active support of the Taliban from a well-educated individual who spoke perfect English than from any of the foreigners associated with Britain's radical Muslim preachers. Even though Butt has claimed that parts of his story were fabrications this does not detract from the fact that he appears to have been operating quite openly on the periphery of a terrorist network.

Iraq

Indignation at the conflict in Afghanistan was kept within a relatively discrete niche of public opinion in the United Kingdom, but indignation against the government's decision to support the American invasion of Iraq cut across communities and political lines. Hundreds of thousands (and maybe more than a million) turned out to march in protest in London alone, including several individuals who would later become involved in terrorism. The events also gave the radical preachers an even greater boost in support, as their predictions of a conflict between Muslims and *kafirs* appeared to become ever closer to realisation. In a particularly fiery speech entitled 'Voting is Kufr and Haram', which was re-released by extremists in the United Kingdom after the election in 2010 was called, Abu Hamza laid out in detail how voting was *haram* since it would mean that you were supporting a system which had allowed the invasion of Iraq to occur.[146]

For young men already in thrall to the nihilistic propaganda spouted by the clerics, some of whom had by this point participated in some level of jihadi activity either at home or abroad, the cause seemed ever more immediate.

But there were key differences between the impacts of Afghanistan and Iraq: in the former case a strong connection to the land already existed, both in the form of networks that had helped British Muslims to fight alongside either the Taliban or Kashmiri fighters, but also in the form of a strong ethnic connection to the almost one million-strong Pakistani community in the United Kingdom, with shared languages and familial links making the journey easier. For Iraq on the other hand, the connection was different: while individuals stirred up by talk of a global *ummah* felt the pain of their Iraqi brethren, there was a very practical problem in that Iraq was an Arabic-speaking country—not a first or even second language for most British Muslims.

Some British individuals did fight in Iraq, including some Iraqi-Britons. A number of support networks were uncovered that helped people to go and fight, and there were even a few instances of British suicide bombers.[147] In 2003 a Yemeni man from Sheffield was reported to have blown himself up in a suicide operation, while in 2005 a French national of North African descent living in Manchester was reported to have detonated himself in Iraq. The British–Yemeni Wail al-Dhaleai, a twenty-two-year-old martial arts instructor, had told his family he was heading to the United Arab Emirates for security work. Instead it was believed he went through Damascus before heading into Iraq; his family were informed of his death there by a series of phone calls from other British fighters in Iraq.[148] US forces in Iraq picked up Mobeen Muneef, a British Pakistani from Tooting who had been spotted at Al-Muhajiroun events in London, after they saw him passing weapons to fighters in December 2004. He claimed to have bribed a taxi driver to take him into Iraq from Syria, where he was studying in Damascus, and had traded his passport for a fake Iraqi ID. He pleaded innocence, claiming to have been in Iraq as an aid worker, but an Iraqi court decided to make an example of him and in 2006 sentenced him to fifteen years imprisonment.[149] The path he took appears to be one that Asif Hanif and Omar Sharif also attempted a few years earlier at the outbreak of war in Iraq. The two men, who are discussed in greater detail in the next chapter, had initially headed to the Middle East intending to join the fight in Iraq alongside Abu Musab al-Zarqawi's group. Both had spent time in Damascus deepening their knowledge of Islam, and in late March or early April went to Syria hoping to get into Iraq, though they were turned away.[150]

In testimony before the Chilcot Inquiry into the war in Iraq in 2010, Dame Eliza Manningham-Buller, a former head of the Security Service, pointed out that at the time of the Iraq War MI5 believed that some seventy or eighty 'young British citizens' were in Iraq fighting British forces. In comparison, an MI5 estimate from around the same time stated that prior to 2002 some 3,000 had gone to Afghanistan and Pakistan.[151] For the overwhelming majority of British jihadis, it was the battlefields of South Asia that were the bigger draw, thanks to both ethnic and linguistic links, as well as the already existing well-trodden path for them to follow. Iraq was enough of a cause celebre to stir up already highly radical individuals into believing that the war for which they had been preparing was almost upon them. As Dame Eliza put it in her testimony (verbatim):

By 2003/2004 we were receiving an increasing number of leads to terrorist activity from within the UK and the—our involvement in Iraq radicalised, for want of a better word, a whole generation of young people, some British citizens—not a whole generation, a few among a generation—who were—saw our involvement in Iraq, on top of our involvement in Afghanistan, as being an attack on Islam.[152]

This expressed itself most violently with the events of 7 July 2005, but, as we shall see, this was not simply an isolated incident, but part of a wave of attempted attacks deflected by a combination of incompetence on behalf of the plotters and effective work by security and intelligence agencies. With hindsight, the groundwork for 7 July had been laid long before the events of September 11 and the invasions of Afghanistan and Iraq, but these events acted as an accelerant to the problem of exporting radicals abroad from the United Kingdom and precipitated the chain of events that led to terrorist attacks at home.

5

7/7 AND THE NEAR MISSES

'I did try leaving before, after Afghanistan happened; I left and went to Pakistan like many emotionally charged brothers, intending never to return, vowing to become the West's mortal enemies. A few months later, circumstances forced almost everyone back...'[1]

In summer 2003 a group of young Muslims, predominantly from the United Kingdom and of Pakistani descent, had gathered in Pakistan to prepare themselves to join the struggle in Afghanistan against the 'crusader' forces that had recently invaded that country. Drawn from among the young men who had been persuaded by British-based radical preachers to participate in the struggle for the global supremacy of Islam, they now wanted to play a more active role. Long-term converts to the extremist cause, they had trained at camps in the United Kingdom and in some cases in South Asia too. This time they were gathering at a facility at their own instigation where they were planning to learn the elements of the modern warrior's trade. The only qualifications needed were that those who attended 'were serious, [and] were going to go on to fight in Afghanistan.'[2] But they remained at heart a rambunctious group of young men on an adventure holiday: prior to departing for the camp near Lahore, neighbours complained to the police about the noise they made, while at the camp one of them earned the sobriquet 'Abu Finish-up' after his repeated calls to the camp latrine.[3]

159

Two plots emerged from among these aspirant warriors that would come to define how Britain understood its Islamist terrorist threat. The first, led by Omar Khyam, one of the key organisers and funders of the trip, was made public in March 2004 when police arrested a group of men in connection with a long-standing investigation code-named Crevice. The second was led by a youth worker from Beeston named Mohammed Siddique Khan.

The group's journey from Britain to the badlands of Pakistan and back in many ways epitomises the broader trajectory described thus far.[4] The men were mostly of Pakistani descent with relations in the Kashmir and Punjab parts of the country, children of first- or second-generation immigrants who had enjoyed the privileges of a reasonable education and for the most part had stable families. Some were married with children and, while their parents may have been practising Muslims, few can be said to have been deeply orthodox or religious in their outlooks. A couple had links to the military in Pakistan and most had spent their childhoods travelling back and forth between families in Pakistan and the United Kingdom. The majority were (or had been) active members in the broad community of extremists in Britain, drawing inspiration from preachers like Abu Hamza, Omar Bakri Mohammed and Abdullah el-Faisal, and with connections to local extremists who provided them with role models in jihadism. They supported their activities and travels through low-level fraud and established local networks of young aspirant warriors around community-based activities and meeting-places.

As we saw in previous chapters, the path of young British men joining the jihad in South Asia was well-trodden. Of this group alone, Mohammed Shakil had in 1999 taken some time off to go travelling around Kashmir, during which time he connected with extremist groups; in January 2000 Omar Khyam had run away from home to join fighters in Kashmir; and in 2001, just prior to September 11, Mohammed Siddique Khan made a similar pilgrimage with a young acolyte in tow. A participant known as 'Imran', later identified as Zeeshan Siddiqui, had gone to Lebanon in 1997 hoping to connect with fighters there. Anthony Garcia, also known as Rahman Adam, or Rahman Benouis as he was originally known, had come to an earlier camp established by Omar Khyam, although his pale complexion had complicated his participation, with people looking on him with great suspicion. Drawn from suburban communities up and down the UK, the path that steered them towards such extremism was a complex combination of their local experiences and external motivations. The radical groups were key, acting as initiators into a jihadi mindset, as were older jihadi veterans towards whom the young men would gravitate. Crawley, a town just outside London from which the main elements of the Crevice plot emerged, is as good a place as any to trace how these elements coalesced.

By the late 1990s, Omar Bakri Mohammed had established a regular presence locally in Crawley. In his 1996 documentary 'Tottenham Ayatollah' Jon Ronson recorded Omar Bakri leading prayers at a local gym and helping a group of young men to train with punch bags, before publicly outing Ronson to the attendant audience as a Jew. Captured rather comically in Ronson's book *Them*, in the course of the discussion Omar Bakri referred to him as an 'infidel', while members of the audience assured him that it was worse to be a Jew than an atheist.[5] Omar Bakri managed to get himself invited to a local school in Hazelwick, where in 1999 the radical preacher led the sixth form assembly.[6] And it was this school that two of the convicted Crevice plotters, Omar Khyam and Jawad Akbar, had attended, though by 1999 they had graduated. Omar's younger brother, Shujah, who was initially arrested alongside him, was still a student there at the time. In retrospect the school recognised the magnitude of its oversight, but even at the time, there had been indicators that the self-appointed sheikh and his group's credentials were towards the extreme end of the scale. In February 1997 Al-Muhajiroun had hosted a series of meetings on the future of Islam in Britain, under the low-profile titles 'Israeli policy and the American green light', 'The joint strategy between USA and Israel', and 'The Western strategy for Israel'.[7] In December 1998, they hosted a session entitled 'Christmas: a Capitalist festival', while in May 1999 they actively urged Muslims to boycott elections declaring that 'for Muslims to vote for any party is forbidden. To delegate somebody to be part of a system which legislates in place of God is not permitted.'[8] Other sessions were rather less controversial, including one in September 1998 titled 'Drink and Drugs, Public Enemy no. 1'. A blend of anti-Zionism and anti-establishmentarianism intermingled with attacks on the dissolute state of society won Omar Bakri some local praise. One local newspaper quoted a priest who agreed with the sentiments expressed about the commercialisation of Christmas.[9]

Others in the community were less accommodating. Talking after the arrests of a group of locals linked to Al-Muhajiroun in April 2004, the

Luton Central Mosque president Mohammed Sulaiman proudly stated he had 'told them to bugger off' when they had made attempts to co-opt believers in his mosque.[10] And there was evidence of similar local responses earlier in 1998 when the group was officially banned from the local Asian Mela celebrations, leading to a vociferous protest campaign focused on their exclusion. It is probably as a result of this that they held in the same month a workshop on the dangers of alcohol and drugs, an innocuous topic that was unlikely to anger people and might even soft-ened concerns about them.[11] Others apart from Omar Bakri were also promoting radical ideas locally: years earlier, in early 1994, Omar Saeed Sheikh, the LSE graduate who would allegedly mastermind the killing of Daniel Pearl, returned to Britain after training in Waziristan and attempted to find recruits and funding. Despatched home by Kashmiri jihadist leader Maulana Masood Azhar to obtain a visa to travel to India, Sheikh wandered around his old stamping ground for a few months, try-ing to incite people to go to train, as well as establishing 'martial arts classes in the Muslim pocket of Crawley'. According to a diary kept by Sheikh at the time, 'Jan–April: Encourage people to go for training. In this time, I collect many items of interest for the camp and also given funds by people (though I don't ask for them).'[12]

By the late 1990s, Al-Muhajiroun had become the public face of extremism locally, with Omar Bakri Mohammed performing for the cam-eras at any opportunity. When in January 2000 stories emerged in the local press of a local youth running away to Kashmir to fight, Omar Bakri did not claim responsibility, though he praised the youngster's actions:

I share the worry of these families, but if my child wanted to go and fight for a noble jihad then I would encourage them. I have received many complaints from families in Crawley and other places, but I tell them it is a Muslim's duty to have military training when they reach puberty. These boys go not because of what I tell them to do, or what their mothers and fathers say, but as an obligation to God.[13]

This particular teenager was to prove a significant fixture in the British jihad. A young cricketer called Omar Khyam, he went on to become the key figure in the first major Islamist terror plot in which British nation-als targeted the United Kingdom in a bombing campaign.[14] Omar has already appeared earlier in the narrative, highlighting the journey and appeal of jihad in Kashmir, but his personal story starts with an upbring-ing in Crawley in a family where his father spent much of the time travelling for business between Belgium and Karachi. In the absence of a father figure, Omar looked after his younger brother Shujah Mahmood, eventually bringing him into his global jihadist plotting. Young Omar was seemingly unaffected by the absent parent, and appears to have lived a humdrum existence growing up; he liked 'cricket, Manchester United and fish and chips'.[15] Omar was a local cricket star, had captained the county team and was even tipped to play for England. But somewhere during his mid-to late teens he was drawn into a community of individuals at the local Langley Green Mosque who were actively involved in promoting extreme ideas and were apparently facilitating travel for young men seeking to train at jihadist camps abroad.

Drawn to meetings organised by Al-Muhajiroun locally, Khyam later recalled on the witness stand watching videos with the group about Bosnia, and the destruction of Grozny in Chechnya. The Bosnian ones were particular striking to the young boy:

The videos I saw of Bosnia were even more graphic than the ones that came from Chechnya, because the aim of the Serbs was just to kill the Muslims, simple as that. That's how it was being portrayed, as a complete ethnic war, and again you would see mosques blown up, you would see people being shot. It was quite graphic pictures.[16]

In early 2000, while still a teenager, Omar told his mother he was heading to France on a school trip and instead travelled to Pakistan. He recalls hopping into a taxi on his arrival and ordering it to 'take me to the office of the Mujahedeen'. Omar claimed to have first come across the Kashmiri warriors a year earlier when on a family trip to Murree, near the Pakistani side of the Kashmir border, when he saw a tent run by the Al-Badr Mujahedeen, a group aimed primarily at jihad in Kashmir that grew out of groups fighting the Soviets in Afghanistan. When he asked if he could join them, he was told he was welcome to train with them, but had to grow a beard and had to dress more like a Muslim. Spurred on by youthful enthusiasm, a familial passion for Kashmir and doubtless the encouragement of his new friends in Al-Muhajiroun, Omar returned the next year with the specific intent of training at a Kashmiri-inspired training camp. There he was taught how to fire AK-47s, pistols, Rocket Propelled Grenades (RPGs), and 'everything I needed to know for fighting guerrilla warfare in Kashmir'. According to Omar, the trainers were from Pakistan's Inter-Services Intelligence agency (ISI) and he saw some of them teaching other recruits how to make bombs. In the end, the young warrior was persuaded by family contacts in Pakistani military intelligence to leave the camp and return to the United Kingdom, receiving a hero's welcome as well-wishers showering him with flowers 'as if I'd just been married', as Omar put it on the stand. According to Omar, it was only his mother who disapproved of his actions—the rest of the family was impressed by his zeal.[17] As Omar put it, 'starting with my granddad all the way down, most of my family are in the military. So—and they all work for Kashmir and they work that cause for liberating that part of Kashmir. So, when they saw their grandson or their nephew had gone there, they were very pleased.'[18]

Operation Crevice

Omar provided this rather romanticised version of his story in court after his arrest as part of Operation Crevice. His trip to Pakistan in early 2000 was the first of many he took with the specific intent of joining and supporting various extremist groups who ran training camps in the mountains of the North West Frontier Province (NWFP) of Pakistan. From there he went into Afghanistan at least once, though it is possible he might have returned. Speaking to BBC journalist Richard Watson after his second trip to the region in the summer of 2001, Omar said he had been 'all over Afghanistan' and that 'the Taliban are the most hospitable people in the world'.[19] The role played by Al-Muhajiroun in all of this is uncertain: when Khyam was arrested in March 2004, local leader Saleem Sultan was approached for interviews a number of times and admitted to knowing Omar. This was not new information, as he had also appeared in the local press years earlier when Omar had first run away to Kashmir, saying 'Omar spent time with our organisation', although he went on to deny they had anything to do with his travels abroad.[20] Omar's uncle, Sajjid Ahmed, was quite certain of what had occurred and laid the blame squarely at the feet of Omar Bakri Mohammed, saying 'they [Al-Muhajiroun] preyed on boys at the mosque and even in the shopping mall, getting them when they were young and impressionable. They showed them videos of the injustices Muslims were suffering, and then channelled their anger into hatred.'[21] However, whether it was Al-Muhajiroun that actually provided him with the contacts to get into training camps in South Asia is uncertain. Certainly, Omar's account in court of simply hopping into a cab and asking them to 'take me to the office of the mujahedeen' seems a fanciful one, especially when taken in conjunction with his later activities and his familial contacts with Pakistan's intelligence services.

What is certain is that Omar was in touch with a circle of individuals who all had some association with Al-Muhajiroun, many of whom went on to become involved in terrorist activity and training in Britain and Pakistan. As we shall see, this network of individuals provided fertile ground for al-Qaeda recruiters, producing a string of aspirant warriors and plots. Shiv Malik, a journalist who has covered a number of the major plots detailed in this chapter, describes Al-Muhajiroun's role in reference to the Crevice group as being that of 'an old boys' network' which provided a structure of individuals who had been cultured into a similar set of values and beliefs, and thus were willing to provide support "once they were ready to act"'.[22] This version is supported by the testimony of Mohammed Junaid Babar, one of the Crevice group who turned the state's evidence against the rest of the group. In his telling, Al-Muhajiroun provided a structure for the men to go to Pakistan, but once there the majority broke off to conduct operations and connect with local extremists, retaining some loose connections to Al-Muhajiroun, but ridiculing them in conversation among each other.[23] Certainly, Omar on the stand spoke of how the group's goals of establishing a global Caliphate seemed 'unrealistic.'[24]

The 'Crevice' group of seven individuals around Omar Khyam in Canada, Pakistan, the United Kingdom and the United States (part of a much wider network, but the focus here is on those who were tried and convicted) was the first to emerge as a direct threat to the United Kingdom. They were all one-time members of Al-Muhajiroun, and with one exception (Rahman Adam, who was of Algerian descent and had changed his name to Anthony Garcia) of Pakistani extraction. Omar Khyam, Waheed Mahmood and Jawad Akbar were all Crawley boys, while Salahuddin Amin was born in Pakistan, but had lived in Luton from the age of sixteen. Adam was born in Algeria, but his family had moved to London in the mid-1980s seeking a better life for the three children. Momin Khawaja was born in Ottawa, Canada, but had lived between Libya, Pakistan and Saudi Arabia before his family re-settled in Ottawa in his mid-teens. Finally, Mohammed Junaid Babar was born in Pakistan, but moved to the US in 1977, when he was very young, and was brought up there, picking up a strong American accent along the way, which made his claims to a British film crew that he was willing to kill US forces if they came to Afghanistan all the more menacing.[25]

All of them can be easily characterised as well-assimilated individuals born to immigrant families, educated to various levels, with parents who held down jobs as café owners, taxi drivers or manual workers in jobs associated with the nearby airports in Gatwick and Luton. Omar Khyam's father had business connections with textile firms in Belgium, where young Omar would occasionally go to visit him. At the time of arrest, none of them was advancing far in his career. Khawaja seemed to have the most promise, as an IT engineer on contract with the Canadian Ministry of Foreign Affairs and International Trade. Mahmood was most recently working in some capacity for Transco, the gas utility company, but had previously been a manager at a Gatwick tiling shop where Omar Khyam, recently returned from Kashmir, also worked. One of the more radical members of the cell, Mahmood seems to have acted as something of a slightly older spiritual guide, spurring the group on to action as the idea of carrying out an attack in Britain started to come together.

Amin was a taxi driver who admitted to attending a couple of conferences of Abu Hamza's at Finsbury Park shortly prior to emigrating to Pakistan in November 2001. Already providing support by putting aside about £5–10 a day to send to 'freedom fighters' in Kashmir, after hearing Abu Hamza speak about the obligation of Muslims to go and support an Islamic state he made up his mind 'to move to Afghanistan and stay there'.[26] Akbar and Khyam were students, while Rahman Adam was a part-time security guard and Tesco employee who dreamed of being a male model.[27] The second of three brothers, Rahman's older brother Lamine was a prominent acolyte of Abu Hamza's and would emulate the preacher's messages and actions.[28] Lamine seems to have led his siblings astray and featured during the Crevice trial when a co-conspirator testified that he had heard stories that Lamine was planning 'on making a bomb and hitting a nightclub'.[29] However, Lamine and younger brother Ibrahim were eventually assessed as not playing a direct role in Crevice, though they were very active on the periphery of the immediate network and were placed on restrictive control orders from which they both absconded in May 2007. Ibrahim partially re-emerged in July 2010 when passport photos of him were found in the possession of a Norwegian–Uighur extremist arrested in Oslo. Security services surmised that the long-missing Ibrahim was eager to travel once again, apparently still using al-Qaeda-linked networks.[30] Whatever plans he had, however, apparently came to an end when it was reported that he had been killed in an American drone strike in Waziristan in November 2011.[31] At the time of writing, Lamine's whereabouts remain unknown.

The final player, who was to turn against the rest of them as well as numerous other members of the network, was Mohammed Junaid Babar, who had abandoned his studies in pharmacology in New York and had a string of odd jobs before leaving for Pakistan in the wake of the September 11 attacks. He first encountered Al-Muhajiroun when the group was trying to establish a US office a year prior to 9/11, quickly becoming an integral part of the group and moving to help at its Pakistan office after the attacks.[32] When he was picked up by the FBI after returning to the US in April 2004, he quickly confessed to his involvement with al-Qaeda and agreed to testify against numerous former friends with whom he had plotted in Waziristan. Much of the basic information that exists about the many plots associated with this network is drawn from testimony by Babar and thus has to be treated carefully, but the fact that numerous convictions for terrorism have been handed down (and much of it is corroborated from other testimony) demonstrates that there was evidence beyond his testimony, and in many cases his accounts have not been substantively disputed by defence lawyers.[33]

The key event to which Mohammed Junaid Babar was witness was a training camp in the summer of 2003 in Malakand in Pakistan, which he helped establish using Al-Muhajiroun activists' networks and their contacts. Confessing his involvement in a New York courtroom in June 2004, Junaid Babar described his role: 'I set up a jihad training camp where those who wanted to go into Afghanistan where they could learn how to use weapons, and also, you know, any explosive devices that they wanted to test out over there. And I also provided lodging and transportation in Pakistan for them, and I transported them to and from the training camp.'[34]

He had initially looked into establishing the training camp at the behest of Tanveer Ali, an East London extremist and member of Al-Muhajiroun who, along with his brother, had been among those who were drawn to Pakistan in the wake of 9/11 to help 'defend Afghanistan'. Ali had returned to Britain after fighting and, according to Babar, wanted to establish a camp where people could train out of sight of everyone, including the Pakistani authorities.[35]

Babar states that in February or March 2003 he headed to Malakand alongside another East London radical called Kazi Rahman, who will be covered in greater detail later, where they liaised with an Al-Muhajiroun leader named Sajeel Shahid. The three men met with a local Maulana to find out about establishing training camps and finding recruits.[36] The Shahid brothers, Sajeel and Adil, were identified during the Crevice trial as important members of Al-Muhajiroun who played roles in establishing both its American and Pakistani branches. Their older brother, Sohail, worked in a senior role in the Pakistan Software Export Board (PSEB), a government affiliate which hired his brothers and others in the Al-Muhajiroun network and which gave them passes permitting them to travel freely about the country, even in the North West Frontier Province.[37]

Having established a location, it took a while for the aspirant warriors to congregate there. One of the young men got married, and they regrouped in Britain where they raised money for their jihadist endeavor. Babar went back to Ali to discuss the costs of establishing a camp. Busy with other projects, Ali had seemingly lost interest and Babar ended up researching how he might instead establish a similar camp for Omar Khyam in Pakistan. Returning to Pakistan, he was joined in May by Khyam who went to obtain explosives training in Kohat, after which he joined other members of the group who had now arrived in Pakistan, including his old schoolmate Jawad Akbar and the Algerian Anthony Garcia, as well as a pair of men from Beeston who identified themselves as Ibrahim and Zubair. Whilst key players involved in establishing the camp—Muhammed Junaid Babar, Omar Khyam and Salhuddin Amin—disagree about how exactly Ibrahim and Zubair came to be invited to the camp, all agree it was not a pre-planned thing. Initially, the camp was intended to be for Omar Khyam's network. He and Waheed Mahmood had been recruiting in East London and Crawley in the months beforehand to find dedicated warriors who deserved to train with them. But when Babar and Omar Khyam went to Islamabad airport to meet a group who had come for the training camp, they found that Salahuddin Amin was already there. Amin had been directed by a contact back in Britain to meet a pair of Britons who were arriving to find out more about the situation in Afghanistan.

Whether by coincidence or not, the men turned out to be on the same flight as the Crawley group. They told Babar that they were from Bradford and had come to find out whether it was possible for foreigners to get into Afghanistan. The men were concerned, according to Mohammed Junaid Babar's later statement, that 'there was a lot of misreporting about

Afghanistan in the UK. [Amin] was going to meet up and tell them what the situation was.'[38] The men were also apparently bringing funds from the United Kingdom, and handed over to Amin 'money amounting to hundreds of pounds for the cause.' Ibrahim and Zubair were in fact respectively Mohammed Siddique Khan and Mohammed Shakil, two Beestonites, both of whom went on to be involved in the network that spawned the 7 July 2005 bombings. Having established that they were moving in the same circles, and trusted by the same people back in Britain, the Crawley group invited the two newcomers to join them at the camp. According to Babar he was the one to invite them, though they both said they had already been trained and felt no need to do it again. Salahuddin Amin and Omar Khyam offered a slightly contradictory account, reporting that they had taken the two men's numbers so that they could later call them and coordinate bringing them to the camp.[39] In Shakil's telling, the men they met at the airport followed them to the house of Mohammed Siddique Khan's uncle where they continued persuading them to accompany them to their camp.[40] Whatever the case, the two men eventually joined the Crevice group in Malakand. Siddique Khan and Shakil ended up staying there for only a few days, and Khyam was particularly wary of letting the outsiders see the Crevice group practise a bomb explosion that was part of their preparations for the attack in Britain. He also made sure the bomb test did not make it into the video the men recorded of themselves in action for recruiting and fundraising purposes. Babar claimed to have subsequently passed the video on to Sajeel Shahid for editing.[41]

By this time, Khyam had made it clear that he wanted to conduct an attack in the United Kingdom. Babar reported hearing this repeatedly. His co-defendant Salahuddin Amin said something similar: 'I didn't know what their intention was, what they were up to, what they were exactly going to do in the UK, but I knew that they wanted to get explosives training to do something in the UK.'[42] In Babar's testimony he suggested that it was Waheed Mahmood who was particularly driven to push the group to conduct an attack, expressing exasperation that 'he didn't understand why all these UK brothers were coming to Pakistan and wanting to go fight in Pakistan [sic] when they could easily do jihad and operations in England.'[43]

While Babar provided a great deal of detail of the plot after the arrests were carried out, the plotters were first brought to the attention of British security services during their investigation of a Luton taxi driver named Mohammed Qayum Khan. A shadowy figure who remains at large at the time of writing, Qayum Khan first became the target of an MI5 investigation when they obtained intelligence about him in early 2003.[44] Qayum Khan was identified as the focal point for a node of extremists operating just outside London, helping raise funds and sending equipment and fighters to Afghanistan. According to Mohammed Shakil, he was a prominent figure in Luton who was known to be helping raise money and support for refugees on both sides of the Afghanistan-Pakistan border.[45] The former president of Luton Central Mosque claimed that Khan was responsible for bringing Omar Bakri Mohammed to Luton.[46]

Babar identified Qayum Khan as Salahuddin Amin (the former Luton taxi driver) and Omar Khyam's 'emir' or leader. In turn, Babar states that Qayum Khan answered to Abdul Hadi al Iraqi, the then head of external operations for al-Qaeda.[47] At the other end of the scale, Omar Khyam acted like the 'emir' of the Crawley cell that he had brought together and tried to assert his leadership over them. According to Babar, having been told by more senior members of al-Qaeda that when they were travelling they were not to pray in public, Khyam made a point of punishing people who did so. When a pair from the group he was leading to the training camp did just that, he castigated them and confined them to their rooms at their guesthouse.[48] Another figure to feature on the periphery of Crevice was a Moroccan-Belgian named Abu Munthir, also identified as an al-Qaeda connected figure who served as a main point of contact for the Crevice group in Pakistan when they were trying to reach out to al-Qaeda.[49] The degree to which he may have helped stir the Crevice group into action is unclear, given that meetings between him and Omar Khyam were not accounted for.

Qayum Khan, charmingly code-named 'Bashful Dwarf' by the security service, was the initial focus of the investigation.[50] Omar Khyam also featured, though initially was thought only 'to be acting as a courier for the network'.[51] By February, MI5 had identified Khan and Omar Khyam as two of the key figures in the network, and believed that the plotters were now intent on attacking within the United Kingdom, rather than simply focusing abroad. What the new intelligence was has not been officially confirmed, but it seems likely to have been a combination of electronic data and a tip-off. On the electronic front, Khyam wrote to Salahuddin Amin in Pakistan asking whether Amin could reconfirm the correct measurements of chemicals required to build bombs. Amin promptly headed off to the tribal regions of Pakistan to make contact with Abu Munthir to pass him some money and equipment and get Omar Khyam his answer.[52] At around this time, an alert assistant at a depot in West London remembered that an Asian man had rented a storage unit that cost £200 a month for over three months in which he left only £100 worth of fertiliser.[53] Having spoken about it with colleagues, they decided to notify the authorities who immediately noticed that the names who booked the storage unit corresponded to Crevice targets. This combination led police to conclude that the men were not simply involved in activity abroad, but plotting a bombing campaign in the United Kingdom using 600 kg of fertiliser as the base for their device.

This was the thread that started to unravel the plot that ended up breaking the Crevice cell and first revealed in a courtroom the extent and depth of radicalisation that had occurred among some young British Muslims. The investigation into Crevice, alongside the information gleaned from Mohammed Junaid Babar's extensive confession, all highlighted a large network of extremists in the United Kingdom (and North America) who were actively plotting with al-Qaeda both to support fighters in South Asia, but also apparently to target the West. The numbers were surprising to British authorities, and during the Coroner's Inquest into the 7 July 2005 bombings, MI5 identified that several operations emerged from information gleaned from the Crevice plot, with a specific operation code-named Scraw launched immediately after the Crevice arrests to pursue twelve particularly wanted individuals in the Crevice network.[54] Having now seen what the Crevice group was capable of, the Security Service had to immediately investigate the broader networks to ascertain whether others might be involved in similar activity.

The group's links to al-Qaeda appear to have taken a number of forms: direct connections to high-ranking individuals like Abdul Hadi al-Iraqi, then al-Qaeda's number three; contact with deputies Mohammed Qayum Khan and Abu Munthir; and connections to the network of camps in Pakistan operated by local extremist organisations like Lashkar-e-Taiba (with whom Khyam claimed to have established a camp in Kashmir) and Harakat ul-Mujahedeen (with whom a number of the wider Crevice cell and the Pakistan-based Al-Muhajiroun group had trained).[55] At one point in his testimony, Mohammed Junaid Babar claims that he went to Abdul Hadi al-Iraqi to try to clarify who was working for whom—the web of connections and links between the various cells had become so complex that they had started to bicker with one other. Babar thought it would be wise to obtain clarification from what he understood was the top of the tree. It was unclear whether he received an answer.[56]

The plotters tended to be young British Muslims (mostly of Pakistani descent) drawn into extremism through the preaching of the clerics profiled previously. Mohammed Junaid Babar recalled attending a session organised by East London radical Abdul Jabbar, to which he had invited Abdullah el-Faisal and Abu Hamza. He attended the event alongside some of the Crawley circle, as well as a number of East London radicals.[57] But while Crevice offered a view into this world, intelligence services were unable to follow up immediately on the wealth of information extracted, due to the prioritisation of another investigation, Operation Rhyme, which stepped up a gear soon afterwards. Among these leads was information that might have helped security services interdict Mohammed Siddique Khan, one of the other men who attended the summer 2003 training camp.

Tel Aviv bombers

According to most interpretations, Crevice is seen as the turning point at which the British police and security services realised the extent of the problem that they were facing. However an event in April 2003 ought to have alerted them to the potential threat posed by groups that had grown out of Al-Muhajiroun's networks.

Having got into Israel bearing their British passports and using other foreign aid workers as cover, Asif Hanif and Omar Sharif visited several sites, collected explosive devices and chose a Tel Aviv club, Mike's Place, as their target. This was to be the scene of the first independently confirmed British suicide bombing, when the two men detonated their explosive packs at the bar. Fortunately for the revellers at Mike's Place, only Asif Hanif's bomb went off; Omar Sharif's seems to have misfired and he instead melted into the crowd. His body was discovered almost two weeks later when it washed up on shore. While it is unclear exactly what had happened to him, it is believed that he may have been attempting to swim to safety and got caught in strong currents.

At the time of the attack, questions about the men's contacts with Al-Muhajiroun and Abu Hamza immediately emerged. Ever eager to capitalise on the event, Al-Muhajiroun spokesman Anjem Choudary expressed no surprise at the bombing in an interview with the BBC, saying 'the feeling for jihad at the current time in the light of Iraq and Afghanistan and the continuing intifada in Palestine is very hot within the Muslim community. People are very eager to support their Muslim brothers and sisters in Palestine and in other areas as much as they can.'[58]

The backgrounds of the two men revealed a strong connection to Al-Muhajiroun networks and a long history of jihadist activity. Described as a gentle giant, Asif Hanif was identified by Omar Bakri Mohammed as having attended a class he taught.[59] Born in Pakistan, the third of four brothers, his family moved to Blackburn, Lancashire when he was very young, before settling in Hounslow where Asif attended nursery school. He appears to have done little to distinguish himself academically, ending his secondary school with a GNVQ in business studies from which he was hoping to progress to a science degree at Kingston University. This plan proved short-lived, and four months after starting he dropped out to travel around the Muslim world, learning Arabic with the aim of becoming a *hafiz*, one who has memorised the whole Koran.

Some time in mid-2000 he ended up in Damascus, where he was to meet Omar Sharif: another young Pakistani Briton who had abandoned a middle class life to become an itinerant holy warrior. Omar Sharif, who was a few years older than Asif, moved to Damascus in July 2000 with his wife and two children, ostensibly to study Arabic and learn about Islam. Born in Derby in 1976, Omar was the son of a Kashmiri immigrant worker who set himself up as a local businessman running a kebab shop and a launderette. His father sent young Omar to Repton Preparatory School, a local private school whose alumni include Roald Dahl, Christopher Isherwood and an Archbishop of Canterbury. Friends recall him being 'a bit of a rebel' who enjoyed joking about the fact he shared a name with a famous actor.[60] He left Repton Prep early for unknown reasons and instead headed to a local comprehensive, where he did well enough to get a place at the prestigious King's College London.

As we saw in Chapter 3, at this time King's College was a prime recruiting ground for Hizb ut-Tahrir. When Omar Sharif arrived there in 1994, he was described by a friend as being 'like an empty bowl' who was rapidly filled by the radical rhetoric that Hizb ut-Tahrir was advancing on campus.[61] According to another Muslim student at the college at the time, by the middle of his first year Omar Sharif was apparently 'attending all, absolutely all, HT-organised circles and even when speakers came from outside he'd be there'.[62] Somewhere along the way he also met his future wife, another Muslim student, Tahira Tabassum, who had also been drawn towards Hizb ut-Tahrir. The two were soon married and Omar dropped out of college, continuing to be drawn deeper into radical circles, following Omar Bakri Mohammed when he broke off from Hizb ut-Tahrir to form his splinter group, Al-Muhajiroun. By this point Abu Hamza had taken over the Finsbury Park Mosque and Omar started to attend sessions there, where it was likely that he was persuaded (or found the contacts) to head to Albania in the late 1990s to train at camps run by mujahedeen warriors still fighting in neighbouring Kosovo—a path similar to that trodden by some of the men whom we met at the beginning of Chapter 4, and who were in the cell linked to Abu Hamza and ended up in a Yemeni jail. Having initially planned to stay there a year, he returned to the United Kingdom three weeks later and eventually moved back to Derby in 1999 with his new family in tow.[63]

He returned as Al-Muhajiroun was enjoying something of a local surge. In March 2000 the group promoted a meeting using a poster emblazoned with the statement 'And kill them wherever you find them', at which Abu Hamza spoke about 'the virtues of jihad in Islam' and 'during which he urged people to take up swords and fight against non-believers in violent situations such as the ones facing Muslims in Bosnia and Grozny'.[64] In October that year the group organised a march through Derby in support of Palestine, and a local spokesman, Abdullah Mohammed, was quoted in the local press as saying 'six people from our city have joined others from Leicester and Manchester to fly to the Middle East. They have all been trained in combat by the Al-Muhajiroun and will be ready to fight alongside their brothers in Palestine.'[65] As an already blooded jihadist warrior Omar would have had a certain local cachet in this environment, which would prove a catalyst to strengthen his conviction about the justness of his path.

Against this backdrop Omar had trouble adjusting to sitting unemployed at home while his wife went to work. According to her testimony, things got so bad that 'he said *talaaq, talaaq, talaaq*…under Islamic law if you say it three times then you're divorced'.[66] Tahira turned to their mutual mentor, Omar Bakri Mohammed, for advice, and while the specifics of what he said are unclear, it was perhaps this that led the family to move to Damascus in July 2000. Here, as we know, Omar Khan Sharif met young Asif Hanif, who was studying in the city with the help of sponsorship from his mosque in Hounslow. This was a fateful encounter, and after returning to their respective homes in England, Omar and Asif were identified as part of a pair preaching jihadism to young children alongside Mohammed Siddique Khan in Manchester.[67] But while the men may have all been spotted together looking for new recruits, they chose to travel separately to Afghanistan that year. Mohammed Siddique Khan had just left with a fellow Beestonite prior to 9/11, while Asif and Omar were among those who were drawn to the fight in the wake of the American assault. Arriving in late October 2001, Omar was recognised by an Al-Muhajiroun organiser at one of their safe houses as an eager martyr, giving away his clothes and belongings and asking others to pray for his imminent martyrdom. In a letter back to his wife he quoted a 'teacher' who reassured him that 'missing your family is natural and not from this evil self; but Allah wants to you sacrifice everything: comfort, nice food, warmth, music, TV all the way up until the ones you love and then yourself will exchange for paradise'.[68]

Asif and Omar did not get their wish this time, and were instead turned back, becoming a more useful funding and equipment pipeline rather than becoming mediocre fighters. Given their backgrounds, it is highly likely that during this period Omar and Asif would have come across some of the figures we met earlier during the Crevice case. Back in Britain, they remained active among the communities of radicals from which they had sprang, with a letter 'on jihad' from Omar with his home address found when police raided the Finsbury Park Mosque in January 2003.[69] Commenting to an undercover journalist about the raid on the mosque and the earlier Ricin arrests at an Al-Muhajiroun base in London, Asif was caught telling a journalist how unfortunate it was that the ricin had been seized before it was used.[70] Already firmly radicalised, the two were pushed into action again when in March 2003 Iraq was invaded. They spoke on the phone the next day in a conversation believed to have concerned their decision to go to fight once again. Soon after they set off for Damascus, planning to use the Syrian capital as a base from which to enter Iraq. Somewhere along the way they were diverted and instead ended their lives in a suicide attack on a beach bar in Tel Aviv.

While it is unclear whether the men knew Omar Khyam or the core Crevice plotters, Asif Hanif had attended high school with Zeeshan Siddiqui, who went by the name 'Imran', who was identified on the periphery of the Crevice investigation as being a participant at the summer 2003 training camp in Pakistan. But at this stage, Operation Crevice had just been launched, and was still focused on 'Bashful Dwarf' and the supply network he was sending to Pakistan. In domestic threat terms, British security services were instead focused on North African networks and assumed that the attack in Tel Aviv was another expression of the now seemingly constant feature of young British Muslims being stirred up to go and fight and die abroad in God's name. The possibility that Omar and Asif's actions might be seen as heralding suicide attacks in the United Kingdom was not considered.

Operation Rhyme

Even if the security services had taken greater note of the attack in Tel Aviv and of the similarities between the plotters' profiles and those in the Crevice network, and their possible links, it is unlikely that they would have been able to connect the dots with any urgency.[71] Almost immediately after the Crevice arrests in March 2004, attention was rapidly shifted to a new high priority plot that was underway. Code-named Operation Rhyme, it focused on one of the more fascinating British extremists to emerge from the British jihad. Dhiren Barot was born in India in 1971, to a Hindu family that moved to West London when he was very young. He sat his GCSEs and obtained a graduate qualification in the tourism industry before converting to Islam sometime in the early 1990s. His turn to religion appears to have moved rapidly to the extreme end of the scale, and in 1995 he quit his job working at an Air Malta office in Piccadilly, London (he was apparently turned down for a transfer) and opted for an itinerant life as an extremist.

What pushed him into action is unclear, although it is likely that he came across radical ideas as an inquisitive and intelligent young man living in London at a time when extreme preachers were given free rein to proselytise. According to press reports based on police interviews with a fellow radical at the time (identified anonymously in the press as 'FC'), Barot met Abu Hamza soon after he had returned from Afghanistan in 1994, and the two young men were captivated by his firebrand preaching. In October 1995 Barot and FC took the preacher's words to heart and headed to Pakistan to fight alongside the mujahedeen in Kashmir against Indian forces—a major departure for the young Hindu-born

Indian.[72] He later wrote about this period in *The Army of Madinah in Kashmir*, published by the Maktabah Al-Ansaar in Birmingham (the company established years earlier by Moazzam Begg with some of his friends from Birmingham).[73] The tract tells the story of Barot's experiences in Kashmir fighting alongside the jihadist warriors, but concludes with a wistful note as he observes the apparent political rapprochement over Kashmir, something he suggests will presage the abandonment of the mujahedeen warriors and violence. As he puts it, 'submission tells people that all those who bravely fought and sacrificed in the occupied territories did so in vain. As such, feelings will seek to be vented through retribution.'[74] This sense of pending betrayal of the Kashmiri cause permeated the thinking of many of the cells at the time: Mohammed Junaid Barbar repeatedly referred to the Crevice group being wary of attending camps run by Kashmiri-oriented groups like Harakat ul-Mujahedeen (HuM), believing them to be filled with Pakistani spies (though Omar Khyam seemed less concerned about this). Mohammed Siddique Khan later turned on the Kashmiri cause and such groups, falling out with his friend Mohammed Shakil over his continued support for them. While these men may have sometimes been drawn to Pakistan by concerns over Kashmir, once there they found the training structures and groups mostly subservient to the Pakistani state and not the pure jihadi organisations that they had imagined them to be. Dedicated to jihadism, and with a global orientation, the men bought into the creed with which Barot concludes the acknowledgements: 'we need the jihad—the jihad does not need us'.[75]

The fact that Barot—who used the pseudonym Essa al-Hindi, a reference to his past religion—was a dedicated convert to Islam impressed those whom he encountered, as is highlighted in the preface of his book. His publisher, Abu Umamah, writes: 'What is most unusual about this book is the author himself. It is so rare for people in our age to take on the struggle for the sake of Allah. So imagine someone who comes from a non-Muslim background, struggling first against himself, then those around him from friends and family and then to take on the most noble of duties in Allah's cause.'[76]

But while it seems that Barot had been active in Britain for a while, it was not until Khalid Sheikh Mohammed, the mastermind of the 11 September 2001 attacks on the US, identified a British al-Qaeda operative named Esa al-Hindi or Esa al-Britani that security services were alerted to his importance. Barot is believed to have first met Mohammed in 1998 when he was working as a trainer at a camp in Afghanistan, and there appears to have been much subsequent communication with a series of important al-Qaeda figures. The following September Barot attended a training camp in the Philippines (his second trip to the nation), and in January 2000 went to Kuala Lumpur with Walid bin Attash—a former bodyguard to Osama bin Laden who may have been in town to attend a terrorist 'summit' at which a number of the September 11 plotters were also present.[77] The group gathered around local senior al-Qaeda plotter Riduan Isamuddin, known as Hambali, who was accused by American investigators of being involved in a series of bombings in Indonesia in Christmas 2000 and was apparently involved in a plot to bomb a series of foreign embassies in Singapore.[78] Under interrogation, Hambali claimed to have given Barot contacts in California and South Africa.[79]

Tantalising hints of conspiratorial knowledge of the 11 September 2001 attacks are further suggested by a series of trips to the United States that Barot made in 2000 and 2001. Having applied in June 2000 to a course at a college in New York that he never attended, he and two accomplices made two separate trips to the United States through New York on 17 August 2000 and 11 March 2001. During the course of these trips they visited Washington, DC and on 8 April 2001 went exploring downtown New York where they shot footage of the World Trade Centre.[80] This film was found in Barot's possession after his capture, buried in the middle of a video of *Die Hard 3*, and was played to the jury when Barot finally came to trial in 2006. Over images of the Twin Towers, a voice can be heard simulating the sound of an explosion.

All of this suggests a high level of involvement with al-Qaeda, as confirmed by Mohammed Junaid Babar's testimony that Barot held enough sway to call a meeting of senior leaders in the tribal areas.[81] Barot's importance was further hinted at by an incarcerated British plotter who was overheard talking about him in very lofty terms, about how senior he was in al-Qaeda.[82] Back in Britain, Barot was plotting alongside a group of young British Muslims, at least some of whom had connections to the broad network of extremists around the radical preachers. In court Junade Feroze was identified as a participant at some of Abu Hamza's sessions,[83] and his phone number was later found in the possession of a mysterious individual named Omar Altimimi. Altimimi, a father of three living in Bolton, was imprisoned for fraud and having in his possession a substantial volume of radical material, including bomb-making plans and information linking him to al-Muhajiroun offshoot al-Ghurabaa. When police picked him up, they found three separate identities linked to him, including fake documentation in the soles of his shoes, as well as connections between him and a flat in Rotterdam where Jerome Courtailler, a French convert who has featured previously as being involved in Britain's radical milieu, had stayed. According to police, Altimimi was also connected to a large money transfer to an Algerian terrorist, as well as to a possible fraud involving the Yemen tourist board. A murky character whose real identity was never confirmed, Altimimi offered no defence during his trial, and police admitted following his conviction that they had no clear idea of his real name, nor of his plans.[84] Arrested while using a Dutch passport, Altimimi had initially entered the United Kingdom in 2002 claiming to be an Iraqi asylum seeker. That he had possession of Feroze's telephone number was kept from the jury, although the fact that he was found with it in August 2006, almost two years after Feroze was picked up, suggests that the two men must have moved in similar circles in northern England (Altimimi was living in Bolton at the time of his arrest, while Feroze was living in Blackburn).

In court it was revealed that Feroze met Barot at an event about Kashmir, and it is likely that, within the context of the cell which Barot drew around himself, it was his charisma and personality that acted as a key radical influence even above that of the radical preachers to which the rest of the plotters around Barot may have been drawn. A blooded jihadist with strong connections abroad, Barot seems to have provided seniority in the cell and given them links to actual jihadists. Junade Feroze acted as Barot's chauffeur and had in 2001 been to a training camp in Pakistan.[85] Barot's book can be described as a key component of the British radical canon that may have helped motivate an unknown number of extremists, and at least two of his co-conspirators were found to have it in their possession. But he was also clearly influenced by others he encountered on the British scene. When he was arrested he had copies of texts by Abdullah el-Faisal in his possession, and, as we saw previously, was impressed when he met Abu Hamza.

Having just detained the Crevice group after running what was at the time the biggest single counter-terrorism operation ever undertaken, the British security services quickly switched their focus to Rhyme following a June 2004 operation in Pakistan suggesting both Barot's seniority and that Britain was a target. Information had already filtered to the security services from detainees that a very dangerous British individual called Essa al-Hindi was on the loose, and they received a detailed drawing of what he looked like.[86] Barot had travelled to Lahore, Pakistan, in early 2004, where he apparently presented the outlines of his terrorist plots to al-Qaeda's leadership, possibly receiving a go-ahead that then led him to return to the United Kingdom on a false passport on 21 April 2004.[87] While Barot's return appears to have been monitored, he demonstrated a very high level of counter-surveillance training and proved very adept at confounding teams following him (he would undertake all sorts of strange manoeuvres in traffic).[88] One former security official involved in the case said Barot displayed 'very impressive tradecraft'.[89] According to court documents in the trial against his conspirators in June 2007, even after Barot and the cell became aware of their police tails they continued in their plotting, and on 28 July 2004 Barot managed to lose those shadowing him completely.[90]

At around this time, security forces in Pakistan captured Muhammad Naeem Noor Khan, a young Pakistani who American and Pakistani intelligence agencies came to regard as a 'treasure trove' of information. Having lived for some time in Reading, Khan spoke English with a British accent and was a computer whiz described as a key hub for al-Qaeda communications.[91] He was also identified by aforementioned Al-Muhajiroun member Sajeel Shahid as a good friend of his who had stayed in a house he ran in Lahore for a while; this same house was identified as a safe house which had been visited by Western journalists and through which a number of British terrorists had passed.[92] Unlike many of his fellow conspirators, however, Noor Khan was helpful to the security services, and provided them with some assistance in tracking down senior al-Qaeda operatives, including Ahmed Khalfan Ghailani, who was wanted for his role in the 1998 al-Qaeda bombings of US embassies in Dar es Salaam and Nairobi. It seems likely that evidence on Ghailani's computer revealed Barot's possible Britain-focused plotting, which led to accelerated British efforts to track him down. On one computer the security services located documents detailing Barot's plans for an operation in London entitled 'Rough Presentation For Gas Limos Projects'. This scheme would involve six men driving three limousines packed with gas cylinders painted yellow (to emulate canisters containing radioactive or other toxic materials to 'spread terror and chaos when the emergency service teams arrive') with pipe bombs taped to the side. As Barot put it, 'this project forms the main cornerstone (main target) of a series of planned attacks that have been prepared for synchronised execution on the same day, at the same time'.[93]

The discovery of the notes on a computer in Pakistan alarmed the British security services, who assessed that Barot would need detaining as quickly as possible. Barot appears to have already suspected that the police had him under surveillance. The prosecution of one of his co-conspirators concluded that Barot had noted the information of the raid in Gujrat in Pakistan in which Ghailani was captured (through internet searches about the event) and therefore likely realised that the plans and information on plotting in the UK he had given Ghailani would now be in government possession. The co-conspirator, Zia ul-Haq, was a construction worker who had known Barot for some time and was one of a group of seven individuals who were charged in a separate trial from Barot's for involvement in his plotting. Like the majority of the group, ul-Haq was a young second-generation Pakistani Muslim who was leading a relatively uneventful life in London's periphery. The level of the men's involvement in the plot remains somewhat unclear, given that they refused to offer any details about the machinery of the plot of which they stood accused. It seems clear, however, that they were all drawn in by Barot's charismatic personality and previous experience. Aside from one, Qaisar Shaffi who pleaded innocent and was later found guilty, the men all pleaded guilty and are currently serving substantial sentences behind bars (varying between fifteen and twenty-six years). Unlike the Crevice plot, the men had not yet apparently begun to move towards assembling a device; in fact, when Barot was arrested, security sources claimed that they had no admissible evidence against him.[94] It required the maximum fourteen days without charge for police to assemble enough evidence from his computers to hand over to prosecutors, who were then able to secure a confession from Barot.

To this day Dhiren Barot remains one of the most intriguing but elusive figures in the history of the British jihad: a convert who managed to rise in al-Qaeda's ranks, he was a warrior–writer whose personality was able to draw a web of individuals into an unspecified plot to cause murder and mayhem.[95] Remaining silent and thus largely an enigma to investigators, speculation has focused on his affiliation with al-Qaeda and his seniority within the organisation. An academic paper written by an American security analyst assessed the data and concluded he was likely to be a major player.[96] This view was supported by discussions with security officials from the time, highlighting that Barot's globetrotting lifestyle was somehow achieved with no discernible evidence of work-related income. And as was mentioned before, other British detainees who had been convicted of terrorism charges identified Barot as a very senior member of al-Qaeda, something corroborated by Mohammed Junaid Babar's testimony. On the other hand, although Barot had a long career involved in radical activity and groups, he never appears to have actually been involved directly in any plots after his time in Kashmir. The plots detailed by the prosecution had been ruminated over intensely by Barot for roughly four and a half years prior to his arrest with no evidence of action. Instead he seems to have enjoyed playing the role of the international terrorist and writing long and detailed plans about carrying out plots, some of which were comically unfeasible. In one particular plot he intended to gather some 10,000 smoke detectors that all contained some small amount of radioactive material and then place them on top of a large explosive.

Nevertheless, Barot remained a concern subsequent to his imprisonment. Letters attributed to him have emerged from prison highlighting how prison guards would keep him away from other prisoners for fear of his charismatic personality influencing them: 'Any time the prison feels that I may have found a "friend" that I may be "overly"' socialising with, more often than not the individual/s concerned are promptly shipped out to other establishments. Why? For irrational fear of "sermonising" or "talent scouting" of course because they believe I have an arresting personality!'[97]

The letter was released soon after Barot had been transferred to a hospital ward, having being attacked in prison by another inmate who poured boiling oil over him. He was allegedly at the core of tensions between a group of Muslim prisoners imprisoned on terrorism charges and other inmates. Others in the prison, HMP Frankland, included Omar Khyam of the Crevice group, who claimed to have had death threats against him and had apparently fought back at one point. The extent of the relationship between Khyam and Barot inside Frankland is unclear, though they must have interacted. Years later, it was revealed that Barot was continuing to have an impact on those around him when a fellow inmate, Michael

Coe, jailed for gang activity involving guns and threatening police officers, emerged from prison as a convert going by the name of Mikael Ibrahim. Jailed in 2006, Ibrahim claimed to have been persuaded to convert to Islam by Barot. Upon his release, Ibrahim was met at the prison gates by a pair of extremists linked to Al-Muhajiroun's latest incarnation and from them on became a fixture at events organised by the group.[98]

Azzam.com

While the cases against the Crevice and Rhyme groups concluded with heavy sentences, at around the same time as Barot was apprehended another British–Pakistani was picked up for a second time: Babar Ahmad. Previously arrested and released by British security forces, Ahmad was detained again soon after Barot in relation to charges against him in the US relating to a website he was allegedly running called www.azzam. com. Named after the 'father of the Soviet jihad' Abdullah Azzam, the website was an information portal for news and stories about the global jihad and was the focal point of a media organisation which also produced videos and cassettes that we saw earlier in detail during the Bosnia section of Chapter 3. Mohammed Junaid Babar, the American who would later turn on his colleagues during the Crevice plot, described it as 'like an online newspaper…where they would report on what's happening in Afghanistan.'[99] Cassettes which detailed the martyrdom of young British men in Bosnia were released by Azzam publications, while the website advertised videos from Bosnia and Chechnya entitled 'Russian Hell' and 'The Martyrs of Bosnia'. As discussed earlier, these videos and cassettes provided young men in the West with a window into the glory of jihad, and spurred an unknown number into joining their Muslim brethren on the battlefields.

According to US prosecutors, the case against Ahmad was built around the fact that email accounts that appeared to belong to him were involved in running the website and maintaining contact between the jihadist leader Ibn al-Khattab, as well as helping to raise funds and guide possible warriors to him in Chechnya, but also to fighters in Afghanistan.[100] A cousin of Mohammed Naeem Noor Khan (the young Pakistani on the periphery of the Rhyme plot discussed earlier), Ahmad was a student when he was picked up in London. He was sentenced by a US court to twelve years in prison after pleading guilty to running the azzam.com website. The trial judge noted however that Ahmad was not an operational terrorist.[101] One piece of information that Babar Ahmad has volunteered about himself in open court is that he fought in Bosnia on three or four occasions during the 1992–95 war.[102]

Established in 1994, azzam.com was one of a number of Britain-based websites to advertise jihad and it provided a portal through which interested individuals could access information or ideas related to jihad in English.[103] Another was Islamic Gateway, guided by preacher Omar Bakri Mohammed and Saudi dissident Muhammed al-Massari, which hosted the online sites of Al-Muhajiroun, Supporters of Shariah and others. Translated texts were provided, as well as regular updates from the battlefield: in September 1999 azzam.com boasted an interview with Saudi-born Chechen fighter leader Ibn al-Khattab. In February 2000 it ran a 'diary' that was alleged to detail the first-person experiences of a Norwegian jihadi who went to Chechnya and which included this desperate appeal:

What I would like to know is where are all the hundreds of Muslim Doctors who for years will fervently pursue their careers in the West so that 'one day' they can help the Muslims? Whilst they are bending over to please their Jewish Consultants and satisfy the whims of the kuffar, great Mujahideen such as *** writhe in unattended agony in some dank basement. Insha'allah Allah will reward the suffering the Mujahideen are enduring for His Pleasure and He will question (Allah knows best) those well fed & paid, smug Doctors about who they cured and pleased whilst the Jihad was going on.[104]

Later it also included the biographies of two 'correspondents' who were regular contributors to the community of azzam.com publications. Known by their battlefield *kunyas* (noms de guerre), Suraqah Al-Andalusi and Masood al-Benini, the two men and their histories appear to have had some influence before the first was martyred in pursuit of jihad in Afghanistan and the second in Chechnya.

Masood al-Benini's real name was Xavier Jaffo, a Frenchman who was close friends with Zacarias Moussaoui. According to investigators quoted by CNN, Jaffo and Moussaoui were friends in London who attended various meetings with radical clerics and who went to Chechnya together at some point in the mid- to late-1990s.[105] Moussaoui returned (not before writing back to Britain with stories of how wonderful his experience there was), but Jaffo stayed for some time, using his IT skills to act as a battlefield reporter for the fighters and, according to his azzam.com biography, learned Arabic to the point that he refused to speak English or French any more, saying that those were 'languages that are primarily used by the disbelievers and have less blessing than the language of the Koran'.[106]

Less is known about Suraqah al-Andalusi, except that given his *kunya* one might expect a link to Spain in his past. His case is particularly striking as, according to the biography provided by the website, he was a married man with two children who chose to go and fight jihad in Afghanistan and was there around the time of the American invasion in 2001. While the details are almost impossible to confirm independently, according to his obituary he fell prey to American cluster munitions that were used in the final battle at Tora Bora in November 2001, from where, it is claimed, Osama bin Laden made his escape from Afghanistan.[107]

Suraqah's obituary is written in the same language that was earlier deployed in Bosnia by Azzam publications to commemorate the young men who fell there, and in fact one of Suraqah's early tasks with Azzam. com was to transcribe the Bosnian tapes. Suraqah's story also seems to have provided something of an inspiration to Mohammed Siddique Khan, the leader of the 7 July 2005 plot, with Khan's will drawing heavily on Suraqah's. Khan was attracted to the parallels he saw between his life and Suraqah's. Both men were young fathers who felt the need to assume responsibility for taking an active role in helping out their Muslim brethren: Khan as a social worker in his local community, and Suraqah reported to be very generous to the many Afghans he met, giving away his belongings and helping those he could. Khan would have seen himself in the azzam.com correspondent, especially as he had attended a training camp in Pakistan and fought in Afghanistan in the months prior to Suraqah's martyrdom at Tora Bora.

7 July 2005

Whether or not the two men met, by mid 2004 Mohammed Siddique Khan would likely have known that the security services were becoming aware of the circles in which he was moving. He knew Omar Khyam, and, according to a report on the BBC, had contacted a mutual friend after Khyam's arrest to 'find out what the security services had found out about [Khyam]'.[108] It is also likely that he would have noticed azzam. com's closure, but it is unclear whether he knew of alleged al-Qaeda 'General' Dhiren Barot's presence in Britain. None of these arrests, however, appeared to deter Khan from his chosen direction in life and in fact the news of discovery seems to have spurred him into further action. According to a document purportedly written by Rashid Rauf, a senior British-Pakistani coordinator for al-Qaeda who we shall encounter later in greater detail, when he met Khan and his co-conspirator Shehzad Tanweer in late 2004 in Pakistan they were apparently 'ready for martyrdom operation'.[109] Aware of the fact that they were probably known to authorities as acquaintances of Omar Khyam and his Crevice cell, the two young Britons expected to be arrested at any moment and had thus decided to go and fight and die in Afghanistan.

In pursuit of this goal, in late 2004 they returned once again to Pakistan to receive what would prove to be their final training. Significantly, they were present in Pakistan at around the same time that both Muktar Said Ibrahim and Abdulla Ahmed Ali were also present in the country—men who would go on to play major roles respectively in the 21 July 2005 copycat attempt (copycat in that the target was the same, though the plot was clearly in motion long before the 7 July attack took place) on London's public transport system and the August 2006 'Transatlantic Airlines plot', which intended to bring down simultaneously some eight flights on transatlantic routes from the United Kingdom. In Rauf's account, he describes the men as all having come over through separate routes and reaching out to them once they were there. In Mohammed Siddique Khan and Shehzad Tanweer's case in particular, Rauf claims to have obtained their phone number from a British Pakistani named Umar, whom he says he trained with al-Qaeda in Waziristan in the use of hydrogen peroxide explosives and who was dispatched back to the United Kingdom to organise a plot. Umar, however, disappeared and it was only from Khan that Rauf discovered that Umar had had a lot of difficulty on his return in recruiting other members to form a cell.[110] The visit in late 2004 was not the first time that Khan had been to Waziristan with the intention of attending a training camp, but this time he did not expect to return. Videos Khan recorded with his wife that were subsequently released show him as a new father introducing his young daughter to his 'uncles' Shehzad Tanweer and Waheed Ali, as well apologising to her for not being there during her childhood. Khan the jihadist was ready to fight and die against the Americans in Afghanistan.

A year prior to this visit, as we saw previously, Khan had visited a camp established by Omar Khyam with Mohammed Junaid Babar. He had come to be in this camp in a somewhat circuitous way, meeting

Salahuddin Amin at the airport in Islamabad under the direction of the aforementioned mysterious fixer, Mohammed Qayum Khan ('Bashful Dwarf'). It seems likely that Mohammed Siddique Khan met the 'Bashful Dwarf' through his travelling partner Mohammed Shakil, who had spent some time in Luton (Mohammed Qayum Khan's base) studying. The 'Bashful Dwarf' himself admitted in an interview with the *Daily Telegraph* that he had met both Mohammed Siddique Khan and Omar Khyam through a charity he was trying to set up.[111] On 25 July 2003 Pakistani immigration authorities record Mohammed Siddique Khan's arrival, at the beginning of a trip that allegedly lasted two weeks, either side of which phone numbers linked to him were in contact with 'Bashful Dwarf'. Meeting at Islamabad airport, the two groups of men from Beeston and Crawley all introduced each other using pseudonyms and went to have breakfast together.[112]

Both Mohammed Shakil and Mohammed Siddique Khan had visited training camps prior to this one. Shakil later testified to having first attended a camp in Kashmir in 1999, where he described the thrill of firing a gun as being akin to a 'bungee jump'.[113] Khan had previously travelled to Pakistan in July 2001 alongside another young acquaintance from Beeston named Waheed Ali. The two of them attended a training camp in Pakistan before crossing into Afghanistan and returned to the United Kingdom a week prior to September 11. Ali later spoke in court of how the camp was run by Harakat ul-Mujahedeen and that 'there were about 200 brothers there and we were treated differently because we had our own hut with two brothers from the United Arab Emirates'.[114] These 'brothers' persuaded Ali and Khan to join them on a planned trip to Afghanistan. They were convinced and all headed off together to the front. Both Ali and Khan fell sick en route, however, and only Khan ultimately completed the trip, while Ali waited behind at a base.[115]

Ali and Shakil were later convicted of attempting to attend a further training camp after they were pulled off an aeroplane to Pakistan in March 2007; both had contact information for training camps as well as camping equipment on them. Both men (and a third Beeston native) were, however, cleared of any involvement in assisting the 7 July 2005 bombers carry out their attack having stood accused of helping them conduct 'hostile reconnaissance' of the eventual targets in London. The information that emerged during the trial, however, showed that they were a part of the community of extremists who gathered around the

Iqra bookshop that Mohammed Siddique Khan helped run in Beeston. During the subsequent 7 July Coroner's Inquest, documents from the Charity Commission were published, showing that some of them were also on the board of trustees of the shop.

The reasons why the Beeston group chose this path of fighting against their country abroad and ultimately conducting terrorist attacks at home has been the focus of a great deal of speculation and press. Numerous public accounts suggest that all the members of his cell suffered from a basic social immobility due to their roots in Beeston, a run-down community on the fringe of Leeds. It is not that they lived in abject poverty, but the opportunities open to them were limited—or at least that might have been the perception. As was pointed out by the defence lawyer in the trial against Waheed Ali and Mohammed Shakil, the men faced the 'sparkling route between shelf-stacker and taxi driver'.[116]

One school friend, Ian Barratt, recalls Khan visiting the US for a few months as a teenager and coming back 'wearing cowboy boots and a leather jacket', for which he was 'pilloried by the other Pakistani lads'. He didn't care, apparently, and was so thrilled by America that he planned to 'finish his exams, pass his courses and go live there'. This dream was not to be realised, however, and when Ian Barratt bumped into him in 1996, after they had both finished school, he discovered that Khan had not gone to the US because 'he couldn't get a visa'. Instead, Khan said he was working at the Inland Revenue auditing companies, a job he admitted was 'a bit boring' but paid a 'good wage'. Clearly not entirely happy with his role, he had played it up for his friend: he was in fact a filing clerk and left soon afterwards to become a learning mentor at Hillside Primary School, where he built on the experience he had gained previously as a youth worker.[117] An ambitious man, he was at the same time studying for a BA in business management at the nearby Leeds Metropolitan University.[118]

But none of this was taking him beyond Beeston and its blocked social mobility. As Waheed Ali put it in court, 'They [the Asian community in Beeston] don't really aspire to anything and I hate that. I always aspired to doing more. I thought life has to be more than this, not staying here in Beeston.'[119] Social troubles were exacerbated by localised drug problems, which tore at the fabric of the closed Asian communities and which Khan and Shakil took a role in trying to improve as social workers and local activists.[120] Rather than simply accept their fate, the young men were eager to do something about their situation: an aspect that might explain why radical ideas of empowerment as a fighter for Islam might have found a greater degree of resonance than either rote learning of the Koran or the Barelwi worship of *pirs* (spiritual leaders). Mohammed Siddique Khan is particularly scathing about his elders during one of the more oddly personalised moments in his martyrdom video, where he derides 'our so-called scholars today [who] are content with their Toyotas and semi-detached houses'. In recounting his experiences meeting with Khan, Rashid Rauf tells of how Khan had for some time followed a Barelwi *pir* around and had ultimately rebelled against him in anger. Khan claimed his family had rejected him as a result of this, throwing him out of the home bitter at his rejection of the family's spiritual leader.[121]

For Khan in particular, this spiritual gap appears also to have been filled in part by love. He met his future wife at Leeds Metropolitan University: she was from a different social stratum (Khan came from a Punjabi family from near Rawalpindi, while his wife was of Gujarati Muslim stock), which meant the relationship was frowned upon by the parents on both sides, doubtless eager to continue the tradition of marrying the young to cousins back in South Asia.[122] So the decision to break from tradition and marry Hasina Patel at the Pakistani Kashmiri Welfare Association office in nearby Batley on 22 October 2001 caused a schism for Khan in his relations with his family and religion, thus adding to the 'cognitive opening' and strengthening his perceived disconnect from the world around him.[123]

While the contours of Khan's narrative captures the backdrop of the 'Beeston three', Siddique Khan, Shehzad Tanweer and Hasib Hussain, and the cell around them, it is not the complete tale for the 7 July 2005 group, which also included Jamaican convert Germaine Lindsay. Although not from Beeston, he was brought up from a very young age in nearby Huddersfield, and thus his story is similar in much of its local background. However, Islam would not have been a direct feature of his household from birth. His father appears to have left when he was young and he converted with his mother in his teens. Soon afterwards his mother left the family to go and live in the US with a new husband, leaving him and his sister behind. According to some reports, he failed to get into one of the better local high schools after his application got lost in the post—leading to a tangible block in his life which might account for the grievance element in his personal narrative.[124]

The backdrop of his ideological journey is similar to that of the Beeston group, though he had a stronger and clearer connection to Abdullah el-Faisal, who is believed to have introduced Khan to Lindsay. Two weeks after Lindsay and his mother converted to Islam, she took him to see Abdullah el-Faisal preach. The young boy was attracted to him, in part thanks to their shared Jamaican black heritage. Having never known his father, this strong and erudite figure became a surrogate parent for the young man. In an interview with the BBC in June 2008, el-Faisal admitted he had taught Lindsay as a student, and claimed to have advised him to go and study in Saudi Arabia the last time they spoke.[125] The influence of the preacher and the radical ideas he espoused were almost immediately visible in the young man, who was noted by teachers to have quite aggressively anti-American views: he is reported to have praised the Taliban and used school computers to seek out information on the 9/11 attacks, which he shared with others at school.[126] He told one friend that he wanted to fight in Iraq, and he boasted of the fact that once he finished his GCSEs his intention was to join the British army to kill his fellow soldiers.[127] Hasib Hussain, while a student in Leeds, also wrote notes in class about 9/11 and threatened his classmates with similar acts.[128]

Lindsay dropped out after completing school in 2002, and in October met his wife at a 'Stop the War' demonstration, following up on contact they had previously made online. The two hit it off and married, moving in together in Huddersfield, where he was a regular at the mosque while also learning Arabic nearby. An interesting figure herself, she was adopted by a local Muslim family in Aylesbury who helped her convert. Samantha Lewthwaite disappeared from public view in the wake of the 7 July 2005 attacks, only to resurface almost seven years later at the heart of an al-Qaeda linked plot in Somalia.[129] At this point, however, the pair seemed normal, a happily married young couple who in 2003 decided to move to Aylesbury, where he took a job as a carpet-fitter. Some time after this he met Mohammed Siddique Khan, and in September 2004 the couple moved into a rented property near to where Khan and his wife Hasina Patel were living.[130] From this point on, it seems as though Lindsay was absorbed into the narrative of the story that Khan was weaving, becoming an integral part of the team. Unlike the others who were still living close to their families, Lindsay seems to have created his own family and then found a further surrogate father in Mohammed Siddique Khan. The four men—Khan, Hussain, Tanweer and Lindsay—were a very close group, who, according to Rauf's account of Khan, would study and train together regularly.[131]

On the periphery of this tight-knit group were a number of other players. Both Waheed Ali and Mohammed Shakil were long-term friends of the 7 July group. Ali was a childhood friend of Shehzad Tanweer, while Shakil was a fellow youth worker at the Hardy Street Mosque where Khan helped out in 1996. Both men were closely tied into the network of radicals that lived in Beeston, and openly declared their support for the Taliban: Ali boasted that his 'ultimate aim' was to fight and kill British and Coalition forces in Afghanistan. Like his friend Mohammed Siddique Khan, Mohammed Shakil was a consumer of azzam.com publications, and an infamous essay posted on the site praising the September 11 attacks called 'Nineteen Lions' was found downloaded on his computer. Arriving in Pakistan on their 'fact-finding' mission to discover the truth about what was going on in Afghanistan and whether foreigners were being allowed in to fight, Khan and Shakil probably felt somewhat like the heroes they had read about who had fallen as correspondents for www.azzam.com.[132]

A couple of years younger than Mohammed Siddique Khan, Mohammed Shakil was born in Kashmir in 1976 to a family that moved to the United Kingdom when he was four years old. As a child he contracted polio, which withered one of his legs, but he proved to be a tough figure and did not let the disability prevent him from leading an active life. In 1995 he married the half-sister of one of the two men with whom he was later accused of plotting (Sadeer Saleem, who was cleared of any involvement), and who also came from the same village as his family in Kashmir. In 1997 he took his family with him down from the north to Luton, where he enrolled on a university course and met Mohammed Qayum Khan; but he abandoned this and decided instead to transfer back north to Huddersfield. Before returning there he headed to Kashmir, drawn by his familial roots in the region.[133] Like many men of his generation, it seems as though videos from Bosnia were key among the materials that drove him to seek out a path as a jihadist warrior.

Both Khan and Shakil were strong-headed young men who were married with children and felt a need to contribute to their communities. Shakil did not let his disability prevent him from attending training camps in remote places: when he and Khan went together, he had to be carried for portions of the journey on the back of a local shepherd.[134] As

191

young men they had hung out together, drinking and smoking drugs, and both had found in fundamentalist religion the salve that helped them overcome these vices. Both had a long-term commitment to training and fighting abroad predating the events of 11 September 2001; and in both cases they appear only to have been spurred on by the subsequent events, attending further camps alongside other members of the network in which they were involved. That Shakil did not become involved in Khan's later plot is possibly explained by the fact that the two allegedly had a falling out after attending the infamous Summer 2003 training camp in Malakand, which brought together the 7 July plotters, the Crevice group, and an assortment of other British extremists. Mohammed Junaid Babar claimed that Shakil had good posture when it came to firing an AK-47 and that he hit his target perfectly when he was chosen to shoot one of two RPG rockets that they had at the camp.[135]

In contrast, Waheed Ali (born Shipon Ullah: he changed his name by deed poll shortly before his arrest) was part of the slightly younger community of men influenced by figures like Khan and Shakil. Soon after arriving in Britain from Bangladesh when he was three years old, both of his parents passed away within a month of each other: his father of a skin disease and his mother of a heart attack. Ali and his three sisters were brought up by family friends in the Leeds area, though it seems clear the young Ali chafed in his new family. He admits to having been a restless young man, who was beaten by his new family for 'messing about', and who was ejected from a school course he was doing in 2001 for 'fighting with [his] best friend'.[136] It was around this time that he apparently first encountered Sadeer Saleem, a slightly older man whom he knew from the area and who approached him on a bus and invited him to come and join the sessions that he and Khan, among others, were helping organise to spread their version of Islam. The impressionable young Ali was a rapid convert and by his own account had within 'a week' swapped the posters of rap artists and footballers in his room to pictures of Kalashnikov rifles, as well as praying three or four times a day.[137]

Alongside his childhood friend 'Kaki', aka Shehzad Tanweer, they would go to the local gyms together and attend sessions at the Iqra bookshop. About this time (in the months after 9/11), young Shehzad had also returned to a more religious identity, with others reporting that he had started to wear prominently Muslim garb and was attending mosque regularly and praying five times a day.[138] From a relatively affluent local family, Shehzad Tanweer was a young man who had been involved in some racial scrapes as a child and had found in Mohammed Siddique Khan a new father figure. The Iqra bookshop was run by local lads that the police and MI5 had noted as individuals of concern. Former soldier and convert Martin Abdullah McDaid lived locally and helped establish both the 'Rays of Truth' and 'Iqra' bookshops in Beeston. Described by others as a fervent convert to Islam, McDaid had been on the security service's radar since 1998 for being involved in what was believed to be 'jihad training'. Others involved in the bookshop at the time reported his paranoia at being watched by the security services, and at some point security officials confiscated his computer.[139] Alongside fellow convert James McClintock, who would later achieve notoriety as the 'Tartan Taliban', and fellow local Tafazal Mohammed, McDaid was alleged to have helped run the bookshops and some rural get-togethers for young men. These were being watched by the security services, though the high number of events taking place at the time, and the fact that it was mostly young men running around the countryside, meant there was nothing for them to do beyond observing them.[140]

Waheed Ali recalled being introduced to videos of events in Bosnia and Chechnya by others at the bookshop and of expressing his desire to train in Afghanistan. Having expressed this one night to Tanweer, the next day his friend told him 'you know that thing you were talking about last night, well Mohammed Siddique Khan wants to go to a training camp'. Raising the money from family and friends, in July 2001 Ali and Khan travelled together to Pakistan to train before attempting to cross into Afghanistan. Ali claimed to have fallen sick and was told to wait behind at a camp while his friend Khan proceeded briefly to the front lines. It was here that he was finally drawn in by the lure of the Afghan jihad, meeting individuals at the camps in Pakistan who persuaded him of the purity of supporting the Taliban rather than the Kashmiri groups infiltrated and controlled by the ISI. Like many of the young men who were drawn to South Asia, Khan and the others were initially drawn by the Kashmiri cause, but once they got there were sometimes disappointed by what they found. As we saw earlier, Dhiren Barot had seen that betrayal was likely to be on the horizon for the Kashmiri jihad, expressing concern at the corruption of the cause that sent young believers like himself to death while the overall war was controlled by political masters in Islamabad whose motives were anything but pure. Khan encountered this first-hand when he went to Pakistan, and upon returning seems to have switched his allegiance firmly in the direction of supporting the Afghan jihad.

Both Khan and Ali were back in Britain by the time of the September 11 attacks, however, a move which, whether by design or not, certainly would have given the men a strong sense of affinity with the Taliban fighters in Afghanistan as they came under attack the following month October. As Khan later read Suraqah al-Andalusi's obituary, he would have remembered the 'hot summer' nights he had experienced in Pakistan as he read a companion of al-Andalusi retelling dreams in which he foretold his own death:

One hot summer's night in August 2001, he woke me up in the middle of the night and said, 'I had a strange dream tonight.' I asked him about what he saw and he said, 'I saw a tall structure that looked like the Eiffel Tower and it had been destroyed and there was a news broadcast saying how thousands of people had been killed.'[141]

The urge in Khan to return to train and fight was strong. Having established firmer contacts with radicals around London, and now persuaded by the purity of the Afghan jihadist cause, Khan and Shakil returned in 2003 at Mohammed Qayum Khan's direction, this time meeting up with Omar Khyam and others. By this time, the men's anger had been further fired up as they watched the United Kingdom join the United States in the invasion of Iraq—a war which had brought millions to the streets across Europe and confirmed the paranoid fantasies espoused by radical clerics like Abu Hamza, Abdullah el-Faisal and Omar Bakri Mohammed (among others) that the West was launching a war on Islam. At the camp in 2003, friendships were forged and connections were made which appear to have laid the groundwork for a series of subsequent terrorist plots in the United Kingdom. Primary among these was the Crevice group, led by Omar Khyam, who as we saw previously used the opportunity presented by this training camp to set in motion the events that led in March 2004 to his arrest, and that of his immediate cell.

The introduction made in Pakistan in the summer of 2003 appears to have blossomed into a stronger connection between Khyam and Khan. Back in Britain, according to MI5 published records, the men met up frequently in the months leading up to the Crevice arrests (from the beginning of February onwards, when MI5 started more intense surveillance of Khyam).[142] The men were recorded discussing petty fraud, how to survive at training camps in Afghanistan and Pakistan, and allegedly mentioning an individual who was 'being tested' but who wasn't yet ready to wage violent jihad.[143] Whether the connection stretched to sharing information about the plot that Omar Khyam had underway is uncertain, though it seems clear that the two men were in confidence by this time. Hinting at a possible forewarning, on 21 February 2004 Khyam was recorded telling Khan that 'in the next month they are going to start raiding big time', though within the context of the conversation it is not clear whether this was referring specifically to something that is about to happen in the United Kingdom. Whichever was the case, by this time the security services had become aware of the advanced nature of the Crevice plot: the team had already purchased a 600kg bag of fertiliser and Canadian co-conspirator Momin Khawaja had already almost completed a detonator. When they were arrested in late March 2004, it is certain that Khan, still in Britain at the time, would have grown concerned about how compromised he had been. In his account to Rauf, Khan stated that he and Shehzad had woken up after the Crevice arrests presuming that they had also been identified and were being followed by police. Over the following weeks the two went to great lengths to mask their religious fervor, going to the cinema and restaurants—activities which would be considered *jahiliyyah*, a state of ignorance of the proper rites of religion—and there make a public scene about how much fun these activities were, thereby hoping to suggest to anyone watching them that they were not pious Muslims.[144] The degree to which his concerns would have been further alerted by the arrests in August of Dhiren Barot and the cell around him is unclear, although it is likely that he might have at least recognised from radical circles in London some of the individuals who had been picked up.[145]

However, rather than dissuading Khan, this fear of detection seems to have driven him into further activity and in late 2004 he headed once again to Pakistan, this time on what he thought was a final journey. During the trial of Ali and Shakil, video footage emerged which showed the proud father Khan saying goodbye to his young daughter with Shehzad Tanweer and Waheed Ali both appearing in the background. At this point it seems likely that the three men knew that they were heading to Afghanistan; at least Khan did not expect to return alive. However, for reasons that remain unclear, Khan and Tanweer headed to Pakistan ahead of Ali, who instead went down to London with Sadeer Saleem and Hasib Hussain (who would go on to blow himself up on a bus in Tavistock Square on 7 July 2005) allegedly to say goodbye to Ali's family before heading off to Pakistan. The Crown Prosecution Service believed that this trip was part of a hostile reconnaissance mission undertaken by the men ahead of the 7 July plot, a conclusion that two successive juries disagreed with, the second clearing the men of any involvement in the 7 July attack (though Ali and Shakil were both convicted for attempting to attend a terrorist training camp in Pakistan).

In Rauf's account there is no mention of this support group. He instead talks about how, after another radical Briton who had passed through the al-Qaeda training camps called Umar passed him Khan's number, he contacted him and arranged to meet with them in Faisalabad. Having watched the two arrive into Pakistan and be welcomed into Shehzad Tanweer's family home in Samundari, a city an hour from Faisalabad, Rauf waited a couple of weeks to see what kind of intelligence attention they were getting. Once they met in Faisalabad he reported driving them around with loud music playing in order to hide their piousness from the family driver. Privately, the men were able to discuss matters more seriously. Rauf was quickly impressed by their piety and learnt at last what had happened to Umar, an aspirant warrior Rauf had helped obtain training to conduct terrorist attacks back in the United Kingdom but who had somewhat fallen off the radar after he returned to Britain. Having established Khan and Tanweer's credentials, the group moved to Islamabad, from where Rauf coordinated their travel into the tribal areas.[146]

Once there the men were put in contact with a man Rauf refers to as Haji, an al-Qaeda leader who clearly held some influence and who may have been Abu Ubaidah al-Masri (a long-term Egyptian jihadist who had fought in Bosnia and spent some time in the 1970s in London, before later claiming asylum in Germany). Meeting Haji had a deep impact on the two men, and it seems that he persuaded them to return home to attack Britain. It might have been some time around this point that Khan wrote to his wife with the surprising news that he was in fact returning. As she recorded in her diary, 'S [Sidique] rang—good news!—back by Feb?'[147] It also seems likely that the men would have come across Abdul Hadi al-Iraqi at some point, the al-Qaeda leader who was eager to use the Crevice cell as a supply line for his forces from the West. They were also introduced to a man called Marwan al-Suri, a Syrian bomb-maker who taught them how to prepare hydrogen peroxide devices. Rauf reports the men were very enthused at having learned to make the devices, though reticent about their capabilities as student bomb-makers. Their teacher was reportedly impressed and considered them good students.[148]

Having completed this training, the men returned to Islamabad, where they tried to record their martyrdom videos. Poor lighting in the house they were renting and some technical problems with reading their scripts to the camera made this difficult. Initially wary of recording videos, Khan and Tanweer agreed since Haji had specifically ordered them to do so. The exact date when these videos were shot is unclear, but by Boxing Day 2004, when Sadeer Saleem and Waheed Ali arrived from the United Kingdom, they claimed their friends Khan and Tanweer appeared to be in a sombre mood. The two pairs of men attended separate camps once they were in Pakistan and while Khan and Tanweer were presumably meeting with Rauf and others, Ali and Saleem claim they were left at a base near the Afghan border, where they did minimal training and ate dal and chapatis. When they finally met up with Khan and Tanweer, the two told them they were heading back to the United Kingdom 'to do something for the brothers'.[149] At some point they may have come into contact with Muktar Said Ibrahim, the leader of the later failed 21 July attempt on London's underground, who was also being led around Waziristan by Rashid Rauf.[150]

By February, the two pairs of men had returned home, with Ali and Saleem leaving a few weeks after Khan and Tanweer.[151] According to Rauf, he contemplated going back with the men, but was unable to get clean documents and was still wanted for questioning by police in Britain.[152] Once back, the men picked up the pace of their former lives, acting normally to make sure they stayed off security radars, and gravitated towards a mosque in Dewsbury, shunning their old friends.[153] Operating as a tight-knit group, the four men increasingly kept to themselves, training heavily at the gym and staying with each other and their immediate families.[154] In early April, Khan and Hussain together rented a flat at 111 Chapeltown Road in Beeston, the landlord later noting that they were regularly unloading goods to bring inside. The three Beestonites were regularly there, with Lindsay reported to have shown up only three times.[155] Eventually, the landlord attempted to get into the flat after hearing of problems with the electricity and noticed that the locks had been changed, causing him to contact Hasib Hussain. The two appear to have had a bizarre conversation in which Hussain claimed to be haunted by

197

an evil spirit that was making him threaten the landlord. Responding to this claim with aplomb, the landlord told Hussain that 'as long as you pay me my fucking rent on time and don't upset the other residents, we won't have any trouble'.[156] The men moved out soon after this, failing to return the keys to the landlord.

Instead, as of June, Lindsay rented a separate location on Alexandra Road, taking it on from some local Arabs who had left the country temporarily.[157] During this time friends reported that the men had noticeablely red and yellowing hair, the result of their cooking down the hydrogen peroxide that they would later use in their devices, though Tanweer told his old friend Waheed Ali that 'chloride in the swimming pool' was to blame.[158] In a separate lie, he instead told his girlfriend that it was the result of bleaching from Pakistan—an explanation that she found curious, but ignored.[159] In fact, the men were having some difficulty in getting the right concentrations of hydrogen peroxide boiled down, something they were able to resolve through contact with Rauf who walked them through their technical difficulties and offered practical advice as to how they could overcome the problem.[160] Their spending patterns became odd and they started to take out loans they had no intention of repaying: Lindsay started buying all manner of spy cameras, anti-bugging devices and gas masks.[161] Throughout this period, Khan was in repeated contact with Pakistan (including a telephone call that reached him after he had detonated his device). Rashid Rauf reports exchanging emails, calls and text messages with Khan, finding Yahoo Messenger the most useful tool for the two of them to communicate and verify details and problems with the preparations for the plot.[162]

By the end of June the men were ready and conducted a reconnaissance mission to London along the route they would use a week later. While they had initially considered targeting the Bank of England with a large truck bomb, they concluded this would be too difficult, as would the alternative—an attack on the G8 Summit in Gleneagles, Scotland. Both scenarios would require overly large quantities of hydrogen peroxide that would be difficult to source. Instead, they decided to time their attack to take place at the same time as the G8 summit, but target London's transport system.[163] CCTV footage shows the bulky men laughing and joking their way around the London transport system. Back home, two of the younger warriors, Germaine Lindsay and Shehzad Tanweer, decided to reach out to recently-met girlfriends (even though

Lindsay was married with a child), trying to entice them into trysts at hotels. Both women declined, but the parallel attempts at physical contact suggest that this may have been a united effort. On 6 July, in an attempt to reconcile with friends who claimed he had been shunning them, Shehzad Tanweer joined a game of cricket Waheed Ali and others were playing, making a special point to talk to his friend and see how he was doing. Ali later told a court that he thought that the men had completed whatever task they were meant to be doing for the 'brothers' they had met in Pakistan: 'I thought that they had done what they needed to do and we would start slowly, slowly chilling again.'[164] However, they had everything still to do, and having made these last gestures of human contact, in the early hours the men headed to Luton and then London to carry out their lethal duty. Once in central London, they embraced euphorically outside King's Cross train station before setting off to their designated tasks.

Fellow Travellers

Khan, Shakil and the Crevice cell were not the only individuals to attend the summer 2003 training camp. Born in 1980 and brought up in Hounslow, Zeeshan Siddiqui claimed to be of Indian descent, his parents reportedly passing away when he was young. According to a report in a local newspaper, in November 1997 aged seventeen he ran away to Lebanon, leaving a note announcing that he wanted to be a 'holy warrior', only to return a couple of months later.[165] Apparently drawn to radicalism from a young age, much was later made of the fact that he came from the same school in Hounslow as Asif Hanif, the Mike's Place suicide bomber. However, while the two appear to have come from the same suburb and attended the same school, Cranford Community College in Hounslow, it is unclear whether they actually were as close as was often suggested in the press. As Siddiqui later claimed, they were at least a year or so apart at school, and he claimed to have 'never developed any friendship [with Asif]. I haven't seen him in the six years since I left school.'[166]

What is known from a statement given by Siddiqui to the British activist organisation Cageprisoners is that on 17 February he headed to Pakistan, allegedly to go on a pilgrimage of sorts as part of a Tablighi Jamaat inspired trip. As we saw in Chapter 1, the organisation has frequently been used as cover by young Muslims travelling abroad whose actions might otherwise appear suspicious. In particular, TJ holds annual conferences in South Asia that Siddiqui claimed to have attended in 2003 and 2004, and 'I would have gone to 2005 but I had been detained by then'.[167]

According to Siddiqui's account, he headed to Pakistan in February 2003 alongside an anonymous individual he referred to only as 'Yayha'. Around this same time Omar Khyam made a trip to Pakistan which, according to fellow Crevice plotter Salahuddin Amin, was at the behest of Mohammed Qayum Khan, in order to help with the funding and equipment pipeline which the men were running to support al-Qaeda and the Taliban.[168] Whether they travelled together or not, according to Babar's account Siddiqui was one of the individuals who attended the camp later in the year, where he was known as 'Imran' or 'Immy'. During this period Siddiqui admits to being in Lahore with Babar, an individual he says he met in Crawley in December 2002, though by the time he had reached Pakistan Siddiqui claims to have taken against him. As Siddiqui described him, 'He seemed very money orientated. He took my passport. He wanted to sell it and split the money. I did not like this. I did not get on very well with him. He had a depraved character. He would often get angry about being reminded to pray.'[169]

According to Babar, Siddiqui was one of the individuals at the camp alongside the Crevice group and Mohammed Siddique Khan (Siddiqui does not account for this period in much detail). In email correspondence later with Momin Khawaja, Omar Khyam discusses the possibility that Siddiqui be deployed in a suicide attack in Israel—though Khyam seems hesitant, at least in discussing the topic further in emails.[170] According to Babar's testimony at the Crevice trial, when he asked Siddiqui if he was willing to become a suicide bomber, the response was 'no, because he thought these guys [the Crevice group] would never carry it out.'[171] No clear plan was laid out for Siddiqui's possible suicide operation, though diaries found in his possession when he was picked up by Pakistani forces in May 2005 appear to confirm that he was interested in the idea, 'do not waver or become weak…This is the only way I can be reunited with Mummy and Daddy.'[172] Siddiqui has disputed the authenticity of the documents.

Under interrogation in Pakistan in 2005, Siddiqui said he had been fighting in Afghanistan and Kashmir for the previous two years, though his later statements claim he was alternatively travelling around as part of Tablighi Jamaat, teaching and doing humanitarian work. He was repatriated to the United Kingdom in January 2006, where he was first held and then released on a control order, before being sectioned under the mental health act. From here he staged a daring escape, jumping out of a window from Belmarsh Prison's hospital unit in October 2006, and at the time of writing in summer 2014 he remains on the run. He had been sectioned as a result of severe flashbacks he claimed to be suffering in the wake of torture he had faced in Pakistani custody.

The case of Zeeshan Siddiqui is a very strange one. He was repeatedly referred to as mentally unstable and was sectioned for a while post-arrest. Press reports at the time of his first foray into jihad in 1997 suggested he suffered from a 'depressive illness', and it has been hinted that he was not used for a suicide attack earlier due to concerns about his mental stability.[173] But at the same time, when he was picked up, he was referred to as being a key aide to al-Qaeda leader Abu Faraj al-Libi and having had contact with the 7 July group.[174] His purported diaries from early 2005 reveal a confused and angry man who was troubled by ill-health and paranoia about the world around him, but at the same time remained constant in his rage against 'enemies of Islam'. Aside from his diary, Pakistani forces also found a circuit board that could be a bomb detonator, as well as contact phone numbers for known members of al-Qaeda and the Crevice cell.[175] Siddiqui remains one of the most cryptic pieces of the British Jihad still at large.

The East London Connection

A final public piece in the Crevice jigsaw can be found in a pair of East London cells that were alternatively disrupted by police or attrited by drone strikes in Waziristan. Made up mostly of South Asians, both cells were identified by Mohammed Junaid Babar in court. Both had been on the periphery of the broader Al-Muhajiroun network for some time, and were respectively led by a Bangladeshi-Briton called Kazi Nuhur Rahman (whom Babar refers to as Abdul Haleem) and a pair of Pakistani-British brothers known as Tanveer Ali and Abdul Jabbar. All feature prominently in Babar's telling as active radicals who had made the transition from Al-Muhajiroun followers to hardened extremists with connections to al-Qaeda's highest echelons, and some appeared in the press as the Al-Muhajiroun group followed their British leader's tactic of actively courting the media.

According to Babar, Kazi Rahman was the first from the Al-Muhajiroun community in Britain to arrive after him in the wake of 11 September 2001. His presence at the time was independently confirmed by a British journalist, Jon Gilbert, who met him as one of a group hanging around Al-Muhajiroun circles, using the name 'Abdul Salam' and saying that 'he "couldn't wait" to kill British soldiers and claimed to have recruited hundreds of UK Muslims for the Taliban'.[176] Footage from the time shows a turbaned young man with a pronounced British accent talking menacingly to the camera. Soon afterwards the brothers Abdul Jabbar and Tanveer Ali arrived, all of them seeking to join the fighting in Afghanistan. Arriving through the Al-Muhajiroun network, the men lived together and would all hang out around the group's Pakistan office, helping with spreading the word and recruiting and training locals. Kazi Rahman in particular was a long-term follower of Omar Bakri Mohammed, and as a young man in East London was one of a group who was picked up by police after the murder of Nigerian Christian student Ayotunde David Obanubi at Newham College. Ed Husain referred to the murder in his autobiographical book *The Islamist*, which blames the influence of Hizb ut-Tahrir and Omar Bakri Mohammed on the campus at the time. While court documents do not mention Hizb ut-Tahrir or Omar Bakri by name, the key individual in the case is identified as having on his possession a name card branding him 'Soldier of Allah', showing at least some religious influence in his thinking. Rahman was not, however, implicated in this murder and appears to have continued to live in East London, graduating from a low-level thug into becoming a plumber and itinerant member of the East London jihadist community.

In Babar's telling, Rahman arrived in Lahore and joined the community loitering around the Al-Muhajiroun office in the Abrar Centre. In January 2002, when Babar got married, he moved to a new flat and Rahman moved in to the one next door to him. Some time after this, Tanveer Ali called Babar inviting him to join him and his brother on a training course they had managed to find in Kashmir. Excited by the prospect of finally going to do something, Babar prepared to join the brothers, only to run into Sajeel Shahid, the local Al-Muhajiroun leader whom we have already encountered, as he was walking out. A figure of some ridicule to others like defector Hassan Butt who identified him as always coming 'into the offices dressed like the Taliban, whereas everyone else agreed to trim their beards and wear Western clothes to be discreet,'[177] Sajeel Shahid seems to have been quite a close friend of Babar's, initially giving him the money he needed when he wanted to come to Pakistan and continuing to stay close to him while he was in Pakistan. He talked Babar out of going with the brothers, pointing out that it was uncertain whom they were going to train with, but also likely eager to keep his Al-Muhajiroun comrade around to help him run the office. According to Babar, the man organising the training for the brothers was none other than Omar Saeed Sheikh, the former British public school boy. A close associate of Harakat ul-Mujahedeen and its successor group Jaish-e-Mohammed, Sheikh helped the brothers train alongside the group and it seems likely that they also saw combat in Afghanistan at the time, with Tanveer Ali reporting back to Babar that while there they were almost killed by a large explosion near them in which some other Britons died.[178]

Much later, an anonymous convert who used the name 'Omar' came forward to fill in the story on what happened with Kazi Rahman, the East London plumber, during this period. Identifying Rahman and his fellow East Londoner Abdul Mukim Khalisadar (after Khalisadar was convicted on an unrelated rape charge), 'Omar' identified having first met Khalisadar in 2001 when the two were fleeing Afghanistan in the wake of the collapse of Taliban defences in Kabul. Somewhere along the way he also came across the East London plumber, and he confirmed that the two men were part of the community of al-Qaeda and Taliban fighters who scattered back into Pakistan following the American-driven attack in late 2001. According to 'Omar' the men were closely linked to Khalid Sheikh Mohammed and Ramzi Binalshibh, the Yemeni al-Qaeda operative who was allegedly meant to be involved in the September 11 attacks, plotting together at safe houses in Khost and Karachi.[179] Such high level contacts are surprising given the later context in which Rahman the plumber appears to have been fishing around for leads to join groups in Afghanistan, but it is possible that in the chaos as the Taliban and al-Qaeda were routed in Afghanistan, Rahman may have come across some senior al-Qaeda figures.

By mid-2002 the excitement around the jihad in Afghanistan had started to ebb among the first wave of recruits, and people started to trail back to the United Kingdom. Both the East London cells returned, with Kazi Rahman telling Babar (who intended to stay behind with his new wife) that he had buried some weapons in the grounds of Punjab

University and that he was to pass them onto Waheed Mahmood of the Crevice cell if he asked for them. According to one report, Rahman had purchased these from Omar Saeed Sheikh.[180] Later, Mahmood appeared with the future Syria suicide bomber Abdul Waheed Majid to collect these weapons.[181] As the year passed Babar watched all his friends go and by late 2002, bored staying in Pakistan living with his new wife, decided to return to Britain. It seems likely that this was also a trip to try to raise funds to support his activities and Babar reports that he went to stay with Kazi Rahman in Hither Green. Rahman was a generous host and introduced Babar to others who would later emerge as part of the Crevice conspiracy, while also taking him to events organised around the radical preachers in London. In one instance, Babar recounts going to an event organised by Abdul Jabbar in East London at which both Abu Hamza and Abdullah el-Faisal spoke, before the group watched videos of the 9/11 hijackers' wills. Some time after this, Babar returned to Pakistan followed by Kazi Rahman, who wanted Babar to help him to forge relationships with people who could help him and his friends train in Afghanistan.[182]

Unable to make direct connections, the men reached out to Waheed Mahmood (jailed as part of the Crevice conspiracy), who lived in Gujar Khan and had at this point been helping send supplies to fighters in Afghanistan. Mahmood generally derided the efforts of the British jihadis to fight in Afghanistan, pointing out to them that 'he didn't understand about why all these UK brothers were coming to Pakistan and wanting to go fight in Pakistan [sic] when they could easily do jihad operations in England.'[183] It is during these meetings that the seeds of what developed into the Crevice operation were born, and around this time that Kazi Rahman, the East London plumber, and Omar Khyam, the leader of the Crevice cell, seemed to get into something of a power struggle. Closer to Mahmood, who could coordinate potential training for the Britons, Khyam demanded that Rahman's cell become subordinate to him, something Rahman refused. The subsequent friction sent the cells in different directions, though they all claimed at various points to work directly for Abdul al-Hadi al-Iraqi.

By April 2003, Mohammed Junaid Babar, the American who later turned informant, had gathered enough information about how to establish a training camp (it would likely cost between $3–5,000) and returned to the United Kingdom to report back to Tanveer Ali (one of the other

East London jihadists), whose suggestion it had initially been. Keen to build on the eagerness of the British community to fight and train, Babar wanted to build some sort of infrastructure so that they could play an active role in supporting jihad in Afghanistan, and to do this he needed money. However, arriving in Britain he found that Tanveer Ali's appetite for the project had diminished—he was busy, he said, building a house, but handed over some money to Babar nevertheless. His brother Abdul Jabbar on the other hand was concerned, as someone had identified Babar in a series of pictures they had been shown by MI5 agents. Clearly unable to get the support he was seeking from the East London brothers, Babar connected with the Crawley crew, who now told him about a parallel camp they were trying to establish for which they were seeking recruits and funding. In a particularly odd instance, Babar recounts being brought to Abdul Jabbar's house by Waheed Mahmood (the older man jailed as part of the Crevice cell) on a fundraising and recruiting mission. Babar dissembled to Mahmood about knowing Tanveer Ali when they were introduced, highlighting that trust between the groups and individuals was in short supply, and that they constantly lied to each other about their identities and what they had done or were doing. Nevertheless, Omar Khyam (leader of the Crevice cell), Waheed Mahmood (also of the Crevice cell) and Babar the informant pooled their efforts at this point to raise money for a camp.[184] As well as going around the country's various jihadist-supporting circles with whom they were in contact, they hosted a barbecue in North London, to which they invited people from the broader community, raising a few thousand pounds to support the cause.[185] It is clear that Babar found Britain a fertile ground for fundraising.[186]

By mid-2003 enough funds had been gathered for Babar and some of the others to return to Malakand in Pakistan and open the infamous camp with which this chapter opened. By this point, East London plumber Kazi Rahman had been pushed to one side in the power struggles between the groups and did not participate, though he stayed involved in jihadist activity. He was finally arrested following an attempt to purchase Uzi submachine guns and rocket-propelled grenades from an undercover security service team in November 2005; he pleaded guilty and was imprisoned in 2006. Following his arrest, leadership for his cell passed to fellow East London jihadist and Afghanistan veteran Abdul Mukim Khalisadar.[187] A part-time teacher, local drugs prevention case-worker and occasional speaker at the East London Mosque, Khalisadar was on police radars as a possible terrorism suspect when in October 2006 they searched his home as part of an investigation into child pornography. Images were found and he was brought to the local police station where a DNA swab was taken, which officers were then surprised to discover matched a DNA sample taken after a brutal rape in Whitechapel, East London in the early hours of 16 October 2005. Khalisadar denied responsibility and called seven friends to provide an alibi that he was at the time giving a speech at the East London Mosque. The group came forward claiming they were all fasting together at the mosque, although it later transpired that they had lied under oath, having elected to coordinate their stories within range of police recording devices. Subsequent raids on their properties further uncovered weapons at two of them, and the group admitted to having lied, while Khalisadar admitted his guilt over the rape. The group were each sentenced to twelve months imprisonment, while Khalisadar was sentenced to ten years.[188] Coming in parallel to the Crevice arrests (and at the same time as numerous other investigations), this effectively disrupted the cell from a policing perspective.

The story of the other East London cell is far less clear, with Tanveer Ali coming to Pakistan in early 2004 to go into Waziristan with Babar to meet with Abdul Hadi al-Iraqi, and allegedly electing to stay with him for a year.[189] It is it not known how much time he spent there, but it seems as though the group remained active in jihadist circles after the Crevice arrests and the 7 July bombings. Close to the brothers of Rahman Adam (aka Anthony Garcia), the lone non-South Asian among the Crevice group, East London brothers Tanveer Ali, Abdul Jabbar and Mohammed Azmir Khan continued to send money and equipment and to travel back and forth. Colleagues and family members were periodically stopped from travelling with substantial amounts of currency that security services assessed were for terrorist purposes. Whilst on intelligence services radars, they seem to have maintained a level of activity for some time before finally in September 2010 it was reported that Abdul Jabbar was killed by a drone strike in North Waziristan in Pakistan. Pakistani intelligence sources told the BBC that Abdul Jabbar had put himself forward as the leader of an al-Qaeda 'splinter cell' that was going to try to launch a Mumbai-style attack on the United Kingdom.[190] Almost exactly a year later, a similar story played out when it was reported that another drone strike in Waziristan had killed both Ibrahim Adam

(Rahman Adam's brother) and Mohammed Azmir Khan (Abdul Jabbar's brother).[191] Their immediate plans were unknown, although photos of Ibrahim Adam had been found a year or so earlier in the possession of another European jihadist, hinting that he was pursuing a new identity to potentially sneak back into Britain. While a few other individuals remain missing from the network around these two families (and others have been tried on various charges), these two drone strikes for the most part destroyed this last element of the broader Crevice network.

All of these connections to South Asian networks came to an apex on 7 July 2005, when Mohammed Siddique Khan led his cell to carry out the first effective Islamist terrorist attack on British soil. It took time for this picture to become clear; the picture post-7/7 was immediately muddied by the appearance exactly two weeks later of a second cell of individuals apparently bent on carrying out a copycat operation but from a very different background.

Finsbury Park and 21 July 2005

On 21 July 2005, London was gradually returning to normal. Speaking afterwards assistant commissioner, Special Operations, of the Metropolitan Police, Andy Hayman said, 'I still worried there might be further atrocities. But so far these had not emerged and I tried to put concerns out of my mind.'[192] The investigation into the 7 July attack was underway and security services were trying to understand how the cell had slipped through, when just after midday reports started to emerge of another series of attempts on London's public transport system.[193] In apparently exactly the same pattern (three on the Underground and the fourth on a bus), and with devices that initially appeared to police to be of a similar construction (Hayman repeatedly refers to the fact that 'a bubbling liquid' was found in both bombs), the attack had 'every sign of being al-Qaeda-inspired'.[194] In fact it went one further, with a fifth plotter dropping out at the last minute and abandoning his bomb in a park in Little Wormwood Scrubs, discovered two days later in a state similar to the misfired devices.

Led by Muktar Said Ibrahim, an Eritrean immigrant who had moved to the United Kingdom when he was twelve, the group were in their mid- to late-twenties and mostly of East African extraction, with strong links to the community of extremists that were drawn to the Finsbury Park

Mosque. His fellow bombers on the day, Hussain Osman (whose real name was Hamdi Adus Isaac), Ramzi Mohammed, Yassin Omar and Manfo Kwaku Asiedu (whose real name was Surmalia Abubakari), were all, like him, immigrants who had arrived during the 1990s from troubled parts of Africa. Asiedu was the exception in having only recently arrived from Ghana on a fake passport in 2003. The others had come earlier, as young children in the case of Yassin Omar and Muktar Said Ibrahim, who arrived respectively from Eritrea and Somalia in 1990. Hussain Osman, on the other hand, left Ethiopia in 1992 aged fourteen, joining his brother in Italy, before fleeing to Britain four years later where he claimed to be a Somali migrant, something he thought would help his chances of obtaining citizenship. Finally, Ramzi Mohammed arrived from Somalia aged seventeen after his mother had sent him and his brother first to Kenya and then to the United Kingdom, after their father was press-ganged into joining one of the militias involved in Somalia's intractable civil war.[195]

In addition to this core group of individuals, a secondary group was also identified and prosecuted on a variety of charges. Adel Yahya, an Ethiopian migrant who at the time of the bombings had moved back to Addis Ababa, pleaded guilty to 'collecting information of a kind likely to be useful for a person preparing an act of terrorism'. He was a school friend of Yassin Omar, and the two were drawn to Abu Hamza's radical Finsbury Park Mosque in 2000–2001, looking to the Taliban's Afghanistan as a model Islamic state. Yahya initially stood trial as one of the bomb plotters accused of being responsible for sourcing the hydrogen peroxide, as well as being the owner of an array of extremist material and other information about obtaining hydrogen peroxide—he pleaded guilty to charges of collecting information useful to a person committing or preparing an act of terrorism.[196] Siraj Yassin Abdullah Ali was brought up for a period in the same foster home as young Yassin Omar, and was also close to Muktar Said Ibrahim; he was found guilty of allowing his flat to be used as a home for the bombers, while they used another flat in the same building as their bomb factory. In his flat, there was evidence that Ibrahim had stayed there, including notes written in Arabic using the heading 'Steps to Martyrdom', as well as 'a notepad bearing Ibrahim's fingerprints with calculations relating to detonators and charges, a handwritten note containing steps to martyrdom, a handwritten list, in Arabic, of bomb-making equipment'.[197]

Having discovered the fifth bomb in the park in north-west London, initial suspicions focused on the fact that the likely aspiring bomber was Wahbi Mohammed, Ramzi Mohammed's brother, who was arrested at the same time, although in a different location to his brother.[198] Instead, Wahbi was convicted of being an active member of the group and of having prior knowledge of the attack. As well as providing food and other support for his brother, he was also allegedly the one who was going to distribute the martyrdom videos that the group had supposedly recorded. A final co-conspirator was Muhedin Ali, another young man who was drawn to radical material. The evening prior to the attempted attack he received a large cache of such material from Hussain Osman, along with Ramzi Mohammed's suicide note the next day, addressed to his family, from Ramzi's brother. Subsequent to the attack, he hosted Osman for a while and was in contact with some of the plotters.[199]

A third tier of individuals were also prosecuted for varying degrees of involvement with the attempt, with most of them standing accused of supporting the group's attempted escape. Yeshiembert Girma, Hussain Osman's wife, and her brother Esayas, her sister Mulu and boyfriend Mohammed Kabashi were all convicted of assisting Osman's escape and shelter in Brighton, and of helping destroy evidence.[200] Osman's brother, Abdul Waxid Sherif, was convicted of giving his passport to his brother to use to escape on the Eurostar train to France, and of being in contact with his brother after his attempted attack. It was also reported that he was apparently seen in a 'euphoric' mood after the 7 July attack, claiming that 'there would be more'.[201] A close friend of the brothers who had met Sherif through college, Ismail Abdurahman was convicted of shuttling Sherif's passport to Osman and of hosting Osman for a couple of nights when he returned from Brighton. He also gave him a ride to the Eurostar station. During this time Osman apparently told him that he was the person appearing in the images of the bombers that were at this point plastered all over the British press, though Abdurahman claimed he 'simply did not believe him'.[202] Finally, Yassin Omar's brand new fiancée (they were engaged in a ceremony—at which she was not present—four days prior to the attack at Finchley Road Mosque, in a move somewhat similar to the last minute trysts that 7 July bombers Shehzad Tanweer and Germaine Lindsay had tried to organise) and fellow Somali, Fardosa Abdullahi, pleaded guilty to facilitating his escape and of lending him her mother's burka to escape to Birmingham.

For the most part relatively new migrants to Britain, none of these individuals held down particularly glamorous or steady jobs. All had only recently become practising Muslims in their short lives. None had entered further education, and a number had troubled pasts involving drugs or petty crime. Cell 'Emir' Muktar Said Ibrahim had a history of run-ins with the police, including a stint in prison as a young man when he was part of a gang carrying out muggings in London. It was while in jail that he found religion, and on his release in 1998 he drifted into radical circles around Abu Hamza and Abdullah el-Faisal, becoming a regular at the Finsbury Park mosque. Somewhere at this time it is believed he met Richard Reid, although it is unclear how close the two men were. He had come to the notice of the police for radical activity several times before, including in May 2004 as part of a group including the three other bombers and Adel Yahya, who attended a camping expedition in Cumbria. Later the same year he was arrested alongside Mohammed Hamid at a stall in Oxford Street, where the two were handing out extremist literature and causing a public disturbance.[203]

Mohammed Hamid, who was later imprisoned as the leader of a training network that was operating in East London, was something of a local celebrity in extremist circles around the Finsbury Park Mosque. Dubbed 'Osama bin London' in the press, a nickname he gave himself after police picked him up in October 2004, he was a former crack addict and petty criminal who had found religion later in life.[204] Hamid was born in Tanzania to a Muslim family that migrated to Yorkshire when he was five, most likely as part of one of the migrations outlined in Chapter 1, but he had hardly practised his religion as a young man. His youth was full of indiscretions, and he moved down to London still in his early teens to enjoy its music scene and a life that rapidly moved into criminal activity. He found his religion, along with his second wife, while on a trip to India to break his addiction to drugs.[205] Back in the United Kingdom he set up home in Hackney, East London, and in 1997 opened the Al Quran Islamic bookshop that he turned into a node of thinking and discussion about radical Islam.[206] He was apparently a student of Abdullah el-Faisal's, and though it is unclear at what date he started to appear at the Finsbury Park Mosque, he would have been attracted to the message he heard there. September 11 proved to be a turning-point for Hamid, and he took to broadcasting sermons from a-top a small ladder at Speakers' Corner in Hyde Park.[207]

Somewhere along the way he met Abdullah Ahmet, a Turkish–Cypriot who took over Abu Hamza's role at the Finsbury Park Mosque following his arrest in May 2004. A physically intimidating individual, Ahmet was regularly seen at Abu Hamza's right hand helping out the cleric and protecting him, and appears frequently in the media coverage that erupted around the cleric following the attacks of September 11. A former junior football coach and gangland strongman, he found Islam in an attempt to atone for his criminal past: he converted in 1998, though he claimed to have actually first found the religion when he heard Arabic six years before that. His notoriety reached a high point when in August 2006 he made a pair of interviews with CNN and Sky News in which he said, among other things, that he loved Osama bin Laden 'more than himself'.[208]

From their vantage points in the Finsbury Park Mosque and Hamid's shop in Hackney, and alongside regular visits to Speakers' Corner and occasional *dawah* stalls around the city, the two men would draw in disenfranchised wanderers who, like themselves, were seeking some direction in their life. Ramzi Mohammed first encountered Hamid at Speakers' Corner, while Yassin Omar, who thought of himself as something of an Islamic intellectual, visited the Al Quran shop one day.[209] The 21 July group was an archetypal selection of individuals that would be drawn to this group: former drug addicts, petty criminals, men who had encountered difficulties in life and were drawn to the camaraderie and sense of purpose offered by activist Islamist extremism. They would then be drawn into a world of training camps, paintballing and other strenuous physical activities which would be supplemented by regular meetings, first at Hamid's shop, and then later at his Hackney home where he would extol the virtues of jihad and boast of wanting to carry out repeated attacks on London.

But these characterisations seem overly dramatic, with Hamid's speeches lacking any of the Arabic fluency or rhetoric of the other radical preachers, with what did emerge sounding more buffoonish than anything else. And on the face of it, much of the activity that the men were organising seemed relatively harmless. When the security services first detected their Cumbrian training camps, they contented themselves with photographing the participants and simply dismissed them as low-level aspirants. Reading the biographies and statements of the group who were involved in the 21 July attempt, and of those who were arrested alongside Mohammed Hamid and Atilla Ahmet when they were rounded up in September 2006, it is easy to draw up a quick mental image of a group of life's unfortunates who had drifted towards extreme religion as a solution to their circumstances. Many had spent time in prison or battled addictions of one sort or another; some were traumatised by previous experiences or from growing up in very difficult environments; some came from foster homes or had been unable to determine what they wanted from their lives.

Nonetheless, the path they had chosen was a hazardous one, and as we saw in the case of Richard Reid, life's misfits could be redirected with deadly intent. What Hamid and Ahmet were in fact running was the latest incarnation of the networks which Abu Hamza had first established, using the mosque at Finsbury Park as a rallying-point while they continued to take young men into the British countryside to help prepare them for fighting overseas. Others did go abroad, though it is unclear how much Hamid and Ahmet were directly responsible for the contacts. Attendees at the May 2004 Cumbria training trip which the 21 July group joined included a cell of individuals who in May 2005 elected to go to Somalia, allegedly as part of a Tablighi Jamaat *dawah* trip. While there is no public evidence that the men went to fight, their explanations for their travels were highly improbable and resulted in some being excluded from Britain while others were placed on control orders.[210] Muktar Said Ibrahim also moved on from the camp to more serious activity. In December 2004, he and two others (Rizwan Majid and Shakeel Ismail, both regulars at Mohammed Hamid's bookshop, with Ismail identified as serving as an assistant to Hamid at the shop) hitched a ride to Heathrow, planning an onward trip to Pakistan laden with camping equipment, where he is alleged to have attended a training camp. Their driver to the airport was an Iraqi who police suspect was acting on instructions from a Syrian British-based facilitator for terrorism who is on a UN and US terrorist list.[211] The Syrian, Mohammed al-Ghabra, remains at large, having only been charged in 2003 on charges of fraud and possession of a document useful for terrorism, while the driver was separately tried and released on terrorism charges. Ibrahim claimed this was not his first trip abroad to train; he stated that he had visited Sudan in 2002 where he allegedly fired a rocket-propelled grenade, something he would show off about to his roomate, Bexhill, who testified against him.[212]

At this point, Rashid Rauf's account of the plot becomes instructive. According to Rauf, Ibrahim and the others were stopped by intelligence services as they tried to fly out of the country. As long-time activists on the British scene, they had prepared for this eventuality and had constructed a cover story in which they claimed to be going to attend one of their weddings. As well as bundles of cash that they claimed were to cover wedding expenses, the men had also brought along a fake wedding ring that they claimed was for the imaginary bride-to-be. Having arrived in Pakistan, they went to the alleged groom's family house while Rauf waited a few weeks before approaching them. They waited a further few weeks before meeting again in Rawalpindi where Rauf organised a trip to Islamabad and then on to the tribal areas. The men were eager to fight in Afghanistan, though, like Khan and Tanweer before them, Rauf directed them to Haji, who persuaded them instead to target Europe.[213]

Haji seems to have taken a direct role in training the men to make explosives. Having mixed up some chemicals, Ibrahim waited at the base camp while Rizwan Majid and Shakeel Ismail went with Haji and others to test the explosives they had made. However, there was an accident and the two men were killed in the subsequent explosion. Haji managed nevertheless to persuade Ibrahim to continue on the path towards an attack and they rushed him through the rest of his training before he went back to Islamabad where he met up with Rauf. Here they had little time rapidly to train Ibrahim in the requisite communication codes and record his martyrdom video before his visa expired. However, while Ibrahim returned to Britain without incident, reporting to Rauf that he had made it, at this point the connection seems to have dropped. Through an anonymous contact Rauf was able to re-establish a connection, though he was able only to ascertain that Ibrahim was at large without any further updates on the status of his plot. In Rauf's telling, as a result of this lack of communication, he was unable to train Ibrahim further in dealing with the problems he would encounter in guaranteeing the concentration of hydrogen peroxide for the bombs, and this is why they consequently failed to explode. It also seems likely that the slightly different ingredients Ibrahim and his team deployed are evidence of a marginally different training method, which might also explain why the bombs misfired.[214]

This account of Rauf's is confirmed by a number of different details. In the first instance, the bombs that Ibrahim attempted to detonate were remarkably similar to those used by the 7 July group, and a type of explosive never deployed previously in the United Kingdom. And while the detonator seems to have worked, the body of the explosive—which would have required the changes to the hydrogen peroxide concentration—was what failed. Additionally, Ibrahim was in contact with a number linked to Rauf after returning to the United Kingdom and the passports of the two men with whom Ibrahim had initially travelled were found at Rauf's house in Bahawalpur.[215] What is not specified in the public domain is who exactly helped Ibrahim get in touch with Rauf, and which intermediaries followed up with Ibrahim after he had returned to Britain and Rauf was unable to make contact. According to Bexhill, Muktar Said Ibrahim's former roommate who testified against the July 21 cell in court, when Ibrahim returned from his trip to Pakistan he was a changed man, had shaved off his beard, and seemingly worried constantly as he prepared his plot.[216]

Operation Overt

Whether Hamid was involved in organising Ibrahim's trips in pursuit of jihad is unclear. He was apparently organising trips for individuals to Morocco, possibly for training of some sort, and had by his own account himself been to Pakistan and Afghanistan in 2002, bringing aid and medical supplies. A relative claimed this was one of many trips to the subcontinent: 'he used to make a lot of trips to Pakistan and India and return to his bookshop in Hackney with lots of packages', although they assumed these packages contained drugs.[217] He claimed that he had the capacity to get people introductions to the camps, but it was unclear whether he actually had the contacts to provide entrance to al-Qaeda or affiliated groups, or whether it was the case that individuals who had contacts would mine his community of radicalised individuals for recruits. This might have been how Muktar Said Ibrahim ultimately made contact with Rauf, through an al-Qaeda recruiter operating on the fringes of the community in London identifying Ibrahim and the other two as individuals ripe for training. Ibrahim also provides the link between Hamid's network of extremists and the cell around the plot described by former Homeland Security Secretary Michael Chertoff as leading to the 'biggest investigation since the Second World War' into a plot which 'would have rivalled 9/11 in terms of the number of deaths and in terms of the impact on the international economy'.[218] The outline of the plot was to bring down around eight airplanes on transatlantic routes using liquid explosives and British suicide bombers, killing thousands and likely bringing transatlantic and global air travel to a halt.

Ibrahim was in contact with this plot's on-the-ground cell leader, Abdulla Ahmed Ali Khan, whom we shall encounter later (Ibrahim called phone numbers linked to Ali Khan and his wife a number of times) and had been in touch with Mohammed al-Ghabra, the burly Syrian mentioned earlier who was repeatedly identified in court documents as being an unconvicted figure in the plot. Whether al-Ghabra was a regular at Hamid's shop is unclear, but he was a known entity at a charity store across the road that was the focal point of the plot. Code-named 'Overt' by authorities, the plotters' aim was to bring down a series of around eight transatlantic flights simultaneously using suicide bombers. The would-be bombers were mostly British Muslims, using devices that were fashioned using hydrogen peroxide, with camera batteries as detonators. The hydrogen peroxide was to be coloured using drinks powder and carefully injected into soft drinks bottles that had been emptied out without breaking the seal. This design is the reason for the ongoing (at the time of writing) ban on liquids in sealed bottles over 100ml in capacity through airport security.

This was not, in fact, the first time such a plot had been envisioned by terrorists with Islamist aims. In the mid-1990s, having attempted to bring down the World Trade Center in New York with a massive car bomb in 1993, Ramzi Yousef, the Pakistani–Baluchi terrorist whose uncle was Khalid Sheikh Mohammed, had a very similar plan drawn up in which he aimed to use liquid bombs on a series of flights concurrently heading from Asia to the US. The specifics of the plan had not been completely worked out, but Yousef and Sheikh Mohammed had identified a series of flights that would be going first somewhere in Asia and then on to the US. It was also unclear whether he was planning on using suicide bombers, though the individual who eventually handed in Yousef claimed that he was about to be used as one of the suicide bombers in the plot. Ultimately, Yousef was caught before he could bring his plan to fruition, but he was able to execute a test run of his explosive on a flight from the Philippines to Tokyo, killing a Japanese businessman.

The method surfaced again in 2003, when police in Northern Ireland identified an Algerian bearing multiple passports as a suspected terrorist hiding out in the province. Abbas Boutrab was initially investigated on unrelated immigration charges, but as they searched his property, they discovered 'floppy discs [that] had been downloaded by the appellant

[Boutrab] from a computer in the Belfast Central library and that they contained information in connection with the making and use of explosives for attacks on aircraft and the manufacture of silencers for firearms'. Among the information collected was a detailed guide about how to create an explosive detonator using the capacitor from a camera flash circuit so that it 'can be accessed on to aircraft without suspicion'. Boutrab was also believed to have been in contact with Abu Hamza and other extremists in Europe, though these connections were tenuous and did not stand up in court.[219] According to Rashid Rauf, Haji seems to have reached quite similar conclusions, with the idea to use an AA battery and a camera flash bulb as the detonator for the new type of device they were designing.[220]

While this hints at the thinking that might be involved in the detonator for the explosive, the idea for the body of the bomb, the liquid hydrogen peroxide, instead seems to have come to Haji and Rauf as they were trying to establish how to get hydrogen peroxide to future plotters in the United Kingdom. Considering that after the July attacks the British authorities would clamp down on purchases of the chemical, the al-Qaeda coordinators tried instead to establish how they could send it to them. Deciding that they would be able to get the material past airport security in sealed rose water bottles, they quickly realised that they might be able to use it on an airplane. This decision made, they moved ahead, using a recently arrived team of young Britons as the vehicle to implement this new plot.[221]

Among the first that they decided to entrust with this new idea was Abdulla Ahmed Ali Khan, a charismatic young man from Walthamstow in East London, who in 2003 went to Pakistan to work in refugee camps, helping people fleeing the conflict in neighbouring Afghanistan. At his trial he appeared well-groomed and cold-eyed, claiming that the misery he saw in the camps reminded him of videos he had seen as a child of events in Bosnia. This was not the only radical influence on Ali Khan: in his mid-teens it appears he met some former Afghan mujahedeen and expressed great pride in the Taliban later in school.[222] When he arrived in Pakistan in late 2004, like the others who had come before him, he told Rauf that he was eager to fight and die in Afghanistan. However, he was persuaded otherwise by Haji and stayed with the fighters in Pakistan for some time while they trained him in using hydrogen peroxide, but also in making gas bombs, given the expected complexities with using hydrogen peroxide after July 2005. Two others who came later, most likely Tanvir Hussain and Assad Sarwar, were also trained in using the hydrogen peroxide and rapidly sent back. Given the enhanced scrutiny by the authorities of young Britons travelling back and forth from Pakistan, al-Qaeda sped up their training.[223]

Yet it was this toing and froing that seems to have unravelled the plot. As police observed a network of extremists in East London, their attention was drawn to their frequent journeys between London and Pakistan, ostensibly to carry out aid work on behalf of an organisation called the Islamic Medical Association (IMA). Until 2004 this was located on the same street as Mohammed Hamid's bookshop, Chatsworth Road in Hackney. During the first trial of Ali Khan and his co-conspirators, the prosecution claimed that it was another former mujahedeen fighter who ran the Chatsworth Road Islamic Medical Association who facilitated a stream of young men to go to Pakistan.[224] A seventeen-year-old relation, Abdul Patel, was among those arrested in August 2006 and was convicted of having 'in his possession a document or record, namely a book on improvised explosives devices, some suicide notes and wills with the identities of persons prepared to commit acts of terrorism and a map of Afghanistan containing information likely to be useful to a person committing or preparing an act of terrorism'.[225] Ali Khan and fellow plotter Assad Sarwar travelled back and forth between Britain and Pakistan with the IMA, visiting the same refugee camp that Mohammed Hamid claimed to have visited in 2002. Others later convicted for roles in the plot, including Umar Islam and Tanvir Hussain, also travelled to Pakistan as part of the charity's network.

After a period of testing, in which they perfected the design of the liquid bomb, Rauf and his al-Qaeda bosses decided it was time to recall Ali Khan to train him specifically in making the new devices. Having concluded that he would be a good on-the-ground leader for the cell, they decided that Sarwar, who appears to have been unwilling to carry out a martyrdom operation, would make an appropriate quartermaster for the plot who could then subsequently be redeployed in future operations. Both men returned to Pakistan and were separately briefed on their roles in the plot.[226] But while Sarwar seems to have slipped through the net, it was after returning from one of these trips in June 2006 that police, who were already watching Ali Khan (according to Rauf they had stopped him on his way to Pakistan) and who had been told by contacts in Pakistan that he had been seen meeting with Rashid Rauf—as counter-terrorism head Andy Hayman put it, 'anyone who has contact personally with Rauf will be under suspicion of potentially being linked to terrorism'[227]—opened his bags and discovered large amounts of Tang, a powdered soft drink, and batteries. This aroused their suspicions and increased the attention paid to Ali and his contacts. As it turned out, the Tang was to both act as an accelerant due to the high sugar content, as well as help dye the liquid peroxide that was being decanted back into plastic bottles to disguise what it was, while the batteries were hollowed out in order to have a small charge inserted in them.[228]

While Ali Khan and Tanvir were the ones who were seemingly running things from Walthamstow, Assad Sarwar used a garage in High Wycombe to boil down the hydrogen peroxide—isolating himself from Ali Khan and the Walthamstow plotters as per his Pakistani commanders' instructions. A large and bumbling individual who was one of five children, he was described by his defence team as a 'Walter Mitty-type character', and had achieved little prior to his involvement in the plot. A self-proclaimed graffiti artist as a young man, he had dropped out of an earth sciences degree at Brunel University and become a postman. By his own account, he first met fellow plotter Umar Islam at the Muslim Education Centre bookshop in High Wycombe, and through him was introduced to the IMA, where he fatefully met Abdulla Ahmed Ali Khan. Sarwar admitted that he had visited Kashmir in June 2006 and met an individual who taught him how to make explosives, all part of a plot that Ali and he claimed to have hatched in January 2006 to carry out a small explosion, which was intended to be part of a scare to wake up the British public to their government's foreign policy. A key part of this was the release of a documentary that would feature the damning martyrdom videos that all six of them had recorded, in which they declaimed their political statements before the black flag of jihad.

Two successive juries had doubts about this story, with the second instead believing the prosecution's case that the men were involved in an al-Qaeda-directed plot. According to the prosecution's case, and supported by Rauf's subsequent documenting of the operation, Ali Khan and Sarwar met in Pakistan with Rauf in 2004–2005. As we have already seen, Rauf by this point was a key al-Qaeda coordinator who was seemingly the first point of contact with the organisation for aspirant British jihadis who were coming over. However, while the success of the 7 July plot seems to have been due to his handiwork as a coordinator, it is the foiled Overt plot that brought him international celebrity. It was as a result of his arrest in August 2006 by Pakistani authorities that British authorities swept in and arrested the British plotters.[229] Well-connected in Britain, Rashid Rauf was a British–Pakistani national who had fled the United Kingdom in 2002 after being sought by police in connection with the murder of his uncle. He was born into a family known locally for its religious leadership and involvement in some of the Kashmiri identity politics in Birmingham at the time. The *pater familias*, Abdul Rauf is believed to have been in contact with Maulana Masood Azhar when he visited Birmingham in the early 1990s, asking the preacher to take some leadership over his errant son Rashid.[230] When the cell was first rolled up in August 2006, a police source told the press, 'The Raufs were targeted precisely because of the family's links to extremist groups in Pakistan that have, over the years, come to work hand in glove with al-Qaeda' and the family had 'been flagged red for months'.[231] The local school that young Rashid attended, Washwood Heath, was identified after his arrest as having been a hotbed of radical thought, with a teacher quoted as saying, 'I'm not at all surprised that someone from the school has been implicated. There were some very influential radical elements there.'[232] In 1996 (while Rauf was a student) a teacher, Israr Khan, leapt up after a rendition of carol singing shouting 'Who is your God? Why are you saying Jesus and Jesus Christ? God is not your God—it is Allah.'[233] While, unlike some other Birmingham Muslims, Rauf does not seem to have joined one of the local gangs, he was allegedly close to the leader of the Aston Panthers.[234] Rauf's parents ran a madrassa in the back of their house, and some stories claimed that young Rashid was being trained to be a preacher. Whatever the case, in May 2002 Rauf and a childhood friend fled Birmingham in the wake of his uncle Mohammed Saeed's murder. The two men had been seen together in February 2002 at an internet café in Portsmouth, 'where they viewed pages relating to a US aviation company and ordered a GPS map receiver and various compass/map CDs using fraudulent credit card details'.[235]

This equipment would prove to be very useful to the two men as they fled to the Bahawalpur region of Pakistan, where Rauf married into the family of Masood Azhar, the Kashmiri militant who established the Jaish-e-Mohammed group following his release from Indian custody alongside Omar Saeed Sheikh. Like Sheikh, Rauf went on to become a notorious British jihadist. Rauf himself claimed that when he fled to Pakistan in 2002 he was seeking to fight in Afghanistan and had connected with Amjad Farooqi, a senior Pakistani militant who put Rauf in touch with al-Qaeda at several levels. While Farooqi was later killed, Rauf maintained his connections, working closely with Abu Faraj al-Libi, the individual who was head of al-Qaeda's external operations networks—a role that Abdul Hadi al-Iraqi and then Abu Ubaidah al-Masri also filled.[236]

Obviously able to impress his al-Qaeda superiors, Rauf seems rapidly to have been entrusted with a relatively senior role and contacts. It is likely that his long-standing connections to extremist groups, together with his Western birth and habits, made him a perfect point of contact for aspirant European extremists drawn to Pakistan by the lure of jihad. While these young men would have been fired up with religious zeal, they would nevertheless have experienced a substantial culture clash and the group would have benefited from having a gatekeeper such as Rauf who could both empathise with their situation in the United Kingdom while also assessing their utility to the group. As we saw in the earlier Crevice plot, the young men who had streamed over from the United Kingdom (and elsewhere) to fight alongside the Taliban and al-Qaeda were hardly paragons of operational security and would have been deeply respectful but slightly uncertain about what to do when confronted with senior al-Qaeda leaders. Rauf's role was probably to try to overcome this tension, vet operatives and also manage plots once they had been hatched from a distance, using his strong connections to al-Qaeda and back in Britain.

This role came to something of an apex in the Overt plot, where, building on the success of the 7 July conspiracy, he worked with senior al-Qaeda plotters to manage an extraordinary plot that would have outdone the 9/11 massacre.[237] Having seen the mixed success of the July plots, this time they decided to guarantee the operation on the ground by using a key individual who was dispatched back to the United Kingdom under the false name Altaf Ravat.[238] Whilst Rauf does not mention this individual in his post-operation assessment documents,[239] in his planning for the 7 July plot, Rauf mentions his eagerness to travel back with Mohammed Siddique Khan and Shehzad Tanweer to help with things on the ground, but being unable to do so due to his difficulty in entering to the United Kingdom. So it is not surprising that he would elect to send someone back to oversee a plot of such a complexity—with two different cells at least to coordinate on the ground. Arriving in the United Kingdom on 18 July 2006 on a flight from South Africa, the British

Pakistani was travelling on a fake South African passport to mask his true intentions, but also because he was wanted alongside Rashid Rauf in connection with the murder of Mohammed Saeed. He was also a childhood friend of Rauf's who had attended Portsmouth University at the same time as him and had been arrested with him. Returning with a fake wife and assuming the identity of a travelling Tablighi, he headed straight to meet with Mohammed al-Ghabra, the tough East London Syrian whom we encountered earlier in connection with Muktar Said Ibrahim's trip to Pakistan in late 2004. According to the security services, al-Ghabra and Ravat met in London and South Africa a number of times during the spring and summer of 2006—which he admitted to in court, claiming it was part of a discussion to import-export leather jackets.[240] It seems that Ali and Sarwar were also in direct contact themselves with individuals back in Pakistan, who were helping direct the plot from a distance. During the second trial into the core group of plotters, the prosecution submitted relevant emails as evidence, showing a high level of control.[241] This is verified by Rauf's account, which refers to four different mobile phones, used to contact three different people in the United Kingdom. On the ground in Britain, the plotters demonstrated counter-surveillance training, regularly changing telephones and choosing to have conversations in seemingly improbable locations. In one instance, Assad Sarwar and Ali Khan were observed going to a park to talk and lying down facing each other to communicate, masking their conversation from eavesdropping.

The final element in the plot was the network of young men that Ali Khan drew upon to act as its footsoldiers. Calling upon numerous old school friends and other locals, Ali Khan deployed his considerable charisma to draw in an unknown number of individuals (according to Rauf's report there were nine 'brothers' ready to go in the operation), of which at least five recorded martyrdom videos alongside Ali Khan. Two of them, Umar Islam, a black former Rastafarian convert who converted in 2001, and Tanvir Hussain, a man referred to as Ali Khan's lieutenant, were both found guilty alongside Ali Khan, while it took three separate trials for a jury to also find Waheed Zaman, Olivier 'Ibrahim' Savant and Arafat Waheed Khan guilty. All of the men recorded suicide videos in the same format, with Ali Khan or Hussain coaching them in the background. The men were all either spotted at the bomb factory in Walthamstow that Ali Khan had purchased for cash, or else identified using forensic evidence found in the apartment.²⁴² Savant in particular was identified in emails using the codename 'half guggie' (a supposed reference to his mixed Indian and English heritage) and 'being well up for it' having done something to alter his appearance in terms of trimming his beard. Umar Islam is believed to have been chosen to carry out a dry run of the planned attack, to see whether the completed device could be snuck past airport security—a detail that panicked security officials on both sides of the Atlantic when they realised while watching the plotters that someone who shared a name with an individual on a terror watch list was on a transatlantic flight. It turned out to be mere coincidence, but it is believed to be the trigger that prompted the American security services to demand that Pakistan arrest Rauf, forcing the British authorities to roll the plot in the United Kingdom up.²⁴³

In contrast to previous plots, connections to the aforementioned radical preachers seem to have been less prominent in this case. While the men had radical material connected to the preachers and Ali Khan was on the fringes of Al-Muhajiroun networks in Walthamstow, they all seem to have been involved in local Tablighi Jamaat and Markaz ud Dawa mosques. Nevertheless, it is unclear to what degree Tablighi was involved in their radicalisation, or whether it was instead something that simply featured in the background in much the same way that we saw it feature in earlier plots in this chapter.

Drawn into the plot for the most part by the appealing and calculating Ali Khan, Waheed Zaman was referred to as the scholar of the group, due to his role as head of a local university Islamic society, while Ibrahim Savant and Arafat Khan appear to have been wayward youths who were attracted by their friend and the possibilities of direction and redemption. Both of these men had histories of drug use, although it is unclear to what degree: Arafat Khan was caught with heroin after the death of his father, while Savant converted when he was sixteen and was then arrested a few years later in possession of cannabis. A further three individuals, Mohammed Shamin Uddin, Nabeel Hussain and Adam Khatib—all Muslims from East London—were convicted of providing a variety of support roles in the plot. Nabeel Hussain was a school friend of Tanvir Hussain who later met Ali through a brother, while Khatib, a much younger man (twenty to Ali's thirty), was introduced to Ali Khan by his older sibling. Ali Khan appears to have taken the young man under his wing (as we earlier saw with Mohammed Siddique Khan and his cell, and Omar Khyam and his younger brother) and brought him along on a trip to Pakistan to use him in the conspiracy, although it remained unclear whether he was meant to be involved in the final attack.[244] A part-time small-time criminal, Nabeel Hussain was jailed for the plot, only to emerge years later when he allegedly tried to get to Syria using a fraudulent passport.[245]

A number of others were also picked up in association with the airlines plot. Another convert named Donald Stewart-Whyte, the son of a local Conservative activist in High Wycombe, was also initially charged as being involved in the plot, though ultimately a jury found him innocent of involvement, despite pleading guilty to possession of a firearm. His primary link to the plot seems to have been through Umar Islam.[246] Cossor Ali, Ali Khan's wife, was also charged with knowing about the plot and failing to warn authorities. She was cleared of any involvement in a trial that exposed Ali Khan as an abusive husband and his family controlling of his wife's life and activities.[247] Others who had been initially picked up and were cleared of any involvement included one of Rashid Rauf's brothers in Birmingham, while a separate investigation into a charity established by his father led to nothing. Finally, an individual identified by security services as a radicalised twenty-year-old British Indian from northern England was believed to represent the northern end of the conspiracy, either as a suicide bomber or as a source for fake documentation. He was allegedly in contact with both Mohammed al-Ghabra and Rauf's childhood friend who had been sent to manage the plot on the ground.[248] According to the security services' assessment, he had travelled to Pakistan twice, in 2004 and 2005 (journeys he has admitted to, while insisting they were innocuous trips), where he is believed to have attended training camps. Moreover, in April 2006 he went to Oman with a man he had met only recently, where he had a strange encounter with a ship of the Royal Navy.[249] While not necessarily connected, but potentially relevant, in Rauf's account of the plot, he refers to a pair of individuals who had trained and were not caught in the wave of arrests that took place when police rolled the cell up.[250]

The crest of the first wave of British jihad

Aside from those who were found guilty, it is difficult to draw any definitive conclusions about many of those believed to be involved in this plot.

223

A number of individuals whom security officials identified as senior players in al-Qaeda support networks remain at large in the United Kingdom at the time of writing. While Ali Khan was portrayed as the leader of the plot, it is more likely that he was the operational leader on the ground, chosen for his personal charisma, something he showed through the ease with which he assembled a large cell of people to support the plot. A man who does not appear to have held down any serious jobs in his life or to have pursued studies with any great intensity, supporting the jihadist cause in South Asia seems to have taken over his life. Responsible for identifying and purchasing the flat in Walthamstow that the group would use as their bomb factory, he then drew into the plot some of his schoolmates and acquaintances, as well as directing aid convoys from East London. While Ali Khan may have been instrumental in bringing the team on the ground in London together, it seems very clear that Rashid Rauf was the key player in the overall operation. His role included vetting potential recruits, guiding Ali Khan around the tribal areas, passing messages between the senior leadership and the team on the ground, and ultimately maintaining contact with a number of players on the ground beyond Ali Khan. However, this has only become clear in the fullness of time, with absolute clarity as uncertain on this as on his possible death in a drone strike in November 2008.[251] In many ways, one of the most disturbing aspects of the plot was the sheer volume of young men willing to provide martyrdom videos and be involved in the plot, and the number who were subsequently convicted for conspiracy to murder.

This is not to say that the entire plot was cooked up by British Muslims: investigators believe it was, in fact, directed by Abu Ubaidah al-Masri, who allegedly masterminded and organised training for the 7 July, 21 July and Overt plotters when they visited Pakistan in late 2004.[252] This seems to be confirmed by documents purportedly written by Rauf and discovered in the possession of German terror suspects, which claimed that Haji (believed to be al-Masri) was the power behind the scenes, while Rauf was the key organiser. Subsequent to his arrest as part of this plot, Rauf escaped from Pakistani custody in December 2007, and disappeared from public view until November 2008, when his death was announced after a Predator drone strike in Waziristan. It was never confirmed officially (reports at the time suggested that in the wake of a Predator strike a radio intercept had been overheard which indicated he had been killed),[253] and for his lawyer, the entire story of his escape and death were part of an elaborate conspiracy.[254] Since then his perceived role in previous al-Qaeda planning has only continued to grow, with links to him being found in all three of the above-mentioned plots, as well as a series of plots that we shall describe in Chapter 6. After escaping from custody, he seems to have returned to his old ways, continuing to play the role of key point of contact for Western extremists coming to Waziristan.[255]

While it is unlikely that we will ever know the full story of Rashid Rauf, or even know whether he is still alive,[256] he was not the only British Muslim to rise to such a position of trust within al-Qaeda's structures, after moving across from the parallel community of Kashmir-oriented radicals. At around the same time as his arrest in August 2006, but to much less fanfare, Pakistani forces intercepted a British Pakistani individual who has already featured briefly in the narrative, named Rangzieb Ahmed. A self-confessed member of Harakat ul-Mujahedeen, Ahmed was born in Rochdale but moved to Pakistan as a young boy. While there, he embraced the Kashmiri jihad, and in 1994 as an eighteen-year-old was picked up by Indian forces, having illegally crossed the Line of Control with a friend. In an interview with the *Manchester Evening News* prior to his release in 2001, he told a reporter, 'When I was in England I heard that the Indian forces were doing wrong, killing children and burning mosques. I was told mothers and sisters were being raped by the Indians. It was my duty to go and fight them. I had to come.'[257] Years later, while Ahmed did not contradict this, the tone of his description to a British prisoner support organisation was a little different: 'Ahmed with his friend Saleem went for one of their walks around the mountainous area of Azad Kashmir. Unbeknownst to them, they had strayed into the line of control and into Indian occupied Jammu Kashmir. They had only wandered one kilometer beyond the line when an Indian patrol ambushed them.'[258]

Whatever the case, Rangzieb was welcomed back to the Kashmiri community of Rochdale in July 2001. The local newspaper had run a campaign to help secure his release and his family, who had shied away from visiting him in India for fear of being incarcerated themselves, greeted him upon his return. He appears to have then settled into a relatively quiet life, although he experienced some paranoia owing to his experiences in India. Sometime in 2002 he was introduced to Habib Ahmed, a local young British Pakistani who had heard of Rangzieb's celebrity and was introduced to him by a relative of another local extremist, Hassan Butt. In his early twenties at this point, Habib Ahmed was a

225

longtime Al-Muhajiroun activist who first encountered the group at Stand Sixth Form College in 1996, where Hassan Butt and his brother Usman had established a local Islamic society with strong links to Hizb ut-Tahrir. After graduating from college, the two brothers went to Wolverhampton University, where they continued their activism and were followed by Habib Ahmed. In 1999 he claims to have joined Al-Muhajiroun, and in July 2000 he was picked up by Manchester police for sticking posters for the group on top of traffic lights in Prestwich. A year later in June 2001 he married a fellow Al-Muhajiroun activist called Mehreen Haji at a ceremony in Wilmslow, presided over by Omar Bakri Mohammed and at which Hassan Butt served as a signatory.

Omar Bakri appears to have had a relatively strong hold over the young men. Habib regarded Omar Bakri's participation in his wedding as an honour; as he put it, 'at that time he was leader of Al-Muhajiroun. We looked up to him so hence for my marriage I wanted him to be present.'[259] He also instructed Hassan Butt to take on a prominent role as a speaker for his group Al-Muhajiroun in Pakistan, though it is unclear when Hassan Butt was there. In October 2001, near Islamabad, Hassan Butt introduced a British journalist to Mohammed Junaid Babar, the American we saw earlier who provided such a wealth of information on the Crevice group, and he was frequently called upon to provide the voice of British Pakistani radicalism in the press.[260] In January 2002 Butt took a step too far, telling the BBC's Today programme that there were many British extremists in Pakistan, and that eventually some of them would return to 'strike at the heart' of Britain. Omar Bakri quickly refuted his claims and announced he no longer spoke for Al-Muhajiroun.[261] This did not stop Butt's tirades, and he returned to Britain where he tried to sell his story repeatedly to the press. In one instance, alongside his old friend Habib Ahmed, they approached the *Daily Mirror* newspaper seeking £100,000 for their story as extremists who had trained at al-Qaeda camps in South Asia and had now slipped back into the country.[262] Habib Ahmed used this story, and testimony from Hassan Butt, as part of a complex defence he mounted in court in which he claimed that he had fabricated much of his story and contacts as part of an effort to make some money. A similar story was disseminated by Hassan Butt, who in December 2008, while testifying at Habib Ahmed's trial, claimed that he had fabricated his entire story. He claimed that he had even gone as far as to stab himself in the arm to prove to a journalist that he had changed his ways, and was now a wanted man by British jihadis he had once helped recruit and support.[263]

While Hassan Butt appeared to have somehow avoided trouble or prosecution (he has been picked up on five different occasions by British police), his childhood friend Habib Ahmed had a different fate. Alongside Rangzieb Ahmed, he was accused and convicted of being part of a three-man al-Qaeda cell on an undefined mission. The men were recorded talking in vaguely coded terms about al-Qaeda in a hotel in Dubai in 2005, where Rangzieb had summoned Habib to collect some notebooks full of contact information for a string of high-level extremists in Europe and Asia. These notebooks ended up forming the central element in the prosecution's case against the two men, highlighting the men's connection to Hamza Rabia, the then operational commander of al-Qaeda, whose death drew Rangzieb Ahmed back to Pakistan in 2006; Mamoun Darkazanali, a Syrian based in Germany; Khalid Habib, a renowned fighter who had appeared in Chechnya, Iraq and was a commander in Afghanistan when he was killed by a Predator strike; Mohammed Zillur Rahman, the alleged third man in their terror cell who had a number of meetings with Rangzieb Ahmed in Bradford and Manchester before leaving the country heading to South Africa; Abdul Rashid Ghazi, the son of the founder of the infamous Lal Masjid (Red Mosque) in Islamabad, who died fighting the Pakistani state in July 2007; Maulana Shah Abdullah Aziz, a leading member of Pakistani Jamaat Islami; and his brother Shah Mehboob Elahi, a member of the governing council of Jamaat Islami.[264] The inclusion of these final two does not necessarily highlight any connection whatsoever of their respective group with al-Qaeda, but it does reveal Rangzieb Ahmed's top-level contacts with very senior Islamists in Pakistan. Most significant about the case against Rangzieb Ahmed and Habib Ahmed was that aside from this laundry list of international extremists, the two men were deeply linked to the community of British radicals who have appeared in the narrative so far.

As we saw previously, Al-Muhajiroun played a major part in Habib Ahmed's life. In many ways, his overheard comments in which he claimed to have seen a list of names that Mohammed Junaid Babar had given up to the police (in which Babar had 'grassed…everyone from A to Z' including himself), highlight the importance of this Al-Muhajiroun–grown network to the wider British jihadist scene.[265] The connections implicit within these comments were strengthened by the parallel list of British extremists to which Rangzieb Ahmed was linked. First among the group is fellow British Harakat ul-Mujahedeen member Omar Saeed Sheikh, who sent Rangzieb Ahmed money in 1996 during his long period in an Indian jail; this detail was revealed by police briefing to journalists during the course of the trial, though it remains unclear whether the two met. Omar Sheikh was a known figure in Al-Muhajiroun circles more broadly, and aside from the connections identified earlier, he was also spotted at an Al-Muhajiroun safe house in Lahore and was identified by Hassan Butt as someone he had met.[266] Furthermore, as we saw on the fringes of the Crevice group, Omar Saeed Sheikh featured as someone helping Kazi Rahman obtain weapons, and also helping the other East London cell, brothers Tanveer Ali and Abdul Jabbar, as well as others, go for training.

But Rangzieb Ahmed's connections went further than Omar Saeed Sheikh. In an intriguing detail, in March 2005 a mobile phone number linked to Yassin Omar, one of the 21 July 2005 attempted bombers, called Rangzieb Ahmed. Furthermore, in Rangzieb's books were the mobile phone numbers of Abdul Rahman and Aslam Awan, two former schoolfriends from Pakistan who migrated to the United Kingdom ostensibly to study, but instead appear to have established a terror support network from their Cheetham Hill house two streets away from Habib Ahmed's home. The two men in their mid-twenties, alongside a further group of local young Muslims, were running a pipeline that was sending over fighters and equipment to Afghanistan. Initially arriving to study biotechnology at university in Dundee, Abdul Rahman appears to have lasted all of a day before concluding he was 'unable to settle into the culture' and moving instead to Manchester where his friend Aslam Awan had been for a few years.[267] Once here he appears to have got a job as a mobile phone salesman, while integrating himself into a local community of young men enthused by jihadist culture. No doubt alongside others, he helped run a number of training camps in the nearby Lake District. Short videos released show the men crawling through the snow while talking about jihad and shouting '*Allahu Akbar*' (God is great). When he was arrested in January 2007, police found him in the middle of packing envelopes to send to Pakistan containing 'combat knives and mobile telephones, mobile phone batteries and two mobile phone chargers'. He had previously, during the same month, assisted a young convert to the cause, named Umar Arshad, to flee a control order which had been imposed upon him after his parents had raised concerns to local police about his growing extremism. He has not been heard of since, though Aslam Awan, who by this point was reported to have risen to senior rank within al-Qaeda under the *nom de guerre* Abdullah Khorasani, was reported to have been killed by a drone strike in January 2012.[268] Alongside the usual assortment of extremist videos, recordings and written material, when he was picked up, Rahman also had in his possession a letter in Urdu by his old schoolfriend Aslam, which described his experiences as a jihadi in Afghanistan and exhorted others to come and join: 'We have to do this work even with our last drop of blood. Please do migrate and encourage others to migrate too. Please invite everybody towards this cause.'[269]

The letter was intended as a rallying call for young Muslims, highlighting the excitement they were missing out on, and specifically called upon six different individuals to assist in particular ways. When police finally intercepted Rahman in early 2007, he was one of the first to be prosecuted under legislation against disseminating terrorist information. Two others, Aslam Awan and Muraad Mohammed Iqbal (another young British Pakistani from Karachi who was running the network alongside Rahman), were instead issued exclusion orders by the British government, forbidding them from re-entering the country.[270] While Awan is believed to have died, Iqbal and the earlier mentioned fighter Umar Arshad have both disappeared into Pakistan's wilder regions or beyond.

In an interesting twist, the connection to the radical clerics and the narrative woven thus far has in some ways evolved since its early days. While Rahman and Awan appear to have been connected to Rangzieb Ahmed, it seems unlikely that the men were directly influenced by the radical clerics or would have been particularly excited by groups like Al-Muhajiroun. For these young men born and raised in Pakistan's tribal areas, it seems much more likely that a figure like Rangzieb Ahmed would have been able to speak directly to them, rather than clerics like Omar Bakri Mohammed or Abdullah el-Faisal, who had no direct experience on the battlefield. The fact that much of their experience of the United Kingdom would have occurred long after the trends highlighted to date reveals how, in many respects, they are part of the second generation of terrorist threats that has emerged.

The trial of Rangzieb and Habib Ahmed, and the parallel set of trials of the Overt conspirators, all marked what might be called the zenith of domestic Islamist terrorism. As the commentator Yahya Birt astutely put it in September 2009 when Ali Khan, Hussain and Sarwar were sent down for their roles in Overt: 'the conviction of the ringleaders of the airliner plot last week represents the end of an era'.[271] While this may be a slight overstatement—indeed, Birt prefaced these comments with a caveat—it is much harder to draw hard and fast links between many of the subsequent plots that have threatened Britain (or that have emanated from it) than it has been up to this point in the story. This is not to say that the threat has evaporated, simply that it appears to have been displaced quite substantially and has now mutated into a variety of forms in different parts of the globe. In Chapter 6 we shall explore how the threat has evolved since then, and what shape it might assume in the future.

6

THE NEXT GENERATION OF BRITISH JIHAD

'I wanted the public to taste what is going on, for them to have a taste of what the decisions of their democratically-elected murderers did to my people.'[1]

The events of July 2005 were a rude awakening for the British government, especially when they realised that several of the key plotters were already on their radar: Mohammed Siddique Khan and Shehzad Tanweer had been seen repeatedly with the Crevice plotters, while Muktar Said Ibrahim had been searched at Heathrow in December 2004 as he flew to Pakistan with two others from Mohammed Hamid's circle and their camping gear, having been dropped off at the airport by an individual under heavy MI5 surveillance. Once it became clear that these men were not only set to become fighters abroad, but were prepared to be suicide bombers at home, the whole threat perception changed. The immediate focus became the broad network of plotters that was uncovered in Chapter 5 and its strong connection with al-Qaeda. These young radicals circled around the mosques, study sessions, bookshops and events run by the radical preachers, as well as other overtly radical elements in the country emanating from the South Asian community in the United Kingdom. Unfortunately this was not the only show in town, and running in parallel to this network were a number of phenomena that increasingly came to characterise the subsequent evolution of jihadism in Britain.

Iraq comes home

As mentioned earlier, the war in Iraq was less of a draw for British jihadis compared to the conflicts in South Asia. Some did go, many tracking a route through Damascus, where they claimed to be going to study Islam, before heading across the border into Iraq to join the insurgency. However, their number was relatively small—the former head of MI5 Dame Eliza Manningham-Buller has estimated some seventy to eighty—while around 4,000 Britons travelled to Afghanistan and Pakistan, from before and after the Taliban's fall up to early 2009.[2] This disparity was reflected in the number of terrorist plots that subsequently emerged from the respective battlefields, with the overwhelming majority tracing links back to Pakistan's badlands, as we saw in Chapter 5, due both to the strong South Asian character of Britain's jihad, and the fact that this was where al-Qaeda's core remained. This changed in 2007, when two Mercedes filled with fuel and propane cylinders were left outside a central London night-club. Already shocked by the arrival of Baghdad-style tactics on British soil, the next day the United Kingdom was struck again when a Jeep filled with a similar mix was driven in a suicide attack into the departure hall at Glasgow International Airport. One driver died, while the other leapt from the vehicle and was tackled by onlookers. As information emerged about the two, what particularly struck people was the integrated nature of the men, Dr Bilal Abdulla and Dr Kafeel Ahmed. Unlike many of those in the former chapters, their formative years had been spent out-side the United Kingdom, but they had strong roots in the country and were qualified medical doctors and research engineers.

Dr Bilal Abdulla was born in 1979 in Aylesbury, Buckinghamshire to a father who was in Britain on an Iraqi government scholarship and a mother who worked as a pharmacist. When he was four the family returned to Iraq where young Bilal did most of his schooling, scoring high marks and ranking eighteenth in national tests. Upon completing high school he decided to follow in his father's footsteps and embarked on a medical career at the University of Baghdad. The backdrop to this academically high-flying childhood was Saddam Hussein's brutal Ba'athist regime. As Abdulla himself put it in court, 'in Iraq the conditions under Saddam's regime were extremely bad. The level of oppression was very high in the country.' He recalled his father taking hormones to enlarge his thyroid gland in an attempt to evade being drafted in the 1990s—a dangerous trick that had killed an uncle who tried it. Even at 'eighteen years old, I did not want to stay in that country. I did not want to stay in Iraq because of the oppression of the regime.'[3]

But it was not only the Hussein regime that Bilal found a curse on his country. During the Gulf War in 1991, the adolescent Bilal fled Baghdad with his family as bombs fell on the city. In his recollection the war coloured the outlook for an entire generation of Iraqis: 'Baghdad was one of the most beautiful cities in the Middle East and it was a ruin. In Baghdad there is a massive river that divides the city into two areas, I do not know how many bridges, but none of them was intact.'[4] The war changed his views of the West, notions that he characterised as being 'the views of the middle class of the country'. He tearfully recalled the damage shown in elevated leukaemia rates among children in Iraq, attributed to shells using depleted uranium, and Madeleine Albright's callous views on the *60 Minutes* television news show in which she said in response to a question about 'half a million children' dying due to the sanctions on Iraq that the 'price is worth it'.[5]

Unlike many of his countrymen, however, Bilal had a way out of Iraq thanks to his British nationality. At fifteen he went to Jordan to claim his British passport, and by 2000 was living in Cambridge with an uncle. He considered sitting A-levels and tried to pursue various avenues to continue his studies in the United Kingdom, but was obstructed by a lack of money. One path he investigated was the army, and he visited a British Army recruiting station in Cambridge to discuss with a colonel there whether the army might be able to pay for his continued medical studies. The discussions came to nothing, and once he had exhausted his possibilities in Britain he returned to his medical studies in Baghdad, graduating in 2004 and returning afterwards to Cambridge, this time to pursue a conversion course to allow him to practise in the United Kingdom. It was here in late 2004 that Shiraz Maher, then a member of Hizb ut-Tahrir, was first introduced to Bilal Abdulla and another immigrant student, Kafeel Ahmed. Recalling meeting them both on his first night in Cambridge at the small mosque that the town's community shared, he recalls Kafeel as a 'very quiet, shy, reticent guy', while Bilal was an intense man with a warm heart who would refuse car rides home from the mosque, preferring to walk home 'even in the rain' while listening to his iPod which was filled with verses from the Koran.[6]

By this time, the United Kingdom had joined the United States' second Iraq War, perhaps hardening Bilal Abdulla's views of the West.

Fortunate to be abroad, he watched as his nation descended once again into chaos and war. Recalling meeting the two men who would later carry out a bombing campaign in London and Glasgow, Shiraz found little sympathy for Bilal's fate, whom he describes as a charismatic and knowledgeable hard-line Islamist who would have heated debates about Iraq and sectarianism. In contrast, Maher found a great sense of responsibility towards Kafeel, a man whom he describes as a follower rather than a leader.[7] The two South Asian men, Shiraz and Kafeel, bonded over the fact that they had spent parts of their childhoods in Saudi Arabia.

Born in Bangalore, Kafeel's parents moved to Saudi Arabia for work while he was still very young. His mother remembered the young Kafeel being deeply affected by the stories emerging from Bosnia at the time.[8] He was sent to India in his early teens, to live with an aunt and pursue his further schooling there (Shiraz, on the other hand, was sent to Birmingham, where he had been born to a Pakistani family, to attend high school). Like his future co-conspirator Bilal, Kafeel excelled at his studies and ended up graduating from the BDT College of Engineering in Davanagere in 2000 with a score of 87 per cent and fifth place in his class. The college principal later recalled Kafeel as a 'brilliant student and very good, not just in academics but extra-curricular activities too'.[9] There followed a move to Belfast to study for a Master's in aeronautical engineering at Queen's University 2001–4. It was here that he may first have come to the notice of the security services. Active in the university's Islamic community, Kafeel appears to have been in Belfast at the same time as Abbas Boutrab, the mysterious Algerian who was picked up by local police on immigration-related charges in 2003 and was found with details of how to fabricate a bomb that could evade airport security. When the connection was made public in the wake of Kafeel's attempted attack, some intelligence sources spoke to the press in very definite terms about the depth of Kafeel's contact with Abbas Boutrab and his impact on the young man's radicalisation. This is contradicted by Shiraz Maher's research, in which he spoke to people who knew Kafeel during his time in Belfast who described him 'condemning Hamas for suicide bombings, even in Israel'.[10] Given the relatively small Muslim community in Belfast and Kafeel's active involvement there, it is perfectly likely that the men might have interacted, although whether this was anything more than a chance encounter is unclear.

Having completed his studies in Belfast, he crossed the Irish Channel to continue his academic career, moving to Cambridge to study for a

PhD in computational fluid dynamics at Anglia Ruskin University. He had just arrived there when Shiraz Maher first came across him in 2004, living at the time with one of Maher's Hizb ut-Tahrir (HuT) 'brothers' in Cambridge. In Kafeel the HuT men found what they thought might be a possible recruit: as Shiraz Maher put it, he 'was not political or radical' but 'a blank canvas'. This was in contrast to the deeply knowledgeable Bilal Abdulla who had memorised half the Koran, could explain obscure theological points to the well-read HuT men and would stand up for his views even if he was the only one in the room who held them. He may have disagreed with the HuT men, but he 'respected them' and as fellow Muslims he was generous whenever they needed his assistance. As Maher recalled Bilal putting it, 'soft hearts for the believers and hard hearts for the non-believers'.[11]

In the meantime, Iraq had descended into chaos. Friends from Iraq reported Bilal as being particularly radical in his anger towards American forces, and one professor reported that Bilal once stood up when the US Army came into the college to tell them, 'you are a *kafir* [unbeliever] and all of you should die'. In another instance the same professor, Ahmed Ali of the University of Baghdad's College of Medicine, reported Bilal telling his peers, 'we should not learn medicine. We should learn how to fight the occupation.'[12] In Cambridge, Shiraz Maher recalls having heated conversations with Bilal about Shia Muslims: 'he was very hot. We used to have a lot of disagreements with him, because he was very *takfiri*. He would say "Shias are *kafir*", and used to support the sectarian attacks against them in Iraq.'[13] It later emerged that some of this fire and brimstone may have come from the influence of Abu Qatada's tapes. Whilst serving in Belmarsh Prison, Abu Qatada, who said he 'felt insignificant' before Bilal and described him as 'a man from the men of Islam, in knowledge action, steadfastness and manhood', reported that Bilal told him he had been greatly influenced by Qatada's tapes.[14]

As a member of a middle-class Iraqi Sunni family, Bilal was at the forefront of the internecine civil war that gripped the nation after the toppling of the Hussein regime, and he claimed that some fifteen family and friends were killed in the violence. His mother recalled him calling home and becoming distraught in phone conversations about the violence and misery he was hearing about. In 2006 it is alleged that he returned home and connected with the insurgency, though it is unclear which group specifically he was linked with. One police report suggested that he had volunteered for a suicide mission, but was rejected on the basis that his British passport and clean record made him more useful for operations abroad.[15] In court Bilal said that he admired insurgents in any form, and in a letter addressed to the 'Soldiers of the Islamic State of Iraq' found after his arrest he stated, 'God knows that the days I spent with you were the best and most rewarding days of my life.'

Returning to Britain, Bilal was imbued with a sense of mission, living in a spartan manner as he completed his medical studies. Visiting his room in Cambridge, Maher remembers it 'was totally sparse. Nothing in there. A mattress on the floor and it was quite a big room, so felt really hollowed out. One shelf, a few medical books, a Koran, a typical big computer with lots of Arabic stuff on it and a prayer mat in the corner.'[16] Kafeel had returned to Bangalore in mid-2005 to look after his sick parents and took a job in a local technology company, his PhD studies appearing to have fallen by the wayside. Family members and Indian police believe that somewhere around this point Kafeel and his brother Sabeel were drawn into the Tablighi Jamaat movement.[17] While he was back in February 2006, his mother recalled her son organising a conference about the atrocities in Bosnia and Chechnya: 'he gathered the people, he distributed the pamphlets, he arranged a big meeting, then he spoke regarding Chechnya; and then he said "Why are Muslims suppressed everywhere? I want to bring awareness to people."'[18] According to the prosecution in the case against Bilal, it was also during this period while he was still in Bangalore that Bilal and Kafeel first started plotting their action—though it seems as though they must have already been considering something prior to this. On 26 February 2007 Kafeel emailed Bilal from India saying, 'Bro, *inshallah* I think we're going to start experiments soon', to which Bilal replied, 'Oh cool…LOL. Probably in a week or so we will have to meet and then establish a timetable.' The two men continued this discussion electronically for the next months, exchanging ideas on detonator mechanisms, and on what the requirements would be for a bomb factory. Kafeel specified 'flat with a garage if possible', which Bilal was able to locate and rent at 6 Neuk Crescent in Houston, Scotland, a short journey from the Royal Alexandra Hospital in Paisley, Glasgow, where he now lived and worked as a trainee doctor in the outpatients clinic.[19]

When on 5 May Kafeel returned to the United Kingdom, Bilal flew down from Scotland to meet him at Heathrow and the two men hired a car to drive back to Glasgow together. Two weeks later they were in London again, scouting for possible targets. As Bilal put it in court it was a day out to the city to find some suitable places to leave the devices, like 10 Downing Street, Parliament, Buckingham Palace, places we had in mind, places we had heard about. Mostly we were wandering around on tour buses. We were looking at how protected these places were and if it is possible to leave a car outside. In conclusion, we decided it was very difficult to leave a car outside prominent Government buildings. We decided to leave the car in central London.[20]

Having concluded their reconnaissance mission, the two men returned to Glasgow where they started to gather all the necessary items for their plot: purchasing nails, gas canisters, containers for fuel and duvet covers to hide the bombs in the vehicles. In early June, using the Autotrader.com website, they located and bought from a variety of locations around the United Kingdom five large vehicles, which presumably they calculated would be able to hold more explosive material. While they were gathering these materials, Bilal continued his work at the Royal Alexandra Hospital, and Kafeel stayed at home designing the detonators for their explosive devices. In fact, Bilal's work kept him so busy that they missed their initial self-imposed deadline to strike as power was being handed over from Tony Blair to Gordon Brown.[21]

Finally, on 27 June, the men worked through the night putting the finishing touches to their devices, with the mobile phone detonators recording an attempt to call them at 3am. Having tested the devices the men rested before setting off the next afternoon for London, driving straight down in a twelve-hour ride in a pair of green Mercedes, stopping off along the way to ensure that their fuel tanks would be full before they left them behind. In London, they headed straight for the Tiger Tiger nightclub in the heart of the city's West End, parking both vehicles in such a way as to inflict maximum damage. But while their mobile phone detonators worked, their devices failed to ignite properly and fizzled out. The vehicles attracted the attention of passers-by and a parking attendant as one of them had been left in a no-parking zone.

Disappointment quickly gave way to concern as the men recognised that they were now in a great deal of trouble: incriminating evidence was all over their bomb-laden vehicles. They set off back to Scotland, pausing only to pick up some belongings and money from another fellow Muslim doctor from their time in Cambridge, Mohammed Asha. Initially on trial alongside Bilal as a supporter of the plot, Mohammed Asha was eventually cleared of any involvement or knowledge of their activities.

Back in Scotland the pair prepared their jeep with a similar mix of explosives to those they had deposited in London. With the police and security services after them, they left the house in Neuk Crescent and went to a nearby loch, where they spent a few hours resting, praying and generally preparing themselves for what was to come. Once ready, the two men headed for Glasgow International Airport, where Bilal claims he thought they were going to catch flights: he was planning to go to Turkey and then Iraq. In reality, however, the airport was their final destination; they would try to drive their vehicle into the busy departure lounge. Like their previous device, however, this one failed to explode properly, and while Kafeel stayed in the vehicle and got badly burned, Bilal leapt from the car only to be tackled to the ground by passers-by. The two men were taken into custody, their point having been made: the war in Iraq had been brought to Britain's streets.

Af-Pak persists

The mid-2007 attempts in London and Glasgow showed that South Asia was not the only incubator (or source) of terrorist plots threatening the United Kingdom. Earlier in the year Birmingham police disrupted a network of older radicals funnelling money and equipment to anti-Western forces in Afghanistan. The men were targeted by police after they appeared to shift from supply network to active plotters: they were planning to film the beheading of a British Muslim soldier whom they were going to kidnap in a British city. Led by a British–Pakistani named Parviz Khan, a thirty-seven year-old unemployed man, the network seems to have been known to the local police as part of the broad community of radicals in the Birmingham area. As we saw in earlier chapters, Birmingham has a long history of extremist elements supporting jihad in Kashmir, and this ideology appears to have transferred itself as successive steps into supporting jihad in Bosnia and later Afghanistan. Bookshops like the Al-Maktabah were centres of radical thought, acting as a congregation point for radicals and publishing extremist material. It was from this milieu that Parviz Khan and his network emerged, coming to police attention by mid-2006.

At the time of his arrest, Khan was found to be in possession of a wide array of equipment useful to fighters living in the mountains between Pakistan and Afghanistan. Sending at least four shipments of equipment to Mirpur in Pakistan during 2004–6, he also brought more delicate items with him when he flew back to Pakistan in person. On one trip back from Pakistan in July 2006 he was stopped with a notepad which allegedly had a list of items requested by his contacts in Pakistan. It seems as though on one of these trips, however, Khan caught the itch to fight himself. In a conversation overheard by a security service bug installed in his house, Khan revealed his disappointment about not achieving much in life beyond small-time success as a young footballer: 'there is no answer... brother was a good footballer...centre midfield...it's not going to be good enough...not good enough. I know if I die now, if I die tonight, if I am not working for Islam full-time...pure hypocrite'.[22]

According to the prosecution, Khan hatched his plan to kidnap and behead a British Muslim soldier some time after his return from Pakistan, having been refused the opportunity to participate in the fighting in Afghanistan since his 'supply network was important'.[23] In many ways, this was similar to the Crevice cell's initial encounters, since they were more useful to Abdul Hadi al-Iraqi as a supply network rather than a terrorist unit. While the lead police investigator was convinced that Khan's plot was 'if not sponsored, then certainly supported by al-Qaeda',[24] it was unclear what form this support took. On the ground, Khan had difficulty getting others in Birmingham involved in his scheme. Not a particularly charismatic man, Khan was on the periphery of a number of radical networks: in London, he attended speeches by Abu Hamza, but also in Birmingham where he was close to some of those running the Al-Maktabah bookshop at the time. The main organiser at the time of the arrests, known as Abu Bakr or Ahmad Faraz, was initially picked up with the rest of the men. Khan does not, however, seem to have been very deeply ingrained within either the Birmingham or London group, as evidenced by the relatively haphazard nature of the plot he was attempting to carry out.

In the end Khan pleaded guilty to the charges against him, along with another fellow plotter, Basiru Gassama, a Gambian immigrant, who pleaded guilty to knowing about the plot and failing to disclose the information to police. Two other men were convicted alongside them of helping Khan run his supply chain to send equipment to Pakistan, while another four men were arrested and later convicted in October 2008, also for providing Khan's network with support. The entire group consisted mostly of men in their early thirties or late twenties, most of whom were in low-level employment or on welfare, and few of whom had achieved much in life. Their drift towards extremism is difficult to chart, but in court one of Khan's co-defendants, Zahoor Iqbal, told of his long-time friend's transformation from someone who 'went out clubbing, drinking, smoking' to someone who got rid of his television and 'became more anti-West, blaming Britain for the Israel–Palestine issue, Kashmir, civilians dying in Iraq and Afghanistan'.[25] By the time Khan was actively plotting he had also drawn others around him who were apparently of the same mindset and eager to conduct attacks. Abdul Raheem, one of the men charged in the second group of individuals, expressed a wish to become a suicide bomber and discussed with Khan the idea of kidnapping aid workers in Pakistan. As he was overheard putting it, 'five of them is worth one brother in Guantanamo Bay'.[26]

Khan's plan was a relatively simple one. He planned to use Gassama's contacts in the Gambian community to identify a British Muslim soldier. Then, while the individual was on a night out, they would lure him away from a crowd 'by winning his interest by the white stuff [cocaine]'.[27] Then, 'two lads will show blades and get him in the car and take him... drag him into the car—there will be three men, they will put him in the car'.[28] Having snatched their target, the plan was to take him to a lockup where they would behead 'him like a pig' in front of a video camera. The resulting film would be published on al-Jazeera and, in Khan's words, 'young Blair's going to go crazy'.[29] The point would be to scare off other Muslims from serving in the British Army in an attack that would also have struck terror in the public at large. Ultimately, the flaw in Khan's network was that he was not entirely persuasive in drawing fellow plotters into his intended action. Gassama did not respond to his advances in July 2006 or November 2006, though he also failed to alert the authorities to what Khan was plotting. In the end, he was the only individual to be convicted alongside Khan for involvement in or knowledge of the beheading plot. It was, according to the leading investigator, this aspect of the network that was more important: 'this is about dismantling what was a well organised, well-established supply line taking equipment, material and finance to terrorists and training camps abroad'.[30]

At this point in the second half of the decade the flow of fighters from the United Kingdom was continuing, though it is unclear at what rate. In April 2008, acting on an intelligence tip, Turkish police intercepted two young Britons travelling through Ankara to Tajikistan, from where they were allegedly planning to walk across the border into Afghanistan.

Once there, Mohammed Abushamma had written to his family saying that he planned to fight 'with a Koran in one hand and an AK-47 in the other'.[31] He pleaded guilty to the charges against him, while his co-defendant was cleared of any involvement. It is unclear how exactly Abushamma had planned to connect with mujahedeen fighters, or how he had been radicalised. During the trial much emphasis was placed on the internet as a radicalising agent, but the case appeared to highlight once again the ongoing allure of Afghanistan as a battlefield in the minds of young British Muslims.[32]

In November 2010, a court cleared a London Underground driver from Ilford of plotting to join the insurgency in Afghanistan in early 2009. Admitting that he knew the Adam brothers, one of whom, Anthony Garcia, was imprisoned during the Crevice trial while the other two remained on the run, the British–Pakistani man had left letters for his wife and child telling them not to be 'upset or depressed' and specifically asking for his wife's 'forgiveness', assuring her that he would see her 'in this life or the thereafter'.[33]

At around the same time as he was allegedly preparing to go to fight, a group of young men from Crawley also attempted to make the trip to Pakistan. Anonymously given the initials BG, BH and CA in court judgments assessing the need for control orders to restrict their movements, the judge concluded that 'I am satisfied that the trip to Pakistan in June 2008 and the attempts to return were for terrorism-related purposes'.[34] These men may have all failed to make it to Afghanistan, but others seemed to have completed the journey, showing the continuing existence of an active link between the insurgency in Afghanistan and the United Kingdom.

The intricacies of this connection were highlighted in a separate case in Manchester around a former Taliban fighter called Munir Farooqi. Farooqi has appeared briefly earlier in the narrative, but his case is worth going into more detail here, in particular the cell he had around him. Born in Pakistan, he moved to Britain as a child in the 1960s and was brought up in northern England. In the wake of September 11 he returned to Pakistan, where he joined the Taliban, was captured by Northern Alliance forces, and then released in May 2002, when Farooqi's wife was able to find him and pay for his freedom. Back in the United Kingdom he was trailed by MI5, and when British border officials stopped him as he returned from Pakistan in 2003, photos were found of him

241

posing with weaponry in the Swat valley. It was not until 2008, however, that they decided to mount a concerted effort against him, sending two undercover officers to collect evidence. The men made contact by approaching two separate *dawah* stalls that Farooqi and his acolytes would run in open door markets in Longsight and Manchester. One of his prominent followers was a twenty-nine-year-old convert called Matthew Newton, a local Manchester lad who had hovered on the edges of Manchester celebrity, photographed socially with members of the Happy Mondays and the stars of local television shows, before finding Islam later in life and being drawn in by Farooqi's influence.[35]

A charismatic man who had both first-hand war stories and bullet wounds to show for his experience, Farooqi would use the stalls to disseminate radical material he was mass producing in his basement and to find lost souls seeking meaning in their lives in a model of recruitment reminiscent of Mohammed Hamid's efforts in London on the fringes of the Finsbury Park mosque. Over a period of months, Farooqi would slowly foster relationships with these individuals (with Newton providing some support), taking them to prayer meetings, telling them more about his experiences as a jihadist and planting the idea in their heads that this was their religious commitment too. As he told one of the undercover officers, 'you know when you've tasted the honey [of jihad] then you only want more…until Allah takes you from this earth.'[36] Israr Malik, another recruit he was in the process of radicalising was later convicted alongside him. Malik was a petty criminal whom he had visited while in prison, bringing him radical material to read. On the outside, he would also point his recruits in the direction of more publicly known local religious leaders at certain mosques, where they would receive affirmation of their duty to fight jihad. Publicly released recordings did not seem to support this, though a local religious figure did tell undercover officers that, as his students, they should follow Munir Farooqi.[37] It is unlikely that the full extent of Munir Farooqi's activity will ever be known: during the trial he was heard talking about at least three followers who had gone to Pakistan and never returned. Local police estimated that Farooqi had sent at least twenty people to Afghanistan, though they did not publicly speculate about over how long a time this had taken place.[38]

In late 2010, in the wake of a scare around a supposed plot connected to a pair of British–Pakistani jihadists who were apparently loose in Waziristan, the Government Communications Headquarters (GCHQ,

Britain's signals intelligence agency) was reported to have estimated that there were some twenty British citizens in the region.[39] One story circulating in the press in June 2009 was an alleged report from a British officer in Afghanistan who claimed that a Taliban body had been found with an Aston Villa tattoo (a Birmingham football team).[40] This apocryphal-sounding story emerged after reports were published of RAF 'listening planes' over Afghanistan picking up chatter in distinctly 'Brummie' (Birmingham) accents; other tales reported Yorkshire, Bradford and Mancunian (Manchester) tones being overheard. When the foreign secretary, David Miliband, visited British forces in Helmand in early 2009, he saw Taliban bomb-making equipment with British components. An explosives officer briefing the foreign secretary told him, 'the devices had either been sent from Britain, or brought over to the country. They ranged from remote-control units used to fly model airplanes to advanced components which could detonate bombs at a range of more than a mile.'[41] While the number of British fighters in Afghanistan was reportedly relatively small, a former British commander in Afghanistan, Brigadier Ed Butler, stated in 2008 that he had seen intelligence of groups in southern Afghanistan plotting with 'Muslim extremists in the UK'.[42] Within the context of this book these are hardly surprising revelations, but the discovery of the Aston Villa tattoo was a particularly striking detail that brought the connection home at a very tangible local level.

Somalia

Stories of British Taliban are elusive and hard to pin down in jihadist videos and other material, with only one fleeting image of a man identified as 'Musa the British' appearing in a video released onto extremist forums honouring fallen 'martyrs' in February 2011.[43] Another image of a British jihadi in AfPak emerged in a video linked to the Pakistani Taliban in which the anonymous individual—identified as 'Umar'—claimed to be involved in the 2009 plot by Jordanian doctor and triple agent Abu Dujana to attack the CIA's base at Camp Chapman in Afghanistan. The same video claimed that 'Umar' was involved in organising the attack and was later killed in 2010 in a drone strike. 'Umar' was later identified as one of the East London group in chapter five.[44] However, these fleeting images were all that emerged from years of activism in Pakistan. In Somalia the presence of British nationals was confirmed when in March 2008 al-Shabaab (The Youth) terror organisation released a video featuring Abdul Ayoub al-Muhajir (Abu Ayyub al-Muhajir), a young English-speaking Somali who purportedly carried out a suicide bombing at an Ethiopian checkpoint on 10 October 2007. The British media subsequently identified him as a British national who had studied business at Oxford Brookes University and worked as a shop assistant prior to his return to Somalia to become an Islamist warrior. In his subsequently released martyrdom video, the young man was quoted as saying, 'Oh my people, know that I am doing this martyrdom operation for the sake of Allah. I advise you to migrate to Somalia and wage war against your enemies. Death in honour is better than life in humiliation.'[45]

The emergence of this footage confirmed something that had long become an open secret among Britain's growing Somali community: that young men were disappearing to fight in Somalia. In summer 2006, a reporter for the *Independent* recalled meeting 'at least half a dozen young men, including two brothers from Wood Green in North London who were acting as bodyguards for Sheikh Yusuf, one of the main Islamist commanders'.[46] The path these men may have followed to get to Somalia was detailed in a case that was briefly mentioned earlier in connection with the 21 July 2005 group. Here, a group of young men of mixed heritage tracked a path from London to Somalia on what they maintained was a 'free-style dawah', a move they claimed to have taken with inspiration from Tablighi Jamaat. The cell was connected to the radicals responsible for the 21 July 2005 attempted bombings, some of whom had attended sessions at Mohammed Hamid's house and the camping trips he had run in Cumbria.[47] They set off for their trip in May 2005, flying through Dubai to Somalia, and once there allegedly spent their time travelling between mosques and supposedly spreading the word of God. While it is unclear exactly what the men were up to, the fact that young men drawn from the milieu of the 21 July group were drawn to Somalia at this time is interesting, showing that it was clearly on the network's mind. Beyond the fact that two of the men convicted of attempting to detonate bombs in London in July were Somali, this second group's trip highlights the potential risk of the Somalia connection to Britain.

It was not until the video released by al-Shabaab in March 2008, however, that this threat started to make itself heard in the public domain. The insular 250,000-strong British Somali community was not forthcoming with information about those who were possibly going to fight in the Horn of Africa, and any stories were largely anecdotal and shrouded in rumour.[48] Then, in November 2010, the BBC broadcast an interview with a British–Somali woman who claimed that her brother, a biology graduate, had announced in late 2009 that he and a friend were travelling to Egypt to deepen their study of Islam. Leaving with few possessions, or explanations as to where he had got the money for this travel, the young man telephoned his family sporadically over the next year, saying first he was in Egypt and then later in Somalia. In mid September 2010, the family received word through his travelling companion that 'a flying missile' had killed him. The family had heard nothing more about his fate since that phone call, nor had they heard anything more about the friend who went with him to Egypt.[49] This sort of travel seems similar to that undertaken by previous generations of young men eager to fight back in their homelands. Just as the Kashmiri cause had drawn young British–Pakistanis, it now seemed as though Somalia was having a similar effect on young British Somalis. And while it is only recently that al-Shabaab has officially joined the al-Qaeda axis, security services have long worried about the connection.[50]

Initially, these concerns seemed to be focused around the fact that young Somalis were being drawn home to fight alongside al-Shabaab. The Ethiopian invasion in July 2006 heightened nationalist sentiments, and many were drawn back to protect their nations from the invading Ethiopian army (a long-standing enmity exists between Somalia, a Muslim nation, and Ethiopia, a largely Christian one). However, with the Ethiopian withdrawal in January 2009 this motivation became irrelevant, and this had a depressing effect on the general tenor of support for the fight in Somalia among diaspora communities. This was most clearly illustrated in telephone intercepts in August 2010 from an al-Shabaab linked case in Sweden: 'The diaspora helped us before, when the Ethiopians came, so that we could drive them away…because they hated Ethiopia so much…when they left, then came the Ugandans… but they hate the Ethiopians more than the Ugandans…they have never heard of the Ugandans…and now we get no help because they do not know what the war is about.'[51]

While nationalism was an important driver among the Somali community, the fight in Somalia was already attracting British fighters from beyond the diaspora. As we saw from the earlier case in May 2005, an ethnically mixed group was drawn to the country, and in early 2009 Kenyan authorities detected a pair trying to enter Somalia. The men, identified as Bilal Berjawi, a British-Lebanese national, and Mohammed Sakr, a British-Egyptian, had been to the country before and were friends with a British-Somali former train driver who was repeatedly detained by British and foreign security forces heading to Somalia. In one instance, he was stopped at Dubai airport in February 2007 with three mobile phones and $4,600 in cash. As he was being questioned he attempted to swallow a piece of paper with some numbers on it.[52] Part of a wider network of Britons going back and forth to Somalia during this period, his current status is unclear.

Much more is known about Bilal el Berjawi,[53] however, an important figure who was alleged to have been involved with senior al-Qaeda members who had been hiding in East Africa with al-Shabaab. Born in Beirut in September 1984, his parents brought him to the UK when he was a baby.[54] Raised in West London, he lived near an Egyptian family whose son, Mohammed Sakr, became his close friend.[55] Characterised as 'two peas in a pod' by fellow Somalia-based foreign jihadist Omar Hammami, the two men's stories are deeply intertwined.[56]

Little is known about Berjawi's youth and his family have shied away from the media in the wake of his death. In their martyrdom notice, al-Shabaab highlighted the fact that he was from West London.[57] He married a Somali girl with whom he later had a child after he had risen up the ranks of al-Qaeda in East Africa (AQEA).[58] According to al-Shabaab's martyrdom notice, he first 'embarked on the caravan of Jihad to protect the honor of Islam after arriving in Somalia in early 2006.'[59] According to a longer martyrdom notice that was published later as part of a series about 'Biographies of the flags of the Martyrs in East Africa' almost a year after his death, Berjawi was trained by senior al-Qaeda in East Africa figures Fazul Abdullah Mohammed and Saleh Ali Saleh Nabhan when he first arrived in Somalia.[60] Under the tutelage of these two, he seems to have flourished, though when the Islamic Courts withdrew, Berjawi was dispatched back to the United Kingdom to fundraise and find ways of sending money back to East Africa.[61] Members of the group praise him in this role, calling him 'brilliant' and allege that he set up many profitable projects for them.[62] According to his martyrdom video released by al-Kataib (al-Shabaab's media wing) soon after the publication of his biography, at some point during his time in London he returned to Lebanon.[63]

Back in London, in February 2009 Berjawi and Sakr headed to Kenya, telling their families their intention was to go on a 'safari.'[64] They were detained in Nairobi having stayed in a hotel in Mombasa where they 'aroused the suspicions of the hotel manager.'[65] Both were deported back to the UK (as British passport holders) and told different accounts of their actions to security officials who met them when they returned.[66] When Mohammed Sakr's father confronted his son about his actions, he told him 'Daddy, it's finished, it will never happen again. It's all done and dusted.'[67]

By October that year, the men decided to try to get back to Somalia, and this time evaded detection and slipped out of the country, along with a third man. According to the East African martyr biography, they had to travel through many countries before reaching Somalia.[68] In November, they were reported by Ugandan authorities as being at the heart of a manhunt for individuals who were allegedly plotting terrorist acts in the country.[69] The two are identified alongside a third British national named as Walla Eldin Abdel Rahman—a name that corresponds with British court documents and a figure alongside whom Mohammed Sakr was arrested in January 2009 at a protest outside the Israeli Embassy in London.[70] Berjawi in particular is identified as having three passports with him.[71]

According to the East African martyrs biography, having returned to Baidoa in Somalia, Berjawi joined a camp and trained diligently alongside others, undertaking 'difficult assignments'—a medical condition notwithstanding.[72] He is described as being supportive of his colleagues and a lover of battles. As time passes he seems to have assumed greater responsibilities, helping organise getting supplies to forces (like clothing and weapons) and to take on responsibility for tending to families left behind by fallen warriors.[73] In early 2010, Mohammed Sakr called his parents from Somalia to reassure them that he was ok.[74]

Later in 2010, a cell linked to al-Shabaab and believed to have been directed by AQEA, conducted a double suicide bombing in Kampala on two bars where people were enjoying the football World Cup final. The attack claimed some seventy lives. According to one report in the Ugandan press, Berjawi, Sakr and Rahman were detected entering the country in July 2010, though it remains unclear the exact role that they played (if any) in the Kampala attack.[75] By this point, Berjawi is repeatedly referred

WE LOVE DEATH AS YOU LOVE LIFE

to in the Ugandan press as being a direct deputy to Fazul Abdullah Mohammed—Fadil Harun—the head of al-Qaeda in East Africa,[76] though he also seems to have been close to others in al-Shabaab. Certainly his East African martyr biography identifies him as being in regular direct contact with Fazul, and even helping him get into Somalia at one point.[77] In September 2010, the British home secretary sent letters to Berjawi and Sakr's parents revoking their citizenships 'on grounds of conduciveness to the public good.'

On 25 June 2011 Berjawi was allegedly injured in a drone strike that may have been targeting Ibrahim al-Afghani, a senior figure in al-Shabaab.[78] This came two weeks after Fazul had taken a wrong turn down a road in Mogadishu and gone straight into a Transitional Federal Government roadblock. According to the East African martyrs biography, after being injured in the drone strike, Berjawi snuck into Kenya to recuperate with Sakr's assistance.[79]

It is unclear at what point Berjawi returned to Somalia, but by early 2012 he seems to have been back in the country, having assumed the mantel of leadership for AQEA from Fazul—though given he was injured so soon after Fazul's death it is not certain how much he would have actually been able to achieve. Nevertheless, this would have made him a target for the foreign intelligence services and, according to a video confession released by al-Kataib, it is at this time that unspecified foreign intelligence services recruited a young Somali named Isaac Omar Hassan to their side.[80] According to Hassan's video confession, he was recruited by the foreign services to plant a telephone in the car that Berjawi was in and turn it on when he was told to by his handlers to direct a drone strike against it. In Hassan's account, Berjawi was the first person that the handlers asked him about when they first spoke to him.[81]

Berjawi's significance within the East African networks highlighted how British nationals remained at the core of a variety of different battlefields. However, his active role in attack planning outside Somalia was never made that clear. Rumours of British nationals connected to plots from Somalia continued to emerge, however, with the clearest evidence of their involvement coming to the fore in early 2012, when it was revealed that a convert called Germaine Grant was on trial in Kenya for his involvement as part of an al-Shabaab linked cell planning an attack in Mombasa. Born in Newham, East London, Grant had converted to Islam while he in Feltham Young Offenders Institution on a rape charge (the same institution from which Richard Reid graduated and through which Muktar Said Ibrahim, leader of the 21 July cell, passed). On his release, he apparently travelled to Pakistan to train before being sent to Somalia to connect with al-Shabaab.[82] More surprising than Grant's arrest, was the revelation that, in parallel to arresting him, Kenyan authorities had been watching a pair of British women who they believed also had some connections with al-Shabaab. One of them was subsequently identified as Samantha Lewthwaite, the widow of the 7 July bomber Germaine Lindsay. Lewthwaite had disappeared after her husband's death, though it seems she had retained his contacts and stayed involved in radical circles. At the time of writing she was apparently still on the loose in Africa with at least one other British woman from Hounslow, and supposedly in possession of currency, detonators, and possibly her children, some of whom she had conceived with Germaine Lindsay.[83]

The path that had brought Grant and Lewthwaite to Somalia bore an increasingly strong correlation to that which had previously attracted so many young Britons to Pakistan. Somali preachers who would later appear alongside al-Shabaab were active among the British Muslim community—including a red-bearded and bespectacled preacher known as Abdulcaadir Mumin, a prominent al-Shabaab-linked preacher who spent some time speaking at mosques in East London, Greenwich, Leicester, and Woolwich.[84] Britain also increasingly became a source of radical material supporting al-Shabaab, with alqimmah.net (al-Shabaab's main website) allegedly run by individuals based in the United Kingdom. In an attempt to disrupt these networks, British security services moved in May 2008 to arrest two individuals in Leicester they assessed to be site administrators. Both men were ultimately cleared of the charges against them, though during the trial one of them was unrepentant about comments he had made online about the deaths of civilians. Openly supportive of the forces in Somalia trying to eject 'invader' forces from their country, the men had made videos with al-Shabaab and accumulated considerable amounts of radical material that they claimed they were going to bring to the fighters in Somalia.[85] One of them was also identified by Swedish security forces as having appeared in previous investigations into radical networks in their country, and when arrested was overheard asking police 'is it the British or Swedish police who want me? In Sweden we were active with the Islamic Courts. My friends are in Sweden.'[86] A UN Somalia Monitoring Group report from March 2010 claimed that subsequent to their release, one of the men had appeared on alqimmah.net participating in an online discussion about their experiences.[87]

The direct impact of these networks in Britain is unclear, although by 2010 it was increasingly obvious that they were providing at least the ideological backdrop, if not practical support, to young Britons who were trying to join al-Shabaab. In November 2010 a video was released by al-Shabaab that included an individual who used the *nom de guerre* of Abu Dujana and claimed to be from the United Kingdom. At around the same time, a Nigerian Briton called Michael Adebolajo, who had been on periphery of a number of investigations around the latest incarnation of Al-Muhajiroun, including brief detention at a protest organised by the group, appeared in Kenya. Along with a group of Kenyan radicals, Michael Adebolajo was trying to get to Somalia to join with al-Shabaab, answering the group's siren call.[88] He would later become infamous as one of the two responsible for the brutal murder of drummer Lee Rigby in Woolwich in May 2013. Back in 2010, however, all this activity came a month after the director general of MI5, Jonathan Evans, noted that there were a 'significant number of UK residents training in Shabaab camps. I am concerned that it is only a matter of time before we see terrorism on our streets inspired by those who are today fighting alongside the Shabaab.'[89] This 'jihadi tourism', as it was referred to in an official discussion between American and British officials in Addis Ababa in December 2009, was of particular concern to British officials, given the large number of Somalis with British passports then in Somalia or its surrounding regions for both legitimate or illegitimate reasons.[90] In May 2011 three Britons of Bangladeshi descent were detained by Kenyan authorities in Garissa county—the men claimed to be travelling to a destination that was not near their actual location.[91] And then in October 2011 a pair of eighteen year-olds, a British Somali and a British Pakistani from Cardiff, were apprehended by Kenyan authorities 5 km from the Somali border.[92]

The threat from Somalia has not yet truly materialised on Britain's streets, although the potential certainly exists for former fighters to return radicalised and cause problems similar to those seen in the Pakistani community. The similarities between the close diaspora connections—the disenfranchised second generation, the tendency to send troubled young men home to sort themselves out, and an Islamist jihadi group leading the fight in Somalia using a globalised rhetoric targeted at young

Western men—paints a very similar picture to that laid out above. Reflecting this potential threat, the British government added al-Shabaab to its list of proscribed terror groups. The Horn of Africa, in particular Somalia and, increasingly Kenya, have continued to be a focus of concern. The rationale behind this concern was crystallised in October 2013 when a video emerged by al-Shabaab which featured a British narrator, eulogising Michael Adebolajo's act and listing a number of British nationals identified as having died fighting alongside al-Shabaab. The group called for people to rise up and emulate Adebolajo's act, as well as suggesting that the ongoing connection between the UK and Somalia remained strong.[93]

The internet

Another threat that has matured is that of the internet serving as a nexus between dangerous radical ideas, training, and the community of young aspirant warriors in the West and United Kingdom in particular. While radicalisation in what one might term the traditional sense has continued in Britain for many years, with an unknown number of young men leaving to train or fight alongside groups abroad, since the beginning of the decade there has been an incremental growth in groups' and individuals' use of the internet to promote radical ideas and to prepare for terrorist activity. As we saw in earlier in this book, the United Kingdom had long been a home for radical websites supportive of al-Qaeda and affiliate groups—in the early 1990s the Islamic Gateway (www.ummah.org.uk) was set up, providing an online home to a number of radical British groups, as well as providing links and information on the Taliban, Osama bin Laden and others. By the mid-2000s, the British security services began to note the increasing importance of the internet as a vehicle to supplement and even displace extremist forums in mosques, bookshops and community centres that until now had seemed the loci of radicalisation in the United Kingdom.

On 19 October 2005, police in Bosnia made a pair of arrests that uncovered a network of extremists with links in Britain. The first strand for British investigators came after Bosnian police burst into a house on the outskirts of Sarajevo that they believed was linked to a radical individual known as Maximus. There they discovered two young men, Mirsad Bektasevic and Abdulkadir Cesur, who were both armed and aggressive.

Bektasevic, aged eighteen at the time of arrest, was born to Serbian parents, but was brought up in Sweden where, according to his mother, he converted to Islam and fell under the spell of local radicals. Abdulkadir, aged twenty at the time, was born to Turkish parents in Denmark. The two men were found to be in possession of weaponry, explosives, a suicide belt and a video that appeared to show them preparing an attack on a nearby NATO base, with a voiceover intoning:

These brothers are ready to attack and, God willing, they will attack the non-Muslims who are killing our brothers and Muslims in Iraq, Afghanistan, Chechnya and in many other countries. These weapons will be used against Europe, against those whose forces are in Iraq and Afghanistan... We are here and we are planning and we have everything ready. This is a message for you.[94]

Bosnian police picked up a further three men afterwards and charged them with helping the young men obtain their weapons, but the most important leads proved to be those who went abroad. As investigators trawled through the men's mobile phone and computer records, they passed on details to their counterparts in Denmark, Sweden and the United Kingdom. Danish and Swedish forces immediately moved to disrupt pockets of extremists that were connected to the men, while in Britain police followed phone numbers provided by Bosnian police to addresses in London.[95] The Metropolitan Police acted swiftly and on 21 October moved on addresses in Bayswater, Chatham and Shepherd's Bush. At the Chatham address they found Waseem Mughal, a twenty-two year-old British-born biochemistry graduate whom they suspected was the head of the network that they had uncovered with links to the Bosnia-based extremists. Mughal, of Pakistani descent, had excelled at a degree in biochemistry at the University of Leicester, obtaining a first class degree, and had served as administrator for the university's Islamic Society website. His CV boasted a capacity to fix and troubleshoot computer problems, and he was in the process of applying for a Master's degree.[96]

Across town in Shepherd's Bush police burst in on Younis Tsouli as he was in the process of tinkering with a website he had designed called YouBombIt, a version of the file-sharing site YouSendIt, changing the tagline to 'The jihadi's favourite uploader online'.[97] Tsouli was a twenty-two-year-old Moroccan national who had moved to the United Kingdom in September 2001 with his family, and in August 2005 had been granted a residence permit with indefinite leave to stay. He had had a transient childhood, born in Casablanca, Morocco, before moving to the US as a child. Following America, the family spent some time back in Morocco, before moving to Brussels, where they stayed for three years and where Tsouli attended school. In 1994, at the age of eleven, the family returned to Morocco, this time staying in the country for seven years, allowing Tsouli finally to put down roots. According to his defence lawyer, and presumably based upon interviews with him, it was during this period that:

He became increasingly interested in Muslim world affairs. He came to learn and genuinely believe that Muslims around the world were being subjected to widespread and systemised persecution, suppression and brutalisation at the hands of various Western powers and those Governments allied to them. He also came to a genuinely held belief that the same powers, via their media interests, were painting for the world a deliberately false picture of that oppression.[98]

Having started down this path, in September 2001 Younis was uprooted once again when his father got a job in London; the student enrolled at the Westminster College of Computing, attending and completing his course in June 2004.[99] Somewhere along the way he discovered Omar Bakri Mohammed and started attending camps and sessions run by the preacher, including one at which he met one of the young men later arrested in Denmark.

Police were stumped at the final address, where they expected to find Tariq al-Daour, a young and recently naturalised British citizen who had been born in the United Arab Emirates and was in the process of applying to do a law degree in Britain. However, having heard about the arrests, and aware that police were looking for him, the following day al-Daour contacted a lawyer and handed himself in to the authorities.

All three men were still living with their parents at the time of arrest, their youthful nature reflected in al-Daour's willingness to hand himself over to authorities, and in the first instance police seemed to think that the focal point of the cell was Waseem Mughal. He appeared to provide the connection between the three, as it emerged that al-Daour and Tsouli had in fact never met or spoken. As police started investigating what they found at the men's properties, and crucially on their computers, they realised that it was in fact Tsouli who was the prize catch. Without realising it, British police had intercepted an infamous online jihadist who used the handle Irhabi007 (*irhabi* is Arabic for 'terrorist'). Irhabi007 had become something of a celebrity among the community of online jihadis and supporters, famed for his abilities to get material from al-Qaeda in

Iraq onto web forums and accessible to the world. He was responsible
for disseminating the video of the beheading of American contractor
Nicholas Berg, a video that marked the crossing of a new threshold by
Abu Musab al-Zarqawi's al-Qaeda in Iraq (AQI). His work was so
respected by the group that in October 2004 Abu Maysara al-Iraqi, considered one of al-Zarqawi's closest aides, praised Irhabi007 in a posting,
saying, 'Bless the terrorist, Irhabi 007. In the name of Allah, I am pleased
with your presence my beloved brother. May Allah protect you.'[100]

Assessments by online terrorist trackers pointed to Irhabi007 being
an important figure in AQI's online presence in particular, both as a poster
and disseminator of material, but also as an administrator of the AQI
supportive online forum al-Ansar.[101] In September 2005 Mirsad
Bektasevic posted a rambling declamation against the West under the
banner of 'Al Qaeda in Northern Europe', to which Irhabi007 responded,
'blood, blood and destruction'.[102] Long discussions were found on his
computer between Bektasevic and Tsouli, and when police raided the
Shepherd's Bush flat they discovered that Bektasevic's number was the
last one called by Tsouli's number. Mughal appears to have played something of a subsidiary role to Tsouli, though he was clearly good with computers, making him an invaluable supporter. He was also in direct contact with Bektasevic, with his phone number in his possession on arrest
and having had online conversations with him. A fluent Arabic speaker,
Mughal was also involved in helping translate some materials from terrorist organisations to make them more accessible to a non-Arabic speaking audience.

Mughal's greatest contribution, however, was in supporting Tsouli's
online activity in support of AQI by helping to source funding. All the
video posting activity, for instance, required investment in web hosting.
And the cell was remarkably efficient at obtaining its funding through
illicit means. Through stolen credit cards and online fraud, the men
ensured a stream of revenue to keep themselves online—as well as bringing Tariq al-Daour into the network. A year younger than the other
men, al-Daour was deeply involved in another online jihadist forum,
At-Tibyan publications, which he claimed to run with 'three other brothers'.[103] An important forum, the At-Tibyan site was a major draw for
young Western radicals who found there an active online community
ascribing to violent Islamist ideals. But within Tsouli's group it was
other online connections that were more important. Al-Daour would

apparently pass information and credit card details to Mughal, who would forward them on to Tsouli. But while Mughal knew why Tsouli was using the money, it is unclear that al-Daour was aware of why he was gathering it, although the anonymous nature of the internet complicates any sort of clear assessment.

In arresting Tsouli and his immediate cell, British police deprived al-Qaeda in Iraq of its most valuable online administrator. They had been alerted to Irhabi007's presence prior to his arrest, in March 2004, after online activists had tracked him to Ealing, London. Their efforts had angered Tsouli, to the point that he had posted a message requesting that if someone killed his pursuers, 'I get to keep a finger or an ear. A little souvenir.' Eager to stop a person they saw as a key online supporter of al-Qaeda, the online trackers, led by an individual named Aaron Weisburd, passed the information on to UK police.[104] At that time it seems likely the latter were over-extended addressing the threat of Operation Crevice (the fertiliser bomb plotters) and the subsequent threat of Operation Rhyme (around Dhiren Barot), and so the information was not followed up. However, once they unravelled the case in 2005–6, they opened the doors to an online network of extremists that crossed the United Kingdom, Europe and North America. A video of sites in the US found on Tsouli's computer linked him to a pair of young men in Georgia, who in turn were in contact with a cell of extremists in Canada.[105] The video was also found in the possession of Aabid Hussein Khan, a twenty-two-year-old British Kashmiri living in Bradford, who was later identified as being a key player and coordinator for the Canadian cell and who had met with one of the young Georgian plotters in Pakistan.[106]

Khan, a young man who was already a career extremist at the age of twenty-two, seems to have played a crucial role in the broader network subsequently uncovered. Described by Crown Prosecution Service prosecutor Karen Jones as the 'Mr Fix-it' of the network, Khan had links to extremist groups in Pakistan (he claimed to have contacts with Lashkar-e-Taiba and Jaish-e-Mohammed) and was an administrator for the At-Tibyan publications websites. From his bedroom in Bradford, Khan reached out to a network of young radicalised individuals, and in some cases ushered them further down the path of radicalisation or helped them attempt to contact active extremists in his native Pakistan. In Canada he connected with a group of young men who were planning a bombing campaign in Toronto, marshalling them further in their plotting, and in the US he contacted Syed Haris Ahmed and Ehsanul Sadequee, the two men who had made the video footage that was found in both Khan and Tsouli's possession. Syed Ahmed was particularly keen to go and fight jihad in South Asia, and in August 2005 arranged to meet Khan in Pakistan. However, Ahmed arrived in combat trousers, conspicuously acting the part of young aspirant jihadi he hoped to become. Demonstrating a security savvy that appeared to correspond with his importance in the eyes of individuals linked to LeT and JeM, Khan quickly realised that Ahmed was likely to attract negative attention, consequently refusing to take him to his extremist contacts.[107] Ahmed returned to Atlanta, Georgia, was quizzed by agents on his return, and was later arrested by the FBI.[108]

In other cases, Khan seems to have used the internet to motivate others whom he had identified as being susceptible to the extremist narrative. Through the At-Tibyan websites, he found in Alva, Scotland, an aimless and dim youth called Mohammed Atif Siddique, a young second-generation Pakistani who used to try to impress his friends with wild claims about having met Osama bin Laden and saying he was plotting an attack in Glasgow city centre.[109] In regular contact with Khan online, chats between the two men seemed to indicate that Khan was 'grooming' Siddique towards further action. What Mohammed Siddique had in mind when he and his uncle set off to the airport for a trip to Pakistan on 5 April 2006 is unclear, but the pair were stopped, searched and turned back by police. Further investigation of Siddique's computer and other electronic material found at his house and school showed that he had helped establish a number of websites, including one called 'Al-Battar' (the name of a mythical sword in Islam), another called 'Mu'askar AlBattar' (the Al-Battar training camp), and a final one called 'Sawt al-Jihad' (Voice of Jihad). The websites had links and copies of al-Qaeda magazines, many of them in Arabic (a language that Siddique did not appear properly to understand).[110]

Closer to home, Khan had also drawn around himself a two-man cell of Mohammed Sultan and Hammad Munshi. Sultan, Khan's cousin, was from the same part of Pakistan as Khan, an area called Attock in the North West Frontier Province (NWFP), and also lived very near him in Bradford. A postal worker, he seems to have been very supportive of Khan's activity, travelling around the United Kingdom with him visiting other extremist friends, paying Khan's way, and acting as his driver to and from the airport as he went to Canada and Pakistan on extremist activity. He was present in Pakistan at the same time as Khan from June to September 2005. Prior to this trip, the two men purchased some replica AK-47 guns, though it is unclear what they did with them. Sultan also introduced Khan to other individuals whom he suspected would be supportive of their activity.[111] One such young man was Hammad Munshi, the teenage grandson of a prominent Dewsbury Shariah court judge. Munshi and Khan met first in January 2005 at a mosque in Dewsbury where the young men were all praying together.[112]

The encounter would prove to be a fateful moment for Khan, and it was this that would earn him subsequent notoriety in the press. Arrested when only sixteen years old while returning home from sitting a GCSE chemistry exam, Hammad Munshi has the dubious honour of being the youngest person to be convicted for terrorism offences in Britain. Online discussions between Khan and Hammad revealed the two discussing how to smuggle swords past airport security, and Hammad prepared documents about how to make napalm that Sultan then shared with Khan. A note found under his bed read: 'One who is not taking part in the battle nor has the sheer intention to die is in the branch of hypocrisy…I don't want to be a person like it has been mentioned about, I don't want to be deprived of the huge amounts or lessons Allah has prepared for the believers in the hereafter.'[113] However, what pushed young Hammad in this direction is unclear to most of those who knew him, including the presiding judge in his case, who cast much of the blame for Hammad's activity on Khan. As the judge put it, 'Were it not for Aabid Khan's malign influence, I doubt whether this offence would ever have been committed.'

The At-Tibyan website of which Khan was an administrator also provided links to a number of other individuals who were convicted of terrorist activity. Yassin Nassari, an Ealing-born man of Belizean and Moroccan heritage, was at Luton Airport with his Dutch–Syrian wife and their young child. In his luggage was a computer hard-drive with details of how to fabricate Qassam rockets from car parts, and a letter purportedly from his wife that seemed to support his desire for jihad and martyrdom. A campus activist who ran the Islamic society at the Harrow branch of Westminster University, Nassari had undergone a transformation following a period in which he disappeared from his cognitive sciences course in 2002–3. Returning to university, his appearance had taken a more religious aspect, and he seems to have become increasingly involved in the university's Islamic Society, inviting along prominent anti-establishment Muslim speakers like Yvonne Ridley and Abdul Raheem Green to an event he had organised entitled 'Weapons of Media Deception'. When he was stopped at Luton Airport, he had just passed through Holland on a journey that he claimed had started in Syria, where he was learning Arabic. While trawling through his computer records, police ascertained that he was also in contact with Tariq al-Daour, Younis Tsouli's money man who had supplied him with credit cards and who claimed to be an administrator of the At-Tibyan forum. Nassari and al-Daour had apparently conversed online through the forum and had shared radical material.[114] Unlike many fellow Britons convicted for such crimes, Nassari was taken down waving his fist in the air in triumph while blowing a kiss to his wife.

This disparate set of cells was disrupted from 2005 onwards, at a time when the internet was increasingly receiving attention as a purveyor of radical ideas. In early 2008, a series of postings on the password-protected Al-Ekhlaas web forum ('sincerity' in Arabic) once again drew the threat to the British public's attention. The first posting appeared on 2 January and purported to be the 'declaration of the creation of the Al Qaeda organisation in Britain'. It outlined the group's goals as 'the elimination of political leaders and top of the list Blair and Brown' and 'huge attacks, God willing, on centres and places of benefit to the crusaders'. Later that same month a second posting appeared, this time from 'Shaykh Umar Rabie al-Khalaila' the leader of 'Al Qaeda in Britain'; the threat demanded the 'complete withdrawal of the British troops from Afghanistan and Iraq' and 'to free all Muslim captives from Belmarsh prison' including 'foremost of them Shaykh Abu Qatada al-Filistini and Shaykh Abu Hamza al-Misri'.[115] This second posting, dated 23 January, put a specific timeline to its response, claiming that if these demands were not answered by the end of March, 'the martyrdom seekers of the organisation of Al Qaeda in Britain will target all the political leaders especially Tony Blair and Gordon Brown, and we will also target all Embassies, Crusaders Centers and their interests throughout the country, with the help of Allah'.[116]

These threats were publicly dismissed by the security community in the United Kingdom: 'this is the stuff we get all the time, background noise … in other circumstances you might regard this person as a bit of a fantasist'.[117] Nevertheless, security services did launch an investigation to try to uncover who was behind the threats and ascertain how serious they might be about there being a genuine organisation known as 'al-Qaeda in Britain'. As it emerged, the threat emanated from Blackburn-born Ishaq Kanmi, a twenty-two-year-old second-generation Pakistani who had written the posts while sitting in Blackburn public library. Later described in court as a 'friendless' child whose 'life was dominated by a strict fundamentalist view of Islam', Kanmi 'had little or no play and recreation in his formative years' at a local private Islamic school.[118]

At the time of his arrest, Kanmi was not completely isolated and was in contact with a group of local Muslims who portrayed themselves as the 'Blackburn Resistance'. Brothers Abbas and Ilyas Iqbal, alongside Muhammad Ali Ahmad (a Caucasian convert who found Islam in 2004, changing his name from Paul Cryer), filmed themselves running through a local park in commando gear and shooting weapons in their garden. This footage was then cut and overlaid with Islamic songs (*nasheeds*), while a voice-over at the beginning intoned, 'They are fighting against oppression, they are the Blackburn Resistance.' Police were alerted to the men after Abbas was stopped at the airport with Ishaq Kanmi as the two were going on a trip to Finland. A *hafiz al Koran* (one who has memorised the Koran), Kanmi was apparently a regular traveller to Finland, although on this occasion when police started to search their belongings they found a mobile phone storage card which had on it pictures and videos of the men acting the part of jihadis. Having stopped them from leaving the country, police then started to search their properties, and at the Iqbals' discovered a cache of radical material, as well as a cupboard full of weaponry (numerous air rifles, knives, machetes, a sword, a cross-bow, various ammunition, books on weaponry and handwritten notes on 'Attack planning' and 'Urban combat'). Abbas' brother Ilyas was picked up soon afterwards, along with Mohammed Ali Ahmad, and a further quantity of radical material was found in their possession.

Nevertheless, the entire case received little serious attention in the public eye. The videos the men had made of themselves had a clownish air to them, and the prosecutor warned the jury, 'Some of the material may at first blush seem almost comical in its amateurishness.'[119] It was very hard to imagine that four rather simple young chaps operating out of Blackburn Library and a local park could really constitute some sort of terrorist threat. The weaponry and films they had made were unimpressive at best, and it seems as though they no connections to anyone of great import. The problem is that through the internet they did seem to connect with someone who might constitute a genuine threat: Krenar Lusha, an Albanian refugee who had entered Britain hiding in the back of a lorry and who had apparently answered Ishaq Kanmi's call for martyrs. As police went through Kanmi's computers and phones they found evidence of contact with Lusha, including online conversations that aroused their concerns. When they went to his house in Derby at 7.30am on 27 August they found him in the middle of downloading a Hezbollah terrorist video, and on searching his property discovered 2kg of potassium nitrate, 71 litres of petrol, fourteen mobile telephones and computers and hard-drives with extremist videos and training films of how to make explosives and mobile phone detonators. Described by police as a 'lone wolf' who 'was off everybody's radar', Lusha claimed to have first come to Britain in 2000 with his brother 'in the back of a wagon'.[120] Their journey started in Albania where he and his brother Ndriqim paid a smuggler $7,000 to get them to the United Kingdom. They were apparently abandoned and spent the next three weeks tracking across Europe via Belgium. Once in Britain they presented themselves to the Home Office and were eventually helped to go to Derby, where they appear to have settled in to low-level lives as factory workers and mechanics.

It is unclear how and when Lusha acquired his taste for extremist material. He claimed to have studied Arabic and Islam as a child in Qatar, and told police that since 2002 he had been studying Arabic to learn the Koran, and that the war in Iraq had made him more religious; but that 'I respect religion. In practice it is not true. My religion was work because all the time I was at work.'[121] This was belied somewhat by his many online postings about extremism and his avid enthusiasm for downloading such material. Furthermore, investigation of his computer uncovered long conversations with women around the world whom he had met on Muslim dating forums where he boasted about his capacities as a sniper and the pleasure he derived from killing Jews and Americans. In court Lusha argued that his actions had merely aimed to attract women, as he put it, 'sometimes women like a kind of Rambo man'.[122] This entire side of Lusha was repeatedly described as being a huge surprise to his neighbours and co-workers, all of whom described him as a pleasant and personable individual. But the jury did not find his explanation adequate, and Lusha was sentenced to seven years' imprisonment to be followed by deportation back to Albania.

Lone Wolves

The case of Krenar Lusha highlights the phenomenon of the 'Lone Wolf' and its frequent connection with the internet. Certainly in Lusha's case it appears that the online world facilitated and even accelerated his radicalisation; though given his somewhat opaque responses and continued denial of activity, it is hard to know exactly what was going on. But it was a much clearer factor in the separate cases of Nicholas Roddis, Nicky 'Mohammed Abdulaziz Rashid Saeed-Alim' Reilly and Andrew 'Isa' Ibrahim, three young men who attempted to cause public disorder using the guise of Islamist extremism. In all three cases, the men were converts to Islam and for all three the internet played a role in their radicalisation. However, unlike many of the other individuals listed so far as violent extremists, these men appear to have had no direct real-world connections to active radicals (police suspected Reilly may have had contact with extremists locally, but no one was charged), meaning that they largely fit, like Krenar Lusha, into the 'Lone Wolf' category of aspirant terrorists.

Before proceeding further into the description of these specific cases, it is worth defining the term 'Lone Wolf' more clearly. A 'Lone Wolf' within the context of terrorism is an individual who attempts to carry out an act of random violence using a mask of political justification as his or her driving motivation. This is a group separate from individuals like Richard Reid, who attempted to carry out his attack alone; he would more likely fall into the category of 'lone attacker'. Lone wolves, on the other hand, appear to have no direct contact with active cells of extremists or other radicals, or if they do, it tends to be through the internet. As the United Kingdom came to terms with the threat from organised groups plotting acts of mass terror, it appeared as though the 'Lone Wolf' terrorist had increased his capacity to plot and attempt to carry out acts of terrorism. This threat is likely to continue to grow in the future.

Three early 'Lone Wolf' cases show the nature of the first expressions of this threat in the UK: Nicholas Roddis, Nicky 'Mohammed Abdulaziz Rashid Saeed-Alim' Reilly and Andrew 'Isa' Ibrahim. All three men claimed at some point to be converts to Islam, and all three attempted or appeared to be on the road to carrying out acts of public disorder in the name of their interpretation of violent Islamism. Crucially, it did not appear as though any of them had any substantial connections in the real world to extremists or radicals who might drive forward their activity. In fact, they appeared for the most part to be a set of unfortunate young men whose lives appeared to be going nowhere and who appear to have been drawn towards the ideas of violent extremism by a blend of curiosity and naivety. They are by no means the only such individuals who became involved in this kind of activity and who might fit the profile, but they show the very varied nature of the potential threat from 'Lone Wolf' types of attackers.

The first of the three to achieve public fame was Nicholas Roddis, who on 8 May 2007 got onto the Maltby–Rotherham bus wearing 'an obviously false beard and glasses' and carrying a plastic bag in which he had placed a few bags of sugar wrapped with tape, wires, nails and an alarm clock. In addition to this rather crude attempt at a fake bomb, he added a note in poor Arabic that said: 'There is no God but Allah. Mohammed is the messenger of Allah, God is great. God is great. God is great. Britain much [sic?] be punished. Signed the Al Qaeda organisation of Iraq.'[123]

When other passengers on the bus examined the bag and found the fake device, they were naturally concerned. Police and bomb disposal units were called in and around fifty houses had to be evacuated while they dealt with the device. No one was apprehended for the crime, but police did pick up a woman they suspected of involvement. A couple of months after this incident, in the first week of July, Roddis showed up at the loan company he used to work at in Sheffield wearing a *keffiyeh* and showing off what he claimed were live ammunition and landmine detonators; in fact they were replica bullets and railway fog signals. When he returned a week later for a job interview, his former employer saw him with a bag and was so concerned that he called the police and evacuated the building.[124] Roddis was picked up and police searched his bedsit in Rotherham, where they found hydrogen peroxide, acetone, fuse wire, radical material he had downloaded, as well as notes he had written on how to make explosives and possible targets in his neighbourhood. Watching this scene from the wall was a large poster of Abu Musab al-Zarqawi, al-Qaeda in Iraq's infamous terrorist leader who was responsible for a number of the beheading videos that were discovered on Roddis' computer.[125]

An average-looking young white man, there was very little about Roddis that suggested he had embraced the radical Islamist message in any serious theological way. He used apparently to hang around Muslims at work, showing off beheading videos he had found online and declaring how terrible US policy was in the Middle East towards 'brothers and sisters'. Somewhere along the line he had apparently claimed to be a convert. But there was little tangible evidence of this and in court the judge largely blamed his actions on personal demons stemming from his parents' divorce and his inability to form social relationships.[126] In court Roddis denied he had ever claimed to be a convert, and afterwards police made a statement in which they highlighted that 'he knew next to nothing about the true nature of Islam and had not been converted to the faith by any person or group'.[127] In justifying his actions, Roddis had little to offer, beyond saying that 'It was just a practical joke. I was bored, I'd lost my job and had nothing to do … I never really thought of the consequences of it.'[128]

Nevertheless, he managed to obtain two of the three ingredients required to make HMTP explosive (acetone and hydrogen peroxide) and admitted to having made efforts to obtain the third: acid. Whether he would have carried through to a terrorist act was unclear, but in the run-up to his conviction, police in Bristol and Exeter were shocked to discover two remarkably similar individuals in their communities who had moved even further down the path towards action than Roddis. On 17 April police in Bristol arrested Andrew 'Isa' Ibrahim, a young convert with a biscuit tin of HMTP in his fridge and advanced plans for carrying out a suicide attack on a local shopping centre. Police had started investigating Ibrahim in the wake of a local community tip-off to a Special Branch officer. Individuals at the mosque were concerned about the fact that Ibrahim had shown up with severe burns and cuts on his hands and was apparently espousing radical ideas. The locals believed that Ibrahim might already be in possession of some explosives and warned police officers of their concerns, setting off an operation to follow the young man. When they located him wandering around the streets, they found he was wearing a rucksack, sparking off further concerns that he might be in the middle of an operation. It emerged that these concerns were exaggerated, and when they grabbed him off the street they did not discover explosives, but instead a USB around his neck laden with radical material. Following up on this investigation they searched his home and there discovered the biscuit tin of explosives in the fridge, and also a suicide vest hanging behind the door as well as tubs of nails, ball bearings and empty bottles of peroxide. Further examination of Ibrahim's telephone revealed a video of him attempting an experiment with some explosives in his room, and police revealed that the flat was covered in hydrogen peroxide residue, evidence of his attempting to make different forms of explosive. Extensive notes were discovered on his phone of the layout of a local shopping mall, which when paired with video footage of him walking around the mall constituted evidence of detailed reconnaissance of his desired target.

Nineteen years old at the time of his arrest, Ibrahim was born a Christian in Bristol to an Egyptian Coptic father and a British mother. His father was a doctor in the affluent Bristol suburb of Frenchay. In what was described by a senior police officer involved in the investigation as 'a perfect example of nature versus nurture', Ibrahim's brother, six years his elder, graduated from Oxford University and got a good job at a City law firm, while Ibrahim got expelled from good schools, became involved in steadily stronger drugs, was obsessed with computer games, and eventually took to selling the *Big Issue* charity magazine in Bristol's city centre.[129] His parents attempted to support him, by paying his rent and backing his various decisions to find some direction, but Ibrahim appears to have rejected all offers of assistance, choosing instead to pursue a variety of obsessive habits. Starting to dabble in drugs at twelve years old by smoking cannabis, he moved up through his teens to injecting heroin and smoking crack cocaine. He later appears to have tried steroids, and developed fixations with computer games, rave music, women's feet, and finally Islamist extremism and terrorism. By his own account, in the summer of 2006 at around the anniversary of the 7 July bombings he converted at the Green Lane Mosque in Birmingham on a visit there with a family friend, though this account is not corroborated by individuals working at the mosque who said they could not find anyone who recognised Ibrahim.[130]

This apparently confused story supports Ibrahim's general approach to his religion, which he seems to have adopted somewhat sporadically. A fellow local drug addict, Jack Everson, to whom Ibrahim was selling his prescription of methadone, recounted how Ibrahim had made him watch videos of Osama bin Laden, expecting him to be 'impressed' and 'find it cool'. Everson reported how Ibrahim used to alternate between wearing Islamic garb and tracksuits, 'depending on how he wanted people to perceive him and how he perceived himself'.[131] According to Ibrahim himself, he could not get more than five chapters into the Koran, focusing instead on the political side that interested him more and made it 'more likely he would stick at it'.[132] Ibrahim was apparently impressed by online preachers like Omar Bakri Mohammed and Abu Hamza, and watched the 7 July bombers and the Tel Aviv pair's videos repeatedly. When he was arrested he was both both fearful and boastful in equal measure, saying, 'my mum's going to kill me' and asking whether he could be 'sent to Belmarsh'—the high security prison where many prominent Islamists, including his apparent idol Abu Hamza, are held.[133]

Ibrahim was a 'Lone Wolf' figure who claimed to have decided to construct a suicide vest as something to keep him busy and away from drugs. Taking himself a step further than Nicholas Roddis, who appeared to have only assembled material and expressed some interest in converting, Ibrahim was seen as an alarming case of how jihadist ideas had ingrained themselves in the United Kingdom. When the case first came to light the focus for the government, however, was that the initial tip-off into Ibrahim's activity had come from members of the local Muslim community in Bristol, who expressed concern about this new figure in their midst. The case was taken as a textbook case of how the government's Prevent strategy was working and how at last the tide was turning towards confronting the terrorist threat.

The problems in the system were rudely highlighted a month later when, on 22 May, Nicky 'Mohammed Abdulaziz Rashid Saeed-Alim' Reilly walked into a Giraffe chain restaurant in Exeter armed with a rucksack containing stacks of nails and three glass bottles of caustic soda and paraffin. He stopped at the bar to order a drink before going to the toilet where he closed himself into one of the cubicles to assemble his bomb. Fortunately for the customers at Princesshay Centre on that spring day, Reilly was unable to get back out of the cubicle in time and his improvised device instead blew up in his face injuring only him and simply scaring all the customers in the restaurant. When an ambulance arrived, he allowed himself to be taken away to hospital where he quite baldly told shocked investigators that he had attempted to detonate a bomb. In his room at his mother's house they located further evidence of this, including a hand-written note explaining the motivation behind Reilly's action:

In the name of God most gracious, most merciful: why I did it.

Everywhere Muslims are suffering at the hands of Britain, Israel and America. We are sick of taking all the brutality from you.

You have imprisoned over 1,000 Muslims in Britain alone in your war on Islam.

You torture and destroy Muslim lives by taking a father or a son or a brother, even you torture Muslim women.

In Britain it's OK for a girl to have sex without marriage and if she gets pregnant she can get an abortion so easily.

When you are getting drunk on Friday and Saturday night your behaviour is worse than animals.

You have sex in nightclub toilets. You urinate in shop doorways. You shout your foul and disgusting mouth off in the street.

It is unacceptable to Allah and the true religion Islam. Britain and USA and Israel have no real rules.

All us Muslims have seen the pictures of Abu Ghraib prison in Iraq, and you all know what you do to our brothers in Guantanamo Bay.

Sheikh Usama has told you the solution on how to end this war between us and many others have as well but you ignore us.

Our words are dead until we give them life with our blood. Leave our lands and stop your support for Israel.

I have not been brainwashed or indoctrinated. I am not insane.

I am not doing it to escape a life of problems or hardships. I am doing what God wants from his mujahideen. We love death as you love life.

Muslims welcome death because we will get *jennah*, *inshallah*, for defending the weak and oppressed Muslims.

You kill one of my people, I kill one of yours.

I have simply seen for myself the brutality and corruption of America, Britain and Israel for myself and my common sense told me it is unacceptable and wrong.

The word is the word of the sword until the wrongs have been righted.[134]

Such language was alien to his family and friends, who while noting his allegiance to Islam, broadly described him as a simple figure in their community. Nicknamed the 'big friendly giant' or 'BFG' (after Roald Dahl's fictional character), Nicky Reilly was born in 1986 to a dysfunctional Plymouth family. His younger brother Luke was imprisoned for six years in February 2008 for robbing and violently kicking unconscious a Polish man, while his mother's partner was remanded in custody for selling heroin to undercover officers in January 2009. The area they lived in was so known for trouble that a neighbour commented that he thought 'it was just another police drugs raid' when local police raided Reilly's residence after his attempt.[135] Reilly, however, was apparently largely omitted from such public misdemeanour, and what difficulty he did get into tended to be in the form of self-harm or stemming from his Asperger's Syndrome and obsessive compulsive tendencies. His mother described how in his mid-teens 'He started self-harming, but then self-harming became the obsession. He'd sometimes go to school and pop into a chemist and buy paracetamol, and take them; cutting—cutting his wrists— buying drink and cutting, so he wouldn't feel the pain. He was contemplating suicide all the time and it was destroying us all.'[136] This led to him being sectioned for his own health and to a session in 2003 with a psychiatrist in which he claimed he wanted to study engineering so he could learn how to make a bomb. Local Special Branch were alerted to these comments by the hospital, but the assessment was that 'this was thought to have been a one-off comment', and that an approach to Reilly might have exacerbated the situation rather than simply letting it fade away.[137]

It was around this time that Reilly converted and in 2004 changed his name to Mohammed Abdulaziz Rashid Saeed-Alim, the name under which he was eventually charged. As with many others who suffer from Asperger's, Reilly was obsessive about his newfound religious faith, and his mother dismissed it: 'In my heart I always believed that it [Islam] was another hobby, another fad, and he'd go onto something else: move on from it.'[138] However, it seems as though he rapidly developed an interest in extremism; it is even possible that part of the reason he developed an interest in the religion was for its violent side. And while it seems as though he may have made contact with elements who were believed by local police to be on the more radical end of the spectrum, the fact that no one else was convicted alongside him suggests that if these connections did exist they were at best circumstantial.[139] As the case progressed, it increasingly seemed that the main radicalising driver in Reilly's case was the community of extremists he encountered on the internet. His YouTube page in particular, which he ran under the name Chechen233, attracted the interest of a pair of radical individuals with whom in early 2008 he shared ideas and plans for carrying out an attack. During his comments summarising the case, Justice Calvert-Smith characterised the discussions as being about 'what sort of person should be targeted in due course, whether public servants such as police officers or other public servants or ordinary citizens. In the end the decision was made to target ordinary citizens in a restaurant.' These contacts appear also to have given him ideas about what kind of a device to construct, and over the next few months 'He [Reilly] bought more than necessary equipment over those months to construct two types of improvised devices, one using caustic soda and the other kerosene.'[140]

The Muslim community in Plymouth is quite small: at the time of the 2001 census it was officially 800, but this number is believed to have swollen to a few thousand in the wake of substantial migrations of Kosovans and Kurds. Others in the community regularly spotted Reilly hanging around Kurdish shops or chatting to Muslim friends in the city, which was not so surprising given the noticeable factors of his size and status as a white convert—a rarity in that particular community. Local mosque leaders recognised Reilly and found him to be a polite and serious character full of questions about his chosen religion. Two days before his attack, Reilly was spotted at the Islamic Cultural and Community Centre in Plymouth, where he was intently examining the Koran.[141] None of them appear to have suspected the path upon which he was embarking, but there was nonetheless a local backlash in the wake of the attack. One report mentioned a Kurdish youth in the local community being heckled in the street with taunts of 'suicide bomber',[142] while another alleged that many had stopped attending the local Plymouth Islamic centre for fear of becoming tarnished by the investigation into Reilly that was taking place.[143]

In many ways, it was this feedback loop of radicalisation and social tensions they helped propagate that was Roddis, Ibrahim and Reilly's greatest contribution to the narrative of jihadism in Britain. None of the men can be considered to have felt in a particularly personal way the larger narrative that has been painted in this book. None of them was anywhere near the large migratory communities where radical ideas had been incubated around the country; none of them was born into Muslim families, or even into families of Middle Eastern or South Asian origin (Ibrahim is the exception to this, of course, but his Egyptian father married a British woman and he was a member of a Christian minority). In fact, none of them really had any contact with any of the extremist communities that have thus far been listed in the United Kingdom. Police may have suspected that Reilly was operating on the fringes of extremism in Plymouth, but this is more likely the product of it being a small community, and in any case no one was actually convicted or charged. Their closest connection to other radicals were online, though unlike the plots around Aabid Khan or Ishaq Kanmi that featured earlier, for Ibrahim, Roddis and Reilly it was a purely virtual relationship. While their expression of the threat through the lone actor style attack—in which undirected plotters carry out attacks against the West purposely distancing themselves from known networks to sneak past security services—became a key strategy that al-Qaeda-linked groups tried to advance subsequently, there was little evidence that it was ultimately connected to any of these three.

Nevertheless, the emergence of these three cases marked the nadir in the evolution of radical Islamist ideas in Britain. The individuals involved were affected by the ideology that was swirling around in society, without the need for direct contact with the influences that drove others towards the violent ideologies that led them to become involved in terrorist activity. Instead they appear to have chosen the ideology in order to lend their lives a sense of direction. They also seemed not to have needed the same real-world (as opposed to virtual) drivers and group dynamics that were encountered in many of the plots discussed earlier in this book. For these three young men, it was enough to imagine that they were connected to the world of radical Islamism through online communities and the hothouses of their own vivid imaginations. All three self-mobilised and indoctrinated themselves with the ideology of radical Islamism online and then converted this into reality by acquiring the necessary ingredients to transform what they found in cyberspace into devices to be used against the communities around them.

There is nothing in their stories to suggest that an extremist Islamist ideology was the only answer to the question that gave their lives a sudden direction. Had a fundamentalist Christian, Jewish or Hindu ideology—or even a leftist, right-wing or some other political faction—been as readily available and alluring, it might have served their purposes equally well. But at the time, as they sought ideas in a world from which they felt roundly rejected, the most pervasive and all-answering ideology they encountered was the extremist Islamist message offered by jihadist ideologues. The combination of an all-encompassing ideology, with the ready availability of messages from ideologues, and the ease with which the internet seemed to offer an immediate access into this world, all meant that three men whose lives were going nowhere could suddenly feel connected to something greater than themselves. In these cases it seems it was less Islamist ideology that had drawn them in, and more the broader outliers of jihadi culture that had emerged around that ideology that offered them the satisfying answers they were seeking. Jihad and jihadist ideas in the United Kingdom had now matured to the point that they were reaching far beyond their initial target community of born Muslims:

instead, troubled young men from across British society were and are being drawn in by the jihadist mindset and broader jihadi culture. Jihad in the United Kingdom has now propagated itself across society.

7

CONCLUSIONS

'We are living at a time of war because the Western world is not letting anyone live in peace.'[1]

In early 2010 British satirist Chris Morris produced a feature film, *Four Lions*, that took a sceptical and humorous view of the problem of Muslim extremism in the United Kingdom. It was released at a time when a sense of ennui seemed to have set it in the coverage of all things Islamist and terrorism-related, as the British public slowly moved beyond the terrible events of 7 July 2005. The concern that had peaked in the mid-2000s seemed to be receding as the security services gained greater insights into the threat with which they were dealing and grew more confident in their ability to counter it. Alert to the dangers of over-confidence, in a speech in September 2010 the director-general of the security service, MI5, said that:

In recent years we appear increasingly to have imported from the American media the assumption that terrorism is 100% preventable and any incident that is not prevented is seen as a culpable government failure. This is a nonsensical way to consider terrorist risk and only plays into the hands of the terrorists themselves. Risk can be managed and reduced but it cannot realistically be abolished, and if we delude ourselves that it can we are setting ourselves up for a nasty disappointment.[2]

Jonathan Evans' comments illustrated that, while the threat may have evolved, it continues to exist and is still a source of concern. In particular, the director general laid out a threat matrix that in many ways was

271

unchanged from the broad trend that had existed over the previous decade and has been laid out in this book, although it now seems to have shifted away from prioritising Pakistan as the major source of terrorist activity targeting Britain. Evans estimated that some 50 per cent of terror-related activity that concerned his service now emanated from Pakistan, down from 75 per cent in 2007–8, while Somalia and Yemen had both gained prominence as sources of 'increased concern'. He emphasised that this did 'not mean that the overall threat has reduced but that it has diversified'.[3] In fact, as we have seen in the preceding chapters, the threat has fragmented from being first and foremost a movement directed by extremists based in Waziristan to being a more scattered wave of extremists, enraged by aspects of British society or policy decisions, choosing to plot terrorist attacks in a variety of different guises. And the threat has continued to evolve since then. In late 2013, Jonathan Evans, successor at the Security Service gave a speech in which he highlighted similar trends to his predecessor, though adding Syria into the mix:

Since 2000, we have seen serious attempts at major acts of terrorism in this country typically once or twice a year. That feels to me, for the moment, unlikely to change. While that tempo seems reasonably even, the ground we have to cover has increased as the threat has become more diversified. Ten years ago, the almost singular focus of the international CT effort was Al Qaida in South Asia. Since that time we have seen violent Islamist groupings in various countries and regions exploiting conflict, revolutions and the opportunity of weakened governance to gain strength and refuge. Some have adopted the Al Qaida brand, becoming franchised affiliates with what at the same time has been a declining Al Qaida core in South Asia. A time-lapse sequence of a world map over the past decade would show outbreaks in Iraq, North & West Africa, Yemen, Somalia, and most recently Syria.[4]

This multifaceted threat continued to make itself felt at the end of the first decade of the new century, with a series of plots or attempted attacks emanating from almost every one of the networks highlighted in the preceding chapters.

In April 2009, police in north-west England conducted a series of coordinated raids at the conclusion of an operation code-named 'Pathway.' The operation was initiated as a result of intelligence that had reached security services which led to agencies targeting for investigation a man in his forties from Pakistan's NWFP who had sought asylum in Britain in 2000 after alleged mistreatment at the hands of the Taliban. Investigators were particularly concerned by the fact that he worked with a hair products company, a position that gave him easy access to hydrogen peroxide, a key ingredient in home-made explosives. As they dug into his life, investigators focused on his roommate Abid Naseer, a young Pakistani who had first come to Britain in 2006, but had failed at his studies and returned to Pakistan.[5] Now back and theoretically studying again, Naseer and his friends spent very little time at university and instead occupied themselves taking pictures of each other in front of rather unremarkable local sites like shopping malls. According to the security services, Naseer was also in close and regular contact with an email account in Pakistan, with which he shared correspondence about girls he had met and possible marriages. However, watchers suspected they were actually observing the closing stages of a terrorist plot. The security services believed that individuals connected to the al-Qaeda core in Pakistan were using the email account to direct both Naseer and his cell, alongside another cell targeting New York's underground system and a rather looser cell in Oslo, Norway.[6]

At the time of writing, all of the men initially arrested as part of Operation Pathway had been released and no charges were pressed, with the exception of Abid Naseer who was extradited to the United States, where he is to stand trial connected with a series of plots whilst remaining of serious concern to British services who concluded he 'was an al-Qaeda operative who posed and still poses a serious threat'.[7] In the wake of Osama bin Laden's death, news was leaked to the press that Naseer's name might have appeared on a list in bin Laden's Abbottabad residence. Naseer was connected to an American-Afghan named Najibullah Zazi, who was arrested by New York police following a tip-off from the British security services, who had continued monitoring the email account that Naseer had been in touch with in Pakistan. According to New York officers, this tip-off from their British counterparts was the first they knew about Zazi, and they leapt into action once they realised that they had an active al-Qaeda-connected cell heading to the city. When arrested, Zazi admitted having been trained by the Taliban and al-Qaeda and of plotting to carry out a suicide bombing campaign on New York's underground system. In his confession, he highlighted that in late August 2008, he and two friends had headed to Pakistan to try to connect with the Taliban to fight in Afghanistan. Their first attempt failed after Pakistani forces turned them back as they tried to drive to the border from Peshawar. Back in Peshawar they managed to contact individuals who took them to Miram Shah where they met with Rashid Rauf, who told them they 'would be presented with a serious decision' and asked if they were interested in becoming suicide bombers. The men initially refused, stating their interest in learning instead to fight in Afghanistan where they had dreams of becoming heroic warriors.[8] Soon after this, Rauf was supposedly killed in a drone strike, bringing his role in al-Qaeda to a close.[9] Zazi and his cell have all been jailed in the United States for their roles in trying to launch the attack on the New York subway system.

Zazi and his colleagues had been persuaded to organise a suicide attack, becoming one of three spokes of a network dispatched to target the West. The other alleged spokes in this network were Abid Naseer and a group led by a Uighur-Norwegian called Mikael Davud that was supposedly planning an attack in Oslo, disrupted much later in July 2010. All three used similar codes in their emails, were in Waziristan at around the same time in late 2008, and Naseer, Zazi and Davud were all communicating with the same email account that had been set up in Peshawar. Zazi confessed to his plot and to meeting Rauf. The others with him were also found guilty, as was Mikael Davud, of plotting an attack in Oslo, while Naseer is due to stand trial soon in the United States.

In August, between the disruption of the northern England and New York plots, British officials observed a strange individual suddenly appearing in a surveillance operation underway in Derby. A tall, burly man with eyes of different colours (one green and one brown), he was an American–Pakistani named Dawood Gilani, or later David Coleman Headley, a former drug dealer and police informant who had radicalised to become a central protagonist in the Kashmiri—and increasingly international—terror network Lashkar-e-Taiba. Having increasingly fallen out with Lashkar in the wake of their November 2008 strike on Mumbai, in which he had played a key preparatory role, Headley had connected with another long-term al-Qaeda commander in Waziristan named Ilyas Kashmiri. Some time during July and August 2009, Kashmiri sent Headley to Derby to connect with a cell of supporters originally from Kotli in Pakistani Kashmir (where Kashmiri was also from) to obtain funds and support for an operation he was planning in Denmark. According to evidence Headley gave the FBI, the two men told him that they known Kashmiri for some time and were angry at the al-Qaeda commander for 'misusing the jihad money'. One of them nevertheless expressed an interest in Headley's plot, and armed with this information and some funds Headley went on to Sweden to connect with another group that Kashmiri had put him in touch with. It was this link in the chain that alerted the British services to Headley and they passed the details on to their American counterparts, who arrested him soon afterwards.

The British-AfPak connection still seemed alive and well throughout 2010. In mid-December 2010 a posting appeared on a jihadist web forum praising the apparent martyrdom of Mahmud Sulaiman Abu Rida, also known as Abu Hanan or Mahmoud Abu Rideh, a Palestinian who had lived for many years in the United Kingdom under a highly restrictive control order. Abu Rideh became something of a cause célèbre for groups like Amnesty International or Cageprisoners, who saw his continued detention under a control order, essentially a very restrictive house arrest, as an infringement of his human rights. After a number of very public breakdowns that included a spell in a secure hospital, he was eventually allowed to leave the United Kingdom, but few among those monitoring suspected terrorists were surprised when he was reported killed on the battlefield and hailed as a martyr. A few months later, an anonymous British fighter nicknamed 'Musa the British' appeared listed as a martyr on the forums in February 2011. On 18 April 2011, in an attack within the Afghan defence ministry in Kabul, a suicide bomber who had apparently been radicalised in a British jail was shot moments before he was able to detonate his device. Atiqullah Mangal had apparently got into the United Kingdom as an illegal migrant in 2001 and was living in the West Midlands before being jailed during a fracas. In prison he was apparently radicalised by fellow inmates and following deportation to Afghanistan joined the Haqqani network.[10] And then in June, British Special Forces raided a house in Herat, Afghanistan where they found two individuals of interest to MI5. Allegedly preparing to return to Britain, they were ultimately released into Afghanistan after Coalition forces were barred from handing them over to Afghan authorities or returning them to the United Kingdom.[11]

The extent of the persistence of the threat from South Asia was brought home in September 2011 when police in the West Midlands arrested a group of men accused of planning suicide bombings in the United Kingdom. Tried in November 2012, Irfan Naseer (nicknamed 'big Irfan' because of his physical bulk), Irfan Khalid (named 'little Irfan' in comparison to 'big Irfan') and Ashik Ali were found guilty of planning 'acts of terrorism on a scale potentially greater than the London bombings in July

2005.'[12] Using plans they had been taught at training camps in Pakistan, the men were building devices that were fashioned out of using chemicals in athletes' cold packs. The cell leader, 'big' Irfan, claimed to have met Abu Zaid al Kuwaiti, a senior al-Qaeda ideologue, in Pakistan and told the others stories of hiding from drones while he was training.[13]

As with many of the plots, there were clownish elements to it. One of the second tier of supporters, Rahin Ahmed (who pleaded guilty), at one point tried to double the money that they group had accumulated through fraudulent charity fundraising by playing foreign exchange markets online. However, he left to get a cup of tea at a crucial moment, leading to the cell losing most of their money as markets fluctuated. On another occasion, a group of four that had been dispatched by Irfan to Pakistani training camps did not particularly enjoy the experience, and phoned home to their families who ultimately alerted the authorities—hardly the behaviour of hardened terrorists. But at the same time, the devices that they were building demonstrated a new technical skill. Irfan was a graduate chemist who was able to design functioning devices and the group had managed to forge firm connections to al-Qaeda leaders who had instructed them to return to Europe and disseminate what they had learned in their training to others.[14] In tune with their predecessors, 'big' and 'little' Irfan had trained at Harakat ul-Mujahedeen camps, though by their own admission, they were not star recruits. In September 2011, 'big' Irfan was overheard showing off to Ashik Ali,

I was like rolling around with pain and that in my stomach. They still go, 'go lesson'. So what it is—guess what we start doing? We go forget it man. If these lot [sic] throw us out, they throw us out. We went upstairs and we got wireless internet…So we were just watching 'J' videos all day. After Fajr [dawn prayers] they used to come to our room. We used to be knocked out—say we were ill. They would come up again. Then, eventually got fed up after two months and threw us out.[15]

And the disruption of the cell proved not to be the end of the West Midlands cluster of terrorists. In June 2012 a group linked to 'big' Irfan was disrupted as the members drove back from Dewsbury, where they had been planning to detonate a homemade bomb and then attack the crowd with guns and knives in their possession. Their target was a march by the far right protest group the English Defence League (EDL)—that they referred to in a letter that was seemingly intended to be released subsequently to show off what they had done, as the 'English Drunkards

League'—that had been born in protest at Al-Muhajiroun's activity in Luton. Individuals who were part of the cell targeting the EDL march had appeared as part of the investigation into Irfan Naseer's group, including as fundraisers for the fake charities that he used as cover to raise money to support his activities.[16] At one point it was discovered that one individual within 'big' Irfan's network, Jewel Uddin, was observed by security services purchasing knives from a supermarket—weapons that were later found in the boot of the car with the weapons and bomb they were planning on using against the EDL.

The conjoined set of cells offered proof that there remains a persistent threat from al-Qaeda in Pakistan, one that can still tap into radical networks in the United Kingdom. The network drawn into the plot was directed by al-Qaeda to launch attacks in Britain, and was also able to generate an off-shoot cell that was equally bent on causing mayhem but was instead more focused on domestic targets such as the EDL.

Anwar al-Awlaki

But even more worrying than the continuous pattern of plots with links to Afghanistan and Pakistan was the growing visibility of the influence of Yemeni-American preacher Anwar al-Awlaki. An increasingly prominent cleric who had been an imam at a mosque in Virginia that two of the September 11 hijackers had attended, al-Awlaki had left America in 2002 and moved to the United Kingdom, which he toured giving presentations to large audiences. Already known on the Salafist scene, al-Awlaki was, according to Usama Hasan, a former radical who heard him speak in the United Kingdom, 'one of the icons of Western Salafism, [he] would pack out every venue he spoke at, people were excited to see him.'[17] By 2004 he had moved on to Yemen, but his impact would be felt years later as he slowly became one of the hubs of international jihadism from his base in the desert under the protection of al-Qaeda in the Arabian Peninsula (AQAP), an organisation that had developed from the remnants of the Islamic Army of Aden-Abyan alongside which Abu Hamza had sent his son to train (see Chapter 4). From his base in Yemen, al-Awlaki's tentacles offered online guidance to his followers around the world, both directly and indirectly. While his target seems to have resolutely been the United States, in many instances the United Kingdom played a key role in radicalising or providing a backdrop for his acolytes.

The most direct example of this is the case of Nigerian student Umar Farouk Abdulmutallab who on Christmas Day 2009 attempted to bring down a flight as it was making its final approach into Detroit airport. Abdulmutallab had studied at University College London and for a period was the head of its Islamic Society. There he helped organise events focusing on the injustices of the War on Terror, but was otherwise described as a quiet Nigerian student who lived in an affluent area. In an investigation conducted after the case, UCL cleared itself of any responsibility, even though several online postings ascribed to Abdulmutallab while he was at UCL hinted at his loneliness and growing radicalisation.[18] In 2009 he moved to Dubai where he was taking Arabic classes and decided to try to contact the Yemeni-American preacher he had long admired from afar. In August 2009 he moved to Yemen from Dubai and when he wasn't taking Arabic classes at schools in Sanaa he spent his time asking worshippers in mosques about who could put him in touch with al-Awlaki. Finally he made a connection to the preacher and after a few security tests, was brought to meet al-Awlaki, whom he told of his desire to participate in jihad. The arrival of a young man eager to strike against America was a pleasant surprise to AQAP, who were delighted to discover that his passport still contained an open visa to enter the United States. Quickly equipping him with a clever device sewn into his underwear that would get past airport security, al-Awlaki sent Abdulmutallab on his way, giving him simple instructions to head to America via a circuitous route and to detonate his device once he was over American territory.[19] Flying through Ghana, Nigeria and then Holland, Abdulmutallab waited until his plane was coming in to land in Detroit to set his device off. Fortunately, as with Richard Reid's shoe bomb, the device failed to go off immediately and a quick-thinking passenger noticed Abdulmutallab trying to detonate his device and leapt on him, dousing it and saving the plane.

A second al-Awlaki connection to the United Kingdom was uncovered two months after Abdulmutallab's failed attempt. On 25 February 2010, British police arrested a Bangladeshi-British IT employee of British Airways in Newcastle. Resident in the United Kingdom since 2006, Rajib Karim was initially charged with supporting Bangladeshi jihadist organisation Jamaat ul-Mujahideen Bangladesh (JMB). A long-time member, Karim and his brother had produced videos in support of the group and undertaken fundraising activities. However, in late 2009, his brother Tehzeeb left Bangladesh for Yemen, apparently to seek out al-Awlaki.

Once he had connected with the preacher he told him of his brother who worked for British Airways. By late 2009 al-Awlaki had definitively connected with the two brothers, recording a message for them after reports surfaced of his death.[20] In early 2010, al-Awlaki wrote to Karim declaring, 'I immediately wanted to contact you and tell you that my advice to you is to remain in your current position. Depending on what your role is and the amount of information you can get your hands on, you might be able to provide us with critical and urgent information and you may be able to play a crucial role.' He went on to ask about airport security, clearly frustrated at having watched Abdulmutallab fail and eager to ascertain what new developments there might have been as a result. Karim responded by telling the preacher some information about the airports and also revealing that he knew 'two brothers, one who works in baggage handling at Heathrow and another who works in airport security. Both are good practising brothers and sympathise towards the cause of the mujahideen and do not slander them. They are of the type who would help with money and moral support but I am not sure if they are at the stage to sacrifice with their lives.'[21]

According to Karim, his aim in telling al-Awlaki this information was to get the preacher onside, as his priority was to try to travel to Yemen and join his brother, the itinerant warrior.[22] As he put it to al-Awlaki, 'leading a life like that [in the West] was really killing me inside, that's why I desperately wanted to make *hijrah* [migration] as I was not seeing any opportunities to do anything in this land.' But for al-Awlaki, the priority was a strike at the United States, and he pressed his new acolyte for support: 'our highest priority is the US. Anything there, even if on a smaller scale to what we may do in the UK, would be our choice. So the question is: with the people you have, is it possible to get a package or a person with a package on board a flight heading to the US? If that is not possible, then what ideas do you have that could be set up for the UK?'[23] Just under two weeks later, Karim was arrested and these emails were later found on his hard drive. While it was unclear whether Karim was planning anything in the United Kingdom (he was not found to have any bomb-making materials and the individuals he had supposedly identified as potential recruits were picked up and quickly assessed as innocent and released), the case revealed al-Awlaki's reach and his single-minded focus on striking America.

In the end, al-Awlaki's direct impact in the United Kingdom proved paradoxically to have been indirect. Rather than through the individuals Umar Farouk Abdulmutallab and Rajib Karim—whom, despite their strong connections in Britain, Al-Awlaki chose to deploy in efforts against America—it was through his online magazines and recordings that Al-Awlaki had the deepest impact in the United Kingdom. Key among these was *Inspire*, a slick publication he produced together with a young Pakistani-American named Samir Khan, who left his American home to join the preacher in Yemen, and died alongside him in a drone strike in September 2011. The magazine was a one-stop shop for the modern jihadi. Focused on ideas of 'Lone Wolf' jihadism, whereby individuals around the world would simply pick up whatever weapons were to hand and launch a terrorist attack, *Inspire* drew heavily on the ideology of Abu Musab al-Suri, the Syrian ideologue of jihad who had spent a considerable time in London. Offering stories from the field in Yemen, messages from al-Awlaki and other senior leaders, and lessons on how to build bombs 'in the kitchen of your mom,' the magazine (which at time of writing was up to issue number 12) acts as a compendium for the aspirant jihadi, the aim being to persuade individuals of the viability of jihad at home rather than the need travel to dangerous lands like Pakistan, Somalia or Yemen where they are likely to be detected.

There was also a British angle to *Inspire* magazine, as Rajib Karim was not the only British webmaster that connected with al-Awlaki. In 2010 a Vietnamese convert called Minh Quang Pham left his residence in London to head for Yemen where he connected with AQAP. A long-time feature of the Al-Muhajiroun community who used the nickname 'Amin', Pham shows up in the background of a documentary about another convert who had joined Al-Muhajiroun called *My Brother the Islamist*. Adept with computers, Pham joined AQAP and trained with AK-47s alongside them, before returning to the United Kingdom in July 2011 to the great consternation of the British security services. In contact with a number of known radical individuals from Al-Muhajiroun, it was not publicly revealed exactly what Pham was intending to do, but he was later revealed to be responsible in part for producing *Inspire* magazine.[24]

By 2010 there was considerable evidence that the magazine was at least providing young people with a clearer idea of how to carry out attacks. Nowhere more so than in the United Kingdom, where on Christmas Day 2010 police arrested a network of individuals in Birmingham, Cardiff, East London and Stoke-on-Trent. Code-named Operation Guava, the investigation was part of a long-term effort to disrupt a domestic network of South Asian British extremists, at least some of whom had spent time as associates of Al-Muhajiroun or affiliated groups. Key among their possessions was *Inspire* magazine, from which they were drawing the design of a bomb that they later admitted they were going to leave in the toilet of the London Stock Exchange.[25]

The 'lynchpin' of the group was a British Bangladeshi from East London called Mohammed Chowdhury who was caught holding up an Islam4UK[26] sign at an event organised by the group, attended a poppy burning ceremony they organised, and who was described in court as 'an obsessive self-publicist.'[27] He made the most phone calls between the group and organised meetings, and online he used the moniker JMB (standing for Jamaat ul-Mujahideen Bangladesh, the group of which Rajib Karim was a member). In Stoke, the individuals were known as the 'local nutters', handing out leaflets for Al-Muhajiroun descendant groups and regularly running stalls on the high street broadcasting extremist ideas and views. It was at these *dawah* (propagation) stalls that they all met, assessing each other's levels of radicalisation and then continuing their discussions online using PalTalk. They then gathered together in late 2010 in Cardiff and Newport to discuss their plans and talk further about jihad. But the various groups involved (in Cardiff, East London and Stoke) all had slightly different agendas. The Stoke group seemed the most active, and had identified a plot of land in Kashmir owned by one of their families that they wanted to turn into a madrassa at which they could train to fight. While they had not decided whether to return to the United Kingdom to carry out terrorist attacks, they did discuss ideas like bombing local pubs. Their priority seems to have been to develop the training camp, and from court documents it appears as though they were most eager to direct the cell in this direction, seeing the others as potential recruits. Of the others, Abdul Miah, a British Bangladeshi who lived in Cardiff with his young family, and who had served time in prison for violent offences, particularly impressed them. While in prison he had been radicalised and upon release he seems to have started to fraternise with Al-Muhajiroun groups in Cardiff alongside his older brother.[28]

On the other hand, the East London group was drifting towards trying to carry out an attack in the United Kingdom. On reconnaissance trips into central London they wandered around the Houses of Parliament and Whitehall looking at potential targets, while continuing to discuss their potential operation. Then on the evening of 19 December 2010, security services overheard them discussing in some detail how to build a pipe bomb using recipes laid out in *Inspire* magazine. Having maintained heavy surveillance over the group for some time and looking for a reason to finally roll the group up, this triggered police into action and the plotters was arrested around the country the next morning. Going through their belongings many more recordings and publications of al-Awlaki's were discovered, although there was little tangible evidence that they had managed to assemble much of a device. Nevertheless, they pleaded guilty to the charges laid against them and all received sentences of between five and twenty-one years.[29]

Much was made in the press subsequently of the relatively amateurish nature of this cell. With a number of prominent Al-Muhajiroun acolytes among their number (hardly the behaviour of discreet terrorists), half-baked plots (they admitted to planning to plant a bomb in the London Stock Exchange, but failed to check that it was going to be open on the day that they were going to leave it there), and their apparent casing of institutions like the London Scientology Center as potential targets, comparisons were made between them and the hapless plotters of *Four Lions*. Clearly this was not a plot on a par with Overt or the many plots listed in Chapter 5, but nevertheless, the cell's disruption highlighted the coming together of a number of strands of narrative of the British jihad. With Pakistani training camps, radical preachers, a mysterious figure called 'the Bengali' who was mentioned in court proceedings as a possible radical contact, prison radicalisation, the internet and classic radical groups linked to Al-Muhajiroun, the cell seemed to encapsulate Britain's jihad. The key difference was an absence of any clear connection to al-Qaeda, beyond the information that they were able to download from the internet. Here was a cell that was born in Britain's radical milieu, took al-Awlaki's ideas and decided to try to move into action by themselves. Fortunately, they proved remarkably inept and had made themselves targets for intelligence focus long before they moved into action.

In stark contrast, on 14 May 2010 a young Bangladeshi girl walked into the MP for East Ham Stephen Timms' office for an appointment she had made over the phone with his assistant. When calling to make the appointment, Roshonara Choudhry had specified that it was her local MP she needed to talk to and not simply an assistant, and security noticed that she seemed 'anxious' as she waited for the MP, who was running behind schedule.[30] Timms, a longtime Labour MP, was somewhat surprised when he came out to meet the woman all in black who came around to shake his hand. As he put it later, 'I was a little puzzled because a Muslim dressed in that way wouldn't normally be willing to shake a man's hand, still less take the initiative to do so.'[31] The handshake was merely a feint, and while with one hand she reached out to the MP, with the other she gripped a knife she had bought at a local supermarket. In describing her actions to the police afterwards, Choudhry said, 'I walked towards him with my left hand out as if I wanted to shake his hand. Then I pulled the knife out of my bag and I hit him in the stomach with it. I put it in the top part of his stomach like when you punch someone.'[32]

The young woman was quickly restrained by others in Timms' office and taken into custody by police. In a remarkably candid police interview after the event, Choudry revealed both her jihadist aspirations and motivations while stating that she had targeted Timms for his support of the invasion of Iraq. 'I wanted to be a martyr', she declared as 'that's the best way to die' and it is 'an Islamic teaching'. She had seen the suffering of the Iraqi people and took it as her burden to do something for them. As she put it, 'as Muslims we're all brothers and sisters and we should all look out for each other and we shouldn't sit back and do nothing while others suffer'.[33] There are clear similarities between these statements and those we saw made earlier by Mohammed Siddique Khan when he assumed responsibility for his community in his action, and their ideological groundings at least seem to have come from similar places. While there is no evidence that Choudhry was interested in Kashmir, she was drawn to the videos and writings of Abdullah Azzam and Anwar al-Awlaki (that she had watched obsessively in the weeks leading up to her attack) and was particularly appalled by the invasion of Iraq. 'I thought that it's not right that he voted for the declaration of war in Iraq', and unlike the legions of protesters who took to the streets, Choudhry chose a path like Khan's, launching an attack in which she hoped to die while avenging her people. Like Khan, she appeared to be a well-integrated person, working as a volunteer teacher in a local Islamic school while she studied at King's College London—a position she had worked her way up to from humble beginnings as one of five children of an East London Bangladeshi tailor. However, sometime during her final year she appears to have undergone a transformation that made her conclude that the only path open to her was to carry out a suicide attack in the name of her religion. In her telling, this was something instigated in part by the watching of Anwar al-Awlaki's videos as a source of inspiration, but since her arrest she has not offered much more detail about her radicalisation. Showing her commitment and reflecting her desire to conduct her action within the context of a martyrdom operation, prior to getting on the bus to Timms' surgery, Choudhry went to the bank and emptied her accounts and cleared her debts, wanting to be ready to enter the next life with a clean slate.

When she finally appeared in court, Choudhry refused to enter a plea and, according to press reports, had not seen any family or visitors for a while since she refused to submit to the extensive strip searches that would be required before and after each visit as a category A prisoner. Jailed for a minimum of fifteen years, Choudhry remained impassive as the sentence was passed, but inside and outside the courtroom extremist supporters shouted 'Allah Akbar', 'Takbeer', 'British go to hell' and 'curse the judge'.[34] She was reported to have smiled. In police interviews she denied any connections with groups or radical networks, but soon after her sentence was passed, al-Qaeda in the Arabian Pensinsula, in an attempt no doubt to claim her actions as part of their movement and thus bask in some of the reflected glory and success, published an article in their *Inspire* magazine online hailing her actions. In offering an explanation for her actions, the article maintained: 'The borderless loyalty is a religious sentiment of the people in your midst. As long as the Muslims remain in your focus, you will remain in ours. No matter the security precautions you may take, you cannot kill a borderless idea.'[35]

Alongside Choudhry, the article also praised another individual who had attempted a terrorist act by himself and been radicalised in the United Kingdom. A month or so after Choudhry's sentencing, Taimour Abdulwahab al-Abdaly strapped on a bomb and planted another in a car, before marching towards a large mall in the middle of Stockholm bustling with Christmas shoppers. Fortunately, al-Abdaly had fashioned his explosive incorrectly and the device blew up killing only him. Shortly before his attack, al-Abdaly had called a number in Iraq, and it is believed he was in contact with, and had possibly trained with, the insurgency there.[36] However, the ideas that had started him down this path were traced to Luton. Living in the city from 2001 to 2004 while studying at the University of Luton (now the University of Bedfordshire), al-Abdaly appears to have changed from a mild-mannered individual to a radical who was eventually expelled from his local mosque for repeatedly espousing extremist ideas. There continued to be a highly radical atmosphere in Luton: in early 2010 a group of local extremists connected to Al-Muhajiroun descendant groups took to the streets during a homecoming parade for British soldiers, waving placards pronouncing the men 'the butchers of Basra', and residents interviewed at the time of Taimour's attempt were full of stories of local radicals. Unlike Roshonara Choudhry's secret radicalisation, Taimour Abdulwahab al-Abdaly's seems to have been a very public one, and one connected to other individuals and fighting in his mother country of Iraq.

The two cases, while grouped together by AQAP as examples of 'borderless loyalty' to their ideas, instead offer something of a contrasting pair: one showing the potential of 'Lone Wolf' jihad instigated by Anwar al-Awlaki's ideology, and the other the more traditional path of a radical milieu in Luton leading to a connection with foreign fighters in Iraq. In both cases, however, the United Kingdom's radical environment provided the backdrop for their actions, highlighting them as merely the latest in a growing list of individuals radicalised as part of the British jihad. *Inspire* magazine tried to isolate this theme and extend it further, showing how individuals could simply pick up tools that are to hand in order to launch an attack. One young British-Pakistani living in Wolverhampton actually beat the magazine to the punch in this message. Bilal Zaheer Ahmad, a part-time Al-Muhajiroun activist who was particularly active on an extremist site called RevolutionMuslim.com, posted inflammatory comments praising Choudhry's action, along with lists of MPs and links to where people could buy kitchen knives like that she used. In comments he declared: 'this sister has put us men to shame. We should be doing this.' Picked up at around the same time as Choudhry was being sentenced, he was later sentenced to twelve years, with the judge describing him as a 'viper in our midst' in his closing remarks.[37] By this point, al-Awlaki's ideas seem to have firmly taken root in the United Kingdom, though it remains an open question as to whether they evolved in this way at the late cleric's instigation, or whether this was a natural trajectory that he and his colleagues at AQAP were able to identify and exploit.

Today

In 2012, London hosted the Olympic Games. A huge global spectacle, they were matched by a massive security operation focused on ensuring that no terrorist plot was able to disrupt the event. Police and intelligence agencies went into overdrive as they moved to protect the foreign athletes and dissuade al-Qaeda from using the opportunity of the global spotlight to humiliate the West and United Kingdom in particular. In the run-up they moved to shut down a number of cells that were under observation, to get them out of the way so they could focus on potential threats to the Games. Two specific plots were unravelled at varying stages of preparation. Codenamed Operation Nimrod and Operation Movie, the two networks were both connected to the broader community to emerge from around Al-Muhajiroun. The two plots were at relatively unformed stages, but demonstrated connections abroad, creative use of tradecraft to mask activity and an interest in launching attacks against local British targets that would have an international resonance.

The first of the two to be disrupted was a cell of four in Luton who had been on security services' radars for some time. The men, three of Pakistani origin and the fourth Bangladeshi, were fixtures at Al-Muhajiroun events in Luton and active supporters of the insurgency in Afghanistan. The cell leader, Zahid Iqbal, was in contact with an individual described by security services as an 'active terrorist' in Pakistan, but who was only identified by his MI5 codename 'Modern Sleeve'. Through this figure, Iqbal tried to arrange for his companion, Mohammed Sharfaraz Ahmed, to join a training camp in Pakistan in March 2011. While a very active radical (beyond his activity as part of this cell, Ahmed had stirred up two cousins in Bradford to prepare to go and train in Pakistan as well), Ahmed was a less impressive warrior and seems to have returned to the UK less than a week after he left. He alleged a difficult security situation and a lack of languages hindered him.[38] Recognising that Pakistan might be too difficult, the group was later overheard discussing how, if they were unable to get into contact with groups in Pakistan, they could instead head to Mali where they knew an alternative al-Qaeda affiliate was brewing.

Upon Ahmed's return, the group seems to have continued its activity, seeking to send support and go and fight abroad. They were recorded going for long walks in Snowdonia, describing it as 'good training for jihad.' Most worrying, however, aside from their contact with 'Modern Sleeve,' was the volume of money they were able to raise through fraudulent activity. This was done through use of a card skimming machine owned by Syed Farhan Hussain, who on arrest was found to have £10,000 in his possession and there was evidence some £180,000 had passed through his account. In April, after Ahmed aborted a trip to Pakistan, the group was overheard discussing bomb-making and some of the ideas for how to carry out attacks provided by *Inspire* magazine. The one that most caught public attention was the comment overheard by Zahid Iqbal that 'I was like driving past the TA [Territorial Army] Centre, if you had a small toy car there's a small gap under the gate. You could drive it under a vehicle that they use.' The group discussed arming this vehicle and thought about doing a test run, though were concerned about how this might attract attention. In the end they were arrested prior to being able to build any devices, and were sentenced a total of thirty-five years incarceration between them.

The second disrupted cell was picked up on 5 July 2012, weeks before the start of the Olympic Games and involved six arrests across London.[39] In the end, three men pleaded guilty to the terrorism charges against them, including one prominent figure called Richard Dart, also known as Salahuddin al Brittani, a tall Caucasian convert who had been the star of a documentary by his step-brother, *My Brother the Islamist*.[40] A prominent attendee of Al-Muhajiroun related events, Dart had formally videoed his conversion to Islam under Anjem Choudary's watchful eye and later featured in the background of a number of interviews with him. Dart seems to have been more prominent in the group when it was using the name Muslims Against Crusades, and a look at the background of some of the videos in which he featured, as well as the *My Brother the Islamist* documentary, shows a number of individuals who were later arrested on terrorism charges. Demonstrating that Choudary was still an important figure to him, when he was stopped at Heathrow en route to Pakistan, Dart was found to have USB stick in his possession that had on it a will in which one of his co-defendants and Anjem Choudary were listed as co-executors.

The plot that Dart and his friends Jahangir Alom and Imran Mahmood were alleged to be planning seemed to mostly involve trying to go abroad, though the men were also overheard talking about launching an attack of some sort at Wootton Bassett, a location in the United Kingdom that achieved fame as the village where the bodies of soldiers who died fighting abroad are returned home. Al-Muhajiroun groups have previously undertaken very aggressive public protests while the soldiers march through the village. Dart and Mahmood were found to have had conversations on a computer (using a relatively innovative method of typing into a word document and then deleting it) discussing the permissibility of attacking the site and of targeting others in the United Kingdom.[41] Dart was overheard telling Mahmood another time 'things have to be done. It doesn't matter if you're in this country or abroad, things have to be done.'[42]

Most of the men's activity, however, seemed to involve activity abroad. Mahmood had spent some time in Pakistan where he had received training—when he was picked up by Pakistani authorities they found traces of explosives on his bags and he later admitted that he had 'received rudimentary training in explosives.'[43] Dart and Alom also tried to make these connections, though were unable to. Alom had, in fact, also served for a year or so in the British Territorial Army and as a police support officer. During his army service he had specifically requested to be deployed in Afghanistan. He was discharged on medical grounds. Dart, on the other hand, seems to have been very keen to join groups like the Tehrik e Taliban Pakistan (TTP) and at one point Mahmood shows off to him that he met the organisers of a plot in which an al-Qaeda and TTP double agent killed nine American CIA operatives in an attack in Afghanistan.[44] In the end, Dart, Alom and Mahmood were collectively sentenced to nineteen years in jail, while Dart's wife Ayan Hadi, pled guilty to charges of not informing the authorities and was given a suspended sentence.[45]

Concerned about Olympics security, British security services used the moment to disrupt a number of these cells, though their ongoing existence demonstrated the persistence of the terrorist threat to the United Kingdom. The cells' connections to Al-Muhajiroun highlighted the security services' focus on the networks around this group and showed how terrorist plotting and a desire to go and fight abroad against British soldiers or join groups close to al-Qaeda continued to be a regular feature of their thinking. It was not until May 2013, however, that the threat came home to roost once again when Michael Adebolajo and Michael Adebowale drove Michael Adebolajo's car into drummer Lee Rigby as he walked outside his barracks in Woolwich. Having knocked the off-duty soldier down, the two men jumped on him with knives and meat cleavers hacking away until he bled to death. As passersby watched horrified, the older of the two, Michael Adebolajo, declared the men's creed for posterity to the many camera phones pointed at them about how they had carried out this brutal act in revenge for actions 'against their people.' When police arrived, the two men pointed the rusty old pistol they had obtained through gang contacts and ran at them likely seeking to die.

Both survived, however, and were later found guilty of the murder of Lee Rigby and given heavy jail sentences. As journalists dug into their pasts, however, it turned out that the two men had long histories as features at events organised by Anjem Choudary and in the background of other investigations. In late 2010, Michael Adebolajo was detained by Kenyan authorities as he tried to sneak into Somalia along with a group of radicalised Kenyan youth. Prior to that he was seen at a number of events organised by an Al-Muhajiroun successor called al-Ghurabaa (the strangers), and was arrested after a scuffle with police outside where another group leader, Mizanur Rahman, was being held. He had also appeared in the backdrop of a number of serious terrorism cases identified by the security services but that came to nothing or were disrupted in ways other than detention and terrorism charges. His younger friend, Michael Adebowale, had a history as a troubled young man who had spent some time at Feltham Young Offenders institution, and had witnessed a brutal knife murder years before. He was also spotted at Al-Muhajiroun linked events, though his degree of activity seemed to be less.

The full details of the two Michaels' links has not yet been mapped out, though they were known to be in contact with a number of the al Muhajiroun figures identified in the book so far, including ones with links in Yemen, Somalia and elsewhere. Both were connected to a number of other plots in the UK, and had almost been arrested before, as well as having been approached by authorities. In many ways, however, the degree of contacts and history merely served to highlight the persistent threat that was posed by such individuals and the community of radicals in the United Kingdom. The attack in Woolwich, the first death of a citizen at home at the hands of Islamist radicals since the 7 July 2005 attacks was a shock, but showed how the trends and threats laid out in this book continue and persist to this day. Both Michael Adebowale and Michael Adebolajo were individuals who had been of some concern for a while, were radical converts who had been involved in extremist groups that have long been of concern, and were eager to try to connect with terrorist groups abroad. For Britain's police and intelligence agencies it merely served to reinforce long-standing concerns and demonstrated again that the threat was one that had not gone away.

And none of this addresses the growing threat from Syria and the radicalised networks of young Britons that have been making their way to the region. This topic is one that is largely left aside in this book, given its current and dynamic nature and the fact that, while many of the trends highlighted in the book appear to be repeating themselves there, with similar networks, recruitment and fundraising and even possibly plots coming back, it is simply too early to write about it with any authority. But at the time of writing the official figures being quoted for Syria from the United Kingdom stated that somewhere 500–700 individuals had gone and fought at some point from 2011 onwards. At least one plot to carry out terrorism in the UK developed since this time shows evidence of having been directed from the battlefield, and up to three others are possibly linked to individuals either inspired by or with some experience of the battlefield. A number of individuals who have featured in this narrative have been reported as going over to fight, or seeking to go over and fight, whilst English-spoken information was increasingly emerging from the battlefield. One seemingly all-British group called Rayat al Tawheed (the flag of oneness) was producing a regular diet of radical material that included at least one video of them participating in a battlefield execution and another that showed images of them with the heads of fallen enemies.

Jihadist networks and ideas continue to be active in Britain, but have developed a great deal from their early incarnations as outlined at the beginning of this book. From large networks of young men stirred up by radical preachers and former fighters to go abroad and connect with Islamist insurgencies, to networks which were then redirected by al-Qaeda to conduct operations in the United Kingdom, the ideas that were brought to Britain in the late 1980s and 1990s are now firmly established and continue to exert influence. The original structure that allowed these ideas to incubate in the United Kingdom has for the most part been disrupted, but similar shadow networks have now evolved to replace old ones, and the internet has allowed an ever-expanding community of individuals to be drawn towards a single narrative offering a globalised vision of violent activism. Radical gatherings still take place in the United Kingdom, but the attention of the security services has engendered a sense of paranoia among communities of extremists who are wary of overstepping the mark and infringing the increasingly rigid legislative framework that has been crafted to prevent individuals from fomenting terrorist activity.

CONCLUSIONS

Undeniably, foreign policy was a forceful driver in motivating established jihadist networks in Britain to turn against their host nation. In retrospect, these networks were already moving in this direction quite early on: the plot disrupted in Birmingham in 2000 and the Yemen cell from 1998 both suggest this, alongside the networks of British plotters or fighters that had fought on jihadist battlefields prior to 11 September 2001. Moreover, 9/11 and subsequent events acted as an accelerant to this trend and encouraged other jihadists to target the United Kingdom. The decision to invade Afghanistan angered already radicalised individuals, but the subsequent decision to go into Iraq suggested to those who had only partially imbued extremist ideas that the West was indeed launching a war on their cherished religion and that they were the only ones who were able and duty bound to protest. What is disturbing is that, more than ten years since this event, while we have witnessed a clear decrease in effectiveness, we continue to see individuals trying to seek jihadi training, with some of them deciding to attempt attacks at home. The facility with which individuals can now enter the congregation of virtual jihadis and become active rather than passive plotters has meant that a whole secondary community of dangerous individuals has emerged who often have no connection to other violent extremists and who often do not even vaguely match the broad parameters of the profiles of previous attackers, yet remain an active menace. The threat has complicated and diversified, and few terrorism-watchers will say that it shows any signs of going away altogether.

But such alarmism must also be tempered. There have several close calls at home, but the May 2013 attack in Woolwich is the only successful attack since the July 7 2005 bombings to emerge from this threat. And while this book has shown how alarmingly large is the community of radicals involved in terrorist activity in the United Kingdom, even a complete tabulation of all the those convicted on terrorism charges in Britain or abroad with links to the British radical scene shows that they account for an infinitesimally small proportion of the wider British Muslim community. However, these figures are not necessarily pertinent to the larger point: we are increasingly seeing a shift away from networks of individuals linked by shared ethnicity to parts of the world where dangerous groups gather, and towards jihadist ideas acting as beacons which draw in both disenfranchised young Muslims but also estranged individuals who were not born into Islam. The continuing presence of relatively recent converts in disrupted cells suggests that this is no longer a problem which is isolated among established Muslim communities, but rather that jihadist ideas within the United Kingdom are becoming the default anti-establishment movement for an increasingly diverse community of individuals.

But as we saw in the Introduction, the mix of drivers that draw people along a path of political violence is a complex one, requiring ideology, mobilisation and grievance. While the messages contributing to the ideological element are still out there, to openly encounter them in the same way that they used to be found in the late 1990s and early 2000s without drawing the attention of security services is increasingly difficult. The same can be said for those who mobilise at home by participating in extremist activity or training camps in the United Kingdom, while those who choose to go abroad and to connect with radical groups often find themselves spotted by alert intelligence agencies or observed when they make contact with others or try to call back home. Intensive American and British communications intercepts mean that calls and emails from Pakistan, Syria, Somalia or Yemen are often heard or seen and answered with a rapid and decisive drone strike. While the internet remains an open domain in this regard, it is still a fraction of an already reduced community that is motivated all the way to violence solely through contact with radical ideas online.

However the threat has not disappeared. Indeed, with events in Syria it appears that the threat may be growing once again. Old narratives playing out again show that the complacency produced by a long period of success is dangerous. The reality is that while the British security services understand much better the networks they are dealing with and what radicalisation looks like, there is still very little understanding of how to counter and de-radicalise. The growing instances of ex-convicts emerging radicalised from prisons, and the very few terrorist prisoners coming out of jail having recanted their views, shows that even when the state holds individuals in a confined space it is unable to prevent extremist ideas from taking root. And among the wider radical community, numerous arrests and lengthy incarcerations have not stopped a steady number of young Britons posting radical material online, attending meetings hosted by Al-Muhajiroun, or seeking out others with similar ideas with whom they can plot and form secret communities. Set against a backdrop of continued fighting in Afghanistan, Pakistan, Somalia, Yemen and

Syria, and the ongoing fall-out from the so-called Arab Spring, it is not hard to see how the radical narrative that was so appealing in the past continues to resonate.

Britain's jihad has been underway for decades, and the appeal of the ideas that underlie it has proved remarkably resilient. As the conflict in Syria drags on and on, and a seemingly endless cadre of young Britons goes to fight there, the potential for some of these individuals coming home to launch attacks in the United Kingdom and elsewhere remains high. The crest of the first wave of British jihadism may have been broken, but the undercurrents of a new storm surge are building.

NOTES

INTRODUCTION: JIHAD UK

1. Author's transcription of the martyrdom video of Mohammed Siddique Khan released by al Qaeda, from which all of the quotes from the video are drawn.
2. Regina vs. Muktar Said Ibrahim et al., trial transcript, Woolwich Crown Court, 19 March 2007.
3. Jonathan Evans, 'Intelligence, Counter-terrorism and Trust,' speech to The Society of Editors, Manchester, 7 Nov. 2007—since this speech the British security services have avoided detailing their metrics so more recent official figures are unavailable.
4. For the complete strategy, see http://security.homeoffice.gov.uk/news-publications/publication-search/general/HO_Contest_strategy.pdf
5. Some of these have been laid out in a book by Mitchell D. Silber, the former head of the New York Police Department's Intelligence Unit, who published a book in 2012 that detailed sixteen al-Qaeda linked plots in the West. Of the ten he lists as having a component of al-Qaeda command and direction over them, six involved British citizens. There are in fact more, as shown in later chapters of this book: Mitchell D. Silber, *The Al Qaeda Factor*, Philadelphia: University of Pennsylvania Press, 2012.
6. This is also not to dismiss the other forms of extremism that have appeared recently in the United Kingdom, including recently a resurgent far right, a persistent problem from Irish-related terrorism, but these are not the focus of this book.
7. For a comprehensive discussion about radicalisation within this context, see Peter Neumann, 'The Trouble with Radicalisation,' *International Affairs*, vol. 89, no. 4, July 2013.
8. This debate is best captured by Dr Bruce Hoffman and Dr Marc Sageman's debate in *Foreign Affairs*: Bruce Hoffman, 'The Myth of grass-roots terrorism', *Foreign Affairs*, vol. 87, no. 3, May/June 2008; and Bruce Hoffman and Marc Sageman, 'Does Osama still call the shots?', *Foreign Affairs*, vol. 87, no. 4, July/Aug. 2008.
9. Marc Sageman, *Understanding Terror Networks*, Philadelphia: University of Pennsylvania Press, 2004.
10. Alan Kreuger, *What Makes a Terrorist: Economics and the Roots of Terrorism*, Oxford: Princeton University Press, 2007.
11. Robert Pape, *Dying to Win: The Strategic Logic of Suicide Terrorism*, London: Random House, 2006.
12. Olivier Roy, *Globalized Islam: The Search for a New Ummah*, New York: Columbia University Press, 2004.

13. Jonathan Githens-Mazer and Robert Lambert, 'Why Conventional Wisdom on Radicalisation Fails: the persistence of a failed discourse,' *International Affairs*, vol. 86, no. 4, pp. 889–901.

14. Quintan Wiktorowicz, *Radical Islam Rising: Muslim Extremism in the West*, Oxford, Rowman & Littlefield, 2009.

15. I owe a note of thanks to Nigel Inkster for this image.

16. Alan Travis, 'MI5 report challenges views on terrorism in Britain', *The Guardian*, 20 Aug. 2008.

17. *Takfirism* is a movement within Islam that call those who do not agree with their views *kafirs* (non-believers), and believe that violence is permissible against them, even if they are Muslims.

18. Ahmed Rashid, *Taliban: the Story of the Afghan Warlords*, London: Pan Macmillan, 2001, p. 2.

19. Jon Ronson, *Them: Adventures with Extremists*, London: Picador Macmillan, 2001, p. 12.

20. Anonymous, 'The Islamic Verdict on Clapping,' http://www.islam4uk.com/islamic-systems/107-the-islamic-verdict-on-clapping, uploaded sometime in Dec. 2008.

21. His regular clashes with local authorities make it unclear where he exactly is, but he is periodically quoted in the British press and elsewhere as broadcasting his extreme views from Lebanon. For example, in Jan. 2012 he told the *Telegraph* 'Al Qaeda are so clever, they can make so many weapons from nothing. They can go to any kitchen, make a very nice pizza bomb and deliver it fresh', 25 Jan. 2012.

22. Andrew Norfolk, 'Hardline takeover of British mosques', *The Times*, 7 Sept. 2007.

23. In fact, some Salafis have been at the forefront of fighting radicalisation and extremism in Britain for a long time.

24. *Ummah* literally means the community of believers.

25. Mohammed Siddique Khan, suicide video, source op. cit.

26. Shehzad Tanweer suicide video, http://www.youtube.com/watch?v=FG6a26uX1eA

27. Wiktorowicz, op. cit., p. 12.

28. Travis, op. cit.

29. Dafna Linzer, 'Suspect in Pearl killing is college dropout who was radicalized by war in Bosnia', AP, 2 April 2002.

30. Quoted in Wiktorowicz, op. cit., p. 91.

31. A heavily redacted section of the Intelligence and Security Committee (ISC) Parliamentary report 'Could 7/7 Have Been Prevented?' on page 77 deals specifically with Al-Muhajiroun, stating that 'whilst membership or links with extremist groups might appear significant, it is not something that would, of itself, greatly influence the actions of MI5', which suggests that not all members are of interest to the security service. In fact, as we shall see later, in a number of cases, individuals actually get angry at groups like Al-Muhajiroun since they see them as all talk and no action.

32. This is a live debate that will be looked at in greater detail later.

33. For more on Aabid Khan and Younis Tsouli, see Raffaello Pantucci, 'Operation Praline: The Realization of Al-Suri's nizam la tanzim?', *Perspectives on Terrorism*, vol. 2, no. 11, Oct. 2008; or Evan Kohlmann, 'Anatomy of a Modern Homegrown Terror Cell: Aabid Khan et al.', *NEFA Foundation Special Report*, http://www.nefafoundation.org/miscellaneous/nefaabidkhan0908.pdf

34. Sageman, *Understanding Terror Networks*, p. 101.

35. Wiktorowicz, op. cit., p. 85.
36. Mohammed Siddique Khan suicide video, op. cit.
37. Early Azzam.com recordings and publications suggest that there may have been other fighters who sacrificed themselves consciously for their causes, but there is no official confirmation of them. Mohammed Bilal is the first to appear in the independent press.

1. FROM ARABIA TO SOUTH ASIA: MIGRATION

1. Jeevan Vasagar, 'Dilemma of the moderates', *The Guardian*, 19 June 2002.
2. There is evidence of pirate activity offshore though. Ansari alludes to this early on, as does D. M. Dunlop, 'The British Isles according to medieval Arabic authors-', *Islamic Quarterly*, 4:1, 1957, pp. 11–28.
3. Humayun Ansari, *The Infidel Within: Muslims in Britain Since 1800*, London: Hurst, 2004, p. 26.
4. Muslim Council of Britain, *Quest for Sanity*, London: Muslim Council of Britain, 2002.
5. Ansari, op. cit., pp. 31 and 58 chart much of Mahomet's history; and Martin Hickman, 'Sake Dean Mahomet: The man who opened Britain's first curry house, nearly 200 years ago', *The Independent*, 30 Sept. 2005 provides some more details. For Mahomet's own account with preface, please see Dean Mahomet, *The Travels of Dean Mahomet: An Eighteenth-Century Journey through India*, ed. with introduction by Michael H. Fisher, University of California Press, 1997.
6. Ansari, op. cit., p. 25.
7. He did not establish the first mosque, however; this was either the mosque built in Woking, London in 1889 (Ansari) or 1890 (Mohammed Anwar, 'Muslims in Western States: The British experience and the way forward', *Journal of Muslim Minority Affairs*, vol. 28, no. 1, April 2008, pp. 125–37) by the ex-registrar at the University of Punjab, Lahore; or else Britain's first mosque was established earlier, in 1860, by what is believed to be a community of Yemeni sailors in Cardiff.
8. Yahya Birt, 'Abdullah Quilliam: Britain's First Islamist?', http://www.yahyabirt.com/?p=136, 25 Jan. 2008.
9. Ansari, op. cit., p. 126.
10. Ansari cites the *Islamic Review*, March 1924, p. 118.
11. Jahan Mahmood, 'Britain's Pakistani communities and their contribution to the Italian campaign during World War II', unpublished paper delivered at All Souls College, University of Oxford, 3 April 2009, accessed Nov. 2009: http://www.britainsmuslimsoldiers.co.uk/images/bms.pdf; Shiraz Maher, *The Ties That Bind*, London: Policy Exchange, Sept. 2011.
12. Mohammed Anwar, 'Muslims in Western States: The British experience and the way forward', *Journal of Muslim Minority Affairs*, vol. 28, no. 1, April 2008, pp. 125–37.
13. Ansari, op. cit., p. 147.
14. Philip Lewis, *Islamic Britain: Religion, Politics and Identity Among British Muslims*, London: I. B. Tauris, 1994, p. 15, and UK Census figures, accessed at http://www.statistics.gov.uk
15. Ceri Peach, 'The Muslim population of Great Britain', *Ethnic and Racial Studies*, vol. 13, no. 3, 1990; Jørgen Nielsen, *Muslims in Western Europe: 3rd edn*, Edinburgh: Edinburgh University Press, 2004, p. 42.; UK Census figures, UK Census figures, accessed at http://www.statistics.gov.uk
16. It is unclear whether the Pakistani-Bangladeshi category includes the Gujarati populations

from East Africa, but in any case Bangladeshis and Pakistanis make up the overwhelming majority of South Asian Muslims in the United Kingdom.

17. According to the UK Islamic Mission's (UKIM) account of its story, it was as a result of the partition between Bangladesh and Pakistan that Dawatul Islam was created in 1978 specifically for Bangladeshi members, thus dividing UKIM's until then pan-South Asian community, 'The Founding Mission,' *Emel*, Dec. 2012.

18. An interesting contemporary note is added with the case of Rajinder Singh, the British National Party's first non-white member whose desire to join the party was driven by his hatred of Islam, the result of losing his father during Partition. Ben Quinn and Jerome Taylor, 'BNP signs its first non-white member', *The Independent*, 20 Nov. 2009.

19. Ansari, op. cit., p. 153.

20. The term 'lascar' refers to men of South Asian descent serving in the navy. The etymology appears to come from *lashkar*, meaning army unit.

21. Mohammed Anwar, *The Myth of Return*, London: Heinemann, 1979, p. 21.

22. Mahmood's study of Indian army deaths in Italy argues that there are strong links between the parts of Pakistan (then India) where soldiers who fought on the Allied side came from and those Britain's Pakistani Muslim communities derive from today. Furthermore, in his research he has located communities claiming to be descended from such individuals. Mahmood, 'Britain's Pakistani communities'.

23. Ansari, op. cit., p. 152.

24. The Change Institute, 'The Pakistani Muslim Community in England: Understanding Muslim Ethnic Communities', Department of Communities and Local Government, March 2009.

25. John Eade and David Garbin, 'Competing visions of identity and space: Bangladeshi Muslims in Britain', *Contemporary South Asia*, vol. 15, no. 2, pp. 181–93.

26. Ceri Peach, 'South Asian migration and settlement in Great Britain, 1951–2001', *Contemporary South Asia*, vol. 15, no. 2, June 2006, pp. 133–46.

27. John Eade and David Garbin, op. cit.

28. Alison Shaw, 'Why might young British Muslims support the Taliban?,' *Anthropology Today*, vol. 18, no. 1, Feb. 2002, pp. 5–8.

29. Ed Blanche, AP, 13 Aug. 1979.

30. http://www.nationalarchives.gov.uk/cabinetpapers/themes/commonwealth-immigration-control-legislation.htm.

31. Salil Tripathi, 'Powers of Transformation', *Index on Censorship*, 2002.

32. *Islamophobia—A Challenge for us All*, London: Runnymede Trust, 1997, p. 14.

33. Quoted in Philip Lewis, *Young, British and Muslim*, London: Continuum, 2007, p. 17.

34. 'How Sir Anwar built an empire in the best way,' *The Grocer*, 22 Oct. 2005.

35. Details found on the International Scholarships site: http://internationalscholarships.ca/asia/pakistan

36. Philip Lewis cites figures for Bradford in 1961 showing all but 81 of 3,376 Pakistanis were male. Philip Lewis, op. cit, p. 16.

37. John Eade and David Garbin, op. cit.

38. Steven Vertovec, 'Islamophobia and Muslim recognition in Britain' in Y. Haddad (ed.), *Muslims in the West: From Sojourners to Citizens*, Oxford: Oxford University Press, 2002.

39. Ansari, op. cit., p. 149. Another example is the global community of Chinese migrants, the vast majority of whom can trace their roots to the Southern Fujian province.

40. Mohammed Anwar, *The Myth of Return*, London: Heinemann, 1979.

41. Philip Lewis, *Islamic Britain: Religion, Politics and Identity Among British Muslims*, London: I. B. Tauris, 1994.

42. Danièle Joly, *Britannia's Crescent: Making a place for Muslims in British Society*, Aldershot: Avebury, 1995.

43. Alison Shaw, 'The arranged transnational cousin marriages of British Pakistanis: critique, dissent and cultural continuity', *Contemporary South Asia*, vol. 15, no. 2, June 2006, pp. 209–20.

44. Author interview, Oct. 2009; anecdotally, it is also the case that the author knows at least two such Pakistani-British couples.

45. Shiv Malik, 'My Brother the Bomber', *Prospect*, 30 June 2007.

46. These are, however, figures compiled in 1992. Fred Halliday, *Arabs in Exile: Yemeni Migrants in Urban Britain*, London: I. B. Tauris, 1992. It is interesting to note that Yemenis are one of the oldest Muslim communities in Britain, and yet very few British Yemenis have been drawn to radical ideas.

47. Ghada Karmi, 'The Egyptians of Britain: a Migrant Community in Transition', CMEIS Occasional Paper no. 57, May 1997.

48. Ansari, op. cit, p. 151.

49. Caroline Nagel, 'Hidden minorities and the politics of "race": the case of British Arab activists in London', *Journal of Ethnic and Migration Studies*, vol. 27, no. 3, pp. 381–400.

50. Rushworth M. Kidder, 'Burnooses among the bowlers: London's wealthy Arab population', *Christian Science Monitor*, 22 Aug. 1980.

51. 'Arabs in London: the big spenders', *The Economist*, 21 Aug. 1976.

52. Kidder, op. cit.

53. Leslie Plommer, 'We like it here', *The Guardian*, 8 Aug. 1994.

54. Ansari, op. cit., p. 161.

55. Plommer, op. cit.

56. Kidder, op. cit.

57. Kidder, op. cit.

58. Stefan Aust, *The Baader Meinhof Complex*, London, Bodley Head, 2008, p. 384.

59. Lewis, *Islamic Britain*, p. 68.

60. Lewis looks in some detail at the situation in Bradford, pp. 67–72, while Danièle Joly, *Britannia's Crescent: Making a place for Muslims in British Society*, Aldershot: Avebury, 1995, pp. 88–95 looks in detail at the situation in Birmingham.

61. Lewis, op. cit., p. 68.

62. Abdul Ala Maududi, quoted in Lewis, op. cit., p. 41.

63. For a comprehensive overview and analysis of Jamaat Islami, see Seyyed Vali Reza Nasr, *The Vanguard of the Islamic Revolution*, Los Angeles: University of California Press, 1994.

64. It is worth noting, however, that these groups have not always been peaceful. JI in Pakistan was a hardline organisation that thrived during the jihad in Afghanistan during the 1980s. Vali Nasr, op. cit., p. 195. With regard to the Muslim Brotherhood, a number of jihadists to emerge from the Arab world appear to have a history of involvement in the group.

65. 'The Founding Mission,' *Emel*, Dec. 2012.

66. Lewis, op. cit., p. 102. The choice of Nadvi as a founding speaker was an interesting one within the wider politics of JI, given his prominent role in the organisation's early days as an opponent of Maududi's. For more, see Seyyed Vali Reza Nasr, *The Vanguard of the Islamic Revolution*, Berkley: University of California Press, 1994, pp. 22–25.

67. 'The Founding Mission,' *Emel*, Dec. 2012.
68. Ibid.
69. Ansari, op. cit., p. 349.
70. Muhammad Anwar, *The Myth of Return: Pakistanis in Britain*, London: Heinemann, 1979.
71. Ibid., p. 346.
72. According to Mehmood Naqshbandi, a surveyor of British Muslims, in 2010 44.6 per cent of mosques are Deobandi and 25.4 per cent are Barelwi. http://www.muslimsinbritain.org/resources/masjid_report.pdf
73. Philip Lewis, op. cit., p. 81–9.
74. Joly, op. cit., p. 91. Joly provides an account of how this style of politics is now being rejected by the later generations, as they start to become properly involved in politics themselves. With regard to the comment about subcontinental politics remaining like this today, one can look to the Pakistan People's Party which was passed from father to daughter (Zulfikar Ali Bhutto to Benazir Bhutto), and then after her death to her widower Asif Ali Zardari, who is holding power until their son, Bilawal Bhutto Zardari, can take over.
75. Lewis, op. cit., p. 36.
76. Stephen Tankel, *Storming the World Stage: The Story of Lashkar-e-Taiba*, London: Hurst, 2010, p. 28.
77. Yoginder S. Sikand, 'The origins and growth of the Tablighi Jamaat in Britain', *Islam and Christian-Muslim Relations*, vol. 9, no. 2, 1998, pp. 171–92.
78. Author interview, Oct. 2009.
79. Abu Musab al-Suri is quoted as saying that Qatada 'had been a supporter of the Tabligh group', Brynjar Lia, *Architect of Global Jihad*, London: Hurst, 2007, p. 185; el-Faisal's activism is referred to in Bruce Hoffman, 'Radicalization and Subversion: Al Qaeda and the 7 July 2005 Bombings and the 2006 Airline Bombing Plot', *Studies in Conflict and Terrorism*, vol. 32, no. 12, pp. 1100–1116 and confirmed in author interviews in London; and Khan's attendance at the TJ mosque in Dewsbury was widely reported.
80. Sean O'Neill, 'Airline bomb plot: mosque has been recruiting ground for 20 years', *The Times*, 9 Sept. 2009.
81. Ahmed Ali Khan et al, trial transcript, June 2008.
82. Ziauddin Sardar, 'Watch this grass-roots group carefully', *New Statesman*, 4 Sept. 2006.
83. Omar Nasiri, *Inside the Global Jihad*, London: Hurst, 2006, p. 110 onwards describes his experience with TJ.
84. Stephen Tankel highlights the difference between AeH and LeT: 'AeH believe jihad is a collective obligation, while LeT believe it to be an individual obligation.' Author interview, Jan. 2010.
85. Seyyed Vali Reza Nasr, op. cit., p. 195; and Ahmed Rashid, *Taliban*, London: Pan Macmillan, 2001, p. 88–90.
86. Author interview (with Azad Kashmiri), London, Oct. 2009.
87. Regina vs. Abdul Qayyum Raja, Royal Courts of Justice, London, 11 Aug. 2004.
88. 'Missing Indian envoy found slain in Britain', AP, 6 Feb. 1984.
89. Richard Ehrlich, 'India to hang convicted murderer', United Press International, 9 Feb. 1984.
90. Ibid.
91. Author interview, Birmingham, Nov. 2012.
92. 'Kashmir comes to Birmingham', *The Economist*, 22 April 2000.

93. Phil Woolas, 'Pakistan: Strategic Challenges and Prospects', Speech to the Royal United Services Institute, 17 April 2007.

94. Author interview, with former British High Commissioner Sir Hilary Synnott, July 2007.

95. Secretary of State for the Home Department and Shafiq ur Rehman, Supreme Court judgement, Case no: 1999/1268/C, 23 May 2000.

96. Daniel McGrory, 'Train bombers "funded by British businessmen"', *The Times*, 17 July 2006.

97. Daniel McGrory, 'British-based charity "funding terror"', *The Times*, 14 June 2002.

98. Author interview, Birmingham, 2009.

99. Author interview, London, 2008.

100. Ceri Peach, 'South Asian migration and settlement in Great Britain, 1951–2001', *Contemporary South Asia*, vol. 15, no. 2, June 2006, pp. 133–46.

101. Adrian Levy and Cathy Scott-Clark, *The Meadow: Kashmir 1995—Where the Terror Began*, London: HarperPress, March 2012, p. 60.

102. A number of sources spoken to suggest it took place. An undated reference in Omar Saeed Sheikh's diary mentions that Azhar met his father in the United Kingdom, though it does not specify the location (thanks to Nick Fielding for providing quotes). A profile of Azhar in the *Kashmir Herald* suggests a visit to Southall in the early 1990s: 'Maulana Masood Azhar', *Kashmir Herald*, vol. 1, no. 8, Jan. 2002. Others spoken to in Birmingham have referred to the trip, while an official Indian source confirmed that they knew Azhar had made a trip 'to the West Midlands.'

103. Author interview with Amardeep Bassey, June 2012.

104. Complete profile of Hafiz Saeed, *Daily Times* (Pakistan), 7 April 2012.

105. U.S. vs. Ali Asad Chandia and Mohammed Ajmal Khan, indictment filed Sept. 2005.

106. Stephen Tankel, op. cit.

107. BBC Monitoring, 3–4 July 1980.

108. Madawi al-Rasheed, 'Saudi religious transnationalism in London' in M. al-Rasheed (ed.), *Transnational Connections and the Arab Gulf*, Oxford: Routledge, 2005, p. 156.

109. Simon Reeve, *The New Jackals*, London: Andre Deutsch, 1999, p. 167.

110. 'Profile: James McLintock', *Sunday Times*, 19 April 2009.

111. In 2008 the author attended a session at the East London Mosque at which Gulbuddin Hekmatyar's brother spoke; while he was not clearly recruiting, the path of former fighters coming to London was still well-trodden.

112. Peter Bergen, *Holy War Inc.*, London: Phoenix, 2002, p. 91.

113. Suha Taji-Farouki, *A Fundamental Quest: Hizb al-Tahrir and the Search for the Islamic Caliphate*, London: Grey Seal, 1996, p. 170.

114. Raffaello Pantucci, 'Al Qaeda's Next Evolution? An Internet of Lone Wolves,' in Manuel Almeida (ed.), *Al Qaeda after Bin Laden: The Western View Point*, Dubai: Al Mesbar Studies Center, 2011.

115. 'The preacher of hate and his pal the terrorist: Pictured—how Abu Qatada is free to walk the streets with car bomb extremist', *Daily Mail*, 2 Sept. 2008.

116. Melanie Phillips, *Londonistan*, London: Gibson Square, 2006.

117. Steve Coll, *Ghost Wars*, New York: Penguin Press, 2004, p. 270. This is also something that former senior British officials have told the author.

118. It also seems likely that these preachers were in communication with the security services, reassuring them that their intentions were not domestic.

2. ALIENATION AND THE SUBURBAN MUJAHEDEEN

1. M. Y. Alam, *Made in Bradford*, Pontefract: Route, 2006, p. 75.
2. Maajid Nawaz, *Radical: My Journey from Islamist Extremist to a Democratic Awakening*, London: WH Allen, 2012.
3. Moazzam Begg and Victoria Brittain, *Enemy Combatant*, New York: The New Press, 2006, p. 28; also repeated to the author in interview.
4. Jon Stock, 'Inside the mind of a seductive killer', *The Times*, 21 Aug. 2002.
5. Nasreen Suleaman, op. cit.; Coroner's Inquest transcript, 14 Feb. 2011, p. 58.
6. Of course, it is almost impossible to know from an outsider's perspective how a person really experiences racism. What seems a small slight to the outsider may in fact cut deep. But the point is that racism as a feature of the social backdrop of the individuals involved in terrorism appears to occur to wildly differing degrees, and thus cannot be used as the sole determinant.
7. Enoch Powell's 'Rivers of Blood' speech, reproduced by *The Daily Telegraph*, 6 Nov. 2007: http://www.telegraph.co.uk/comment/3643823/Enoch-Powells-Rivers-of-Blood-speech.html
8. Yasmin Alibhai-Brown, 'Wake up Mr Straw. You're continuing the tradition of racist immigration laws', *The Independent*, 28 Oct. 1999.
9. A Bradford Muslim born in 1980 in the Manningham part of the city told the author racism was not something she had noticed as a child in school.
10. Quintan Wiktorowicz, Quintan Wiktorowicz, *Radical Islam Rising: Muslim Extremism in the West Oxford*, Rowman & Littlefield, 2009, p. 91.
11. Author interview, Oct. 2009.
12. Adam LeBor, *A Heart Turned East*, London: Little, Brown, 1997, p. 129.
13. Hanif Kureishi, 'Bradford in Trouble Again', *Granta*, no. 20, 1986, pp. 149–70.
14. Yasmin Hussain and Paul Bagguley, 'Citizenship, Ethnicity and Identity: British Pakistanis after the 2001 "Riots"', *Sociology*, vol. 39, no. 3, 2005, pp. 407–25.
15. Philip Lewis, *Young, British and Muslim*, London: Continuum, 2008, p. 29.
16. Philip Lewis, *Islamic Britain*, London: I. B. Tauris, 2002 edn, Preface.
17. D. Phillips, 'The Changing Geography of South Asians in Bradford' found at: http://www.bradford2020.com/pride/docs/Section5.doc
18. Marta Bolognani, *Crime and Muslim Britain*, London: Tauris Academic Studies, 2009, p. 49.
19. M. Y. Alam, op. cit., pp. 78–9.
20. Philip Lewis, op. cit., p. 10.
21. Humayun Ansari, *The Infidel Within: Muslims in Britain Since 1800*, London: Hurst, 2004, p. 345.
22. Ray Honeyford, 'Education and Race—An Alternative View', *Salisbury Review*, 1984, republished in *The Daily Telegraph*, 27 Aug. 2006.
23. Ghazala Bhatti, *Asian Children at Home and at School*, London: Routledge, 1999.
24. Stewart Payne, 'Extremists "are targeting children"', *The Daily Telegraph*, 15 Sept. 2001.
25. This was anecdotally mentioned to the author in conversations in Bradford, Birmingham, and East London.
26. 'Headteacher who never taught again after daring to criticize multiculturalism,' *The Daily Telegraph*, 27 Aug. 2006. Almost a decade later, questions were again raised in the West Midlands when attempts were made to take over local schools in Birmingham by individuals

pushing for fundamentalist beliefs to guide the curriculum. See Richard Kerbaj and Sian Griffiths, 'Islamist plot to take over schools,' *Sunday Times*, 2 March 2014.

27. Philip Lewis, op. cit., p. 62.

28. Marta Bolognani, op. cit., p. 50; she defines 'multiple deprivation' as 'a situation of disadvantage in more than one field: poor housing, overcrowded households, malnutrition, illiteracy, educational underachievement, unemployment, etc.'

29. M. Y. Alam, op. cit., p. 27.

30. Robin Richardson and Angela Wood, *The Achievement of British Pakistani Learners: A Work in Progress*, Stoke on Trent: Trentham Books, 2005, p. 2; they quote the Oldham 'Ritchie Report' from 2001 as an example.

31. M. Y. Alam, op. cit., pp. 168–9.

32. Shiv Malik, 'My Brother the Bomber', *Prospect*, 30 June 2007.

33. Documents obtained by German authorities believed to be authored by British extremist Rashid Rauf.

34. For an exploration of the issues around arranged marriages in Britain's Pakistani community, see Alison Shaw, 'The arranged transnational cousin marriages of British Pakistanis: critique, dissent and cultural continuity', *Contemporary South Asia*, vol. 15, no. 2, June 2006, pp. 209–20. The author has also spoken to a number of young British South Asians who have been involved in arranged marriages with cousins—in at least one case, the author was told the British man involved was less than willing, while in another, the girl asked her parents to help her find a husband demonstrating the complexity of the issue. Author interview, Bradford 2009.

35. Paul Bagguley and Yasmin Hussain, 'The Bradford "Riot" of 2001: A preliminary analysis', paper presented to the Ninth Alternative Futures and Popular Protest Conference, Manchester Metropolitan University, 22–24 April 2003.

36. Paul Bagguley and Yasmin Hussain, Sociology (their emphasis in the quote).

37. Robin Richardson and Angela Wood, op. cit., p. 1.

38. Philip Lewis, *Islamic Britain*, p. 68.

39. Ibid., p. 177.

40. Mehmood Naqshbandi, a well-known surveyor of British Muslims, stated that in 2010 44.6 per cent of mosques in the United Kingdom are Deobandi and 25.4 per cent are Barelwi. This broadly reflects the breakdown of Britain's Muslim community, http://www.muslimsinbritain.org/resources/masjid_report.pdf

41. Adam LeBor, *A Heart Turned East*, London: Little, Brown and Company, 1997, p. 122–123.

42. A report by the University of Chester for the BBC showed that only 8 per cent of imams preaching in British mosques were born in the United Kingdom, and only 6 per cent spoke English as their first language. 'Ban foreign language imams—peer', BBC News, 6 July 2007, http://news.bbc.co.uk/2/hi/6275574.stm (accessed Nov. 2009). A later report from the Quilliam Foundation by Anya Hart-Dyke, *Mosques Made in Britain*, London: Quilliam, 2009, concluded that 97 per cent of imams or mosque leaders were from overseas, and 92 per cent educated abroad, 'mostly in Pakistan or Bangladesh'.

43. Author interview, Leicester, Oct. 2009.

44. Peter Mandaville, *Transnational Muslim Politics: Reimagining the Umma*, London: Routledge, 2004, p. 133.

45. Author interview with prominent Muslim demographer, London, Oct. 2009.

46. Seán McLoughlin, 'Mosques and the Public Space: Conflict and Cooperation in Bradford', *Journal of Ethnic and Migration Studies*, vol. 31, no. 6, Nov. 2005, pp. 1045–66.

47. Philip Lewis, *Islamic Britain*, p. 178.

48. Author interview, Usama Hasan, July 2012.

49. Philip Lewis, *Young, British and Muslim*, p. 29.

50. Tahir Abbas, 'An analysis of race equality policy and practice in the city of Birmingham, UK', *Local Government Studies*, vol. 31, no. 1, Feb. 2005, pp. 53–68.

51. Moazzam Begg and Victoria Brittain, op. cit., p. 29.

52. Tahir Abbas, 'Ethno-Religious identities and Islamic political radicalism in the UK: a case study', *Journal of Muslim Minority Affairs*, vol. 27, no. 3, Dec. 2007, pp. 429–42.

53. Begg himself is something of a polarising figure: some from Birmingham report that he is not held in high esteem, while others appreciate his more recent activities and the organisations that he has established. At time of writing Begg was in jail awaiting trial for his alleged support of terrorist groups in Syria.

54. Yahya Birt, 'Beyond Sidique', *Prospect*, no. 135, 30 June 2007.

55. Shiv Malik, op. cit.

56. Cahal Milmo, 'Close friends of 7/7 bombers cleared of scouting attacks', *The Independent*, 29 April 2009.

57. Regina vs. Mohammed Shakil, Wahid Ali and Sadeer Saleem, Crown Court at Kingston upon Thames.

58. Quoted by Dhiren Barot, a Hindu convert who trained in the 1990s with Lashkar-e-Taiba, and later published by the bookshop that Moazzam Begg helped set up: Esa al-Hindi, *The Army of Madinah in Kashmir*, Birmingham: Maktabah al-Ansaar, 1999, p. vi.

59. Author interview, Leicester, Oct. 2009.

60. It should be highlighted that Saleem admitted going to a camp before it was illegal.

61. Andrew Norfolk, 'Iqra: the backstreet bookshop that taught frontline war', *The Times*, 29 April 2009; Coroner's Inquest transcript, 14 Feb. 2011, p. 71 onwards.

62. Shiv Malik, op. cit.

63. Coroner's Inquest transcript, 14 Feb. 2011, p. 144.

64. Coroner's Inquest transcript, 14 Feb. 2011, p. 65.

65. Coroner's Inquest transcript, 16 Feb. 2011, p. 16.

66. Andrew Norfolk, 'Iqra: the backstreet bookshop that taught frontline war', *The Times*, 29 April 2009.

67. Coroner's Inquest transcript, 14 Feb. 2011, p. 70.

68. Laura May, '7/7 accused "tried to join fighters helping Taliban"', Press Association, 20 May 2008; Regina vs. Mohammed Shakil, Wahid Ali and Sadeer Saleem, Crown Court at Kingston upon Thames.

69. Abul Taher, 'Tartan Taliban linked to bombers,' *Sunday Times*, August 14 2005.

70. Coroner's Inquest transcript, 16 Feb. 2011, p. 69.

71. Moazzam Begg and Victoria Brittain, *Enemy Combatant*, New York: The New Press, 2006, p. 75.

72. Tahir Abbas, 'Ethno-Religious identities and Islamic political radicalism in the UK: a case study', *Journal of Muslim Minority Affairs*, vol. 23, no. 3, pp. 429–42.

73. Moazzam Begg and Victoria Brittain, op. cit., p. 81.

74. Guantanamo memorandum on continued detention of detainee, Rhuhal Ahmed, US9UK-000110DP, 28 Oct. 2003, http://www.wikileaks.ch/gitmo/pdf/uk/us9uk-000110dp.pdf

75. Dominic Casciani, 'Liquid bomb plot: What happened', BBC News, 9 Sept. 2008, http://news.bbc.co.uk/2/hi/uk_news/7564184.stm

88

NOTES pp. [72–81]

76. 'Bookseller Ahmed Faraz jailed over terror offenses,' *BBC News*, 13 Dec. 2011.
77. Moazzam Begg and Victoria Brittain, op. cit., p. 76.
78. Duncan Gardham, 'Former Taliban jailed for recruiting young men on the streets of Britain,' *Daily Telegraph*, 9 Sept. 2011; 'Longsight market Taliban fanatic sent more than 20 recruits to fight British forces in Afghanistan,' *Manchester Evening News*, 10 Sept. 2011.
79. Navid Akhtar, 'Torn between cultures, Britain's "orphans of Islam" turn to terror', *The Observer*, 23 Oct. 2005. The term is one Akhtar says radical preachers deploy to describe the community of young second-generation Muslims in the United Kingdom.
80. There are a number of instances in which individuals seem to have been born into radical families that may have encouraged them down a path that would invariably lead to violence. In some of these cases, the individuals have ended up in terrorist groups, while in others they have eventually changed their minds and taken a very different path. Examples are awkward to name for legal reasons.
81. This number has now grown further with more recent arrests, though Bradford remains relatively under-represented amongst the ranks of locations that have generated terrorist plotters within the UK.
82. Houriya Ahmed, Robin Simcox and Hannah Stuart, *Islamist Terrorism: The British Connections*, London: Centre for Social Cohesion Press, July 2010.
83. Both men have featured prominently in the press, but relatively comprehensive self-narrated biographies can be found in Peter Stanford, 'Preaching from the converted', *The Independent on Sunday*, 16 May 2004.
84. At time of writing, another convert graduate of Feltham Young Offenders Institution (where Reid was radicalised) was facing charges in Kenya of being involved in a plot to conduct a bombing campaign in Mombasa.
85. Jon Stock, op. cit.
86. Peter Gee, Omar Saeed Sheikh's cellmate for eighteen months in an Indian prison, was quoted as saying that Omar had faced racial taunts as a child; reported in Jon Stock, op. cit. as well as Bernard Henry Lévy, *Who Killed Daniel Pearl?*, New Jersey: Melville House Publishing, 2003.
87. Marc Sageman, *Understanding Terror Networks*, Philadelphia: University of Pennsylvania Press, 2004.

3. EARLY EXPRESSIONS: FROM THE RUSHDIE AFFAIR TO JIHAD IN BOSNIA

1. Iqbal Sacranie, quoted in Peter Murtagh, 'Rushdie in hiding after Ayatollah's death threat', *The Guardian*, 18 Feb. 1989.
2. While admittedly unscientific, a search on http://www.amazon.co.uk of the words 'Rushdie Affair' throws up 776 hits (in March 2012).
3. 'Al Qaeda condemns Rushdie honour', BBC News, 10 July 2007, http://news.bbc.co.uk/2/hi/middle_east/6289110.stm (the video can also be found here).
4. 'Archive on 4: The Book Burners', BBC Radio 4, 13 Feb. 2009.
5. 'Koran and Country: How Islam got political', BBC Radio 4, 10 Nov. 2005, transcript available: http://news.bbc.co.uk/nol/shared/spl/hi/programmes/analysis/transcripts/10_11_05.txt
6. Syed Shahabuddin, quoted in Lisa Appignanesi and Sarah Maitland (eds), *The Rushdie File*, London: Institute for Contemporary Arts, 1990, p. 3.

305

7. Malise Ruthven, *A Satanic Affair: Salman Rushdie and the Rage of Islam*, London: Chatto and Windus, 1990, p. 1.
8. Kenan Malik, *From Fatwa to Jihad*, London: Atlantic, 2009, p. 4.
9. Robin Lustig, Martin Bailey, Simon de Bruxelles and Ian Mather, 'War of the Word', *The Observer*, 19 Feb. 1989.
10. 'Archive on 4: The Book Burners', BBC Radio 4, 13 Feb. 2009.
11. Idem.
12. Peter Lennon, 'Religious Tolerance: Climate of Reason', *The Guardian*, 30 Nov. 1994.
13. Quoted in Kenan Malik, op. cit., p. 28–9.
14. 'Ayatollah sentences author to death', BBC News, 14 Feb. 1989, http://news.bbc.co.uk/onthisday/hi/dates/stories/Feb./14/newsid_2541000/2541149.stm
15. Inayat Bunglawala, 'I used to be a book burner', *The Guardian*, 19 June 2007.
16. Robin Lustig, Martin Bailey, Simon de Bruxelles and Ian Mather, op. cit.
17. Author interview, Leicester, Oct. 2009.
18. Kenan Malik, op. cit., p. 124.
19. Kalim Siddiqui, quoted in Kenan Malik, ibid., pp. 124–5.
20. Ghayasuddin Siddiqui quoted in Kenan Malik, ibid., p. 7.
21. Kalim Siddiqui, unreferenced quote in 'Archive on 4: The Book Burners', BBC Radio 4, 13 Feb. 2009. In Kenan Malik's book, pp. 7–8, Ghayasuddin Siddiqui makes reference to the same meeting, stating that the minister in question was Mohammad Khatami.
22. Andrew Anthony, 'How one book ignited a culture war', *The Observer*, 11 Jan. 2009.
23. Author interview, Leicester, Oct. 2009.
24. Ziauddin Sardar and Wyn Davies, *Distorted Imaginations: Lessons from the Rushdie Affair*, London: Grey Seal Books, 1990, p. 198.
25. Kalim Siddiqui, *The Muslim Manifesto—A Strategy for Survival*, London: Muslim Institute, 1990, http://www.muslimparliament.org.uk/MuslimManifesto.pdf
26. It was initially not to be called the Muslim Parliament, but rather 'The Council of British Muslims'; however, the press started referring to it as the 'Muslim Parliament' (which also features in the description of the Council in the Muslim Manifesto), and it stuck. Author interview with Muslim Parliament founder, Jan. 2010.
27. Kalim Siddiqui, op. cit., p. 10.
28. Peter Murtagh, 'Rushdie in hiding after Ayatollah's death threat', *Guardian*, 18 Feb. 1989.
29. According to Christopher Andrew's authorised biography of MI5, there were a 'series' of Iranian 'inspired operations to target Rushdie'. *The Defence of the Realm: The Authorized History of MI5*, London: Allen Lane, 5 Oct. 2009, p. 801. In one case an apparent agent managed to simply blow himself up in a London hotel room.
30. Ed Husain, *The Islamist*, London: Penguin, May 2007, p. 70.
31. Kathy Evans, 'Radical time-bomb under British Islam', *The Guardian*, 7 Feb. 1994.
32. Nineteen-year-old Kysar Shahnawaz, quoted in Sean O'Neill, 'Keeping faith with a circle of awareness', *The Guardian*, 2 Aug. 1989.
33. It seems as though a Palestinian, Fouad Hussein, may have been the first HuT member in the United Kingdom, but it was not until Omar Bakri and Farid Qassim that the organisation actually developed some substance. Suha Taji-Farouki, *A Fundamental Quest: Hizb al Tahrir and the search for the Islamic Caliphate*, London: Grey Seal, 1996 provides a comprehensive account (pp. 171–87) of its establishment in the United Kingdom.
34. Jon Ronson, *Them*, London: Picador, 2001, p. 5. The chapter about Omar Bakri Mohammed

is based on an earlier documentary that Ronson had filmed in which he trailed him around London in the late 1990s.

35. From his official profile on Al Muhajiroun's latest website: http://www.salafimedia.net/sheikh-omar-bakri-muhammad.html
36. Quintan Wiktorowicz, op. cit., p. 7; however, this is contradicted by an interview Bakri Mohammed gave in 2004 (Wiktorowicz interviewed him in 2002) in which he claimed that he was in fact seventeen when he left the Muslim Brotherhood to join HuT. This is important, as such discrepancies are common among Bakri Mohammed interviews.
37. *Who Are the So-Called 'Salafi Youth for Islamic Propagation'?*, http://www.salafimanhaj.com; also a number of interviews with official sources and former radicals show a general shadow of doubt over Bakri's time at Al Azhar.
38. Quintan Wiktorowicz, op. cit., p. 7. A note also on Juhaiman al-Utaiba, who was the messianic leader of a plot to overthrow the Saudi regime in 1979 in which he and an army of followers took over the holy site of Mecca. For a detailed account of the event, see Yaroslav Trofimov, *The Siege of Mecca: The Forgotten Uprising in Islam's Holiest Shrine*, London: Penguin, 2008.
39. Ibid., p. 7.
40. Mahan Abedin, 'Al-Muhajiroun in the UK: An interview with Sheikh Omar Bakri Mohammed', *Jamestown Foundation Terrorism Monitor*, 22 March 2004.
41. Ibid.
42. Quintan Wiktorowicz, op. cit., p. 8.
43. Mahan Abedin, op. cit.
44. Quintan Wiktorowicz, op. cit., p. 8.
45. Mahan Abedin, op. cit.
46. Author interview, London, Oct. 2009.
47. Mahan Abedin, op. cit.
48. Hizb ut Tahrir Britain Press Release, 'Omar Bakri was not the founder of Hizb-ut-Tahrir', 9 Aug. 2005, accessed: http://www.hizb.org.uk/press-centre/press-release/omar-bakri-was-not-the-founder-of-hizb-ut-tahrir.html
49. Suha Taji-Farouki, op. cit., p. 171.
50. Mahan Abedin, op. cit.
51. Sean O'Neill, 'Keeping faith with a circle of awareness', *The Guardian*, 2 Aug. 1989.
52. Robert S. Leiken, *Europe's Angry Muslims*, New York: Oxford University Press, 2012, p. 157.
53. Author interview, June 2011.
54. Suha Taji Farouki, 'Islamists and the threat of jihad: Hizb al-Tahrir and al-Muhajiroun on Israel and Jews', *Middle Eastern Studies*, vol. 34, no. 4, Oct. 2000, pp. 21–46.
55. 'Hizb ut-Tahrir Britain: media information pack', undated, available at: http://www.hizb.org.uk/hizb/images/PDFs/HT_media_pack.pdf
56. Adam Lebor, 'They could have been Christians; Islam has all the answers I need', *The Independent*, 30 Oct. 1990.
57. Peter Stanford, 'Preaching from the converted', *The Independent on Sunday*, 16 May 2004; also, author interview, Oct. 2009.
58. Ed Husain, op. cit., p. 79.
59. Author interview, London, Dec. 2008.
60. Many former Hizb ut-Tahrir members interviewed by the author attested to this. Certainly,

in Ronson's documentary, Bakri Mohammed comes across as quite an affable person and not the hate-monger that he is often described as in the press.

61. Robert Lambert, 'Salafi and Islamist Londoners: Stigmatised minority faith communities countering al-Qaida', *Crime, Law and Social Change*, vol. 50, no. 1–2, Sept. 2008.

62. Jonathan Birt, 'Wahhabism in the United Kingdom' in Madawi al-Rasheed (ed.), *Transnational Connections and the Arab Gulf*, Oxford: Routledge, 2005, p. 172.

63. Ed Husain, op. cit., p. 71.

64. Johann Hari, 'Renouncing Islamism', *The Independent*, 16 Nov. 2009.

65. Usama Hasan's account is taken from an interview with Johann Hari, op. cit.; and an author interview from July 2012.

66. Author interview, Usama Hasan, July 2012.

67. Author interview, Usama Hasan, July 2012.

68. Ed Husain, op. cit., p. 75.

69. Coroner's Inquest transcript, 14 Feb. 2011, p. 121.

70. Regina vs. Mohammed Shakil, Wahid Ali and Sadeer Saleem, Crown Court at Kingston upon Thames.

71. Ruth Fisher, 'Hitler's Heirs incite Islamic students', *The Observer*, 13 March 1994.

72. Author interview, Usama Hasan, July 2012.

73. Johann Hari, op. cit.

74. Author interview, Usama Hasan, July 2012.

75. Ibid.

76. Author interview, London, Oct. 2009.

77. Raymond Whitaker, 'Crisis in the Gulf: Hundreds of Muslims in London protest march', *The Independent*, 25 Feb. 1991.

78. It is highly likely that this Omar Mohammed is Omar Bakri Mohammed: he was known to have used the affiliation 'International Islamic Front' on a number of occasions.

79. *Le Monde*, 18 Feb. 1991.

80. Tahir Abbas, 'Ethno-Religious Identities and Islamic Political Radicalism in the UK: A Case Study', *Journal of Muslim Minority Affairs*, vol. 27, no. 3, Dec. 2007, pp. 429–42.

81. Lucy Johnson, 'Religion: Muslims isolated by West's "demonization" of Islam', IPS-Inter Press Service, 11 Aug. 1993.

82. Author interview, Leicester, Oct. 2009.

83. The author is unable to track down the original quote for this line, but it has been repeatedly attributed to the Secretary of State.

84. Alan Philips, 'New "arc of crisis" fuels fears over Muslim aggression', *The Daily Telegraph*, 8 Oct. 1992.

85. Evan Kohlmann, *Al Qaida's Jihad in Europe*, London: Berg, 2005, p. 16.

86. Alison Pargeter, *The New Frontiers of Jihad: Radical Islam in Europe*, London: I. B.Tauris, 2008, pp. 40–41.

87. 'Seventh Session of the Muslim Parliament', *British Muslims Monthly Survey*, vol. 1, no. 6, June 1993, pp. 3–4.

88. Iqbal Siddiqui, 'Fundamental principles behind Kalim Siddiqui's establishment of the Muslim Parliament', *Crescent International*, undated, accessed: http://muslimedia.com/archives/special-edition/ks-thought/ksthot1.htm

89. 'Fund-raising for "Arms for Bosnia"', *British Muslims Monthly Survey*, vol. 1, no. 8, Aug. 1993, pp. 9–10.

90. Chris Hastings and Jessica Berry, 'Muslim militia training in Britain: Bin Laden groups to join mujahedeen for various wars, including Chechnya', *Ottowa Citizen*, 7 Nov. 1999.
91. Online posts to the Google groups, soc.religion.islam, author in possession of copies.
92. Author interview, Oct. 2009.
93. Ed Husain, op. cit., p. 75.
94. Ed Husain, op. cit., p. 75.
95. Author interview, Leicester, Oct. 2009.
96. Regina vs. Mohammed Shakil, Wahid Ali and Sadeer Saleem, Crown Court at Kingston upon Thames
97. Author interview, London, Oct. 2009.
98. Author interview, June 2011.
99. Ibid.
100. Johann Hari, op. cit.; and the sentiment was repeated in an interview with the author.
101. Author interview, Jan. 2010.
102. Dafna Linzer, 'Suspect in Pearl killing is a college dropout who was radicalized by war in Bosnia', AP, 2 April 2002.
103. Dafna Linzer, 'Suspect in Pearl killing is a college dropout who was radicalized by war in Bosnia', AP, 2 April 2002.
104. Nick Fielding, 'The British Jackal', *The Sunday Times*, 21 April 2002.
105. In 1993 alone, the *British Muslims Monthly Survey* charts separate fundraising efforts up and down the country in Jan., March, May, June, July, Aug., Oct. and Nov..
106. Tahir Abbas, op.cit.
107. Ibid. Elements of this story were further repeated in a personal interview with the author in May 2009.
108. Moazzam Begg and Victoria Brittain, *Enemy Combatant: My Imprisonment at Guantanamo, Bagram, and Kandahar*, London: The New Press, 2013.
109. Some short mention is probably necessary to highlight that non-Muslim Britons also went over to fight in Bosnia, as mercenaries or as part of the 'international brigades' who popped up, emulating the foreign fighters who had gone to fight General Franco in Spain before the Second World War. For more detail on the phenomenon, see David Williams and Chris Brooke, 'Mercenaries death riddle', *Daily Mail*, 9 Feb. 1993 and R. Fox, 'Bosnia lures the soldiers of fortune', *Courier Mail*, 13 Feb. 1993.
110. 'In the Hearts of Green Birds', London: Azzam Publications, Nov. 1997.
111. 'Under the Shade of Swords', London: Azzam Publications, Nov. 1997.
112. Ibid.
113. 'Terror suspect Babar Ahmad is "no al Qaeda Rambo",' BBC News, 9 May 2011.
114. Ehsan Masood, 'Selfless victim of Serbian attack', *The Guardian*, 28 Sept. 1992.
115. 'Mujahideen riddle over Briton killed in Bosnia', *Daily Mail*, 22 Sept. 1992.
116. 'Moslem fighters "led by Briton",' *Daily Mail*, 14 June 1993.
117. 'Abu Ibrahim', quoted in Evan Kohlmann, op. cit., p. 94.
118. Regina vs. Abdulla Ahmed Ali et al., trial transcript, June 2008.
119. Regina vs. Mohammed Shakil, Wahid Ali and Sadeer Saleem, Crown Court at Kingston upon Thames
120. Richard Watson, 'The One True God, Allah', *Granta*, 103, Autumn 2008, p. 45.
121. Craig Whitlock, 'Trial of French Islamic radical sheds light on converts' role', *The Washington Post*, 1 Jan. 2006.

122. Extract of transcript from Sean O'Neill, 'British terrorist suspect "fought in the Bosnian war",' *The Times*, 15 Sept. 2005.

123. Nick Craven and Laura Peek, 'Targeted by the tourist of terror', *Daily Mail*, 24 Sept. 2005.

124. Guantamano detainee assessment form, Binyam Mohammed, 26 Dec. 2008.

125. https://www.aclu.org/files/assets/Decl.StaffordSmith.FINAL_.121207_wexhibits.pdf

126. Nick Craven and Laura Peek, op. cit.

127. Author interview, Oct. 2010.

128. Criag Whitlock, 'Converts take on larger roles in militant Islam,' *Washington Post*, Jan. 1, 2006.

129. Richard Watson, op. cit., p. 58.

130. 'Terrorism Conviction', *Metropolitan Police News Bulletin*, 26 Sept. 2005, accessed: http://cms.met.police.uk/news/convictions/terrorism/terrorism_conviction

131. Chris Evans, 'Revealed: The sordid truth about the Sheikh of Finsbury Park', *Daily Mail*, 28 Jan. 1999.

132. Sean O'Neill and Daniel McGrory, *The Suicide Factory*, London: Harper Perennial, 2006, p. 12. Unless otherwise indicated, much of Hamza's biography is drawn from this authoritative account.

133. Ibid., p. 6.

134. An account of Hamza's time in Brighton as told by the then-imam of Dyke Road Mosque, Dr Abduljalil Sajid, is provided in an extended interview by Brendan Montague: 'You can feel a violent person when they speak…but no action was taken', *Brighton and Hove Argus*, 28 May 2004. While some elements of the article support the inference that Hamza's radicalisation was stoked during his time at Brighton, the timing concerned does not fit with other accounts of Hamza's time.

135. Sean O'Neill and Daniel McGrory, op. cit., p. 16.

136. Ibid., pp. 24–26.

137. Omar Nasiri, *Inside the Global Jihad*, London: Hurst, 2006, p. 221.

138. 'Underground Algerian newsletter withdraws support for GIA', Agence France Presse, 30 Sept. 1997.

139. An interview with Q News, undated, but used as a 'profile' for Abu Hamza on the Supporters of Shariah website, and later extremist websites in the UK. Last found at: http://www.salafimedia.com/index.php/media/shuyukhduaat/sheikh-abu-hamza-al-masri/profile-sheikh-abu-hamza-al-masri

140. Evan Kohlmann, op. cit., p. 191.

141. O'Neill and McGrory, op. cit., p. 32.

142. Quoted in Kohlmann, op. cit., p. 191.

143. According to one source from Luton, Hamza was initially invited to the town by the Muslim Welfare Center. Author interview, June 2012.

144. David Sharrock, 'Ousted Imam of Luton takes mosque rivals to high court', *The Guardian*, 27 May 1992.

145. 'Illegal flyposting', *British Muslims Monthly Survey*, Sept. 1996, vol. IV, no. 9, p. 3.

146. Accessed Nov. 2009: http://www.angelfire.com/bc3/johnsonuk/eng/sos.html

147. Robert Lambert, *The London Partnerships: an insider's analysis of legitimacy and effectiveness*, (unpublished draft PhD), Sept. 2009, p. 205.

148. Mahan Abedin, op. cit.

149. *Mail on Sunday*, 12 Nov. 1991.

150. One HuT member at the time estimated that some 300 followers went with Bakri Mohammed into his new group. Author interview, Oct. 2009.
151. *British Muslims Monthly Survey*, Dec. 1996, vol. 4, no. 12, p. 16.
152. Jon Ronson, *Them: Adventures with Extremists*, London, Picador, 2001, p. 4.
153. A leader of Al Gamaa al Islamiya, Omar Abdel Rahman, the 'blind sheikh', was imprisoned for his role in the 1993 World Trade Centre bombing, with a network of plotters active in New York in the early 1990s.
154. Author interview, Usama Hasan, July 2012.
155. Interview with Asharq al Awsat, 22 Aug. 1998.
156. 'Abu Hamza trial: Defence claims radical worked with MI5,' BBC News, May 8, 2014.
157. Regina vs. Faisal Mostafa, 7 Nov. 1996.
158. Michael Whine, 'Is Hizb-ut-Tahrir Changing Strategy or Tactics?', *Center for European Policy Occasional Research Paper*, Hudson Institute, Aug. 2006; repeated in author interview, London, Jan. 2010.
159. Regina vs. Moinul Abedin, May 14, 2004.
160. Christopher Andrew, *The Defence of the Realm: The Authorized History of MI5*, London: Allen Lane, 5 Oct. 2009, p. 807.
161. Dame Eliza Manningham-Buller, testimony before the Chilcot Inquiry, 20 July 2010, accessed: http://www.iraqinquiry.org.uk/media/48331/20100720am-manningham-buller.pdf
162. 'My son is no terrorist', *Manchester Evening News*, 26 March 2009.
163. 'Iraq protest student jailed for Petrol Bomb attack', Press Association, 5 March 1999; Michael Whine, 'Al Muhajiroun: the portal for Britain's suicide terrorists', 21 May 2003.
164. 'Al Muhajiroun Ban', *British Muslims Monthly Survey*, vol. 5 no. 10, June 1997, pp. 11–12.
165. This plot was in fact echoed fourteen years later when a group of Luton men, some of whom were linked to groups that were descended from al-Muhajiroun, were charged with, among other things, plotting to drive a remote control car laden with explosives into a Territorial Army base. Duncan Gardham, 'Men appear in court charged with plotting to attack Territorial Army with model car', *The Daily Telegraph*, 30 April 2012.

4. 9/11 AND THE LONDONISTAN LINKS

1. USA vs. Richard Reid, transcript provided by CNN, 31 Jan. 2003, http://edition.cnn.com/2003/LAW/01/31/reid.transcript/
2. *Al Jihad* newsletter, Oct. 1998.
3. Omar Nasiri, op. cit., p. 290.
4. *Al Jihad* newsletter, Oct. 1998.
5. Rory Carroll, 'Yemen trial to start this week', *The Guardian*, 25 Jan. 1999.
6. Kim Sengupta and Gary Finn, 'Defiant shouts end a strange saga of international intrigue and conspiracy', *Independent*, 10 Aug. 1999.
7. Robert Lambert, *The London Partnerships: an insider's analysis of legitimacy and effectiveness* (unpublished draft PhD), Sept. 2009, pp. 205–11.
8. Sean O'Neill and Daniel McGrory, op. cit., p. 225.
9. Robert Lambert, op. cit., p. 210.
10. Combatant Status Review Tribunal Transcript, 'Nabil Hadjarab', 'Summarized detainee statement', p. 1 (undated, between July 2004 and March 2005).

11. US vs. Mustafa Kamel Mustafa, indictment filed at the Southern District Court of New York, 19 April 2004.
12. 'Abu Hamza: Home Secretary Theresa May hails guilty verdict,' BBC News, May 20, 2014.
13. Sean O'Neill and Daniel McGrory, op. cit., p. 179.
14. This was not the only way that Abu Hamza advocated taking over mosques. In Robert Leiken's *Europe's Angry Muslims*, New York: Oxford University Press, 2012, p. 175, the author quotes a tape of Abu Hamza's in which he states that the way to take over a mosque was to 'give a couple of punches for the cause of Allah. That's it. Don't ask anybody for your right. The Masjid (mosque) is a house of Allah. Anybody hindering the cause of Allah inside the Masjid, he should be thrown out.'
15. Sean O'Neill and Daniel McGrory, op. cit., p. 97.
16. Jason Burke, 'AK-47 training held at London mosque', *The Observer*, 17 Feb. 2002.
17. Sean O'Neill and Daniel McGrory, op. cit., p. 84.
18. 'Gist re: Martin McDaid', information from West Yorkshire Police released during the 7 July Coroner's Inquest.
19. Coroner's Inquest transcript, 14 Feb. 2011, p. 106.
20. Coroner's Inquest transcript, 15 Feb. 2011, p. 48.
21. 'Terror Training camps trial marks another first for the Crown Prosecution Service', *Crown Prosecution Service*, 26 Feb. 2008, http://www.cps.gov.uk/news/pressreleases/112_08.html
22. David Heath, "'I love bin Laden…I hate Bush": man connected to Ujaama, hijacking suspect speaks out', *Seattle Times*, 3 Sept. 2002.
23. Les Zaitz, 'Jihad unravels at Oregon ranch', *Sunday Oregonian*, 18 Oct. 2009.
24. Robert Lambert, op. cit., p. 208.
25. Sean O'Neill and Daniel McGrory, op. cit., pp. 201–14, and Feroz Abbasi's diary that was written when he arrived in Guantanamo.
26. US vs. Mustafa Kamel Mustafa, Oussama Abdullah Kassir and Haroon Rashid Aswat, Indictment S204 Cr. 356 (JFK).
27. The connection to Ressam may have also gone through Abu Qatada, Abu Hamza's teacher, who was known to be close to Abu Doha, a prominent Algerian extremist active in the United Kingdom at the time. In American court documents, Ressam admits to having received a lot of support from Abu Doha who was residing in London at the time where he was helping run Algerian networks having completed some time at training camps in Afghanistan.
28. Quintan Wiktorowicz, op. cit., p. 142.
29. Ibid., p. 141.
30. Author interview, Oct. 2009.
31. http://www.al-bab.com/yemen/hamza/suspects.htm
32. Aswat was originally meant to be deported alongside Abu Hamza, however the court decided to delay his case to better assess his schizophrenia. James Pheby, 'Abu Hamza set for extradition to US,' *AFP*, 25 Sept. 2012.
33. Sean O'Neill and Daniel McGrory, op. cit.
34. While this appears in a number of cases, it was most clearly on display during the Crevice trial where in testimonials, members of the group are repeatedly quoted as having conversations about 'what a joke' Al-Muhajiroun was. Regina vs. Omar Khyam et al.
35. Abu Qatada and Home Secretary, Special Immigration Appeals Commission (SIAC) judgment, 8 March 2004.

36. 'Q&A with Muslim cleric Abu Qatada', CNN, 29 Nov. 2001, transcript found at: http://archives.cnn.com/2001/WORLD/europe/11/27/gen.qatada.transcript.cnna/
37. Brynjar Lia, Brynjar Lia, *Architect of Global Jihad*, London: Hurst, 2007, p. 185.
38. Author interview, East London, Oct. 2009.
39. http://www.theguardian.com/world/2008/jun/18/terrorism.humanrights
40. Abu Qatada and Home Secretary, Special Immigration Appeals Commission (SIAC) judgment, 8 March 2004, accessed: http://www.siac.tribunals.gov.uk/Documents/outcomes/documents/sc152002qatada.pdf
41. Author interview, Usama Hasan, July 2012.
42. Combatant Status Review Tribunal transcript, Richard Dean Belmar, accessed *New York Times* Gitmo Docket.
43. Abu Hamza, 'Be Aware of Takfir!' undated, accessed: http://www.kalamullah.com/Books/Beware%20of%20takfir%20-%20Abu%20Hamza%20Al-Misri.pdf
44. Patricia Tourancheau, '*Kamel Daoudi, du rap à la Kalachnikov*', *La Libération*, 18 Oct. 2001.
45. Omar Nasiri, *Inside the Global Jihad*, London; Hurst, 2006, p. 282.
46. Sean O'Neill and Daniel McGrory, op. cit., pp. 89–90.
47. Combatant Status Review Tribunal transcripts, Sufyian Barhoumi and Nadil Hadjarab.
48. The text of the Fatwa is hard to find these days, but a version is included in—the admittedly biased—Shaykh Abdul Mallik ar-Ramadaanee al-Jazaa'iree, *The Savage Barbarism of Aboo Qataadah*, 2007, http://www.salafimanhaj.com/pdf/SalafiManhajQataadah.pdf
49. Abu Qatada and Home Secretary, Special Immigration Appeals Commission (SIAC) judgment, 8 March 2004, accessed: http://www.siac.tribunals.gov.uk/Documents/outcomes/documents/sc152002qatada.pdf
50. Réda Hassaine, 'Undercover Agent,' *The Sunday Times*, 17 July 2005; At the time of writing it seemed as though Abu Baseer had returned to Syria to fight against Bashar al-Assad's forces there.
51. Brynjar Lia, op. cit., p. 121.
52. Brynjar Lia, op.cit., pp. 149–81; Chapter 6 provides a comprehensive description of al-Suri's activities in London.
53. Abu Qatada and Home Secretary, Special Immigration Appeals Commission (SIAC) judgment, 8 March 2004, accessed: http://www.siac.tribunals.gov.uk/Documents/outcomes/documents/sc152002qatada.pdf
54. Omar Nasiri, op. cit., p. 273.
55. Réda Hassaine, op. cit.
56. Jason Burke, *Al Qaeda: The True Story of Radical Islam*, London: Penguin, 2004, p. 184.
57. Abu Qatada and Home Secretary, Special Immigration Appeals Commission (SIAC) judgment, 8 March 2004, accessed: http://www.siac.tribunals.gov.uk/Documents/outcomes/documents/sc152002qatada.pdf
58. Sean O'Neill and Daniel McGrory, op. cit., p. 29.
59. Abu Hamza, 'Be Aware of Takfir!', undated, accessed: http://www.kalamullah.com/Books/Beware%20of%20takfir%20-%20Abu%20Hamza%20Al-Misri.pdf
60. Paul Williams, 'A biography of international intrigue', *Jamaica Gleaner*, 11 June 2007.
61. This biographical sketch is drawn from Faisal's own reported statements in Regina vs. El Faisal, Case No: 2003–01869-C2, 4 March 2004; and Sam Lister, 'Profile: El Faisal, the sheikh of race hate', *Times*, 24 Feb. 2003.
62. Author interview, Usama Hasan, July 2012.

63. It is unclear exactly when Faisal first came to the United Kingdom, though it is possible it may have been before 1993. For example, Abu Hamza refers to Faisal arriving in the United Kingdom in 1991 in his book 'Be Aware of Takfir!' Court documents simply refer to him arriving in the United Kingdom 'about ten years before' 2002.

64. Donu Kogbara, 'Caught between the book and the look', *Sunday Times*, 28 Feb. 1993.

65. Robert Lambert, op. cit., p. 151.

66. Ibid., p. 177.

67. Abu Hamza, 'Be Aware of Takfir!' undated, accessed: http://www.kalamullah.com/Books/Beware%20of%20takfir%20-%20Abu%20Hamza%20Al-Misri.pdf

68. For example, in his speech 'The Role of the Masjid', he says 'today noses are being broken in the mosque; on many occasions noses were broken in Brixton Mosque if you go there.' In 'The Devil's Deception of the 21st Century House Niggers', he says, 'these house niggers they break noses of people in different mosques, especially in Brixton Mosque.' In 'The Devil's Deception of the Saudi Salafis', he says 'they break noses in Brixton Mosque on three occasions.'

69. Robert Lambert, op. cit., p. 158.

70. Regina vs. El Faisal, op. cit.

71. Abu Hamza, op. cit.

72. Accessed online Jan. 2010, http://www.youtube.com/watch?v=xi4AdOPzUqQ

73. Author interview East London, Oct. 2009.

74. Alan Cowell, 'Kenya seeks to deport Muslim cleric to Jamaica,' *New York Times*, 4 Jan. 2010.

75. Damien Gayle, 'Deported preacher of hate transmits terror rants to UK from sun-soaked Caribbean exile,' *Daily Mail*, 13 March 2012. The site is intermittently taken down and moved. At the time of writing in late 2012 it seemed to have moved to http://www.authentictawheed.com/authentictawheed/

76. Author interview, East London, Oct. 2009.

77. 'Cleric supporter jailed for rape,' BBC News, 4 July 2003.

78. Daniel Sandford, 'Hate preacher "knew 7/7 bomber"', BBC News, 20 June 2008, http://news.bbc.co.uk/2/hi/uk_news/7465201.stm

79. Abdullah el-Faisal, 'The Devil's Deception of the Murji', Side B (undated).

80. Ibid.

81. USA vs. Richard Reid, transcript provided by CNN, 31 Jan. 2003, http://edition.cnn.com/2003/LAW/01/31/reid.transcript/

82. USA vs. Reid; Alan Cullison and Andrew Higgins, 'Account of spy trip on Kabul PC matches travels of Richard Reid,' *Wall Street Journal*, 16 Jan. 2002.

83. An alternative option is that he was given them by radical networks that were helping him operate in France and Holland at the time. However, according to testimony by Saajid Badat, his fellow shoe bomber, the two were given the bombs by al-Qaeda directors.

84. US vs. Zacarias Moussaoui, Criminal No. 01-455-A, 'Stipulation Regarding Richard Reid', undated.

85. Chris Gray, 'Richard Reid: How eager convert was turned into a suspected terrorist', *The Independent*, 27 Dec. 2001.

86. Sean O'Neill and Daniel McGrory, op. cit., pp. 215–35.

87. Theodore Dalrymple, 'I see Richard Reids in jail every day', *Sunday Telegraph*, 30 Dec. 2001.

88. Chris Gray, op. cit.

89. Olga Craig, 'From tearaway to terrorist—the story of Richard Reid', *Sunday Telegraph*, 30 Dec. 2001.

90. Author interview with Usama Hasan, July 2012.
91. Peter Herbert, 'I knew exactly what I was doing', *The Guardian*, 24 Aug. 2006.
92. Quoted in Robert Leiken, *Europe's Angry Muslims*, New York, Oxford University Press, 2012, pp. 173–175.
93. Ambrose Evans-Pritchard, 'Al Qaeda bomb plot leader jailed,' *Telegraph*, Oct. 1, 2003.
94. US vs. Nizar Trabelsi, indictment before grand jury, Nov. 3, 2006.
95. Saajid Badat testimony during United States vs. Adis Medunjanin, 29 March 2012.
96. 'British national indicted for conspiring with "Shoe Bomber" Richard Reid', Department of Justice Press Release, 4 Oct. 2004.
97. Badat testimony, 29 March 2012.
98. Ibid.
99. Ibid., More detail on Babar Ahmad in Chapter 5.
100. Sean O'Neill and Daniel McGrory, op. cit., p. 230.
101. Badat testimony, 29 March 2012.
102. Ibid.
103. Ibid.
104. Ibid.
105. Alan Cullison and Andrew Higgins, 'Account of spy trip on Kabul computer matches travels of Richard Reid,' *Wall Street Journal*, 16 Jan. 2002.
106. Badat testimony, 29 March 2012.
107. Asra Q. Nomani, *The Pearl Project: The Truth Left Behind*, January 2011, p. 19; the report cites interviews from Guantanamo with Khalid Sheikh Mohammed, and only specifically refers to Reid. http://pearlproject.georgetown.edu/
108. Badat testimony, 29 March 2012.
109. Ibid.
110. Ibid. and Asra Q. Nomani, *The Pearl Project*, p. 19.
111. Asra Q. Nomani, *The Pearl Project*, p. 19.
112. Badat testimony, 29 March, 2012.
113. Paul Cruickshank and Nic Robertson, 'US Officials: No link seen between missing jet and 2001 Malaysian hijack plot,' CNN, March 18, 2014.
114. Rosie Cowan, Steven Morris and Richard Norton-Taylor, 'British would-be shoe bomber admits plot to blow up plane,' *The Guardian*, 1 March 2005.
115. Badat testimony, 29 March 2012.
116. NEFA Foundation, 'KSM's Transatlantic Shoe Bomb Plot', Sept. 2007, accessed: http://nefafoundation.org/miscellaneous/shoebombplot.pdf
117. 'Shoebomb plotter given 13 years', BBC News, 22 April 2005.
118. Badat testimony, 29 March, 2012.
119. Ibid.
120. Badat testimony, 29 March, 2012.
121. Jason Burke, op. cit., p. 208.
122. Author interview London, Oct. 2009.
123. Steve Bird, 'Quiet existence in Leicester suburb masked a complex terror network', *The Times*, 2 April 2003.
124. Lawrence Archer and Fiona Bawdon, *Ricin!*, London: Pluto Press, 2010, p. 103.
125. Reda Hassaine and Sean O'Neill, 'I was tortured, says ricin plotter,' *The Times*, 9 May 2005.
126. Ibid., p. 104.
127. Regina vs. Bourgass, 19 July 2005.

128. "'Mini-arsenal" find at UK mosque', CNN, 21 Jan. 2003, http://edition.cnn.com/2003/WORLD/europe/01/20/mosque.raid/

129. Jason Burke, Paul Harris and Burhan Wazir, 'War on Terror: The British recruits; The UK connection: "we will replace the Bible with the Koran in Britain"', *The Observer*, 4 Nov. 2001.

130. Ibid.

131. Richard Watson, 'The One True God, Allah,' *Granta*, no. 103, Autumn 2008.

132. 'Fundamentalist links', *Crawley Observer*, 7 Nov. 2001.

133. The BBC interview is quoted in Thomas Abraham, 'British Muslim youth being trained to fight in Kashmir', *The Hindu*, 29 June 2000. It is uncertain, but likely, that this Abu Yahya is the same one who was later convicted for leading an extremist protest outside the Danish Embassy in 2006 and continued to be at the forefront of Al-Muhajiroun descendant group events. A long-term acolyte of Omar Bakri, he was identified as Abdul Rahman Saleem, who according to his wife trained in Pakistan and later claimed to her that he had met al-Qaeda second-in-command Ayman al-Zawahiri. Christian Gysin, 'Muslim fanatic jailed for preaching race hate now accused of swindling benefits', *Daily Mail*, 30 Dec. 2010; Polly Dunbar, 'My husband sold the TV, threw away CDs and even tried to take a second wife', *Daily Mail*, 30 Jan. 2011.

134. Thomas Abraham, 'British Muslim youth being trained to fight in Kashmir', *The Hindu*, 29 June 2000.

135. Chris Hastings, 'Terrorist camp calls for recruits: fanatics in Britain receive firearms training in US and are eligible to join fighting units in places like Chechnya', *Sunday Telegraph*, 21 May 2000.

136. It is unclear what his name actually was: Mohammed Bilal, Abdullah Bai, Bilal Ahmed and Asif Sadiq are all variants that have appeared in the media.

137. Daniel McGrory, 'Suicide bomber's British family fear for safety', *The Times*, 29 Dec. 2000.

138. Peter Foster and Ahmed Rashid, 'Muslims still looking for martyrs', *The Daily Telegraph*, 29 Dec. 2000.

139. *British Muslim Monthly Survey*, 1999, vol. 7, no. 11, pp. 2–3.

140. Ibid.

141. Dominic Casciani, 'The man from Martyrs Avenue who became a suicide bomber in Syria,' BBC News, March 20, 2014, http://www.bbc.co.uk/news/magazine-26452992.

142. Jason Burke, Paul Harris and Burhan Wazir, op. cit.

143. Regina vs. Mohammed Shakil, Wahid Ali and Sadeer Saleem, Crown Court at Kingston upon Thames.

144. Abu Abdullah, aka Atilla Ahmet, quoted in 'Five Years Later: Are we Safer?' Anderson Cooper 360 Degrees, CNN, aired 23 Aug. 2006, 23:00ET, accessed: http://transcripts.cnn.com/TRANSCRIPTS/0608/23/acd.02.html

145. Nick Parker, '1,000 Brits want to die for bin Laden', *The Sun*, 29 Oct. 2001.

146. http://salafihd.com/videos/Sheikh-Abu-Hamza-Audios/Voting%20is%20Kufr%20and%20Haram.mp3

147. The anonymous cases of AH, AE and Bestun Salim all highlight Home Office and Security Service concerns that the individuals were involved in support networks targeting Iraq. The case of AH is particularly convincing, given his proximity to Muktar Said Ibrahim and another prominent East London Islamist. Bestun Salim was initially only known by the code name LL, but having repeatedly absconded on his control order, he finally disap-

peared and his anonymity was lifted. AE vs. Secretary of State for the Home Department (SSHD), [2008] EWHC 585 (Admin), Case No. PTA/34/2006; PTA/20/2007; PTA/21/2007, handed down 20 March 2008; AH vs. SSHD, [2008] EWHC 1018 (Admin), Case No. PTA/8/2006 & PTA/6/2008, handed down 9 May 2008; 'Control Order Absconder Named', BBC News, 25 May 2007.

148. Daniel McGrory, 'School for suicide bombers may be based in England', *The Times*, 17 Nov. 2003.

149. Daniel McGrory, 'Briton is jailed for 15 years in Iraq as a warning to foreign insurgents', *The Times*, 20 April 2006.

150. 'The Road to Martyrdom', Journeyman Pictures, first broadcast BBC 30 May 2007.

151. David Leppard and Hala Jaber, '70 British Muslims join Iraq fighters', *The Sunday Times*, 26 June 2005.

152. Dame Eliza Manningham-Buller, testimony before the Chilcot Inquiry, 20 July 2010, accessed: http://www.iraqinquiry.org.uk/media/48331/20100720am-manningham-buller.pdf

5. 7/7 AND THE NEAR MISSES

1. Mohammad Momin Khawaja, convicted co-conspirator of the Crevice group, quoted in Regina vs. Mohammad Momin Khawaja, Ontario Superior Court of Justice, Reasons for Judgment, No.04-G30282, 29 Oct. 2008.

2. Regina vs. Omar Khyam et al., 27 March 2006.

3. Sarah Knapton, 'Anatomy of a Bomb Plot', *Ottawa Citizen*, 1 May 2007; Daniel McGrory, Nicola Woolcock, Michael Evans, Sean O'Neill and Zahid Hussain, 'Meeting of murderous minds on the backstreets of Lahore', *The Times*, 1 May 2007. See also Regina vs. Omar Khyam et al., 5 April 2006.

4. At least two of the individuals were not from the UK: Mohammed Junaid Barbar was from New York, while Mohammad Momin Khawaja was Canadian, though both were also of Pakistani descent.

5. Jon Ronson, *Them: Adventures With Extremists*, London: Picador, 2002, pp. 34–5.

6. Richard Watson, 'The One True God, Allah,' *Granta*, Vol. 103, Autumn 2008.

7. 'Al Muhajiroun meetings', *British Muslims Monthly Survey*, Feb. 1997, Vol. 5, No. 2, p. 12.

8. 'Al Muhajiroun boycott elections', *British Muslims Monthly Survey*, May 1999, Vol. 7, No. 5, p. 8.

9. 'Al Muhajiroun Christmas campaign', *British Muslims Monthly Survey*, Dec. 1998, Vol. 6, No. 12, p. 10.

10. Chris Millar, Patrick Sawer and Keith Dovkants, 'The ordinary home-grown boys and lure of a "holy war"', *Evening Standard*, 31 March 2004.

11. 'Al Muhajiroun meeting', *British Muslims Monthly Survey*, Aug. 1998, Vol. 6, No. 8, p. 9.

12. Quotes taken from Omar Saeed Sheikh's signed confession to Indian security forces after his arrest in late 1994, and his diary. The author is grateful to journalist and writer Nick Fielding for passing on both extracts.

13. 'Fears for boy recruited for "jihad"', *British Muslims Monthly Survey*, Jan. 2000, Vol. 8, No. 1, p. 8.

14. Arguably, of course, this was the third plot: as we saw at the end of Chapter 3, Moinul Abedin was already plotting before 9/11, though his targets were never made clear. Similarly,

Kamel Bourgass was captured over a year prior to the Crevice arrests, but again his targets were unclear and he appeared to be plotting a random series of poisonings of questionable efficacy.

15. 'It must be a mistake—these boys are Man Utd fans and love fish and chips', *The Daily Telegraph*, 1 April 2004.

16. Regina vs. Omar Khyam, 14 Sept. 2006.

17. Ibid.

18. Ibid.

19. Richard Watson, op. cit., p. 48.

20. 'Al Muhajiroun member answers questions', *British Muslims Monthly Survey*, Feb. 2000, Vol. 8, No. 2, pp. 2–3.

21. Richard Watson, op. cit., p. 47; 'Family backs terror arrest men', BBC News, 31 March 2004.

22. Shiv Malik, 'The missing links', *New Statesman*, 7 May 2007.

23. Regina vs. Omar Khyam et al.

24. Ibid.

25. Jon Gilbert, 'The Supergrass I helped create', *The Times*, 3 May 2007.

26. Regina vs. Omar Khyam et al., 21 Nov. 2006.

27. Regina vs. Omar Khyam, 25 Sept. 2006.

28. Jonathan Githens-Mazer and Robert Lambert, 'Why conventional wisdom on radicalization fails: the persistence of a failed discourse', *International Affairs*, Vol. 86, No. 4, July 2010.

29. Martin Beckford, 'Fertiliser bomb plotter's brothers missing', *The Daily Telegraph*, 24 May 2007.

30. Raffaello Pantucci, 'Manchester, New York and Oslo: three centrally directed al Qaeda plots', *CTC Sentinel*, Vol. 3, No. 11, Aug. 2010.

31. Duncan Gardham, 'Britain's most wanted killed in a drone attack,' *The Daily Telegraph*, 18 Nov. 2011.

32. Shiv Malik, 'The al Qaeda supergrass and the 7/7 questions that remain unanswered', *The Guardian*, 14 Feb. 2011.

33. Further evidence of the importance of Babar's confession comes from a comment recorded by police listening to Habib Ahmed, another Al-Muhajiroun member who was later imprisoned on terrorism charges. Following Babar's arrest and confessions, Ahmed was recorded saying that he had been included on the list of names provided by Babar and that 'he [Babar] has grassed. Everyone from A to Z.' Cited in Kim Pilling, 'Bogus charity dinner hid terror fund-raising, jury told', Press Association, 26 Sept. 2008. New questions were raised in 2011 when Shiv Malik published a piece which suggested that Mohammed Junaid Babar may have been an American intelligence agent during the period in which he was helping organise the camping trip in the summer of 2003. At the time of writing, this remained uncorroborated; Shiv Malik, 'The al Qaeda supergrass and the 7/7 questions that remain unanswered', *Guardian*, February 14, 2011.

34. Trial Transcript, 'US vs. Mohammed Junaid Babar', US District Court, Southern District of New York, 3 June 2004, p. 40.

35. Regina vs. Omar Khyam et al., 24 March 2006.

36. Regina vs. Mohammad Momin Khawaja, Ontario Superior Court of Justice, Reasons for Judgment, No.04-G30282, 29 Oct. 2008.

37. Jeevan Vasagar, 'Supergrass crucial to fertiliser bomb convictions', *The Guardian*, 30 April 2007; Nick Meo, 'First Person: Disaffected youth seduced by notion of holy war', *San Francisco Chronicle*, 17 July 2005. Regina vs. Omar Khyam et al.; Richard Watson, op. cit.

38. Mohammed Junaid Babar statement, released during the 7 July Coroner's Inquest, http://7julyinquests.independent.gov.uk/evidence/docs/INQ10300–41.pdf

39. Mitchell Silber, *The Al Qaeda Factor*, New York: Oxford University Press, 2012, pp. 98 and 119.

40. Regina vs. Mohammed Shakil, Wahid Ali and Sadeer Saleem, Crown Court at Kingston upon Thames.

41. Regina vs. Omar Khyam et al., 28 March 2006.

42. Extracts of police interview (Salahuddin Amin), Paddington Green Police Station, 8 Feb. 2005.

43. Regina vs. Omar Khyam et al., 24 March 2006.

44. Intelligence and Security Committee (ISC), *Could 7/7 Have Been Prevented?*, London: The Stationery Office, May 2009, p. 7.

45. Regina vs. Mohammed Shakil, Wahid Ali and Sadeer Saleem, Crown Court at Kingston upon Thames.

46. Ian Cobhain and Jeevan Vasagar, 'Free—the man accused of being an al Qaeda leader, aka "Q"', *The Guardian*, 1 May 2007.

47. Regina vs. Omar Khyam et al., 28 March 2006.

48. Regina vs. Omar Khyam et al., 3 April 2006.

49. Regina vs. Mohammad Momin Khawaja, Ontario Superior Court of Justice, Reasons for Judgment, No.04-G30282, 29 Oct. 2008; Regina vs. Omar Khyam et al.

50. Intelligence and Security Committee (ISC), *Could 7/7 Have Been Prevented?*, p. 7.

51. Ibid.

52. Regina vs. Omar Khyam et al., 30 Nov. 2006.

53. 'Is self-storage vulnerable to terrorists?,' BBC News, 1 May 2007.

54. Witness G, testifying before the Coroner's Inquests into the London Bombings of 7 July 2005, 22 Feb. 2010, http://7julyinquests.independent.gov.uk/hearing_transcripts/2202 2011am.htm; Furthermore in the ISC report four operations are mentioned (among which is Scraw and others to be touched upon later) which 'resulted directly from Crevice,' Intelligence and Security Committee (ISC), *Could 7/7 Have Been Prevented?*, p. 13.

55. Regina vs. Mohammad Momin Khawaja, Ontario Superior Court of Justice, Reasons for Judgment, No.04-G30282, 29 Oct. 2008; BM vs. Secretary of State for the Home Department, [2010] EWHC 264 (Admin), handed down 16 Feb. 2010.

56. Regina vs. Omar Khyam et al., 24 March 2006.

57. Ibid.

58. 'UK Muslims shocked by "bombers"', BBC News, 1 May 2003.

59. Martin Bright and Fareena Alam, 'Making of a martyr', *The Observer*, 4 May 2003.

60. Nick Fielding, 'Passport to terror', *The Sunday Times*, 4 May 2003.

61. Shiv Malik, 'NS Profile—Omar Sharif', *New Statesman*, 24 April 2006.

62. Ibid.

63. 'Road to Martyrdom', Journeyman Pictures, first broadcast 30 May 2007.

64. 'Fears expressed about Derby meeting', *British Muslims Monthly Survey*, March 2000, Vol. 8, No. 3, p. 8.

65. 'Protests against Israel around the UK', *British Muslims Monthly Survey*, Oct. 2000, vol. 8, no. 10, p. 6.
66. 'Road to Martyrdom,' op. cit.
67. Jonathan Calvert and Claudio Franco, 'July 7 ringleader linked to Tel Aviv bombers', *The Sunday Times*, 9 July 2006.
68. 'Road to Martyrdom,' op. cit.
69. Sean O'Neill and Daniel McGrory, op. cit., p. 60.
70. Claudio Franco, ISN Security Watch, 21 July 2005.
71. A security service document published during the 7 July Coroner's Inquest showed that a quarterly summary of 28 May 2004 by the International Counter-Terrorism section of the service showed that they had sixty-one operations underway under eight categories (meaning that the total number of plots might be lower since some plots covered two categories). Nevertheless, this highlights the volume of threat analysis that the service was undertaking. http://7julyinquests.independent.gov.uk/evidence/docs/SYS11077–1.pdf
72. Sean O'Neill, 'How young Hindu turned to Islam and Abu Hamza', *The Times*, 8 Nov. 2006.
73. According to Lashkar-e-Taiba expert Stephen Tankel, the title of the book is a reference to Lashkar-e-Taiba, suggesting Barot fought alongside Kashmiri fighters.
74. Dhiren Barot, *The Army of Madinah in Kashmir*, Birmingham: Maktabah Al Ansaar, 1999, p. 144.
75. Ibid., p. viii.
76. Ibid., p. v.
77. According to a biographical note on the back cover of *The Army of Madinah in Kashmir*, 'Brother Esa now resides in South Thailand where he emigrated to in 1998, having married there.' This has not been independently verified, but it would seem to provide further circumstantial evidence that he was in South East Asia in the late 1990s.
78. 'Summary of evidence for Combatant Status Review Tribunal—Hambali, Riduan bin Isomuddin', US Department of Defense, 28 March 2007.
79. Duncan Gardham, 'The Police Hunt', *The Daily Telegraph*, 8 Nov. 2006. However, in Ken Conboy's authoritative account of Jemaah Islamiyah, he instead suggests that it was Barot who gave Hambali the contacts in California and South Africa, further elevating Barot's potential importance to the AQ network. Ken Conboy, *The Second Front*, Jakarta: Equinox Publishing, 2006, p. 87.
80. US vs. Dhiren Barot, Nadeem Tarmohamed, and Qaisar Shaffi, indictment from US District Court, Southern District of New York.
81. Duncan Gardham, 'Average student who met 9/11 mastermind', *The Daily Telegraph*, 15 June 2007.
82. Author interview London, Oct. 2009.
83. 'Computer "geek" and Thai boxing champion—members of the "dirty bomb" plot gang', *Daily Mail*, 15 June 2007.
84. 'The terrorist in our midst', *Manchester Evening News*, 5 July 2007.
85. 'Operation Rhyme: Defendents, Junade Feroze,' Metropolitan Police factsheet, http://www.nefafoundation.org/file/FeaturedDocs/FerozeFactSheet.pdf
86. Author interview London, Oct. 2009.
87. Duncan Gardham, 'Average student who met 9/11 mastermind', *The Daily Telegraph*, 15 June 2007.
88. 'Barot operation posed complex challenge,' Press Association, 7 Nov. 2006.

89. Author interview London, Oct. 2009.

90. Regina vs. Bhatti et al., trial transcript, 15 June 2007, p. 20.

91. Douglas Jehl and David Rohde, 'Captured Al Qaeda figure led way to information behind warning', *The New York Times*, 2 Aug. 2004. Some suggestion of Naeem Noor Khan's importance can be found in the confessions of an Indonesian plotter named Gun Gun (younger brother of the more infamous Hambali), who was picked up in Pakistan sometime before Khan, and described Khan, under his *nom de guerre* of Abu Talha, as taking over as the key go-between for al-Qaeda and helping Gun Gun and a group of South East Asian extremists plot the kidnapping of some American oil executives. Ken Conboy, *The Second Front*, Jakarta: Equinox Publishing, 2006, p. 210.

92. Nick Fielding, 'The Terror links of the Tottenham Ayatollah', *The Sunday Times*, 24 July 2005.

93. 'Full details of Barot's murderous plans to attack UK', Press Association, 7 Nov. 2006.

94. Author interview London, Oct. 2009. Peter Clarke, the then head of Counter Terrorism Command, has repeatedly said that at the time of the arrest they had 'not one shred of admissible evidence' http://www.publications.parliament.uk/pa/ld200708/ldhansrd/text/80708-0002.htm

95. He is not the only convert from the West to rise in the group's ranks during the pre-9/11 period. German–Pole Christian Ganczarski is a white convert who appeared at around the same time and was eventually imprisoned in France for his involvement in a deadly plot in Tunisia. For more information: Raffaello Pantucci, 'Polish-born Muslim convert sentenced for leading role in Tunisian synagogue bombing', *Terrorism Focus*, vol. 6, no. 6, 25 Feb. 2009.

96. David Carlisle, 'Dhiren Barot: was he an Al Qaeda mastermind or merely a hapless plotter?', *Studies in Conflict and Terrorism*, vol. 30, no. 12, Dec. 2007.

97. First published on Al-Istiqmayah.com

98. The video in which Ibrahim speaks of his conversion by Barot can be accessed here: https://www.youtube.com/watch?v=I5EVYHbE7b8; the story was also covered by the BBC, Raphael Rowe, 'From jail to jihad? The threat of prison radicalization,' *BBC Panorama*, May 12, 2014.

99. Regina vs. Omar Khyam et al.

100. US vs. Babar Ahmad, affidavit in support of request for extradition of Babar Ahmad, No. 3:04M240 (WIG).

101. 'Two Britons who pleaded guilty to US terror charges seek access to secret files,' *The Guardian*, 4 April 2014.

102. 'Terror suspect Babar Ahmad is "no al-Qaeda Rambo",' BBC News, 9 May 2011.

103. Though it does not include a specific mention of azzam.com, Gary Bunt, 'islam@britain.net: "British Muslim" identities in Cyberspace', *Islam and Christian-Muslim Relations*, vol. 10, no. 3, 1999 provides a good overview of the online Muslim scene in the UK at the time, including prominent mentions of Abu Hamza's Supporters of Shariah website and the Islamic Gateway, which was featured in Chapter 3 in relation to support for events in Bosnia.

104. 'Diary of a Foreign Mujahid in Chechnya,' Azzam Publications, published 14 Feb. 2000.

105. 'France opened Moussaoui file in '94', CNN, 11 Dec. 2004.

106. 'Shaheed Masood al-Benin', azzam.com correspondent, Azzam Publications.

107. 'Suraqah al-Andalusi', Azzam Publications, published 3 April 2002.

108. BBC Radio 4, *File on Four*, first broadcast 25 Oct. 2005.
109. The documents in question were found with Maqsood Lodin and Yusuf Ocak, respectively Austrian and German, who were detained in May and June 2011. However, it took until the following February for the information about the documents to come into the public domain. Amongst the papers found on a memory stick hidden in their underwear was a pair of documents that appear to be post-operation de-briefs of the 7 July, 21 July and 2006 Transatlantic Airlines plot. German, British and American authorities all believe the documents were written by Rashid Rauf, and biographical information within them seems to confirm this. The quotes here included are all drawn from an assessment of the documents received by the author. From here on they are referred to as the 'Rauf documents.'
110. Ibid.
111. Duncan Gardham, 'Bomb plotters "Al Qaeda link" still in Britain', *The Daily Telegraph*, 1 May 2007.
112. Documents released during the 7 July Coroner's Inquest, flight information for Gulf Air GF434 on 25 July 2003 to Islamabad: http://7julyinquests.independent.gov.uk/evidence/docs/manifest-24022011.pdf, and summary of Mohammed Junaid Babar's testimony: http://7julyinquests.independent.gov.uk/evidence/docs/MPS4-63.pdf
113. Regina vs. Mohammed Shakil, Wahid Ali and Sadeer Saleem, Crown Court at Kingston upon Thames.
114. Ibid.
115. Ibid.
116. Laura May, '7/7 accused "tried to join fighters helping Taliban"', Press Association, 20 May 2008.
117. Nasreen Suleaman, 'Biography of a Bomber', BBC Radio 4, first broadcast 17 Nov. 2005, available online at: http://julyseventh.co.uk/media/BBCRadio4-Koran-and-Country-Biography-of-a-bomber-KHAN.mp3
118. Coroner's Inquest transcript, 14 Feb. 2011, p. 61.
119. James Sturcke, 'July 7 plot accused stayed near Afghan frontline', *The Guardian*, 20 May 2008.
120. Shiv Malik, op. cit.
121. Rauf documents
122. Shiv Malik, op. cit.; Nasreen Suleaman, op. cit.
123. Shiv Malik makes much of this breakage, suggesting that a family move to Nottingham in 2001 was part of a final effort to break Khan away from his extremist circle and un-approved wife.
124. Farah Stockman and Donovan Slack, 'For Jamaican native, life path led from success to extremism', *Boston Globe*, 22 July 2005.
125. Daniel Sandford, 'Hate Preacher "knew 7/7 bomber"', BBC News, 20 June 2008.
126. Coroner's Inquest transcript, 14 Feb. 2011, p. 112.
127. Ibid., p. 113.
128. Ibid., p. 122.
129. 'Samantha Lewthwaite: Missing widow of the 7/7 bomber,' BBC News, 5 April 2012, the story was told as part of BBC Radio 4's 'The Report' series of shows.
130. Coroner's Inquest transcript, 14 Feb. 2011, p. 114.
131. Rauf documents.

132. On the stand, Shakil denied that he had intended to go to a training camp in the first place, and claimed that he was not responsible for the material on his computer.

133. 'July 7 trial: the defendants', *The Daily Telegraph*, 28 April 2009; '7/7 trial: how acquitted trio came to embrace radical cause', *The Times*, 29 April 2009. Regina vs. Mohammed Shakil, Wahid Ali and Sadeer Saleem, Crown Court at Kingston upon Thames.

134. Regina vs. Mohammed Shakil, Wahid Ali and Sadeer Saleem, Crown Court at Kingston Upon Thames.

135. Regina vs. Mohammed Shakil, Wahid Ali and Sadeer Saleem, Crown Court at Kingston upon Thames.

136. Ibid.

137. Jbjd.

138. Coroner's Inquest transcript, 14 Feb. 2011, p. 100.

139. Testimony by Martin Gilbert at the 7 July Coroner's Inquest.

140. 'Gist re: Martin McDaid', West Yorkshire Police report released during the 7 July Coroner's Inquest.

141. 'Suraqah al-Andalusi,' from azzam.com publications. Found at: http://www.islamicawakening.com/viewarticle.php?articleID=713&pageID=236&pageID=233&

142. Intelligence and Security Committee (ISC), *Could 7/7 Have Been Prevented?*, London: The Stationery Office, May 2009, pp. 20–21.

143. Ian Cobhain, 'Cousin of 7/7 leader: I'm not the fifth bomber', *The Guardian*, 19 May 2007; it seems likely that, having guessed that Siddique Khan 'Saddique ***' was in fact Mohammed Siddique Khan, they thought that 'Imran' was his wife's cousin Imran Motala. Security service documents released during the 7 July Coroner's Inquest, 'Amended Gist: Saddique *** and Imran'. Later assumptions seem instead to point to the possibility that this 'Imran' may in fact be Zeeshan Siddiqui, whom Mohammed Junaid Babar identified as being a possible suicide bomber and who was apparently at the training camps alongside the Crevice men. Regina vs. Mohammed Momin Khawaja, Ontario Superior Court, Court file no.: 04-G3028, 29 Oct. 2008, p. 16; Regina vs. Omar Khyam et al.

144. Rauf documents.

145. This assertion is based on the fact that Khan had attended sessions with the radical preachers, at which at least some of Barot's accomplices had been.

146. Rauf documents

147. Coroner Inquest transcript, 14 Feb. 2011, p. 88.

148. Rauf documents.

149. Regina vs. Mohammed Shakil, Wahid Ali and Sadeer Saleem, Crown Court at Kingston upon Thames.

150. Rauf documents

151. Regina vs. Mohammed Shakil, Wahid Ali and Sadeer Saleem, Crown Court at Kingston upon Thames.

152. Rauf documents

153. Coroner Inquest transcript, 14 Feb. 2011, p. 105; Regina vs. Mohammed Shakil, Wahid Ali and Sadeer Saleem, Crown Court at Kingston upon Thames.

154. Coroner's Inquest transcript, 16 Feb. 2011, p. 65.

155. Coroner's Inquest transcript, 14 Feb. 2011, p. 92.

156. Coroner's Inquest transcript, 15 Feb. 2011, p. 57.

157. Coroner's Inquest transcript, 14 Feb. 2011, p. 94.

158. Coroner Inquest transcript, 14 Feb. 2011, p. 106.; Regina vs. Mohammed Shakil, Wahid Ali and Sadeer Saleem, Crown Court at Kingston upon Thames.

159. Coroner's Inquest transcript, 15 Feb. 2011, p. 76.

160. Rauf documents.

161. Coroner's Inquest transcript, 14 Feb. 2011, p. 117.

162. Rauf documents.

163. Rauf documents.

164. 'Bombers "pushed 7/7 accused away"' BBC News, 21 May 2008.

165. David Rohde and Mohammed Khan, 'Jihadist's self-portrait: Alone and seething', *The New York Times*, 9 Aug. 2005.

166. Letter by Zeeshan Siddiqui in 'Briton held in Pakistan wants chance to prove his innocence', *The Daily Telegraph*, 5 Oct. 2005.

167. 'Testimony of Zeeshan Siddiqui', Cageprisoners, 23 Dec. 2008.

168. Regina vs. Omar Khyam et al.

169. 'Testimony of Zeeshan Siddiqui', Cageprisoners, 23 Dec. 2008.

170. Regina vs. Mohammed Momin Khawaja, Ontario Superior Court, Court file no. 04-G3028, 29 Oct. 2008, p. 16.

171. Regina vs. Omar Khyam et al.

172. Siddiqui's diary was quoted primarily in two news stories: David Rohde and Mohammed Khan, 'Jihadist's self-portrait: Alone and seething', *New York Times*, 9 Aug. 2005; Dominic Casciani, 'Jihadi diary: Inside the mind', BBC News, 14 June 2007.

173. Regina vs. Omar Khyam et al. Dominic Casciani, 'Jihadi diary: Inside the mind', BBC News, 14 June 2007.

174. 'Pak, Lashkar, Jaish link to 7/7 blasts,' *The Times of India*, 17 July 2005. The story quotes the information as coming from Pakistani intelligence sources.

175. David Rohde and Mohammed Khan, 'Jihadist's self-portrait: Alone and seething', *The New York Times*, 9 Aug. 2005.

176. Jon Gilbert, 'The Supergrass I helped create', *The Times*, 3 May 2007.

177. Richard Watson, op. cit.

178. Regina vs. Omar Khyam et al. While not all the details are verifiable, the link between Khalisadar and Rahman has been confirmed to the author by security sources in interview in Oct. 2009.

179. Martin Bentham, 'Do you want to become a martyr, the Al Qaeda chief asked…', *Evening Standard*, 31 March 2008. While not all the details are verifiable, the link between Khalisadar and Rahman has been confirmed to the author by security sources. It is also likely that Khalisadar was one of the individuals mentioned during the Crevice trial—though it is unclear exactly who.

180. Richard Watson, op. cit.

181. Abdul Waheed Majid later appeared as Britain's first confirmed suicide bomber in Syria. When he first went to Syria, he went as part of an aid convoy with his childhood friend Raheed Mahmood, Waheed Mahmood's brother.

182. Regina vs. Omar Khyam et al.

183. Regina vs. Omar Khyam et al.

184. Regina vs. Omar Khyam et al.

185. Shiv Malik, 'Jihadi House Parties of Hate,' *The Sunday Times*, 6 May 2007.

NOTES

186. Regina vs. Mohammed Shakil, Wahid Ali and Sadeer Saleem, Crown Court at Kingston upon Thames.

187. Author interview London, Oct. 2009.

188. Regina vs. Abdul Mukim Khalisadar, 11 Feb. 2008.

189. USA vs. Mohammed Junaid Babar, letter submitted to the court by Preet Bharara, 23 Nov. 2010.

190. 'Drone death man "being groomed to head UK terror group",' BBC News, 5 Oct. 2010.

191. Duncan Gardham, 'Britain's "most wanted" killed in drone attack,' *The Daily Telegraph*, 18 Nov. 2011.

192. Ibid.

193. Andy Hayman and Margaret Gilmore, *The Terrorist Hunters*, London: Bantam Press, 2009, p. 139.

194. Ibid., p. 143.

195. Bios drawn from: 'The Four Guilty July 21 bombers', *The Daily Telegraph*, 10 July 2001; Profile: Adel Yahya, 13 Nov. 2007; Profile: Manfo Asiedu, 9 Nov. 2007; Profile: Hussain Osman, 9 July 2007; Profile: Yassin Omar, 9 July 2007; Profile: Ramzi Mohammed, 9 July 2007; Profile Muktar Said Ibrahim, 9 July 2007', all from BBC News.

196. Profile: Adel Yahya, BBC News, 13 Nov. 2007.

197. Regina vs. Adbul Sherif, Siraj Ali, Muhedin Ali, Wahbi Mohamed, Islmail Abdurahman, Fardosa Abdullahi.

198. Andy Hayman and Margaret Gilmore, op. cit., p. 169.

199. HMG vs. Adbul Sherif, Siraj Ali, Muhedin Ali, Wahbi Mohamed, Islmail Abdurahman, Fardosa Abdullahi.

200. HMG vs. Yeshiembert Girma, Esayas Girma, Mulumebet Girma and Mohammed Kabashi, case no. B3/2008/3988; C1/2008/3085; C5/2008/3939; C5/2008/3901, 15 May 2009.

201. 'The July 21 helpers', Press Association, 4 Feb. 2008.

202. HMG vs. Adbul Sherif, Siraj Ali, Muhedin Ali, Wahbi Mohamed, Islmail Abdurahman, Fardosa Abdullahi.

203. 'Leaders of terrorist recruitment cell jailed', Press Association, 7 March 2008.

204. Ibid.

205. Duncan Gardham, 'Mohammed Hamid is "evil personified",' *The Daily Telegraph*, 26 Feb. 2008.

206. 'Childhood love of camping grew into terrorist training sessions', *The Yorkshire Post*, 27 Feb. 2008.

207. 'Chances to stop July 21 bombers missed by police', *The Daily Telegraph*, 27 Feb. 2008.

208. 'Profiles: Mohammed Hamid and his followers', *The Guardian*, 26 Feb. 2008; 'Chances to stop July 21 bombers missed by police', *The Daily Telegraph*, 27 Feb. 2008; 'Then: Happy soccer coach posing with his players', *Evening Standard*, 11 Sept. 2006.

209. Duncan Gardham, 'Mohammed Hamid "is evil personified"', *The Daily Telegraph*, 26 Feb. 2008.

210. Secretary of State for the Home Department and AP, [2008] EWHC 2001 (Admin), 12 Aug. 2008. Others they encountered (including Bilal Berjawi and Mohammed Sakr) were killed alongside al-Shabaab, a Somali affiliate of al-Qaeda, some of whom were celebrated in a later video released by the group.

211. http://www.un.org/sc/committees/1267/NSQI22806E.shtml The UN designation which

325

was listed in Dec. 2006 also specifies: 'Al Ghabra has played a central role in radicalizing young Muslims in the United Kingdom, through direct contact and also through his distribution of extremist media. After radicalizing these individuals, he recruited them to the Al-Qaida cause and often facilitated their travel and, through his extensive range of contacts, arranged for them to attend Al-Qaida training camps. Some of these individuals went on to engage in overseas terrorist attack planning from the United Kingdom.'

212. Regina vs. Muktar Said Ibrahim et al, Jan. 2007.
213. Rauf documents.
214. Ibid.
215. Duncan Gardham, 'Rashid Rauf's connections to terror,' *The Daily Telegraph*, 8 Sept. 2009.
216. Regina vs. Muktar Said Ibrahim et al, Jan. 2007.
217. Duncan Gardham, 'Mohammed Hamid "is evil personified"', *The Daily Telegraph*, 26 Feb. 2008.
218. Richard Greenberg, Paul Cruickshank and Chris Hansen, 'Inside the terror plot that "rivaled 9/11"', MSNBC, 8 Sept. 2009.
219. His phone number was found in the possession of an extremist who was at the time in a French jail awaiting extradition to Holland on terrorism charges, and his phone had been called by a number within Abu Hamza's home. He also admitted to having visited the Finsbury Park Mosque in London, and was found in possession of an Underground ticket which supported this. All information on Boutrab drawn from Regina vs. Abbas Boutrab (aka Youcef Djafari; Abbas Fawwaz; Brahmin Ahaoui), [2005] NICC 36, Ref: WEAF5406, 24 Nov. 2005.
220. Rauf documents.
221. Ibid.
222. 'Ringleader of airline plot dreamed of jihad since his teens', *The Guardian*, 8 Sept. 2009; Regina vs. Abdullah Ahmed Ali Khan et al
223. Rauf documents.
224. 'Airlines plot: al Qaeda mastermind "is still alive"', *The Daily Telegraph*, 10 Sept. 2009.
225. CPS Press Release: 'CPS authorises charges in alleged aircraft terror plot', 21 Aug. 2006, http://www.cps.gov.uk/news/press_releases/149_06/
226. Rauf documents.
227. 'The Liquid Bomb Plot', *National Geographic*, screened 25 March 2011.
228. Ibid.
229. There has been considerable controversy about Rauf's arrest, with many in the British security community angry at what they see as America's instigation in getting Pakistan to arrest Rauf and thus forcing them to make their arrests sooner than they wanted.
230. Adrian Levy and Cathy Scott-Clark, *The Meadow: Kashmir 1995—Where the Terror Began*, London: Harper Press, March 2012, p. 60.
231. Ian Fisher and Serge Kovaleski, 'In a British inquiry, a family caught in 2 worlds', *The New York Times*, 20 Aug. 2006.
232. *Daily Mirror*, 15 Aug. 2006.
233. 'Muslim teacher in carol concert tirade is made Ofsted inspector,' *Daily Mail*, 30 Sept. 2006.
234. Author interview, Amardeep Bassey, June 2012.
235. Secretary of State for the Home Department vs. AY, [2010] EWHC 1860 (Admin), judgment handed down 26 July 2010.

236. 'Sources: UK terror plot suspect forced to talk,' NBC News, 18 Aug. 2006.

237. Some 2,996 people are believed to have died on 11 Sept. 2011. If this plan to bring down eight transatlantic airliners, each of which may have had around 400 people on board, had gone ahead, then the total casualty count could have been as high as 3,200.

238. Interviews with former senior officers confirm this, as well as an ongoing control order against him.

239. Rauf documents.

240. Secretary of State for the Home Department vs. AY, [2010] EWHC 1860 (Admin), judgment handed down 26 July 2010; Regina vs. Ahmed Abdulla Ali Khan et al., trial transcript, Nov. 2008.

241. Republished by the *Wall Street Journal*, 7 Sept. 2009.

242. Regina vs. Abdulla Ahmed Ali and Others, [2011] EWCA Crim 1260, judgment handed down 19 May 2011. Regina vs. Ahmed Abdulla Ali Khan et al, trial transcript, Nov. 2008.

243. 'The Liquid Bomb Plot', National Geographic, screened 25 March 2011.

244. Regina vs. Abdulla Ahmed Ali and Others, [2011] EWCA Crim 1260, judgment handed down 19 May 2011.

245. 'Terrorist freed from jail early after plotting to blow up transatlantic planes caught trying o get to Syria,' *Daily Mail*, March 15, 2014.

246. 'Convert turned accused bomber keeps his faith,' BBC News, 5 March 2010.

247. 'Airline bomb plotter's wife tells of abuse,' BBC News, 18 Feb. 2010.

248. Secretary of State for the Home Department vs. AY, [2010] EWHC 1860 (Admin), judgment handed down 26 July 2010; Secretary of State for the Home Department vs. AM, [2009] EWHC 3053 (Admin), judgment handed down 21 Dec. 2009.

249. According to court documents, he was enjoying a peaceful boat ride off Oman with some new friends when a Royal Navy helicopter suddenly appeared and seized all the men. Secretary of State for the Home Department vs. AM, [2009] EWHC 3053 (Admin), judgment handed down 21 Dec. 2009.

250. Rauf documents.

251. 'UK militant "killed in Pakistan"', BBC News, 22 Nov. 2008.

252. Secretary of State for the Home Department vs. AY, [2010] EWHC 1860 (Admin), judgment handed down 26 July 2010.

253. Jason Burke, 'US kills alleged transatlantic airline plot leader, reports say', *The Guardian*, 22 Nov. 2008.

254. Ibid.

255. Convicted American terrorist Najibullah Zazi identified meeting Rauf, using the pseudonym 'Ibrahim' when he went to Miram Shah in North Waziristan seeking to connect with al-Qaeda and the Taliban in 2008. Rauf was among the al-Qaeda figures pushing the Americans to return home to launch plots at home. USA vs. Adis Medunjanin, March 2012.

256. Senior official sources in both the US and UK seem quite convinced he is dead; however, the lack of any DNA evidence and the seeming complexity of his story cast some doubt on this.

257. 'Briton home after Indian prison ordeal', BBC News, 13 July 2001.

258. Cageprisoners statement by Rangzieb Ahmed.

259. 'Taxi driver posed as terrorist for cash', Press Association, 5 Nov. 2008.

260. Jon Gilbert, 'The supergrass I helped create', *The Times*, 3 May 2007.

261. 'UK "terror target" claim dismissed', BBC News, 7 Jan. 2002.
262. Kim Pilling, 'Taxi driver posed as terrorist for cash,' *Press Association*, 5 Nov. 2008.
263. 'British Muslim tells court he fabricated Islamist past,' Reuters, 9 Feb. 2009.
264. 'Links to global terror network', *Manchester Evening News*, 18 Dec. 2008.
265. Kim Pilling, 'Bogus charity dinner hid terror fund-raising, jury told', Press Association, 26 Sept. 2008.
266. Unfortunately, as with many things from Hassan Butt, it is difficult to verify this information, since during the course of Habib Ahmed's trial he claimed to have made everything up. There is a whole layer of articles that he produced with a prominent British journalist that appear to highlight the deep connections between Al-Muhajiroun and al-Qaeda but are therefore compromised.
267. Kim Pilling, 'Jailed terrorist lived close to Al Qaeda suspects', Press Association, 10 April 2009.
268. Duncan Gardham, 'Al Qaeda attack planner lived in Manchester for four years,' *The Daily Telegraph*, 20 Jan. 2012.
269. Kim Pilling, 'Jailed terrorist lived close to Al Qaeda suspects', Press Association, 10 April 2009.
270. Regina vs. Abdul Rehman; Regina vs. Bilal Mohammed, Neutral Citation Number: [2008] EWCA Crim 1465; Case No: 200800022A1, 200802151B, 8 July 2008.
271. Yahya Birt, 'Don't repeat this mistake', *The Guardian* Comment is Free, 14 Sept. 2009, http://www.guardian.co.uk/commentisfree/belief/2009/sep/14/islam-extremism-far-right-terrorism

6. THE NEXT GENERATION OF BRITISH JIHAD

1. Bilal Abdulla, quoted in Chris Greenwood, 'Doctor wanted to give Britons "a taste of fear"', Press Association, 12 Nov. 2008.
2. Kim Sengupta, 'Exclusive: Army is fighting British jihadists in Afghanistan', *The Independent*, 25 Feb. 2009; MI5 sources quoted in the press put the number prior to 2002 as up to 3,000. David Leppard and Hala Jaber, '70 British Muslims join Iraq fighters', *The Sunday Times*, 26 June 2005.
3. Chris Greenwood, 'Terror suspect supports Iraqi insurgency, court told', Press Association, 11 Nov. 2008.
4. Ibid.
5. The clip is still accessible online, please see: http://www.youtube.com/watch?v=omnskeu-puE
6. Author interview, Shiraz Maher, Oct. 2009.
7. Ibid.
8. Mark Daly, 'The international trail of terror', BBC Scotland, 16 Dec. 2008.
9. Duncan Gardham, 'Glasgow bomb plot: profile of airport terrorist Kafeel Ahmed', *The Daily Telegraph*, 16 Dec. 2008.
10. Author interview, Shiraz Maher, Oct. 2009.
11. Ibid.
12. Olga Craig, 'The people who cure you will kill you', *The Sunday Telegraph*, 8 July 2007.
13. Author interview, Shiraz Maher, Oct. 2009.

14. Abu Qatada, 'Statement to the Muslims from Abu Qatadah, Umar bin-Mahmud Abu-Umar, Commenting on the decision by the British House of Lords to Approve His Handover to the Jordanian Government', republished by *Al Quds al Arabi*, 20 March 2009 (translated version 23 March 2009). The authenticity of this document is difficult to ascertain, though it certainly accords with Qatada's style. It was also not the only time that Qatada was linked from inside prison to events outside. In another instance a group of Spanish terrorists linked to the Madrid bombings of March 2004 called Qatada while he was in prison to ask his permission to kill themselves since they were surrounded by police. He authorised the act, though it is unclear how they managed to get through to him (details confirmed to the author from security sources).

15. Andrew Alderson, Ben Leach, Duncan Gardham, 'Bilal Abdulla: Doctor by day, terrorist by night—the secret life of a new breed of terrorist', *The Daily Telegraph*, 20 Dec. 2008.

16. Author interview, Oct. 2009.

17. 'Sabeel, Kafeel had joined Tabligi-Jamaat: Bangalore Police', *Hindustan Times*, 6 July 2007.

18. Mark Daly, 'The international trail of terror', BBC Scotland, 16 Dec. 2008.

19. Duncan Gardham, 'Glasgow bomb plot: How airport terror plotters shared common cause of Iraq', *The Daily Telegraph*, 16 Dec. 2008; and other accounts of the trial.

20. Chris Greenwood, 'Doctor wanted to give Britons "a taste of fear"', Press Association, 12 Nov. 2008.

21. Ibid.

22. 'Khan radicalized on trips to Pakistan', Press Association, 18 Feb. 2008.

23. Duncan Gardham, 'Plot to behead Muslim soldier "like a pig"', *The Daily Telegraph*, 30 Jan. 2008.

24. 'Detective certain Khan would have carried out threat', Press Association, 18 Feb. 2008.

25. 'Defendant tells court of fears friend had become brainwashed', Press Association, 5 Feb. 2008.

26. 'Three jailed for equipping terrorists', Press Association, 9 March 2009.

27. 'Terror plot to behead solider, jury told', Press Association, 29 Jan. 2008.

28. 'MI5 agents bugged terror cell', *Birmingham Evening Mail*, 30 Jan. 2008.

29. Duncan Gardham, 'Plot to behead Muslim soldier "like a pig"', *The Daily Telegraph*, 30 Jan. 2008.

30. Vikram Dodd, 'Life sentence for the extremist who plotted to murder soldier', *The Guardian*, 19 Feb. 2008.

31. 'Student Jailed for trying to fight British in Afghanistan', *Evening Standard*, 18 June 2009.

32. Abushamma was charged alongside another man who was later detained and placed on a control order after he managed to get out of the country to fight in Somalia.

33. 'Terror Tube driver with Al Qaeda links walks free', *Evening Standard*, 9 Nov. 2010.

34. CA vs. Secretary of State for the Home Department, High Court Judgment, [2010] EWHC 2278 (QB), handed down 27 and 28 July 2010.

35. John Scheerhout and Steve Robson, 'Revealed: how "quiet" boy from Stalybridge became a hate-filled Islamic extremist,' *Manchester Evening News*, 10 Sept. 2011.

36. 'Dad told cop: "I want to fight holy war again," terror jury hears,' *Manchester Evening News*, 7 May 2011.

37. Duncan Gardham, 'Former Taliban jailed for recruiting young men on the streets of Britain,' *The Daily Telegraph*, 9 Sept. 2011.

38. 'Longsight market Taliban fanatic "sent more than 20 recruits to fight British forces in Afghanistan"', *Manchester Evening News*, 10 Sept. 2011.
39. 'Pakistan: Dozens of Europeans in Terror Training', AP, 3 Oct. 2010.
40. 'Taliban fighter found with Aston Villa tattoo', *The Daily Telegraph*, 15 June 2009.
41. Kim Sengupta, 'Exclusive: Army is fighting British jihadists in Afghanistan', *The Independent*, 25 Feb. 2009.
42. Con Coughlin, Duncan Gardham and Thomas Harding, 'British Muslims "fighting with Taliban in Afghanistan"', *The Daily Telegraph*, 1 Aug. 2008.
43. http://depositfiles.com/files/d9w6u17l9
44. Nicola Smith and Saleem Mehsud, 'British Taliban "martyr" masterminded suicide attack on CIA,' *Sunday Times*, 11 Nov. 2012.
45. Jonathan Rugman, 'Somalia: the new Pakistan for terror recruitment?', Channel 4 News, 16 Feb. 2010.
46. Kim Sengupta, 'British nationals accused of funding Islamist fighters in Horn of Africa', *The Independent*, 10 Jan. 2007.
47. AP vs. Secretary of State for the Home Department, case no: PTA/2/2008; PTA/7/2008; PTA/26/2008, judgment handed down 12 Aug. 2008.
48. Author interview, London, Oct. 2008.
49. 'My brother and the deadly lure of al-Shabaab jihad,' BBC News, 2 Nov. 2010.
50. The British security community most prominently flagged Somalia up as a risk in late 2007 when MI5 Director General Jonathan Evans mentioned it in a speech, claiming that there was 'no doubt' that 'training activity and terrorist planning … focused on the UK' was taking place there. Jonathan Evans, 'Intelligence, Counter-Terrorism and Trust,' speech to The Society of Editors, 5 Nov. 2007.
51. Court documents from Gothenburg, 8 Dec. 2010.
52. BX vs. Secretary of State for the Home Department, [2010] EWHC 990 (Admin), Case No: PTA/54/2009, handed down 10 May 2010.
53. Berjawi and Sakr's tale is repeated and expanded in its fuller context in Raffaello Pantucci, 'Bilal al-Berjawi and the shifting fortunes of foreign fighters in Somalia,' *CTC Sentinel*, 24 Sept. 2013.
54. Barbara Among, 'Police foil another bomb attack in Kampala,' *New Vision*, 25 Sept. 2010; Chris Woods, 'Parents of British man killed by US drone blame UK government,' *The Bureau of Investigative Journalism*, 15 March 2013 http://www.thebureauinvestigates.com/2013/03/15/parents-of-british-man-killed-by-us-drone-blame-uk-government/
55. Chris Woods, op. cit.
56. This quote is based on a twitter conversation between the author and the @abumamerican twitter handle, believed to have been Omar Hammami. April 19, 2013.
57. 'A drone strike pronounces a martyr,' Harakat al-Shabaab al Mujahideen Press Office, 21 Jan. 2012.
58. Chris Woods, op. cit.
59. Harakat al-Shabaab al Mujahideen Press Office, op. cit.
60. The series can be found here: http://jihadology.net/category/biography-of-the-flags-of-the-martyrs-in-east-africa/
61. 'Biography of the Martyred Figures in East Africa 5: Bilal al-Birjawi al-Lubnani (Abu Hafs)', http://jihadology.net/2013/04/15/new-release-biography-of-the-martyred-figures-in-east-africa-5-bilal-al-birjawi-al-lubnani-abu-%E1%B8%A5af%E1%B9%A3/

62. Ibid.
63. Ibid., Al-Kataib video.
64. Chris Woods, op. cit.
65. BX and the Secretary of State for the Home Department, Royal Courts of Justice, 10 May 2010.
66. Ibid.
67. Chris Woods, op. cit.
68. Biography of the Martyred Figures in East Africa 5: Bilal al-Birjawi al-Lubnani (Abu Hafs)'
69. Milton Olupot, 'Security hunts for Somali terrorists,' *New Vision*, 8 Nov. 2009.
70. J1 and the Secretary of State for the Home Department, Royal Courts of Justice, London, 27 March 2013; Another man arrested at the same protests, Mohammed el Araj, also from West London, was later killed in Syria. 'British Muslim from West London among four killed fighting in Syria,' *Evening Standard*, 21 Nov. 2013.
71. Milton Olupot, 'Security hunts for Somali terrorists,' *New Vision*, 8 Nov. 2009.
72. AQEA bio.
73. Biography of the Martyred Figures in East Africa 5: Bilal al-Birjawi al-Lubnani (Abu Hafs)'
74. Chris Woods, op. cit.
75. Barbara Among, 'Police foil another bomb attack in Kampala,' *New Vision*, 25 Sept. 2010.
76. Fazul Abdullah Mohammed or Fadil Harun, a senior member of al Qaeda's East African cell who had helped establish al Shabaab, was involved in the 1998 bombings in a distant way and acted as a senior shepherd for the many foreigners who went out to join the group fighting in Somalia.
77. Biography of the Martyred Figures in East Africa 5: Bilal al-Birjawi al-Lubnani (Abu Hafs)'
78. Thomas Joscelyn and Bill Roggio, 'Senior Shabaab commander rumored to have been killed in recent Predator strike,' *Long War Journal*, 9 July 2011 http://www.longwarjournal.org/archives/2011/07/senior_shabaab_comma_1.php
79. Biography of the Martyred Figures in East Africa 5: Bilal al-Birjawi al-Lubnani (Abu Hafs)'
80. Confession video—it is worth noting that in the video the group alternates between accusing the CIA or Britain's MI6 being responsible for handling Hassan.
81. Ibid.
82. Dipesh Gadher, 'Britons "spearhead Kenya terror wave",' *The Sunday Times*, 8 Jan. 2012.
83. David Brown, 'Inside the 7/7 widow's African lair,' *The Times*, 3 March 2012; '7/7 bomber's widow will not escape, say Kenyan police,' *The Times*, 6 March 2012.
84. Raffaello Pantucci and A.R. Sayyid, 'A Profile of Sheikh Abdulcaadir Mumin: Al-Shabaab's Leading Theological Guide,' *Militant Leadership Monitor*, vol. 2, no. 11, Nov. 2011.
85. 'Money was for orphans, says terror charge Imam', Press Association, 17 June 2009.
86. 'Man arrested in Leicester kept books on how to make bombs, court is told,' thisisleicestershire.co.uk, 1 Oct. 2010.
87. Report of the Monitoring Group on Somalia pursuant to Security Council resolution 1853 (2008), March 2010, p. 30.
88. Gabriel Gatehouse, 'Woolwich suspect Michael Adebolajo's Kenya links,' BBC News, 29 May 2013.

89. Jonathan Evans, 'The Threat to National Security', address at the Worshipful Company of Security Professionals, 16 Sept. 2010.

90. Wikileaks cable from US Embassy Nairobi, 'Doing more with less; UK Africa regional counterterrorism conference', 2 Dec. 2009 http://wikileaks.ch/cable/2009/12/09NAIROBI 2434.html

91. 'Al-Shabaab suspects arrested in Garissa,' *Daily Nation*, 23 May 2011.

92. 'Cardiff teenagers held by Kenyan anti-terror unit to be deported,' Walesonline.co.uk, 19 Oct. 2011.

93. Video accessible: https://ia601509.us.archive.org/25/items/EidMessage1434/EidMsg 1434_En_HQ.mp4

94. Transcript taken off news reports.

95. Nicholas Wood, 'Bosnia: Haven for Islamic radicals?', *International Herald Tribune*, 28 Nov. 2005.

96. Regina vs. Tsouli, Mughal and Al Daour, [2007] EWCA Crim 3300, No: 2007/3990/A3, 2007/3991/A3 & 2007/3993/A3, handed down 18 Dec. 2007.

97. Court transcript Regina vs. Tsouli, Mughal and Al Daour, sentencing remarks, p. 52.

98. Court transcript Regina vs. Tsouli, Mughal and Al Daour, sentencing remarks, p. 19.

99. Regina vs. Tsouli, Mughal and Al Daour, [2007] EWCA Crim 3300, No: 2007/3990/A3, 2007/3991/A3 & 2007/3993/A3, handed down 18 Dec. 2007.

100. Sandro Contenta, 'Terrorist 007 off-line', *Toronto Star*, 17 June 2006.

101. Ibid.

102. Court transcript Regina vs. Tsouli, Mughal and Al Daour, sentencing remarks, p. 11.

103. Ibid., p. 60.

104. Sandro Conteta, op. cit.

105. USA vs. Syed Haris Ahmed, 'Specific findings of fact', 1:06-cr-0147-WSD-GGB, filed 10 June 2009.

106. Evan Kohlmann, 'Anatomy of a Modern Homegrown Terror Cell: Aabid Khan et al.,' *NEFA Foundation Paper*, Sept. 2008 http://acsa2000.net/TW/samples/Kohlman.pdf.

107. Peter Taylor, 'Generation Jihad', BBC 2, first broadcast 8 Feb. 2010.

108. USA vs. Syed Haris Ahmed, op. cit.

109. Her Majesty's Advocate vs. Mohammed Atif Siddique, Appeal No.XC878/07, [2010] HCJAC7, handed down 29 Jan. 2010.

110. Ibid.

111. Regina vs. Muhammed, [2010] EWCA Crim 227, judgment handed down 19 Feb. 2010.

112. Evan Kohlmann, 'Anatomy of a Modern Homegrown Terror Cell: Aabid Khan et al.,' http://www.nefafoundation.org/miscellaneous/nefaaabidkhan0908.pdf

113. Quoted in 'Britain's youngest terrorist, Hammaad Munshi, faces jail after guilty verdict,' *The Times*, 18 Aug. 2008.

114. 'Man jailed under Terrorism Act', Metropolitan Police Press Release, 18 July 2007.

115. Full text in possession of author, dated 23 Jan. 2008.

116. Ibid.

117. 'Skepticism greets "Al Qaeda in Britain" founding', Reuters, 16 Jan. 2008.

118. Kim Pilling, 'Man jailed for urging Blair and Brown assassinations', Press Association, 24 June 2010.

119. Kim Pilling, 'Three accused were "intoxicated by evil of terrorism"', Press Association, 18 Feb. 2010.

120. Lucy Collins, 'Failed asylum seeker jailed for terrorist offences', Press Association, 15 Dec. 2009 and Lucy Collins, 'Terror suspect "was smuggled into UK in lorry"', Press Association, 30 Nov. 2009.

121. Shaun Jepson, 'Iraq war made suspected terrorist "more religious"', *Derby Evening Telegraph*, 4 Dec. 2009.

122. Shaun Jepson, 'Terror trial accused told women he wanted to kill Jews and US troops', *Derby Evening Telegraph*, 2 Dec. 2009.

123. Regina vs. Nicholas Roddis, [2009] EWCA Crim 585, no: 2008/4229/B5, judgment handed down 12 March 2009.

124. 'Convert in bus bomb scare', *The Star*, 1 July 2008.

125. Regina vs. Nicholas Roddis, op. cit.

126. 'Seven years for Yorkshire bus bomb hoaxer', *Yorkshire Post*, 18 July 2008.

127. Ibid.

128. 'Hoax bomb suspect blames boredom', BBC News, 11 July 2008. Roddis was later re-arrested on similar charges, but cleared.

129. Duncan Gardham, 'Andrew Ibrahim: how a public schoolboy became a terrorist', *The Daily Telegraph*, 18 July 2009.

130. Ibid.; email communications with individuals at Green Lane, Aug. 2009.

131. Peter Taylor, 'Generation Jihad: Part 3', BBC 2, first broadcast 22 Feb. 2010.

132. 'Bristol terror suspect had Keira Knightley foot fetish', *Bristol Evening Post*, 24 June 2009.

133. 'Would-be terrorist "just hours from bombing Bristol"', *Bristol Evening Post*, 18 July 2009.

134. The entire letter is reproduced here: http://www.thisisexeter.co.uk/Bomber-Nicky-Reilly-s-suicide-note/story-11795579-detail/story.html

135. Diana Prince, 'City man is held after terror blast', *Plymouth Evening Herald*, 23 May 2008.

136. 'Why I'll always support my son', *Plymouth Evening Herald*, 31 Jan. 2009.

137. 'Police warned about Exeter bomber in 2003', BBC News, 8 Feb. 2010.

138. 'Why I'll always support my son', *Plymouth Evening Herald*, 31 Jan. 2009.

139. Two individuals who were picked up by police to great fanfare in the wake of Reilly's arrest were both cleared of any terrorism charges.

140. Carl Eve, 'It could have been us', *Plymouth Evening Herald*, 16 Oct. 2008.

141. 'Nicky Reilly: from BFG to failed suicide bomber', *The Guardian*, 15 Oct. 2008.

142. Tom Palmer, 'Kurdish community faced backlash after bombing bid', Press Association, 15 Oct. 2008.

143. 'Kurds need a community focal point', *Plymouth Evening Herald*, 13 Sept. 2008.

7. CONCLUSIONS

1. Bilal Mohammed, cited in Peter Taylor, 'Generation Jihad: Part 1', BBC 2, first broadcast 8 Feb. 2010.

2. Jonathan Evans, 'The Threat to National Security', address at the Worshipful Company of Security Professionals, 16 Sept. 2010.

3. Ibid.

4. Andrew Parker, 'The Threat from Terrorism,' address to the Royal United Services Institute for Defence and Security Studies (RUSI), 8 Oct. 2013.

5. Special Immigration Appeals Commission (SIAC) Open judgment, Abid Naseer, Ahmad Faraz Khan, Shoaib Khan, Abdul Wahad Khan and Tariq ur Rehman vs. Secretary of State for the Home Department, appeal no: SC/77/80/81/82/83/09, 18 May 2010.

6. Raffaello Pantucci, 'Manchester, New York and Oslo: Three Centrally Directed al Qaeda plots,' *CTC Sentinel*, vol. 3, no. 5, Aug. 2010.

7. SIAC Open judgment, Abid Naseer, Ahmad Faraz Khan, Shoaib Khan, Abdul Wahad Khan and Tariq ur Rehman vs. Secretary of State for the Home Department, appeal no: SC/77/80/81/82/83/09, 18 May 2010. Mosi Secret, 'Pakistani in terror case is extradited to New York,' *New York Times*, 3 Jan. 2013.

8. Mitchell Silber, *The Al Qaeda Factor*, Philadelphia: University of Pennsylvania Press, 2012, p. 160.

9. Speculation around whether he had died or not continued for some time after this, though his family finally allowed a case be opened against the British government for murder in Oct. 2012 suggesting they at least had confirmation of his death. Amardeep Bassey, 'Family of al Qaeda terrorist Rashid Rauf to sue British government for murder,' *Birmingham Mail*, 27 Oct. 2012.

10. Francis Elliott, 'Afghan bomber was radicalized in jail, say investigators,' *The Times*, 3 June 2011.

11. Duncan Gardham, Con Coughlin and James Kirkup, 'Extremists plotting attacks on Britain freed from detention,' *The Daily Telegraph*, 17 Oct. 2011.

12. Regina vs. Irfan Naseer et al., Nov. 2012.

13. Ibid.

14. Regina vs. Irfan Naseer et al., Nov. 2012.

15. Ibid.

16. 'Six admit planning to bomb English Defence League rally,' BBC News, 30 April 2013. Regina vs. Irfan Naseer et al., Nov. 2012.

17. Quoted in Alexander Meleagrou-Hitchens, *As American As Apple Pie: How Anwar al-Awlaki Became the Face of Western Jihad*, London: ICSR Press, 2011, p. 27.

18. 'Umar Farouk Abdulmutallab: Report to UCL Council of Independent Inquiry Panel', University College London, Sept. 2010, available at www.ucl.ac.uk/caldicott-enquiry/caldicottreport.pdf

19. Government's Sentencing Memorandum, USA vs. Umar Farouk Abdulmutallab, 10 Feb. 2012.

20. 'British passport "important key" in terror,' Press Association, 2 Feb. 2011.

21. Emails published during the trial. The emails were reproduced in the *Daily Telegraph*: http://www.telegraph.co.uk/news/uknews/terrorism-in-the-uk/8353402/Internet-messages-reveal-al-Qaeda-leader-grooming-British-Airways-worker-for-attack.html

22. Eid letter by Rajib Karim, 17 April 2011, http://aseerun.org/2011/04/17/rajib-karim-april-4–2011-april-17–2011/, the authenticity of this letter is unfortunately uncertain, but it provides a very high level of detail that makes it very credible.

23. Emails quoted in Jenny Purt, 'Exerpts from Karim messages,' *Press Association*, 28 February 2011.

24. USA vs. Minh Quang Pham, indictment.

25. Regina vs. Mohammed Chowdhury & Ors, sentencing remarks by Mr Justice Wilkie, 9 Feb. 2012.

26. Islam4UK is the latest in a long list of names that Al-Muhajiroun has adopted. As the names become proscribed, the group shifts to another, using websites and statements that look remarkably similar to the previous ones and continues as normal. At time of writing

the most popular name being used was Ummah United, previous ones have included Saved Sect, Al-Ghurabaa (the strangers) and Muslims Against Crusades. Islam4UK has since been added to the proscribed terror list, though it was still operational when Chowdhury was caught on camera with the sign.

27. Sentencing remarks of Mr Justice Wilkie, Regina vs. Mohammed Chowdhury et al., 9 Feb. 2012.

28. 'London terror plot: the four terrorists,' *The Daily Telegraph*, 1 Feb. 2012.

29. Regina vs. Mohammed Chowdhury & Ors, sentencing remarks by Mr Justice Wilkie, 9 Feb. 2012.

30. 'Stephen Timms stabbing: how internet sermons turned a quiet student into fanatic',' *The Daily Telegraph*, 2 Nov. 2010.

31. Ibid.

32. Roshonara Choudhry police interview: http://www.guardian.co.uk/uk/2010/nov/03/roshonara-choudhry-police-interview

33. Ibid.

34. In a letter from Choudhry dated 11 Jan. 2011 published online she thanked those who had chanted in court, saying that 'it literally took my breath away when I heard your voices. Alhumdulillah, the sound of that takbeer filled my heart with such euphoria.' http://www.ansar1.info/showthread.php?t=33212

35. Muhammad al-Sana'ani, 'Roshonara and Taimour: Followers of the borderless loyalty', *Inspire*, Jan. 2011.

36. High court of Justiciary at Glasgow, indictment against Nasserdine Menni, 16 Nov. 2011.

37. 'Blogger who encouraged murder of MPs jailed,' BBC News, 29 July 2011.

38. Regina vs. Zahid Iqbal et al

39. 'Richard Dart: British Muslim arrested in West London appeared in BBC documentary,' *Press Association*, July 6, 2012.

40. The full documentary can be accessed here: https://www.youtube.com/watch?v=viGivP3OcGY

41. Regina vs. Dart et al.

42. Ibid.

43. Ibid.

44. Ibid. In a curious twist, a video released by TTP emerged in 2012 in which a British figure identified only as Umar was reported to have been mastermind of the plot, and to have subsequently been killed in a 2010 drone strike. Nicola Smith and Saleem Mehsud, 'British Taliban "martyr" masterminded suicide attack on CIA,' *Sunday Times*, 11 Nov. 2012.

45. 'UK trio jailed for preparing acts of terrorism,' BBC News, 25 April 2013; 'Terrorist Richard Dart's wife gets suspended jail term,' BBC News, 16 Aug. 2013.

INDEX

INDEX

Guča Gora Monastery, Bosnia and
  Herzegovina 106
Gujar Khan, Punjab 204
Gujaratis 25, 37, 44, 83, 127, 130,
  144, 189
Gujrat, Punjab 181
Gulf War (1990–1) 30, 62, 97, 102,
  233
Guyana 135

Habib, Khalid 227
Hackney, London 73, 210, 211, 212,
  214, 217
hadith 9, 10, 36, 105
Hadjarab, Nabil 124, 133
hafiz 88, 173, 259
hagiographies 106
Haifa, Israel 30
Hajj 112
al-Hajri, Kadhi Abdullah 32
halal (permissible) 49
Halliday, Fred 27, 83
Hamas 16, 234
Hambali 178
Hamid, Mohammed 73, 126–7,
  210–12, 214, 217, 231, 244
Hammami, Omar 246
Hanif, Asif 16, 157, 172–6, 199
Happy Mondays 242
Haqqani network 275
Harakat ul Mujahedeen (HuM) 43,
  44, 69, 97, 103, 153–5, 171, 177,
  187, 203, 225, 228, 276
haram (forbidden) 9, 156, 161
Hardwood, Jamal 91
Hardy Street Mosque, Leeds 60, 191
Harley Street, London 112
Hasan, Usama 66, 94–7, 102, 135
Hassaine, Reda 134
Hassan, Isaac Omar 248
Hassan, Zak 111

al-Hayat 31
Hayman, Andy 207, 218
Hazelwick School, Crawley 161
Headley, David Coleman 274–5
hearts and minds 3
Helmand, Afghanistan 243
Helping Hands 106
Herat, Afghanistan 275
Hezbollah 260
High Wycombe, Buckinghamshire
  218, 223
Hillside Primary School, Beeston
  188
al-Hindi, Esa 71, 76–7
Hindoostane Coffee House,
  Portman Square 20
Hinduism 25, 40, 62, 71, 176
Hither Green, London 204
Hizb ut-Tahrir (HuT) 48, 51, 66,
  76, 87–93, 96–7, 102, 116, 118,
  137, 173, 202, 226, 233, 235
Holland *see* Netherlands
Home Office 111, 112
Honeyford, Ray 52–3, 57–8
Hoshiapur, Punjab 23
Hounslow, London 173, 175, 199,
  249
Houston, Scotland 236
Huddersfield, West Yorkshire 54,
  189, 191
Husain, Ed 87, 93, 94, 96, 100, 107,
  202
Hussain Shar, Maroof 36
Hussain, Dilwar 64
Hussain, Hasib 70, 96, 189, 196,
  197–8
Hussain, Nabeel 222–3
Hussain, Syed Farhan 286–7
Hussain, Tanvir 217–18, 221, 230
Hussain, Yasmin 61
Hussein, Saddam 32, 97, 115,
  232–3, 235

347